Robert Ward, Thomas Lowe, William Whitby

Life among the Maories of New Zealand

Being a Description of missionary, colonial, and military Achievements

Robert Ward, Thomas Lowe, William Whitby

Life among the Maories of New Zealand
Being a Description of missionary, colonial, and military Achievements

ISBN/EAN: 9783337153991

Printed in Europe, USA, Canada, Australia, Japan

Cover: Foto ©ninafisch / pixelio.de

More available books at **www.hansebooks.com**

LIFE

AMONG THE

MAORIES OF NEW ZEALAND.

BEING A DESCRIPTION OF

MISSIONARY, COLONIAL, AND MILITARY ACHIEVEMENTS.

BY THE

REV. ROBERT WARD,

Twenty-six Years a Resident in the North Island.

EDITED BY
REV. THOMAS LOWE AND REV. WILLIAM WHITBY.

" Uirtuti non armis fido."

LONDON :

G. LAMB, SUTTON STREET, COMMERCIAL ROAD, E.
CANADA: W. ROWE, TORONTO.
AND ALL BOOKSELLERS.

1872.

CONTENTS.

Chapter I.

THE DISCOVERY.

Chapter II.

THE COUNTRY.

Chapter III.

NATURAL PRODUCTIONS.

Chapter IV.

THE MAORIES IN THEIR HEATHEN STATE.

Chapter V.

MISSIONARY TRIALS.

Chapter VI.

MISSIONARY SUCCESS.

Chapter VII.

THE COMMENCEMENT OF THE COLONY.

Chapter VIII.

EARLY STRUGGLES.

Chapter IX.

GROWTH OF THE COLONY.

Chapter X.

COUNTRY LIFE.

Chapter XI.

TOWN LIFE.

Chapter XII.

RELIGIOUS ASPECT.

Chapter XIII.
NATIVE SUSPICIONS.

Chapter XIV.
APPOINTMENT OF A KING.

Chapter XV.
TARANAKI WAR.

Chapter XVI.
A LULL IN THE WAR STORM.

Chapter XVII.
CESSATION OF HOSTILITIES.

Chapter XVIII.
RE-COMMENCEMENT OF THE WAR.

Chapter XIX.
THE WAR IN WAIKATO.

Chapter XX.
THE TAURANGA CAMPAIGN.

Chapter XXI.
THE WEST COAST HOSTILITIES.

Chapter XXII.
THE PAI MARIRE DELUSION.

Chapter XXIII.
WAR WITH THE HAU HAUS.

Chapter XXIV.
MILITARY SETTLEMENTS.

Chapter XXV.
A FRESH OUTBREAK.

Chapter XXVI.
CONCLUDING REMARKS.

PREFACE.

SUPPOSING that the British public must be more than ordinarily interested in the events of New Zealand, where so many brave men of all ranks have found a soldier's grave, where so many representatives of every county in Great Britain and Ireland have fixed their home, and where the hopes and fears of the friends of Christian missions have been so strongly excited,—the author has prepared the following pages for the press. In doing so he has endeavoured to place the Mission to the Native people in a fair and honourable point of view; and the trying circumstances to which the Maori race were exposed by being brought into contact with colonization, the hopes which they raised and the reverses of their subsequent history, will be found truthfully described. The remarks on the fitness of the country for British colonization, the various features of colonial life, including its religious characteristics, with suggestions for intending emigrants, will he hopes be accepted as satisfactory and useful. In writing on the war he has had no object beyond placing this unhappy subject fairly before the public—a subject the importance of which will be admitted, when it is remembered that the insurrection will always form a necessary chapter, although a melancholy one, in the history of New Zealand.

No pains have been spared to obtain correct information for this work. The long residence of the author in the colony, the post of observation he has occupied throughout the war, the more valuable from the fact that he was a non-combatant, and his freedom from partisanship of any kind, are considerations which entitle his pages to respect and authority. Some discrepancies may possibly be found in the military department, between the statements here given and the reports of the Newspaper press. This need not cause surprise; for the excitements of the battle-field are not favourable to correct information. Nor have official dispatches been always the most reliable, as subsequent information has sometimes modified their statements.

If this volume exhibits an intelligent view of the "New Zealand Question," if it presents such a picture of colonial life as may be distinctly understood in England, if it be found serviceable to the intending emigrant, and if it places fairly before the friends of Christian Missions the work which has been done, and the work which remains to be done,—the object of the author will be accomplished.

R. W.

INTRODUCTION.

THIS splendid volume is almost exhaustive on New Zealand Life. The author makes no pretensions to high literary culture and finished style; but these deeply interesting sketches are chastely, tersely, graphically, and eloquently written. This book is not a mere missionary journal of denominational enterprise. The author's broad Christian sympathies are unfettered and unconfined by any sectarian peculiarities, characteristics, and ecclesiastical lines of demarcation. He is a true Christian gentleman, one of the " highest style of men," a truly apostolic missionary, of whom any Church in Christendom might be justly proud. For more than a quarter of a century he has been the faithful and able representative of the Primitive Methodist Missionary Society in New Zealand. In the spring of 1871, he visited his native land for a short time, to relate the story of his glorious missionary apostleship at the antipodes.

This book will be found to possess more than missionary interest. The geographer, the ethnographer, the philologist, the linguist, the botanist, the mineralogist, the geologist, the ornithologist, the naturalist, in fine, the most profoundly learned savant, may peruse and study its pages with great advantage. From the ample and varied MSS. in our possession, we might have added considerably to the sketches and data of this work, but its pages are, we opine, sufficiently bulky, copious, and multifarious. If this volume meets with the appreciation and patronage which it merits, a second will be published, at the earliest possible convenience, of equal interest. Many works of travel and adventure, are light, superficial, desultory, and ephemeral. In this work we have indications of thoroughness, intelligent observation, careful research, calmness, and soundness of judgment, and a masterly grouping of character, fact, and incident, from sources the most reliable.

In the chapters that relate to the Maori war, the author often rises to the true dignity of history. We have the clearness and comprehensiveness of Livy, the burning force of Tacitus, and we have a naturalness, a chasteness, a picturesqueness of descriptive power, reminding us occasionally of the splendid sketching of Macaulay and Bancroft, so far, at least, as this volume claims to be historical. It will be seen that its records and details are brought down to the latest possible date, A.D. 1870, a short time prior to the author's visit to his native shores, for the last time. Since the completion of this work for the press, during the past two years, several events worthy of note have transpired in relation to New Zealand pacification, progress, and prosperity. One of the most notable is the submission of the Maori king, Wiremu Kingi, who, twelve years ago bearded Governor Browne, and raised the standard of revolt at Waitara, near New Plymouth, and thus became the typical embodiment of Maori discontent.

The ferocious Kereopa has been arrested, dragged to justice, and expiated his horrible crimes on the scaffold. It is a pleasing fact that some hundreds of the Maories who about four years ago were burning villages, and murdering the out-settlers, are now helping to make roads into their very fortresses for Government wages, and working as railway navvies.

There are four Maori members of the House of Representatives, men of high ability, so popular that it is now proposed to admit native members to the Legislative Council, and also to the Executive Council. According to the recent census, the total population of the various provinces of New Zealand is, 256,393 : males, 150,356, females, 106,037. This is exclusive of aborigines. Live stock, sheep, 9,700,629 ; head of cattle, 436,592 ; horses, 81,028; pigs, 151,460; poultry, 872,174. Dairy produce, in 1871, 5,199,072 pounds of butter; 2,547,507 pounds of cheese.

The Taranaki iron sand has been proved by Government experiments to be extremely useful, and is capable of yielding the finest steel. Among the isles of the vast Pacific that "wait for God's law," not the least in importance and moral glory, are, Eaheianowmawe and Tavia Poenamoo, the rudely euphonious names by which the splendid islands of New Zealand were first known to the Maories.

We have given the MSS. and printed proofs the most careful revision; but such is the range of the matter forming the twenty-six chapters, so varied and ample the data and details relating to persons, places, and historical dates, and so frequent and numerous the recurrence of Maori names and phrases, that we fear that some inaccuracies may be discovered undetected by us. We therefore solicit the intelligent reader's kind indulgence. An imperative sense of duty to—in many respects—a great man, and a great work, influenced us to undertake the risk of this publication. We have expended considerably more than we contem-

plated in the first instance, in order to do full justice to
the talented author, and his splendid book—one of the
best books extant—on that once most barbarous and
interesting people, among the ashes of whose horrid
cannibal fires our holy Christianity has built its altars
and fanes, blunted the points of their battle-spears, split
their murderous clubs, and tamed their savage, hostile
passions.

THOMAS LOWE,

Primitive Cottage, Alford, Lincolnshire,

WILLIAM WHITBY,

19, Grove Street, Retford, Notts,

Editors.

August 21st, 1872.

LIFE AMONG THE MAORIES

OF

NEW ZEALAND.

CHAPTER I.

THE DISCOVERY.

" Then slowly peer'd the rising moon,
    Above the forest-height,
And bathed each cocoa's leafy crown
    In tides of living light ;
To every cabin's grassy thatch
    A gift of beauty gave,
And with a crest of silver cheer'd
    Pacific's sullen wave."

NEW ZEALAND has engaged the attention of the
British public, not only as a field for scientific
research, and as an appropriate sphere for Christian
Missions, but on account of its flourishing colony. In
addition to immigration from Great Britain and Ireland,
hundreds of families from the continent of Europe and
the northern parts of America have found a home on its

B

shores, and have been naturalized as the subjects of our
Queen. Additional interest has been felt in the colony
through the war, occasioned by the efforts of several
native tribes to throw off their allegiance to the Queen,
and to form themselves into an independent kingdom.
The evils of the war have fallen most heavily upon the
Maori race ; but the colony has suffered the loss of life
and property to a fearful extent. Yet the energy of the
settlers has risen with the trial to which they have been
exposed, and instead of folding their arms in despair,
they are encouraging hopes of a bright and prosperous
future.

Much has been written about New Zealand by men
who have spent only a few months in the country.
Some of these works are respectable publications, and
we know of some which are worthy of all confidence ;
but many of them fail in the attempt to portray real
colonial life—its trials and hopes, its joys and sorrows.
Such persons are obliged to collect their information
from whatever sources may be within their reach, whether
reliable or otherwise ; and from books, the value of
which they are not always prepared to determine. They
may have walked a few miles into the dense forest, and
ridden over a few thousands of acres of open land ; they
may have conversed with the farmer in the country, and
mingled with society for a few weeks in the town ; the
native people may have attracted their attention, as
they disposed of their produce to the settlers ; and,
possibly, they may have entered a Maori pah, and slept
in a *raupo whare ;* but their experience and observations
are too crude, with rare exceptions, to enable them to
give a fair view of New Zealand and its inhabitants.
Other books on the same subject have been compiled by

persons who never left the shores of Great Britain. Many of these are open to many objections; for while much valuable information is embodied, a good deal will be found calculated to mislead. We do not insinuate that a false impression is intended to be made; but such an impression is certainly the natural consequence of loose, defective, and one-sided information. But other books, altogether trustworthy, and replete with intelligence on the subjects discussed by their respective authors, have been published. Of these the present writer has endeavoured to make a proper use, so far as they have been within his reach. And a residence of twenty-six years in the colony—in a suitable post for observation, especially during the late native insurrection—has secured advantages which it is hoped will prevent him from presenting fiction for facts, and from misleading the public mind in its estimate of New Zealand, past and present.

The object which we propose is to present such a view of New Zealand as may illustrate the grace and providence of God towards both its aboriginal people and the race which is destined to shed the blessings of civilization and Christianity from the North Cape to Stewart's Island. The Missionary enterprise, conducted in its early stages amidst heavy trials and fearful risks, and followed in numerous instances by decisive and satisfactory results, shall be properly exhibited. The colony, in its formation, growth, and prospects, together with its claims upon the attention of intending emigrants, shall be described. The native race, as they were made known to the world by the early circumnavigators of the globe; their progress in the appropriation of useful arts; their connexion with the colonists, and their recent unhappy attempt to maintain their nationality by an appeal to arms, and the war to which this attempt has given rise—shall be fairly treated. And the whole will be considered as a part of the plan by which God intends the waste places of the earth to be cultivated, and by which those tribes of mankind who have, till a recent period, been living beyond the reach of the Churches of Christ, are to be gathered into the fold of the Great Shepherd.

At the time the Old Testament was completed. the civilized world lay within a comparatively narrow compass. The Mediterranean was the only "great sea" with which they were familiar; the Atlantic ocean was scarcely known, and the wider Pacific was to them a total blank. There was total ignorance of the great American continent, extending from the North Polar Sea to Cape Horn, which faces the wintry blasts from the Antarctic Circle; and of the numerous groups of islands which beautifully studded the bosom of the South Sea, and perhaps at that time supported a numerous population. Geographical knowledge was improved at the time the events transpired which are recorded in the New Testament; but even then, Britain was spoken of as being separated from the whole world, and more remote countries were little more than *terræ incognitæ*. But nearly three thousand years ago the veil was occasionally lifted by the hand of inspiration, and glances of the future history of distant lands were obtained. The prophets taught that the " ends of the earth " were to " see the salvation of our God ;" the isles were to " wait for His law ;" and all nations were to serve Him. The commission which Christ gave to His Apostles embraced the whole world ; and the effects which have been produced by the Gospel in every part of the earth, among men crushed beneath the heaviest curses, and groaning under the most cruel and revolting forms of heathenism, show that the provisions of Divine grace were calculated to meet the wants of all mankind.

The Divine Sovereignty is distinctly seen in the history of our race. Several thousand years passed away before man was able to make an intelligent survey of the earth which he was commanded to subdue and replenish. During that time extensive countries, full of inhabitants, held no intercourse with the known world. Their wants were comparatively few; they roamed in the primeval forests, drank the water from the unbridged rivers and brooks, procured food either by rudely cultivating the ground, or by the chase of the wild animals which came within their reach, and died without knowing whence they came, or whither they were going. Why was it that so many centuries elapsed, after the Christian Church had received her commission to go into all the world, and preach the Gospel to every creature, before many of the lands which have recently been the scene of Gospel triumphs, remarkable for their grandeur and extent, were discovered? We can only reply—"Even so, Father; for so it seemed good in Thy sight."

But when the period arrived in which the Church was to enlarge her boundaries, according to her great commission, both the agents and the instruments were prepared. The discovery of the magnet, the construction of the chronometer, the invention of printing, the desire to search unknown seas, and the anxiety of the Christian Church to carry the Gospel into distant countries, were the signs of the times—tokens that God was about to pour upon all nations the blessings of saving grace. The first voyage round the earth was a great event, not only as a demonstration of science, and as a novel and dangerous enterprise, but because of the blessings which were designed to follow in its wake. Commerce, with its well-appointed fleets; the Christian missionary, with the glad tidings of salvation ; and the adventurous colonist, with the seeds of a civilized state —owe a debt of gratitude to the early circumnavigators of the globe, as pioneers in their path.

The honour of fitting out a ship for the first voyage of discovery in modern times, belongs to Portugal. This occurred in 1412, under the auspices of Don Henry, Duke of Viseo, son of John I. In the course of the next seventy-four years the Madeiras were discovered and colonized, and settlements were formed along the coast of Africa. Under the direction of John II., an expedition, consisting of three ships, was prepared for a voyage of discovery in the South. The command was given to Commodore Diaz, who sailed in August, 1486. He doubled the Cape of Good Hope, and sailed several hundred miles along the Eastern coast of Africa. The stormy weather which Diaz encountered off that great promontory, led him to call it " Il Cabo dos Tormentos " —the Cape of Storms; but on his return to Portugal, the King was so delighted with the grandeur of the discovery, and the prospect of reaching India by that route, that he called it, " Il Cabo del Bueno Esperanza " —the Cape of Good Hope. About six years afterwards the indomitable energy and plodding perseverance of Columbus were rewarded by the discovery of the West Indian Islands, and then of America, along whose coast he sailed as far as the Isthmus of Darien. A southern ocean occupied the thoughts of Columbus ; its existence appeared extremely probable, but he was not permitted to gaze upon its waters.

The following lines, illustrative of the growing intelligence of this period, may be quoted from a poet of Florence, who flourished in the latter part of the fifteenth century. The general idea that had been entertained was, that the Pillars of Hercules—Gibraltar—were the utmost limits of the world, and to this the poet thus refers :—

> " Know that this theory is false ; his bark
> The daring manager shall urge far o'er
> The western wave—a smooth and level plain,
> Albeit the earth is fashioned like a wheel.
> Man was, in ancient days, of grosser mould ;
> And Hercules might blush to learn how far
> Beyond the limits he had vainly set,
> The dullest sea-boat soon shall wing her way !
> Men shall descry another hemisphere :
> Since to one common centre all things tend,
> So earth, by curious mystery divine,
> Well balanced, hangs amid the starry spheres.
> At our antipodes are cities, states,
> And thronged empires, ne'er divined of yore :
> But see, the sun speeds on his western path,
> To glad the nations with expected light !"

In those days Spain was a great maritime nation, and attracted by the report of gold being found in abundance in America, she planted colonies there. Adventurous persons, from the highest rank to the lowest plebeian, sought the land of gold. A man of good family and cultivated mind, but of profligate habits, was appointed Governor. This was Vasco Nunez de Balboa, to whom the honour was given of making known to the world the Pacific Ocean. The existence of this ocean was related to him by the natives of the country, and taking some of them as guides, he prepared for a journey across

the Isthmus of Darien, for the purpose of verifying the
Indians' report. A powerful chief opposed his progress,
but having a strong escort, the effect of his fire-arms
was seen in the destruction of several hundreds of
natives. It is painful to reflect on the fact, that, in
numerous instances, the advancement of science and
civilization have been attended with a great loss of
human life. His heart throbbing with excitement,
Balboa climbed the mountains of the Isthmus, and on
the 26th of September, 1513, the great Southern ocean
opened before him. "He fell on his knees, and amid
floods of joyful tears, extending his arms to the ocean,
and lifting up his eyes to heaven, he offered a prayer of
thanksgiving to the Most High, that on him, of all
Europeans, had been conferred the signal honour of
first beholding the Great Pacific. He then beckoned
the approach of his attendants, who advanced, and, on
beholding the wondrous sight, a priest of the company
struck up the *Te Deum*, in which the whole united on
their bended knees."* With buoyant step Balboa
hastened to the beach, and, while the tide laved his
feet, took possession of the newly-discovered ocean, and
of all the lands washed by its waters, in the name of the
King of Spain.

Six years later, a fleet, consisting of five ships and
two hundred and thirty-six men, left Spain on the first
voyage round the globe. Magellan, a Portuguese by birth,
offered his services for this hazardous undertaking to
Charles V., and was appointed the commander. The
horrors which the crews sustained from disease and want
of provisions, cannot be described. Insubordination
contributed to the general distress. But Magellan was

* "Maritime Discovery," &c., by Dr. Campbell.

equal to the emergency; and had his conduct towards the natives whose lands he visited been governed by the proper feelings of humanity, he would not only have deserved a place among the greatest benefactors of mankind, but, probably, would have returned to Europe to reap the honours which he had so nobly earned. He passed through the strait which bears his name, lying between the most southern part of the American continent and Tierra del Fuego, in October, 1520, and entered into the Great South Sea. Months of suffering were yet before him and his brave companions; but in the following March they reached the Ladrone Islands, where they met with abundance of provisions. The thievish propensity of the natives determined the name by which that group of islands is still known, and was the occasion of a severe punishment which was inflicted on them by the crews of Magellan. The Philippines were soon after discovered. The number of inhabitants, their tattooed decorations, their well-finished and strange instruments of war, and their loquacious and easy habits, made a favourable impression on the Commander, which was increased by the beautiful scenery, abundant provisions, and delightful climate, peculiarly refreshing to men who had been so many months upon the bosom of unknown seas. This led to a so-called Christian exhibition, in which a company from the ships went on shore, for the purpose of saying Mass, and erecting a cross, which was "garnished with nails, and mounted by a crown of thorns." When Mass was said, a volley of musketry was fired, and the cross was offered to the bewildered natives as an object of worship, with a promise of immunity from all extraordinary evils so long as they continued to adore it! This was the first time that the attention of the South Sea Islanders was drawn towards Christianity; but it was nothing better than an endeavour to substitute one form of idolatry for another. An attempt to christianize the natives of another island was made a few days afterwards. A temporary chapel was built, Mass was said, and guns were fired, and many of the natives, without understanding the object, submitted to baptism. The influence of Magellan appears to have been immense, for a little time. Then a reaction took place; his demands on the people brought him into collision with their warriors, when he fell a prey to their ferocity. Eight men fell dead with him, and twenty-two more were wounded. It is to be deeply regretted that a man who had done so much for the advancement of science, and the progress of society, in opening the way for colonizing those remote parts of the earth, and introducing the religion of Christ (but not by the efforts which he made in erecting crosses, as so many idols) in its purity and power, should come to such an untimely end. Several captains and chief officers also were killed; but the ships, notwithstanding, proceeded on their course of discovery. Other countries were visited, and other dangers befell them. Five ships comprised the expedition, but only one returned to Spain; and of two hundred and thirty-six persons who sailed on this dangerous enterprise, not more than sixteen saw their native country again. "This handful of survivors, on reaching Seville, walked to Church in their shirts, barefooted, with burning tapers in their hands, to return thanks to the Most High for their wondrous preservation."* They sailed from San Lucar September 20th, 1519, and

* "Maritime Discovery," &c., by Dr. Campbell.

returned September 6th, 1522, after sailing, in the course of these three years, about forty thousand miles.

Within the thirty-six years preceding the conclusion of this voyage, an immense addition was made to geographical knowledge. The whole of the Western coast of Africa was traced; the much-dreaded Cape was doubled, and the eastern coast was visited. Vasco de Gama sailed in command of a fleet fitted out by Emmanuel of Portugal, for the purpose of finding a passage to India by the Cape of Good Hope. With the usual amount of suffering incident to long voyages in those days, arising from scurvy and the want of wholesome provisions, this intrepid commander reached Calicut, on the Malabar coast, on the 20th May, 1498, and returning by the same course, arrived in Portugal after an absence of more than two years. But of the one hundred and eight men who left their home under his command, only fifty were permitted to return to enjoy the honours, and still more substantial favours, of their king and country, in return for the advantages which were expected in consequence of their successful voyage. The southern extremity of America had then been explored, and a passage found into the vast ocean which washed the eastern coast of that continent. The sails had been freely spread, and the ship's course directed into the heart of the great Pacific, where group after group of beautiful islands, full of inhabitants, were discovered. During the same period, the great discoveries of Columbus had been made, and settlements formed, not only on some of the West Indian islands, but also on the continent of America. We see much to deplore in the hardships which were endured by those adventurous sons of the ocean, and in the cruelties which were sometimes inflicted upon the astonished people whom they visited; but we must never forget the debt of gratitude which all succeeding generations owe to them, and the high honour which God has put upon them, in appointing them to be His agents to prepare His way, that the ends of the earth may rejoice in His salvation.

While thus God was preparing a highway across the oceans, to the most distant parts of the earth, His providence at the same time was raising up agents, through whose instrumentality the sacred Scriptures were to be freed from the fables and superstitions, which had long perverted and corrupted them. Martin Luther was a little child when Bartholomew Diaz first saw the Cape of Good Hope; and no connexion could then be traced between that great discovery, and the little German child. While De Gama was rejoicing at the success which attended his efforts to reach India by doubling the African Cape, and partaking of the hospitality of eastern monarchs, Luther was a student, so poor that he was often seen in the streets of Isenach singing in front of the houses, for a morsel of bread to appease his hunger. No connexion was then discernible between the heroic navigator, and the hunger-bitten student. Just as Columbus, rich in real honours, but crushed beneath a nation's neglect, and the foul tongue of obloquy, was approaching the grave, Luther found a Bible. It was the first he ever saw; its contents aroused his whole soul, and throbbings of a great purpose were soon felt. It is not difficult now to see a close connexion between the discoveries of the great seamen, and that of the student of Erfurt; theirs, exhibited the works of God spread out on the broad bosom of nature, his displayed the grace of God spread out in a divine revelation; the records of one revealed extensive countries, which were destined to be covered with the arts and comforts of civilization, while those of the other proclaimed the doctrines of grace, through which the earth is to be covered with the beauty of holiness. While Magellan was recruiting the health of his crews at the Philippine Islands, where he ingloriously fell, Martin Luther was summoned before the Diet of Worms, to answer the charge of writing books of heresy. There stood Luther before Charles, " whose dominion embraced two worlds, surrounded by six electors of the Empire, eighty dukes, eight margraves, thirty prelates of various rank, seven ambassadors, the deputies of five cities, a number of princes and sovereigns, counts and barons, with the Pope's nuncios and a few others." The question submitted to Luther was, " Will you, or will you not retract? " His noble reply can never be forgotten : " Since your most Serene Majesty, and your High Mightinesses, demand a simple, clear, and explicit answer of me, I will give it. I cannot submit my faith either to pope or councils, since it is as clear as the day, that they have often fallen into error, and even into great contradictions with themselves. If, then, I am not convinced by testimonies from Scripture or by evident reasons, if I am not persuaded by the very passages I have cited, and if my conscience be not thus made captive by the Word of God, I can and will retract nothing; for it is not safe for the Christian to speak against his conscience. HERE I AM ; I CANNOT DO OTHERWISE ; GOD HELP ME. AMEN ! " *

The voyages we have already described were followed

* " The Penalties of Greatness," by Dr. Furguson.

by several others, in which further discoveries of importance were made ; but it is remarkable that the Islands
of New Zealand were not known till 1642 ; except the
country visited by Juan Fernandez, in 1575, was, as
some suppose, a part of the New Zealand coast. He
describes the country which he saw as being fertile and
well cultivated, and the inhabitants as being of a brown
colour, and wearing fine clothing; but the identity of
the island cannot now be satisfactorily determined. As
the dog and pig were found in New Zealand at the time
when the earliest accounts of it were penned, it is not
improbable that the land in question was some part of
its coast, and that a few animals of these kinds were
put ashore at that time. This accords with a tradition
which is held by the Maories, that their ancestors did
not bring the dog and pig from the country whence they
emigrated, but that they came from a ship which visited
their coast a very long time ago.

The first reliable account which we have of this
country is given by the Dutch navigator, Abel Jansen
Tasman. Two ships, the Heemskirk and the Zeehaan,
were placed under his command in 1642, and from his
account of the voyage, the special object which he had
in view may be perceived. It commences as follows :—
" Journal or Description by me, Abel J. Tasman, of
a voyage from Batavia, for making discoveries of the
unknown south land, in the year 1642. May God
Almighty be pleased to give His blessing to this voyage.
Amen."

The pious and manly manner in which he commenced
his voyage is very commendable, and that the blessing
sought was obtained is what all Christian minds will
fully credit. He gave the name to the New Zealand

Islands, by which they will probably always be known ; and from his own name, the large and beautiful island, formerly known as Van Dieman's Land, with its flourishing colony, is now called Tasmania.

Tasman reached New Zealand, but supposed that it was part of the great southern Continent. His description of the natives is peculiarly interesting, as being the first account which we have of them. He anchored in a small bay and wrote as follows :—" We found here abundance of inhabitants ; they had hoarse voices, and were very large made people. They durst not approach the ships nearer than a stone's throw ; and we often observed them playing on a kind of trumpet, to which we answered with the instruments that were on board our vessel. These people were of a colour between brown and yellow, their hair long and black, and almost as thick as the Japanese, combed up and fixed on the top of their heads with a quill, or some such thing, that was thickest in the middle, and with a white feather stuck upright in the knot. These people cover the middle of their bodies, some with a kind of mat, others with a sort of woollen cloth ; but as for their upper and lower parts, they leave them altogether naked."

The natives came alongside the ships in double canoes, from which Tasman was apprehensive of danger. Being on board the Zeehaan, and seeing several of those canoes full of men approach the Heemskirk, and some natives go on board, he sent a quartermaster and six men in a shallop to apprise the crew of that vessel of their danger, with orders not to let many canoes go alongside. But as soon as the boat got clear of the ship, an attack was made by the natives ; the quartermaster and three of the men were killed, and another mortally wounded,

and one of the bodies was taken ashore by the natives.
From this painful occurrence the place was called
Massacre Bay.* In Tasman's Journal a drawing is
given of this attack, with the two ships lying at anchor.
This unhappy event determined him to leave the bay,
and though he afterwards saw different parts of the
coast, he says in his Journal—" As for New Zealand,
we never set foot on it."

Painfully interesting as the foregoing account is, it
supplies but little information, besides the fact that New
Zealand was inhabited by a robust and fierce people;
and one hundred and twenty-seven years passed away
before we have any further reliable information concerning it. There is a tradition among the Maóries, that a
large ship visited the southern part of the North Island
about the year 1740, and that the natives killed the
crew, and plundered the ship; but we know not what
credit is to be given to this story. A singular fact is
related by the Rev. R. Taylor, of the Church of England
Mission, concerning a bell which was found by some
natives under the roots of a large tree, which was blown
down in a storm. Mr. Taylor saw the bell. It had a
legend around it in square characters, which he supposed
to be Japanese. The bell was used by the natives to
boil their potatoes; but on account of its singular history, it was purchased by a gentleman belonging to the
Church Mission. Has this bell any connection with the
ship, said to have been plundered by the natives more
than a century ago?†

* This is now called Golden Bay, from the fact that the first
New Zealand gold-field was discovered on its shores.

† Since the above was written, it has been ascertained that the
characters on this bell are Tamil, and that the translation of them

The man to whom we are indebted for the first intelligent account of New Zealand, is Captain James Cook; and owing to the valuable information which he collected, the familiar terms on which he and his crew lived among the natives, the animals which he landed, the wholesome vegetables which he introduced, and the consequences which flowed from his voyages, the following historical remarks will be found interesting.

He was born at Marton in Yorkshire, on the 27th of October, 1728, his father being a village labourer. His youth was spent on board vessels engaged in the coal trade; but in 1755 he entered on the service of a man-of-war. His devotedness to his profession led to an appointment, four years after, as master of the Mercury, which was engaged within a little time at the siege of Quebec. His next employment was to survey the river St. Lawrence and the coast of Newfoundland. About this time he appears to have entered very earnestly upon the study of mathematics, astronomy, and other branches of science; and a paper, describing some observations which he made on an eclipse of the sun, August 5th, 1766, was approved by the Royal Society, made him known as an able astronomer,, and led to the appointment which was followed by such splendid results. In 1768 he was made a Lieutenant in the Royal Navy, and appointed to the command of an expedition to Tahiti, for the purpose of observing the transit of the

is as follows: "The Bell belonging to the Moheiden Box." As it appears that "Moheiden Box" is a common name of vessels plying between Ceylon and Southern India, it is probable that, by some means, such a ship found her way into the Pacific Ocean, and was wrecked on the New Zealand coast; but the time when, and the circumstances under which this may have taken place, we have no means of ascertaining.

c

planet Venus over the sun's disc. Mr. Green, Mr. Banks (afterwards Sir Joseph Banks), Dr. Solander, and other scientific gentlemen, formed part of the expedition. The voyage was made in the Endeavour, four hundred and fifty tons measurement, and carrying altogether seventy-two persons. After staying at Tahiti three months, during which time their astronomical observations were satisfactorily made, they left Matavai Bay in search of other lands.

On October 7th, 1769, the expedition reached the east coast of the North Island of New Zealand. The Captain mentions the country as being agreeable beyond description, and the streams of water as being extremely good. The attention of the gentlemen was attracted by beautiful parrots, and by a bird whose note resembled the English blackbird. Pahs, with fences round them; houses built of reeds, and covered with thatch; stages for drying fish; crops in regular plantations; and ugly dogs, with long, tapering ears—formed the picture of the Maori homesteads of that time. A canoe, sixty-seven feet long, six feet wide, and four feet deep, with its sides and head curiously carved, lay on the beach. Tattooed men and women, anointed with red ochre and fish oil, were numerous—the former carrying wooden spears, and weapons formed of stone, with a string through the handle. Several canoes came alongside the Endeavour, bringing abundance of fish and other articles for the purpose of barter. Some of the natives tried to cheat while trading, and others were detected while in the act of stealing, which led to the discharge of muskets; but as the Maories were not sufficiently intimidated by this course, some of the men were fired at with small shot. Several attempts were made to attack the ship's crew;

but by the discharge of a four-pounder, loaded with grape-shot, and the firing of muskets, by which some were killed, their design was frustrated. After about a month's cruising off the coast, Captain Cook, on the 15th November, took formal possession of the newly-discovered country in the name of George III., weighed anchor, and again stood out to sea.

The account which the Maories have preserved of this visit, which will be read with interest, is as follows:— " They saw, with wonder and fear, first a white speck on the horizon, which, rapidly increasing in size, seemed to glide as a cloud, silently but rapidly, into the bay. Anon, the phenomenon became stationary; by degrees it folded its snowy wings. Their wonder grew with every change in its appearance, and reached its climax when they discerned forms resembling human beings, now rapidly mounting upwards, and again, to all appearance, swinging in mid-air. Soon a bark, not unlike their own canoes, was seen approaching the shore, followed by another, and yet another. Consternation reigned throughout the pah. With trembling eagerness the warriors snatched up their rude weapons, and prepared for the defence of their homes; matrons raised their discordant cry above the din and hubbub of voices, as they gathered their respective offspring ready for flight, while yet, impelled by womanly curiosity, they lingered to gaze upon the novel danger ; maidens and children rushed hither and thither, now clinging to lover, to brother, or parent, now rending the air with their ' aue !' —that thrilling, piercing cry of mental agony and despair which none who have once heard can ever forget. Suddenly, amidst the uproar, the startling blast of the *Putata*—conch-shell trumpet—was heard, as the signal for deadly strife. In stentorian tones their leader shouted a war-cry, too often heard in those troublous times, ' *He whakaariki! He whakaariki!* ' The spell was broken. The courage of one man inspired the rest, and with headlong speed they rushed out to meet the foe. Nearer and nearer the strangers drew, their barks impelled onwards by rowers who, strange to relate, sat with their backs to the prow. A form rose in the stern of the foremost one; he waved his hand; yes, unmistakeably, he was a man; but with what a complexion! Verily he was a *korako* (albino), perchance one of the *patupaiarehe* whom Maori fable represented as rivalling the snows of Hikurangi in whiteness. By his side stood another, not unlike a Maori, but fairer—fair as the far-famed *Hinekikoia*. Waving his hand gracefully, he addressed them : *Taiao!* (friends; the customary Tahitian salutation). No response was heard from the savage band who, their awe and anticipation of a supernatural visitation being overcome, glared with hideous ferocity upon him and his companions. . . . . . When the foreigners attempted a landing, they showed so bold a front that the intruders were compelled to retire. . . One warrior in particular strove to out-rival his fellows in shewing his contempt for the enemy. A weapon was levelled at him. Supposing that his antagonist was about to hurl a spear, he threw up his left arm, covered with a heavy mat, to parry the stroke. A jet of flame burst from the weapon, followed by a loud ringing report, and he felt through the garment a concussion like that occasioned by a handful of gravel thrown with great force. For an instant he was paralyzed; wonder and fear by turns took possession of his mind; but finding himself unhurt, he became still more insolent. Again

the weapon was levelled at him ; again he threw up his
heavy mat ; again the flash ; again the report—but not
again was he scatheless. With a wild, piercing cry he
bounded in the air, and, with a heavy plash, fell
writhing in the waters which laved the rock on which
he had stood. His comrades gathered round him. The
weapon itself had not been projected ; no, the stranger
still held it in his hand; but from a small orifice the
warrior's life-blood was pouring forth, dyeing the waters
around him. Revenge, the darling passion of the savage
mind in all countries, overcame fear. Again they rushed
on the intruders ; and the foremost fell with a heavy
groan. Fear fell upon them, and with even greater
speed than they had sallied forth, the panic-stricken
warriors retired within their *pah*. The strangers also
withdrew, and ere long the discomfited Maories saw a
cloud of smoke issue from the strange object—the *motu
tawhiti* (foreign island)—then a sound like the roar of
tchatitiri, followed by a heavy crash, and large splinters
of rock, from an island near their *pah*, were hurled into
the air. To their great satisfaction, they soon perceived
a movement in the *motu tawhiti*. It spread its wings
abroad, and was wafted out of their sight."* The rock
which was struck is still pointed out to the traveller as a
memorial of the first visit of the white man to the country of the Maori.

It is probable that there is now no native living who
witnessed the first contact of the white man and the
Maori; but its history is written, and will never be
forgotten. Events such as no man then living could
foresee have taken place in the country, and given
increasing interest to the incidents of the discovery.

* Mr. W. Baker.

Some of the old men delight to talk on this subject. Taniwha, a very old chief, who died near Auckland a few years ago, took a pleasure in relating the circumstances of Captain Cook's first visit to Mercury Bay. The chief says, that when they saw the boats approaching the shore, they thought the men had eyes behind their heads, as they paddled with their backs in the direction of their course. The natives received from the ships, as articles of barter, nails, pieces of iron, axes, knives, and calico. Two handfuls of potatoes were given them for seed. Some of these were planted by Taniwha's father, and after tapuing them for three years, they had a feast, at which the first potatoes were eaten. A spike nail was given to Taniwha—then a boy of twelve years—who wore it round his neck for several years, and found it very useful as a carving instrument. A native, called Marutu-ahu, endeavoured to steal a piece of calico; but while he was paddling away with it, a gun was fired, and killed him. The death of Marutu-ahu caused a great consternation, and a public meeting was convened. The facts of the case being ascertained, the theft was acknowledged by the friends of the delinquent, and the punishment inflicted was considered as an act of justice. The stolen calico was, of course, tapued, and became the winding sheet of the corpse. This unpleasantness soon passed away, and the white men landed, and spent some time on friendly terms with the natives. At the request of the Captain, the natives drew a chart of the coast with a piece of charcoal; and a copy of the chart, with the names of the principal places, were written in a book. Supposing Taniwha's story to be correct—and we know no reason why we should doubt it—Captain Cook and the gentlemen who sailed with him little thought of the altered state of the country, in which an account of their visit would be narrated by one who then, as a little boy, stood looking on in fear and wonder.

Captain Cook continued to cruise along the New Zealand coast, naming its principal bays and headlands, till he had sailed round the two large islands. And after a long time spent in unknown waters, and having passed through dangers both seen and unseen, this remarkable voyage was brought to a close on June 13th, 1771, having been conducted through the space of nearly three years.

His second great voyage was commenced July 13th, 1772, with two ships, the Resolution and the Adventure —the latter being commanded by Captain Furneaux. Several gentlemen of great scientific attainments, with instruments of all kinds for their use, were on board, and no expense was spared by George III. to make the voyage beneficial to the maritime interests of the world. The principal object of this expedition was to determine the existence of a southern continent—the grand problem which previous voyages had failed to solve.

Captain Cook spent some time on different parts of the New Zealand coast, landed sheep, goats, pigs, and fowls, and supplied the natives with various kinds of valuable seeds, among which were potatoes, wheat, beans, peas, cabbage, turnips, onions, carrots, and parsnips. In Queen Charlotte's Sound, Captain Furneaux lost a boat's crew of ten men, who were killed and eaten by the Maories. Having ascertained that there is no southern continent, except too near the pole to be of any service to mankind, the Resolution returned to England ; and such were the intelligent measures made use of by Captain Cook for the preservation of his crew, that in the course of a voyage which extended from fifty-two degrees north to seventy-one degrees south, and which was continued more than three years, only one man died through disease.

On July 12th, 1776, the last voyage of this great navigator was commenced, in command of two ships, the Resolution and the Discovery. A distinguished officer in the previous voyage, Mr. Clarke, was appointed Master of the Discovery. The principal object of this equipment was to find a north-west passage out of the Pacific into the Atlantic ocean. This enterprise has been long pursued, at a great cost of life and property. It is now, we suppose, set at rest for ever; but not until the loss of Sir John Franklin and his noble crews has added painful interest to its history. That there is a water-passage from the Pacific into the Atlantic ocean, is now placed beyond a doubt; but being in such high latitudes, it is of no use for the purposes of traffic. Captain Cook again visited New Zealand, and put ashore pigs and goats, and received, to his enjoyment, the produce of the garden seeds which were sown on his previous visit to Queen Charlotte's Sound. This renowned navigator subsequently fell a victim to the turbulence of the natives of Hawaii, one of the group of islands which he had discovered a little time before, and named the Sandwich Islands, in honour of the Earl of Sandwich. The circumstances — those preceding his death, and those immediately connected therewith—are of such a painfully interesting character, and teach us lessons of so much importance, that we will briefly relate them. When the ships anchored in a pleasant bay, on the west side of the island called Hawaii—written

in Cook's voyages, Owhyhee—the people were wild with
excitement and joy. They covered the ships' sides, decks,
and rigging; large numbers swam around the vessels,
and the beach was lined with spectators. The voyagers
were surprised, as they had seen nothing like it before.
But an explanation may be found in a tradition which
the natives had long preserved—that their god Rono,
who had left the country, gave a promise that he would
return on a floating island, and bring with him everything necessary for their happiness and grandeur.
The fulfilment of this promise had been long and
anxiously expected, and when the ships sailed into the
bay, the people concluded that the floating island—
the object of promise — was before them, and that
Captain Cook was their God Rono, and by this name
he was generally called.

The idols of this people were carved wooden images,
with distorted features, and wrapped round with pieces
of red cloth. Soon after the Resolution was anchored,
an old native priest approached Captain Cook in the
cabin with great veneration, covered the Captain's
shoulders with a piece of red cloth, presented the offering
of a small pig, and delivered a long address. On going
ashore with some of his officers, the Captain was conducted to a *morai*—a sacred inclosure, containing idols,
which were covered partly with red cloth, and a number
of human skulls. He was then placed on a high stage,
with red cloth wrapped around him, and a baked pig was
presented to him, the men who brought it prostrating
themselves with all reverence. After this he was led to
the chief image, and at the priest's request, prostrated
himself and kissed it! Offerings of fruit and a baked
hog were presented by other companies of natives,

accompanied by chants in regular responses, the burden of which seemed to be the praise of Rono; and groups of worshippers prostrated themselves as he and his companions left the *morai* to return to the ship.

This is the great blot on the memory of this truly great man. Nothing can be said to justify those proceedings, and but little in palliation of them. It is a subject of deep regret; but it need not excite our astonishment, that the people whose worship he received should be permitted to become his murderers. On Sunday, Feb. 14th, 1779, in less than a month from his first arrival in the fatal bay, Captain James Cook, the chief of British navigators, fell at Hawaii beneath the blows of the infuriated natives.

The name of Captain Cook will always be associated with that of New Zealand. His ship was the first which sailed round its coasts; he introduced useful animals and vegetables into the country, presented to the world a clear and faithful description of its inhabitants, and was the pioneer of Christian missions and British colonization, through which the whole country of these splendid islands will, we trust, be covered with the blessings of civilization and true religion.

CHAPTER II.

THE COUNTRY.

" The mountain wooded to the peak, the lawns
And winding glades high up, like ways to Heaven,
The slender coco's drooping crown of plumes,
The lightning flash of insect and of bird,
The lustre of the long convolvuluses
That coil'd around the stately stems."—TENNYSON.

TWO large islands, called the North Island and the Middle Island, separated by Cook's Strait; and a small one, called Stewart's Island, separated from the Middle Island by Foveaux Strait, compose the country of New Zealand. Scores of islets are found within a few miles of the coast. Some of these are covered with trees, and are occasionally inhabited by Sawyers. From others a considerable quantity of copper has been exported; but many of them are only barren rocks, on which numerous sea birds find a home.

Lying between the parallels of thirty-four and forty-eight degrees of south latitude, and between one hundred and sixty-six and one hundred and seventy-nine degrees of east longitude, its situation is favourable for commerce. The important colonies of Australia and Tasmania lie within about a week's sail from any of its ports, and several interesting groups of the South Sea Islands may be reached in little more than the same time. As the country extends nearly a thousand miles from north to south, it embraces a considerable variety of climate. In the Auckland province, snow is perhaps never seen—mountains excepted; certainly it never falls

at the North Cape ; but in the provinces of Otago and
Southland it is very common, and sometimes forms
avalanches, which roll down the sides of mountains with
great force, and bury unconscious sleepers under a mass
which forms their grave.

A few hundred miles eastward of New Zealand, and
under its government, are a cluster of islands known as
the Chatham Islands, which were inhabited by a people
inferior to the Maori race. "They went naked, and
their houses, if they might be called such, were made
with a few poles set up together, over a circular pit two
or three feet deep, with *toë-toë* or sods on the outside,
thus forming a cone-shaped hut ; in these miserable
places they sat huddled together, with their children
squatting between their legs for warmth. It is remarkable that this miserable people could make canoes in a
most ingenious way, of a large kind of broad-leaved sea-
weed, which they converted into air tubes, by making a
small orifice through the outer skin and then inflating
it, when one skin separated from the other ; this being
done the hole soon closed, and they were placed in the
sun to dry, and always afterwards retained their form.
A light framework of flax stalks was then made, with a
double keel, and the air tubes were lashed in parallel
rows, and the interstices filled with moss ; so that the
whole was watertight, and so buoyant that it could not
sink—thus forming a regular lifeboat. The air tubes
thus dried were always used as jars, to contain water or
oil, and also their reserves of potted birds for winter
use."*

Nearly forty years ago a number of adventurous
Maories emigrated from New Zealand to the Chatham

* Rev. M. Stack.

Islands, killed many of the aborigines, and made slaves of the remainder. These poor creatures, called Moriories, are still held in slavery by their Maori conquerors; but within the last few years their circumstances have been substantially improved. The islands were visited by a gentleman belonging to the Wellington Provincial Government in 1861, from whose report the following facts have been gathered. The population then consisted of only one hundred and sixty aborigines, four hundred and thirty Maories, seventeen half-castes, and a few Europeans. There are horses, cattle, and sheep, which with proper care would soon become numerous. A large quantity of potatoes has been exported, and grain crops ought to be raised in abundance. Fruit trees and garden vegetables thrive well. It has been for some time a victualling place for the south-sea whaling ships, and has been recommended as suitable for a penal settlement.

The Chatham Islands have recently received an unlooked-for accession to their inhabitants. The prisoners of war taken on the East Coast of New Zealand, have been transported thither. This is of course a cheaper plan than keeping them on board a hulk in the New Zealand harbours, and it is thought that they are not so likely now to effect their escape, but this is of course uncertain.* As their wives and children are with them they

* Our surmise has proved correct. In July, 1868, the Maori prisoners, with their families, seized a schooner, killing one man who resisted them and binding others, and covering the captain and crew with firearms, compelled them to take the vessel to New Zealand, where they landed in safety not far from their former homes. This spirited enterprise was conducted by Te Kooti, a man who was little known up to that time, but who has since made himself infamous, by the massacres of men, women, and children of both races perpetrated by his orders.

may possibly stay, and as they will find abundant provisions with their usual industry, the punishment may possibly be easily borne. But what effects the Pai Marire faith may have upon the people there we do not know. The writer saw a number of men and women from the Chatham Islands in Taranaki in 1865, claimants of some of the confiscated land. Their healthy appearance, European clothing, orderly conduct, and respectable conversation, made a decided impression in their favour ; and give us hope that the Maories lately transported thither will not deteriorate. They met with a hearty welcome ; the fact that they had faced the Pakeha in the battle field would not lessen their influence ; while their defeat would probably be attributed to the superior equipment of the white man. We have made this digression supposing that the information given would be interesting, and will now return to our proper subject.

New Zealand possesses a few good harbours, in which a large fleet might ride in safety ; there are others of less value on account of the bar at their entrance, requiring much caution in reference both to the tide and to the wind. Much might be done to remedy the defects of our harbours, and lessen the number of wrecks which take place. The most melancholy loss of this kind occurred on the 7th of February, 1863, when H.M. Steam Corvette Orpheus, 21 guns, 1,700 tons, and 400 horse power—having on board Commodore Burnett, with 259 officers and men—was wrecked in an attempt to enter the Manakau in the middle of the day, and with smooth water. The cause of the terrible disaster lay in mistaking the proper channel. Commodore Burnett and 189 other persons, including 22 officers, were drowned ; and within a few hours from the time when the ship struck, nothing remained as a memorial of the spot where so many souls were hurried into the eternal world.

Lofty mountains lift their heads above the snow line in both of the larger islands. The cone of Mount Egmont is 8,270 feet above the level of the sea; Tongariso, an active volcano in the centre of the Northern Island, is 6,500 feet above the sea level, and Ruapeha, only ten miles distant, rises to nearly 10,000 feet. But the highest mountain ranges are found in the Middle Island, rising from 11,000 to 13,000 feet. These are the New Zealand Alps. On their massive sides lie some of the largest glaciers in the world. One—the Tasman glacier—is eighteen miles long, and nearly two miles broad. On the west coast the glaciers descend within 705 feet of the sea level, while on the east side they keep at the respectful height of 2,774 feet. From these masses of ice and snow innumerable streams take their rise. The energy of the colonists must command respect when it is known that a coach-road has been made across these mountains, from Christchurch to Hokotiki. About one hundred miles of it cost nearly £1,500 per mile, or £145,000. On this road—extending 150 miles—coaches regularly run. Taking advantage of breaks in the mountains, the highest part of the road is only 3,038 feet above the sea. The engineering difficulties were great, but skill and perseverance overcame them.

The mountain scenery is attractive to the traveller from the deck of a coasting vessel. In one direction the snow-clad peaks pierce the clear blue sky, or are lost in the clouds; while in others the snow sheet presents a pleasing contrast against the dark green foliage of the forests which lie beneath. Very beautiful is the mountain scenery, and pleasingly varied, as the morning sun lights up the snow-clad summits, before a ray is seen elsewhere; or as the last beams of the setting sun linger upon their lofty pinnacles, after he is hidden beneath the western waves. At other times the snowy tops are seen in solitary grandeur while masses of rolling clouds hang midway down the bulky slopes. Adventurous persons—ladies not entirely excepted—occasionally climb to the highest peaks of some of them, and if the weather be suitable enjoy an atmosphere peculiarly bracing, and gaze upon a panorama painted by the Divine hand, in which mountain, plains, and rivers are delightfully intermingled, while beyond the line of coast the sea appears like a vast plain, till it sinks below the distant horizon. Many advantages are secured by the means of these mountain ranges; they are the source of a great number of streams, some of them small and rapid, and others comparatively large, which pour their blessings upon the surrounding country, producing in the fertile waste lands an exuberant vegetation, and considerably increasing the value of the plains through which they run for the purposes of the farmer, especially in grazing districts.

Although the country is intersected by water-courses, there are but few rivers on which an inland navigation can be conducted to any extent with ordinary vessels; this is owing partly to the shallows and rapids, which are not likely to be remedied, and to the trees and other substances which are embedded in the stream, but which might be removed by well-directed labour. But as the Maories conduct their canoes along these rivers, it is probable that when the country is fully opened for the traffic of both races, a class of boats will be constructed to suit the navigation of the interior part of the country, carrying up the rivers the articles of comfort and convenience imported from Great Britain, and returning laden with the rich productions of the soil, to be exported to distant lands. Many streams in different parts of the country are capable of supplying a power to machinery to almost any extent. Advantage has already been taken of them to work flour-mills and saw-mills, but colonial enterprise in this direction is at present only in its infancy.

Several kinds of metals abound. A considerable quantity of copper was exported some years ago from the Kauwau, an islet near Auckland : it is found in other places also, and will probably become a source of colonial wealth. The sea beach at Taranaki is lined with a very rich iron sand : specimens have been analysed and smelted, and several kinds of edge tools made of it with complete success ; it will, in the course of time, secure the attention which it deserves : but hitherto the plans which have been formed for smelting the sand on a large scale have failed, owing partly to the disturbed state of the natives, and partly to a course of mismanagement, which will not be much longer continued. As iron is found in many parts of both the Northern and Middle islands, it will possibly become at no very distant period, a valuable article of export.

Gold is the most exciting deposit of the present day—the means by which a numerous population has been drawn to cover extensive tracks of land that lately formed a mere wilderness, with the pleasant scenes of industry—the smiling country homestead and the crowded city—where the young may be instructed in various kinds of knowledge, and institutions are

D

formed to relieve the miseries of mankind, and churches planted whose influence will extend to distant lands. California startled the world at the discovery of its hidden wealth; Australia became its rival; and New Zealand opened her treasures with an unsparing hand.

Some idea of the value of our gold-fields may be formed from the fact, that the quantity of gold exported, according to the Government statistics, to the 31st of December, 1864, amounted to 1,749,859 ounces, most of which was sold at £3 17s. 6d. per ounce; the total value of which was £6,771.730. Of that amount, only £29,875 was sent from the Northern Island; but this proved to be the first fruits of the Thames gold-field, and has been followed by an abundant harvest. While we write, the *Wellington Independent* announces the following as the quantity and value of gold exported from New Zealand from April 1st, 1857, to June 30th, 1870 :—

	Ounces.		Value.
Auckland	266,831	...	£877,538
Picton	35,667	...	137,470
West Coast (including Nelson,			
Hokotiki, &c.)	2,349,969	...	9,258,575
Otago	2,597,288	...	10,121,886
Southland	28,234	...	111,638

The above includes 30 ounces, value £120, exported from Wellington during the first half of the year 1870, shewing that there is gold in this province, but not in payable quantities, so far as present researches have been extended.

The colony of Victoria sent to the International Exhibition in London, in 1862, a gilded obelisk of ten feet square at the base, and forty-five feet high. Had it been a solid mass of gold, it would have weighed eight hundred tons. It represented the volume of gold produced by the colony from October 1st, 1851, to October 1st, 1861, whose value was £104,000,000. And another obelisk was exhibited at Paris in 1867, by the Commissioners of Victoria, ten feet square at the base, and sixty-two feet five inches and a half high, representing the enormous sum of £146,057,444, the golden produce of that colony, and from ground which had furnished but a scanty provision for a few native wanderers, or herbage for a few thousand sheep.

Within the last quarter of a century, and principally through the gold discoveries, towns and cities have sprung up as if they had been produced by a magic wand. Among the masses who find their way to the colonies under such an excitement, are many persons whose principles and practices are dangerous to society; but a much larger class of industrious and respectable immigrants seek their home in these distant lands, and lay the foundation of an honoured and thriving community. The vicious soon seek new fields for their adventures, or are weeded out by the officers of justice, while the really valuable reap the reward of their toil.

The value of our forests is a noticeable feature. In the year 1853, the quantity of timber exported realized £92,984; and although this export did not reach such a height in any other year, it continued for some time among our chief articles of native produce. The value of timber exported during twelve years ending December 31st, 1864, amounted to £328,231. When it is remembered that various kinds of furniture-wood, that timber suitable for building purposes, not to mention those of the shipwright, and that spars adapted for the navy, may be obtained in almost any quantity, we trust that the claims of our forests will be admitted.

Among the natural products of the country, and an article, so far as we know, peculiar to New Zealand, is the Kauri Gum. This is found only in the province of Auckland, and as a branch of industry it is confined almost entirely to the Maori people. In the year 1864, the quantity exported was two thousand two hundred and twenty-eight tons; the value of which was sixty thousand five hundred and ninety pounds sterling. The value of Kauri Gum exported from the colony, according to the Government returns, from January 1st, 1853, to December 31st, 1864, amounted to two hundred and sixty-two thousand four hundred and sixty-four pounds sterling. We know no reason why this branch of industry —the labour consisting only in digging it out of the ground, removing any soil which may adhere to it, and carrying it to market, which is done with canoes—should fall off, but could suggest several reasons, were it necessary, why it may be expected that Kauri Gum will continue to be a valuable article of export.

It was thought for some years that, valuable as the land is for producing grain, it was not adapted for sheep farming on an extensive scale. This is probably the case in the Auckland and Taranaki provinces; but in the Southern provinces, both the plains and hilly country, covered with native herbage, have answered admirably as sheep-runs. Those who made the experiment of sheep farming in New Zealand, were encouraged, in 1853, by an exportation of wool, to the value of sixty-six thousand five hundred and seven pounds sterling. Eleven years later, viz., in 1864, the quantity of wool exported from the colony was sixteen million six hundred and ninety-one thousand six hundred and sixty-six pounds; the value of which was one million and seventy thousand nine hundred and ninety-seven pounds sterling.

Petroleum has been discovered in different parts of both the principal islands; and in Taranaki, near the Sugar Loaves, within two miles of New Plymouth, the indications were so satisfactory, that three companies were formed to sink wells. It would be premature at the present stage of their operations to say more on this subject than that the expectation of intelligent men runs high, as the boring machine works its way through the hard rock, which comes up ground to sand and saturated with oil. *

Suitable materials for building purposes may be found in abundance, the extensive forests supplying timber to any extent, and the rocks, from which different kinds of stone may be quarried, lying in large masses in various directions. Up to the present time houses are generally constructed of wood, except in the heart of some of the principal towns; and as buildings of this kind can be erected at a smaller expenditure than would be required for more durable edifices, it will probably continue to be the chief building material for many years to come. One kind of granite has been wrought into mill-stones, and other kinds of stone have been used in the erection of large and beautiful buildings. In some of the provinces excellent bricks may be made in any number; but in other places, as in Taranaki, the clay is not found suitable for the purposes of the brick-maker. Shells are found in such quantities in some districts that they are used for making lime; but a better material for this invaluable article may be found in extensive lime-stone rocks. And when the resources of the country are

* Since the above was written, the Petroleum Companies have been wound up, without obtaining a sufficient quantity of oil to meet the amount of money expended in boring.

properly developed, materials for different kinds of pottery will probably be found.

Coal is widely distributed ; it may be seen jutting out on the face of the cliffs in some places, and in others it lies so near the surface that the soil is washed off it by heavy rain.   When proper means shall be used to secure the best kinds, the steam-furnaces of the colony will doubtless be supplied with its own coal; it will also be used in the forge of the smithy, and will form a general article of domestic consumption.

The fertility of the soil varies very much ; some being exceeding rich, capable of producing any of the cereals, grasses, and edible roots in abundance, with proper management ; and in other places it is so barren that a fair return for the labour bestowed on it cannot be ex- pected.   The Middle Island presents many tracts of hilly country, quite unfit for agriculture; and in the North Island, especially in the province of Auckland, there are wide plains, whose barrenness is proverbial. The reason of this is stated to be the intense heat of the destructive fires which swept the Kauri forests once covering them entirely away, by which the quality of the ground was so much injured as to cause its sterility. Yet these plains are the source of that considerable article of export, which we have described as Kauri Gum. As a rule, it may be said that the soil of New Zealand will be found rich in the qualities that constitute a fertile country, and when it can be generally cultivated, will yield abundance for millions of inhabitants.

Volcanic action was, no doubt, carried on with terrible effect in both the islands at no very remote period.   This was probably the cause of the numerous gullies that are met with, some of which are so deep and precipitous that large trees growing at the bottom do not reach the ordinary level land ; so that the spectator, standing on the edge of those gullies, looks down upon the tops of a number of gigantic forest trees ; forming a picture truly unique and beautiful. Earthquakes are still felt with some violence in the neighbourhood of Cook's Strait, and also, though less severely, many hundred miles both north and south.

The Rev. R. Taylor, a gentleman of extensive geological knowledge, and well acquainted with New Zealand, contributes interesting information on the volcanic action of the country. Referring to *Otana*, near the Bay of Islands, he says—"An immense crater rises above the level of the surrounding country, with steep precipitous cliffs of pipe-clay, which, on the summit, incline inwards, so as to form a vast bowl several miles in diameter. This appears to have been formerly one huge crater, but when that became exhausted, a series of smaller ones broke out on the sides, which are still more or less in operation, and are chiefly filled with water of great depth, from which streams of sulphurous hydrogen gas escape in every part. One of these crater lakes contains white mud, which bubbles up in all directions ; in another the heated gas is emitted from innumerable pores, the highest degree of temperature being 196 Fahr. . . . Near Pa Karaka there is a remarkable volcanic cone, upwards of four hundred feet high. The mountain is hollow, and may be descended full three hundred feet. . . . But the grand centre of volcanic action in this (the North) Island is at Roturoa. This, indeed, may be considered as the chief focus of action ; for it extends over a distance of full seventy miles in length, as far as Tongariro. The number of boiling gulfs, solfatara, and boiling mud pools, is extraordinary. They are seen in every direction—in the forest, in the plain, and in the water. A large number of them are concentrated at a place called Tikitere, and a most extraordinary assemblage of them is found at Ohinemato, which renders that place one of the most remarkable in New Zealand. Rotomahana, a warm water lake of considerable size, is surrounded with innumerable boiling gulfs; in fact, it is itself nothing but a crater, the sides of which are full of action. It is, perhaps, one of the most remarkable places in the world; its boiling gulfs and natural snow-white terraces, formed from silicious deposits, are most wonderful. Thence to Hohake and Rotokawa there is nothing to be seen but jets of vapour; and so on to Taupo, where fearful boiling gulfs abound at the two extremities of that noble lake: at Rangatira and Tokahua. Again at Roto-aira, a beautiful lake at the base of the Tongariro range, boiling springs abound. Tongariro itself attains an elevation of perhaps sixteen thousand feet,* and from its lofty cone constantly belches forth a volume of smoke, and occasionally flame, which has been distinctly seen at a distance of one hundred and fifty miles. . . . One spring at Taupo possesses the power of turning whatever substance is immersed in it into stone, preserving all the original characteristics of its nature, but completely converting it into a beautiful silicious stone."†

Another scientific gentleman, Dr. Thomson, who resided in the colony many years, says,—"New Zealand is an admirable geological school; there travellers may

* This altitude is over-rated; the height is 6,500 feet.

† "New Zealand and its Inhabitants," by Rev. R. Taylor, M.A., F.G.S.

see the form of Vesuvius, the dome-shaped summits of Auvergne, the elevated craters of the Caraccas, and the Geysers of Iceland. Taupo, Tongariro, Rotomahana, Rotoroa, and White Island are almost unrivalled geological curiosities. Above the entombed village of Te Rapa, on the border of the Taupo lake, basaltic rocks may be seen in the process of conversion into soft clay by heat and chemical action ; where the Tongariro river falls into the lake travellers may observe how rapidly pumice stone and other deposits are lessening the size of this inland sea. Grand and beautiful geysers, ejecting water two degrees above the boiling point of pure water, and holding various silicates in solution, are found around the lakes of Rotomahana and Rotoroa. This water on cooling encrusts every substance it comes in contact with, and birds thrown into it are brought out like pieces of flint. On looking down through the clear smooth water of the Te Tarata geyser on lake Rotomahana, the silicious matter is observed deposited at the bottom like the hills on the eastern side of lake Taupo, a formation which, when seen from a canoe on the lake, suggests to the eye waves of lava suddenly cooled. Near the geysers at Rotomahana a noise is heard similar to the sound in a large steam-engine room. Adventurous travellers may sail on the lake on hot water, and luxurious ones swim in baths of various temperatures, the sides of which are lined with flint, white as snow and smooth as glass."*

The natives cook their food in those boiling springs ; and resort to the ponds of warm water as a means of enjoyment, when the toils of the day are past ; and there, while the young people indulge in all kinds of aquatic sports, their seniors sit down quietly relating tales

* The Story of New Zealand, by A. S. Thomson, Esq., M.D.

of past days, and discussing the events which are
now taking place around them. The mineral waters
are said to produce disease among the Maories who
generally use them; but when they shall be used
according to the instructions of competent medical skill,
they will probably be found of great value in a variety of
cases. And we may indulge the hope that the time will
come when a journey to the hot springs will be easily
accomplished, instead of being, as it has been, a
dangerous and expensive undertaking; and so bring the
benefits which these singular waters may afford within
the reach of all classes of the community.

When the adaptation of the climate and country to
the constitution and habits of British emigrants is fairly
considered; the crops of corn and abundance of fruit
which may be obtained; its rivers and small mountain
streams; its beds of coal and glittering metals, lying
exposed to the eye of the traveller; its long line of coast
and goodly harbours; its herds and flocks, fattening in
some places on the uncultivated grassy plains, and in
others on the rich pastures produced from English seeds;
no doubt can be entertained concerning the fitness of
New Zealand for the general purposes of a flourishing
and important colony. The language which Moses used
when describing the Land of Promise to the ancient
Israelites may be applied to the New Zealand emigrant:
"The Lord thy God bringeth thee into a good land, a
land of brooks of water, of fountains and depths that
spring out of valleys and hills; a land of wheat and
barley . . . and honey; a land wherein thou shalt
eat bread without scarceness, thou shalt not lack any
thing in it; a land whose stones are iron, and out of
whose hills thou may'st dig brass."*

Deut. viii. 7—9.

It is not likely that the native people, without any foreign assistance, could ever appreciate the natural advantages which their country possesses. In their former state they were conscious of comparatively few wants, which were easily supplied. God had prepared the land for another race—a race which is destined, we trust, to lift up the Maori people to the enjoyment and usefulness of civilization, and to contribute to the advancement of the moral and religious welfare of the southern hemisphere.

CHAPTER III.

"Verdurous glooms, and winding, mossy ways—
Glory in the grass, and splendour in the flower."

THE Rev. R. Taylor states that this prolific and lovely region has a botanic centre of its own; that the number of plants already known is six hundred and thirty-two, and of these three hundred and fourteen are dicotyledonous or exogenous plants, while the other three hundred and eighteen are monocotyledonous and cellular plants; that while England does not produce more than thirty-five native trees out of one thousand four hundred species, New Zealand produces trees and shrubs, above twenty feet high, to the number of one hundred and thirteen, besides one hundred and fifty-six shrubs and plants having woody stems.

The botanical researches of Mr. Banks—afterwards Sir Joseph Banks—who accompanied Captain Cook on his first voyage to these shores, were rewarded by a number of new specimens. Several gentlemen, acquainted with this branch of knowledge, have added others; and all agree that both the forest and open lands are deeply interesting fields for study. The only object contemplated is, to give the reader an intelligent account of the natural productions of this country, not for scientific examination, but to enable him to form a general estimate of the subject.

Some parts of the country present extensive plains, covered naturally with coarse kinds of grass, on which both sheep and cattle thrive well. Other portions of the

open country, and these the most extensive, are covered
with fern, or a small shrub which the natives call *ti*. The
species of fern are very numerous. Some are trees, with
clean straight stems, twenty feet high, and from six to
twelve inches in diameter, headed with a beautiful tuft
of long branching leaves, bending gracefully down on
all sides. The trunks are often used by the settlers as
posts for their rural houses, on account of their durability. Other kinds of fern are so fragile and beautiful,
being finer than the finest muslin, that they are always
admired. Some of the ferns are creeping plants, and
find their way up to the top of the trees, their beautiful
fronds, of various shape, hanging from their thread-like
stems, fluttering in the breeze. A common kind yields
an edible root, on which the Maories used to subsist
largely in seasons of scarcity. The root was roasted on
hot stones, and then beaten till its fibres became soft.
It is said to be nutritious ; many of the natives' pigs
feed principally upon it. In fertile ground the common
fern grows eight or ten feet high, but in poor soil it does
not much exceed eighteen inches ; and the same remark
may be made in reference to the *ti* plant.

The grasses and rushes, including the large coarse
kinds which the natives use to thatch their houses, and
others which grow up into a kind of tree, are numerous.
Of these the Raupo—*Typha Augustifolia*—is commonly
met with in swamps, and forms the principal material
used by the natives in constructing the walls of their
houses.

There are some plants which remind the Englishman
of the wild flowers of his native land. It is true that
he does not see the banks covered with primroses and
violets, nor the hedges white with flowering hawthorn,

except in select spots where these imported treasures
have been planted; but he looks with pleasure upon a
little modest flower, not much unlike the far-famed
daisy, and the butter-cup, with its yellow head, challenges his observation. The common sow-thistle
abounds, and affords food for cattle and other animals.
The natives also eat its tender shoots when boiled.
Water-cress is often seen growing on the margin of
streams. The farmer complains of the Bur of his sheep-
runs, on account of the injury which it does to the wool.
Dandelion has spread so rapidly, that many of the
meadows are covered with it, causing the quantity of
grass which they produce to be much reduced. Care is
needed to prevent the dock from spreading widely. Sorrel
is one of the plagues of which the farmer and the gar-
dener loudly complain ; but the large prickly thistle,
known among the settlers as the Scotch thistle, causes
the most trouble. In some places it has been suffered
to shed its seeds so abundantly, and these seeds have
been wafted by the winds to distant spots, that large
tracts of ground have been covered with them. It is
difficult to decide, in some cases, whether the plants
which are so familiar to an English eye be indigenous
or not, as they are not only found growing wild in the
neighbourhood of the colonial settlements, but are
found also in places whither it seems unlikely that seeds
should be carried.

But it is in the forest that vegetation is most luxuriant and interesting. A scramble into the dense shade
of the bush is peculiarly exciting. It cannot be called
a walk, unless a pathway has been cut ; for the tangled
undergrowth arrests the progress of the traveller at almost
every step. There are trees of various ages and sizes, from

the tender seedling, rising only a few inches from the surface, to the giant parent tree, lifting its proud and noble head a hundred and fifty feet above the ground. Parasites grow upon the lofty and spreading branches, and climbing plants—some with a stem so fine that it is used by the natives to make the meshes of their fishing nets, and others so thick that it resembles a ship's cable—cling to the massive trunks and spread themselves among the topmost branches. The atmosphere is always humid, for the sun's rays cannot pierce through the thick shade. The flap of the wood pigeon's wings is perhaps the only sound which is heard, or, possibly, a few other birds may strike up the note of wonder at the intrusion which has been made upon their quiet domain. It is a suggestive situation, favourable for devout meditation. " Lo, God is here!" The noble intertwining forms of life and beauty which display the forest splendour, proclaim His wisdom, goodness, and glory. He who has clothed the solitary places with so much varied beauty, will not be unmindful of the souls which He has redeemed by the precious blood of Christ; and as He lavishes His·riches upon places scarcely ever trodden by the foot of man, may it not be inferred that the everlasting dwelling place of His people is garnished with indescribable glory ?

The climbing plants meet the traveller in every direction, and so obstruct his way that the application of a small axe is often necessary. The supple-jack—*Ripogonum parviflorum*—the Kareau of the natives—is the most common. It is a useful article in all kinds of coarse basket work, in thatching, and in hurdle making. Some kinds, with a very small strong stem, and others several inches in diameter, reach the tops of the trees, and when cut through near the ground, are often seen hanging from them, like so many cords of different sizes. They furnish berries on which the wood pigeon and other birds fatten.

The largest tree of the forest is the Kauri—*Dammara Australis.* Its trunk is sometimes found without a limb to the height of nearly one hundred feet, and often measures thirty feet in circumference. Kauri spars have for many years been shipped to England, for the use of the Royal Navy. In the province of Auckland, it forms the timber which is in general use for carpenters' work. Posts cut from the heart of the tree resist the influences of the soil and weather for a long time, and they are consequently much used in fencing, and as piles on which wooden houses are built. It is also split into shingles, with which the houses are generally covered, instead of tiles or slates. Ship carpenters use it in constructing coasting vessels, and cabinetmakers work it up into useful furniture. One kind, having a mottled appearance, caused, perhaps, by some disease in the tree, looks very beautiful when well finished and polished. But the Kauri timber is not in such repute in the southern parts of the colony, each province being partial to the kinds of wood which are found in its own locality ; and the Kauri is not found growing south of Kawhia, while further north it is one of the most common of the forest trees. The Kauri belongs to a family of pines, which constitute a large portion of the New Zealand bush, and it is the only one which produces a cone. A resin exudes from this tree in considerable quantities, and is exported from Auckland under the name of Kauri Gum. Many of the natives are employed in searching for it in plains which were once covered with bush, with pointed iron rods. It is dug up in lumps, washed, and brought to market in flat baskets.

The Rimu—*Dacrydium Cupressimum*—is an elegant and beautiful tree, and in some parts of the colony it supplies timber for general purposes. It is more durable than the Kauri, but is wrought with more difficulty. As a material for elegant cabinet-work, the following description of Rimu may be accepted :—" It varies in colour and shade from a bright rich light brown, tinged with yellow, and thickly marked or veined with dark reddish brown, shaded with a still darker and deeper colour, and marked with chocolate colour, or reddish black. It is very close grained, rather hard and brittle, inclined to split, and difficult to work. The Rimu takes polish very quickly, and leaves a good face."

The Totara—*Podocarpus totara*—is a noble tree, and grows to the height of one hundred feet. It is a very durable wood. The Maories sometimes make canoes, seventy feet long and five feet wide, of a single tree. " The lower parts of the tree near the roots, and the top parts near and in the forks, are beautifully grained, varying in shade and depth of colour so suitable for the cabinet-maker." A very handsome sideboard was made of this wood for the King of Prussia. " It is of a peculiar knotted grain, of singular beauty, and varied in its character in a manner that is truly remarkable. The colour is not less rich and effective than the grain, and the texture of the wood is such as to ensure its durability. The new wood requires but to be known to come into great demand, and to ensure that practical recognition shown by the King of Prussia."

The Kahikatea—*Podocarpus dacrydioides*—called by the settlers white pine—grows to the height of nearly

E

one hundred and fifty feet, with a trunk seventy or eighty feet without a limb. The timber is not of much value, at least in the Northern part of the colony, except for inside work.

Several species of the laurel family are found here. Of these the most prized is *Korinocarpus,* called by the natives the Karaka, which, according to their tradition, they brought with them when they first came to New Zealand. The timber is useless, but the beautiful leaves, of a rich green colour, are excellent food for cattle. It produces a berry, the stone of which is as large as an acorn. The pulpy substance which surrounds the stone was palatable to the early settlers, before European fruit could be produced. If proper pains were taken with it, the Karaka fruit might probably be improved, and in the course of time might form a wholesome and well-favoured desert.

One of the most hard and durable kinds of wood is the Puriri—*Vitex littoralis*—generally called by the settlers Ironwood. It grows about fifty feet high, and five or six feet in diameter. As piles for bridges, the foundation of wooden houses, posts for fencing, or for any other purpose in which there is much exposure to the weather, the Puriri is in great repute. But it is prized chiefly in the northern part of the colony, as it does not grow in the south.

The Rata—*Metrosideros robusta*—is a singular tree. It is first a climbing plant, and clings to a tree for support. This course is continued till the Rata becomes so large and strong, that the arms by which it clung to the tree grasp it so tightly as to kill it. The Rata then continues to grow till it becomes a large tree, and may sometimes be seen holding in its giant arms the dead trunk on which it hung in the days of its helplessness; and at other times it may be seen hollow, the crushed tree which had supported it having rotted away. This singular tree reminds us of persons who, after being the chief support of the young and helpless, fall a prey to their withering influence. The Rata furnishes very useful wood for shipbuilding.

Some of the smaller kinds of trees are deserving our attention. The Nikau—*Areca Sapida*—often called the New Zealand palm, is a very handsome object. It has a straight trunk, from twenty to thirty feet high, and is headed with a tuft of leaves, six feet long, hanging gracefully down on all sides. This is the only representative of tropical vegetation. A species of fuschia grows to the height of thirty feet, and looks beautiful when it is covered with blossoms. It produces a fruit which is eaten by children. The fuschia is almost the only tree which sheds its leaves, and looks bare during winter. The Tutu—*Coriaria sarmentosa*—is a dangerous shrub, and is very common in some districts. It bears fruit in large bunches, which are black when they are ripe. The berry contains a stone which is poisonous; but if the stones be carefully removed, the fruit may be safely eaten, and is eaten in large quantities by the natives. Several accidents have occurred among the children of the settlers through eating Tutu berries. The leaves and young shoots are good food for cattle, *when they become accustomed to it*—care being taken that they do not eat them when they are very hungry. Many head of cattle have been poisoned by eating the young vigorous shoots of the Tutu bush; and other animals* also are

* An elephant was imported not long since for exhibition, but was killed through eating freely of the Tutu as it was led along the

endangered by it, notwithstanding the efforts which the settlers make to prevent it.

The most useful plant growing in the open lands is the New Zealand flax—*Phormium Tenax.* It grows in almost every kind of soil—on hills and in swamps, on the sand hills by the sea-shore and on the rich soil of the interior parts of the country. It grows in large tufts, and in the centre a stalk rises eight or ten feet high, and is crowned with flowers and seeds. The leaves of the flax are from three to six feet long, thick, and of a dark green colour. They are very strong, but may be divided lengthways into fine threads. This plant was in general use before the country was visited by Europeans. Mats were made of it, some of which were very beautiful; others were coarse, and served for general purposes. In the early days of the colony, these mats were commonly used by the settlers instead of carpets, and the finer kinds were bought for table covers. The Maori baskets, still in general use among both races, are made of flax, and are called *Kets.* Some of the finer kinds are very pretty and marked with different colours, and the larger kinds often supply the place of sacks. The Phormium Tenax is indigenous also in Norfolk Island and the Chatham Islands; but it is not found, as a native plant, anywhere else. The value of it is acknowledged for all kinds of cordage, a considerable quantity having been used for these purposes both in the colonies and in Europe, and efforts have repeatedly been made, both by individuals and by companies, to bring it fairly into the market, but, from various causes, without complete success. As there is not a little differ-

coast of the Middle Island. Its skeleton may be seen in the Wellington Museum.

ence between the fibre in different kinds of flax, not only in its length, but particularly in the silky gloss and extreme fineness which are sometimes met with, the time will probably come when plantations of flax will be carefully made, the different kinds assorted, and in addition to cordage, the superior material will be wrought into elegant fabrics. While we write, the flax trade is receiving much more attention than it did in former years. Steam mills are engaged in different parts of the country, and the amount of fibre prepared for the American and the European markets has given it an important place among our principal exports.

A species of gourd, called by the natives *Hue—Lagenaria Vulgaris*—is cultivated by the Maories. It is said that they introduced it on their arrival in New Zealand. The fruit, if it be eaten young, is esteemed as a delicacy; but it is in the form of the calabash that its usefulness chiefly appears. The calabash is made by scooping out the inside of the ripe fruit, through a small hole which is cut at the top, and which afterwards forms the mouth of the vessel. The calabash was almost the only vessel for carrying and holding water among the natives before their acquaintance with the white race. It was also used as a common drinking cup, and for containing oil, or any other liquid, and was occasionally marked with approved forms of the tattoo. The Taro—*Arum esculentum*—a species of yam, is highly prized by the Maories. Their tradition states that this plant was introduced on their first coming to New Zealand. Much care, a sandy soil, and a warm situation, are necessary in its cultivation. The Kumara—*Convolvolus Batatus*—often called the sweet potato, was widely cultivated some years ago by the natives, and formed a wholesome article of food.

The Bulrush-Caterpillar—*Sphœria Robertsia*—is a 'very remarkable little plant. It grows from the nape of the neck of a caterpillar, rising from six to ten inches above the ground; and if the stem be broken off, a fresh one grows from the same spot. The growth of the plant commences during the life of the insect, probably from seeds which adhere to the latter. When taken out of the ground entire, it presents a singular appearance—a living plant, with its stem and branches, and a dead caterpillar forming its root.

New Zealand was singularly free from quadrupeds, before the ships from Europe visited its shores, the only three kinds being the *Kiori*, a small rat, and the *Kuri*, a poor degenerate kind of dog, besides the pig. It is said that the two former animals are now become extinct; the Kiori having been destroyed by the common rat, brought to different parts of the country in our ships; and the Kuri has been superseded by several breeds of the English dog. The colonists of New Zealand are favoured above those of many other countries in their freedom from wild animals. Insects are numerous, some of them are troublesome, but none which we have met with are dangerous. The most troublesome kinds are the mosquito, and the *namu*, or sand fly. The former is very annoying by night in "clearings" which are made in the bush, and the latter is a savage little creature, found in countless numbers in the hot days of summer.

Among the birds found in the country, the most extraordinary was the *Moa*, which is now nearly, if not entirely, extinct. Dr. Hochstetter, who belonged to the Austrian Scientific Expedition which visited New Zealand in 1859, obtained a considerable quantity of fossil remains of this remarkable bird. He observes,—" These

gigantic birds belong to an era prior to the human race,
to a post-tertiary period, and it is a remarkably incom-
prehensible fact of the creation that, whilst at the very
same period in the old world, elephants, rhinoceroses,
hippotami; in South America, gigantic sloths and ar-
madilloes; in Australia, gigantic kangaroos, wombats,
and dasyurus were living; the colossal forms of animal
life were represented in New Zealand by gigantic birds,
which walked the shores then untrod by the foot of any
quadruped."

A writer in the New Zealand Magazine states, concerning the Moa, that "the remains of eight species
have been found, all of which have had a very recent
existence :—1. The *Dinornis Gyganteus*, in size and height
rivalling the camelopard, and probably resembling it
in its habits, feeding on the tops of the young cabbage
palms. 2. The *Dinornis Elephantopus*, whose thick
frame nearly approached in size that of the elephant.
3. The *Dinornis Robustus*. 4. The *Dinornis Crassus*. 5.
The *Dinornis Ingens*, which must have been fairly nine feet
high. 6. The *Dinornis Didiformis*, a bird four feet high.
7. The *Patapteria Ingens;* and the *Aptornis.*" Moa bones
are often found in caves, and generally small heaps of
pebbles are found near them; it is supposed that the
small stones were swallowed to assist the bird in digest-
ing its food. Bones and egg-shells of the Moa are also
found occasionally in old Maori ovens. An egg has been
seen measuring nine inches in diameter, twenty-seven
inches in circumference, and twelve inches long ; but of
course the egg varied in size according to the species of
the bird.

The *Nelson Examiner*, June 21, 1861, reported that
some gentlemen belonging to the survey department,

between the Riwaka and Takaka valleys, observed the foot-prints of a very large bird. The size of the foot-prints was fourteen inches in length, with a spread of eleven inches, the distance between them being about thirty inches. Supposing this report to be correct, and allowing these foot-prints to correspond with those of the Moa, it is probable that a remnant may be left in the unfrequented parts of the Middle Island; and if it be so, the Moa is undoubtedly the largest bird now in existence on the earth.

An interesting Moa relic has just been discovered. A workman engaged at the Kaikoras in excavating for the foundation of a house, came into contact with a Maori burial place. On carefully removing the earth, a human skeleton was found, in a sitting posture, with the elbows resting on the knees and the hands grasping a Moa's egg. The egg is described as being of a dirty white colour, slightly pencilled, and resembling that of a goose; it is about ten inches in length and seven inches in diameter, and the shell is about one-sixteenth of an inch thick.

The Kiwi, *Apterix Australis*—another singular bird allied to the Moa though much smaller—was recently common in some parts of the country; but it is now rarely seen, and within a short time it will probably become extinct. Having only the rudiments of wings, it cannot fly. It has a long beak, with the nostrils at the end; enabling the bird to find its food in the earth by the sense of smell, which is supposed to be very strong. The legs and claws are formed for strength, to enable it to tear open the ground in search of worms. Its colour is a dark brown, and the head and eye have a savage expression. The egg of the Kiwi is remarkably large, and the feathers resemble coarse hair. It is rarely seen in its wild state by day, the construction of its form and the peculiarity of its senses leading it to seek its food by night, and it is not easily caught as it runs very fast. The Kiwi is not a handsome bird, but its appearance is so singular, and it is met with so rarely, that it is always esteemed as an interesting creature.

Birds of passage visit New Zealand, but not in large numbers. There is a small species of Owl, and numbers of small Bats make their graceful evolutions in the summer evening twilight. Several kinds of sea-shore birds frequent every part of the coast. It is amusing to see some standing on the top of a rock upon one leg, undisturbed by the surf which dashes against the rocks around them. Others are seen in flocks, flying from one fishing place to another. A species of Hawk is the terror of the domestic fowls, having their chickens around them. Several kinds of small birds are very pretty, especially the Fan-tailed Fly Catcher. In the open land a bird not much unlike the English Lark, but without its song, is common; and at the edge of the forest, the beautiful little green Parrot is found in large numbers, and is a serious enemy to the bush farmer, when his crops of corn are nearly ripe. The Tui is most noted as a singing bird, and is often caged, on account of its melodious notes, in the cottages of the settlers. Its colour is black, with a few long white feathers hanging from its breast, which causes it to be often called the Parson bird; its size is about that of the Thrush. A species of Pigeon is found in the forest, and at the autumn season it becomes very fat, and is good for food. Water Fowls, of several kinds, are common in large swamps, and along unfrequented parts of rivers.

Many of the insects which are very destructive to the field crops and the gardens, have been unhappily introduced by the colonists, but of course unintentionally, and other kinds belong naturally to the country. The number of grasshoppers is immense; and the destruction which they cause is sometimes very great; some are small, and others are large and winged.

The New Zealand waters produce an abundance of fish which are good for food; but we have not met with any of so rich a flavour as the salmon, mackerel, and some other kinds, which are so well known in Great Britain. The *Kawai* is something like the English mackerel in appearance, and is often described, but improperly, as being equal to it. The fisheries of New Zealand were in a more flourishing state some years ago than they are now. Seals were numerous, especially on the coast of the Middle Island, and many of the white men who came to the country forty years ago were engaged as sealers. Several whaling companies were established in different parts of both the islands, and whalebone and oil formed important articles of export. The sperm, the hump-back, the fin-back, the pike-headed, the large-lipped, and the black whale, were found around the coast. From May to October was the whaling season, this being the time when the cow whales visit the coasts with their young calves. It was very interesting to see the whale throw up the water, with all the gracefulness of a fountain, in the act of breathing; and more interesting still to witness from the shore, as was sometimes done, the capture of this noble fish. Not many kinds of employment require more caution, more energy, more skill of a certain character, nor more perfect command of the nerves than whaling. We have stood upon the beach watching with intense anxiety this dangerous work, and have seen the ponderous black mass, a little while before so instinct with life, and threatening destruction to any boat which might have the temerity to approach it, succumb to the harpoon, and then towed ashore to be cut up *secundum artem.* The whalebone of commerce was taken from its monstrous jaws, its flesh, resembling beef in appearance, was hung up by the natives to dry as food for future use, and its fat or blubber was "tried down" for oil; a whaling station at such a time was a busy scene, but it is seldom witnessed in the present day.

Several species of Sharks are common, not only along the coast, but also in the harbours, which makes sea bathing sometimes a hazardous exercise; and in more than one instance persons have been drawn down by these savage creatures. A species, called by the natives Mako, and which is said to be found nowhere but in the latitude of New Zealand, is much prized by them on account of its teeth, which are used by the Maories as ear ornaments.

Shell fish of different kinds are abundant. Craw fish are large and good, cockles and mussels abound. A small kind of crab is plentiful, but is of little or no use. Oysters are good, and adhere to the rocks in some places in immense quantities. Shrimps are numerous, and eels are caught in large numbers both in the swamps and in the streams. No kind of reptile is found but the lizard, and that is harmless.

From the brief and imperfect account which we have given of the country and its natural productions, it will be readily admitted that, as a field for British enterprise, New Zealand possesses important advantages. Not locked up by the frosts of a Canadian winter, nor sweltering under the heat of a tropical sun, but supplied by abundant rain from heaven, falling upon a generous soil, and fanned by the bracing breezes of the vast Pacific ; and instead of breathing a deadly malaria, which no expense and caution could prevent, a salubrious atmosphere being graciously provided for their health and happiness, the people of such a country have more than common cause for gratitude to Him, who giveth them all things richly to enjoy.

·

ROWERA.

A FAIR SPECIMEN OF A LARGE CLASS OF NATIVE WOMEN.

CHAPTER IV.

THE MAORIES IN THEIR HEATHEN STATE.

" When wild in woods the untutored savage ran."

WHATEVER interest may be felt in the examination of the earth—its great divisions, diversified features, hidden treasures, and various forms of animal and vegetable life—much more interest must be taken in the careful study of mankind. The general history of the most influential kingdoms, which have acted their part and passed away, has been written. The steps by which several of them rose to power and extensive dominion; the luxury and ease which followed their successful military campaigns; and their consequent decline and fall; are familiar subjects. But there were large portions of the human race living beyond the descriptive pen of the historian, whether sacred or profane. Some of these were in very early ages formed into a compact people, and others became scattered tribes, entirely cut off from the sympathies and knowledge of the rest of mankind. At what time their migrations took place, and under what circumstances; by what means, and in what numbers they removed; by what route they reached the countries which lie far from the scene of the general dispersion of mankind; and from what portions of the longer settled countries the present inhabitants of many islands of the ocean emigrated; are questions which cannot be satisfactorily answered, except in a few instances. Nor do we know the steps by which the numerous tribes that inhabited the great continents of Africa and America, and others who had spread themselves over the islands of the Pacific Ocean, left the usages and comforts of civilization. So completely were they sunk when the world was first apprized of their existence that no idea of letters remained, nor had they any knowledge of countries beyond their own, only as a dim tradition ; and the metals which were spread around them, and which would have saved them much labour if they had known their worth, lay untouched, except in the case of a few tribes. In the early ages of the world it appears that much attention was given to the art of building ; this is sufficiently shown in sacred history ; and the substantial manner in which some of their public edifices were erected may be inferred from the remains which are in existence at the present day. We might have reasoned, *a priori*, that as the early colonists went out into the wide world they would take with them the builder's art ; and that in whatever countries they might find a home, substantial works would be erected, modified to suit their change of climate and circumstances. It is possible that to such a cause the extensive remains of masonry found in the heart of the American Continent, and in some other countries may be traced. But in the course of time they lost their interest in these things ; indolence succeeded industry, mere animal enjoyment was preferred to the nobler exercises of the mind, generation after generation went lower down the scale, till the type of wretchedness was complete, in which the people were found by the early circumnavigators of the globe. But all the people whom the voyages of discovery made known to us were not sunk to the same level. Among some the cultivation of grain and edible roots was attended to with success ; canoes were constructed, in which they made considerable voyages; their weapons of war were finished with much skill; and although they had entirely lost the knowledge of stone, bricks, and mortar in the construction of houses, they made dwelling-places of frail materials, which were proof against the wind and rain; and, either from the bark of their trees, or from the leaves of plants growing around them, they formed garments for use and ornament. But there were other races discovered so low sunk that the idea of cultivating the soil, or building even temporary houses sufficient to keep out the winter storm, seems never to have entered their minds. We need not wonder at the prevalence of idolatry among such people; but the intelligent, enterprising nations from whom they sprung may well excite our astonishment when we read of *their* unblushing idolatry.

For about one hundred years after the flood "the whole earth was of one language, and of one speech." The command which was given to Adam, to be "fruitful and multiply and replenish the earth," was repeated to Noah and his family when they left the ark. But apparently with a resolution not to obey this command, and probably with an idolatrous purpose in view also, a tower was planned in the land of Shinar—the site of Babylon—whose "top was to reach unto heaven," lest, they said, "we be scattered abroad upon the face of the whole earth." But God prevented them from accomplishing their purpose by confounding their language, and led them to form settlements in different countries, "every one after his tongue, after their families, in their nations."* Within a short time of this general dispersion, influential nations sprang into existence. Egypt

* Gen. x. 5.

rose into power, and was marked by superior intelligence; the foundation of the great Assyrian empire was laid; India teemed with inhabitants, and assumed its national character; and China, the strange, reserved, and populous China, commenced its singular course. Streams of emigration flowed in other directions; we have no means of tracing them, but some centuries after their results are seen in the people who were settled in different and distant countries. It is remarkable to see some portions of our race, only a few centuries after the confusion of Shinar, sunk to the condition of "savages," while other portions rise in every thing which constituted a great people. Europe was a long time inhabited by uncivilized tribes; the aborigines of Italy are described as hordes of savages, without laws, and living upon the natural production of the forest, and the animals which they could capture. Homer speaks of Sicily as being inhabited by savages and monsters:—

> " The land of Cyclops first; a savage kind,
> Nor tamed by manners, nor by laws confined.
> Untaught to plant, to turn the glebe, and sow,
> They all their products to free nature owe.
>
> . . . .
>
> By these no statutes and no rights are known,
> No council held, no monarch fills the throne;
> But high on hills or airy cliffs they dwell,
> Or deep in caves, whose entrance leads to hell.
> Each rules his race, his neighbour not his care,
> Heedless of others, to his own severe."

The distinctions of the races into which mankind have long been divided, is a deeply interesting study. The colour of the negro's skin, and the peculiarity of his hair, were the same three thousand years ago as they are in the present day. The peculiar features of the Jews, the Hindus, and other races, are seen in the ancient portraits which have been preserved to our time. Negroes are seen portrayed on some of the Egyptian monuments, and their skulls are found among the mummies of that remarkable country. Six hundred years before Christ, the prophet Jeremiah asks—" Can the Ethiopian change his skin, or the leopard his spots ?" shewing that the colour of the different races was then as distinct and fixed as it is now. " Microscopic anatomy has recently shown very satisfactorily that the colour of the skin exists in the epidermis only, and that it is the result of the admixture of pigment cells with the ordinary epidermic cells. The office of these pigment cells appears to be the withdrawing from the blood, and elaborating in their own cavities, colouring matters of various shades ; and all the different hues which are exhibited by the eleven races of mankind, depend on the relative quantity of those cells, and the colour of the pigment deposited in them."

The divine intention has been remarkably fulfilled in the numerous migrations which have been continued, till there is no uninhabited country now known of any considerable extent. From the regions near the North Pole to Cape Horn, and in every degree of longitude where he could · find a home, man has long been found. He flourishes in countries which are so cold·that mercury freezes, and hundreds of thousands enjoy the heat of a vertical sun. The very heart of the continent is his home, and his dwelling-place is also in the isles of the ocean. When the enterprising seamen touched the unknown groups of islands, in parts of the great Pacific far distant from any other land, they found inhabitants

F

both numerous and healthy. Two distinct races were met with, differing in colour, formation, hair, and language ; and it is not a little remarkable, that each race is not found in the groups of islands which lay nearest to each other ; but, in some cases, in islands as far distant as seven thousand miles. One of these races, often called the *Papuan* race, is assimilated somewhat to the Negro, but the other race is lighter in colour, and has straight hair. To this race the Maories—the natives of New Zealand—belong. The question has often been asked, " To which of the great divisions into which the human family is thrown does the Maori people belong ? and from what country did they emigrate, when they reached New Zealand ? " In the present day, so long after the islands have been peopled, and in the absence of any written history, it is impossible to answer these enquiries satisfactorily.

It is very probable that the Maori race have not inhabited New Zealand more than six hundred years ; their traditions, and the enumeration of their principal chiefs, lead to this conclusion. They generally speak of *Hawaiki* as the island whence they came, and describe it as lying a very long way off, and in a north eastern direction. The general opinion is that *Hawaii* in the Sandwich Islands, is the *Hawaiki* of the Maories. The objection which strikes the attention of every one is, that the native canoes were ill-fitted to traverse such an extent of the ocean. But to this it may be replied, that canoes have been met with by ships many hundred miles from any land, after they had been blown about the sea for several months ; and it is no uncommon thing for natives to be driven by the force of the winds and currents to the coasts of islands, distant from the land which they wished to reach. The difference between the language spoken at the Sandwich Islands and in New Zealand is not much, the names of headlands, bays and rivers, are the same in both countries. Some of their traditions further state, that they stayed for some time at an island called *Rarotonga*, and that when their numbers so much increased that there was not room for them, large canoes were built, and they, sailing in search of another home, reached New Zealand. The language of Rarotonga, one of the Hervey group, and New Zealand, is very similar. From whatever country they came, their canoes must traverse many hundreds of miles of sea ; it is impossible to suppose that they could come by any intelligible course, but having committed themselves to the winds and the waves, with a stock of provisions, in search of a home, were guided by divine providence to the eastern coast of the North Island of New Zealand. The Rev. John Williams found some people at Manua, one of the Navigators Islands, who had been drifted about the sea for three months, during which time twenty persons died, and the survivors at last landed nearly two thousand miles from their native island. Mr. Williams mentions a native teacher who, with his family, was drifted from Rurutu to Keppel's Island, a distance of nearly two thousand miles. By such means there is no doubt that the isles of the vast Pacific were peopled ; what may appear to. us as accidental is no doubt a part of the divine purpose, the restless waves and " stormy wind fulfilling His word. "

The traditions of the migration from Hawaiki are very particular. The cause of their leaving is said to have been quarrels and war. Thirteen canoes are named : the chiefs who came in each, the articles brought in each, and the tribes which sprang from the crew of each canoe, are distinctly remembered. On leaving Hawaiki an old chief is said to have addressed the emigrants as follows:—" Now do you, my children, depart in peace; and when you reach the land you are going to, do not follow after the deeds of Tu, the god of war, for if you do you will perish, as if swept away by the winds. Follow rather quiet and peaceful occupations, then you will die quietly a natural death. Go, then, and live in peace with all men, and leave war and strife behind you. Depart and dwell in peace. War and its evils are driving you from your father-land; live then in peace where you are going to. Conduct yourselves like men; let there be no quarrellings amongst you; but build up a great and powerful people." *

New Zealand appears to have been inhabited by an inferior race when the Maories landed on its shores. On this subject the following quotation from a lecture delivered in Auckland by the Rev. Mr. Stack, may be accepted:—" The real aborigines of these islands is not the Maori, but a Nigretto, more nearly allied to the African than to the Asiatic in colour, feature, and hair; much inferior to the Maori in stature and intellect, and occupying a far lower station in the scale of civilization, and most probably identical with the natives of Australia and Tasmania.

" From Maori traditions it appears highly probable that, when their canoes arrived from Hawaiki, this ancient race was thinly scattered over the entire group of the New Zealand isles; that being inferior to the new comers they were subdued, and either reduced to slavery or destroyed; and from the admixture of race seen in

* W. Swainson, Esq., "New Zealand and its Colonization."

the Maori, they may still be traced in the woolly hair, short stature, and chocolate colour, which is not un-frequently met with, especially amongst the Ngatikahua, and to which the derisive name of Pokorekahu—black Kumara—is applied.

"Some portions of this aboriginal race may have long survived in the Northern Island, and maintained its independence amongst the mountain ranges, where they are still remembered as the Maero, or wild men of the mountains; they are supposed even yet to survive on the Tararua range, but their existence is imaginary. It is in the Middle Island that the remnants of this people are to be looked for, amidst the natural fastnesses of the Maori Alps, where they were known as the Ngatimamoe. In former years, such was the dread which this degraded race had of the fierce Maori, that immediately they beheld them approach they fled; they were, however, occasionally captured and made slaves, for which purpose they were much prized. The Ngatimamoe do not appear to have cultivated the ground, or to have had any means of support beyond that of hunting and fishing, and the indigenous fruits and roots of the forest." But our opinion, however, is that the wild tribes mentioned in these extracts were degenerate Maories, rather than remains of an aboriginal people.

No idea of a Supreme Being appears to have entered into the Maori mind. The word *Atua*, which is now used for GOD, was applied to the several gods who were supposed to control particular events. According to their teaching "Rangi, the heavens, and Papa, the earth, had six children: Tumatauenga, the god and father of men and war; Haumiatikitiki, the god and father of the food of men which springs without cultivation ; Tangaroa, the god and father of fish and reptiles ; Tawhiri-ma-tea, the god of winds and storms ; Rango-matane, the god and father of the cultivated food of men ; and Tane Mahuta, the god of forests and birds." * Other gods were added, among whom were the ancestors of the tribes, and particularly those who were remarkable for valour.

New Zealand native religion had its priesthood, to which considerable influence was attached. The Tohunga, or priest, was probably the most intelligent man of his tribe, the supposed duties belonging to his office making it necessary to examine the subjects which were brought before him very carefully, in order to support the honour of his profession. The Maori oracle was in much re-pute, and the Tohunga was the medium through which it was consulted. The following specimens of appeals made to the oracle are given from a work recently pub-lished in the colony.† A man left his home for a con-siderable time, in consequence of a domestic quarrel, and his family not knowing whether he intended to return, consulted the oracle to ascertain his purpose, and re-ceived the following answer :—" He will return ; but yet will not return." As several months passed after re-ceiving this answer without witnessing the return of the wanderer, some of his friends visited him with terms of reconciliation ; they found him dying, stayed till he had breathed his last, and then conveyed his corpse to his former home ; the honour of the oracle was therefore preserved. The captain of a large vessel, bound for a distant country, having completed his cargo, sailed with a Maori girl on board. The Tohunga was consulted as

* Dr. Thomson, "Story of New Zealand."
† "Old New Zealand." By a Pakeha Maori.

being the only assistance within the reach of the excited and aggrieved neighbours, and the following announcement was given by the oracle :—" The ship's nose (bows) I will batter out on the great sea." Nothing was heard of the ship for about ten days, but at the expiration of that time she returned, having sprung a leak in her bows, two hundred miles from land.* This event of course contributed not a little to support the influence of the Tohunga.

The Tohunga, or priest, was employed in any extraordinary undertaking, as in the naming of a child, particularly the child of a chief, and at the interment of a corpse. Connected with the naming of a child a remarkable ceremony was performed, called Iriiri or Rohi. Before the infant was a month old he was taken to the side of a stream, named, dipped in the water, or sprinkled with water from a branch broken off a tree, and the following chant was sung :—

CHANT SUNG AT THE NAMING OF A MALE CHILD.

" Let this child be strong to grasp the battle axe,
  To grasp the spear,
  Strong in strife,
  Foremost in the charge,
  First in the breach,
  Strong to grapple with the foe,
  To climb lofty mountains,
  To contend with raging waves,
  May he be industrous in cultivating the ground,
  In building large houses,
  In constructing canoes suitable for war,
  In netting nets."

Similar ceremonies were performed at the naming of a
* " Old New Zealand." By a Pakeha Maori.

female child, but the chant sung was varied so as to suit her future duties,—

CHANT SUNG AT THE NAMING OF A FEMALE CHILD.

"May she be industrious in cultivating the ground,
   In searching for shell-fish,
   In weaving garments,
   In weaving ornamental mats,
   May she be strong to carry burdens."

How melancholy to see a whole people dedicating their infant charge to the things of this world only; and but two objects, even of a worldly kind, did they place before them as being worthy of their attention—work and war. Not a moral idea seems to have entered into their mind. Success in the battle-field was the highest aim of the men, and industry around their homesteads. was the highest aim of the women—they were really "without God and without hope in the world."

The ceremonies connected with death were still more dark and sad. Not a ray of light illumined the tomb. Natural affection was sometimes strong, and was shown in shocking expressions of blood and anguish; but no hope was entertained of a reunion in a world of perfection and glory. The heathen mother little thought as she wept over the lovely form of her departed babe, that her child was already in the paradise of God. But sad and gloomy as this was for the mother to meet, the thick darkness which hung over the country hindered not the departed babe of the rich inheritance which Christ had prepared. "Suffer little children to come unto me," even from heathen lands, from the thick darkness, "where Satan's seat is;" "let them come, and forbid them not," is the language of Jesus. It is a pleasing reflection that all the infant class, who die in the dark and cruel places of the earth, inherit celestial glory.

The corpse was often interred by the side of a stream, in which a staff was fixed. If the departed person was a man of note, the number of persons who attended the funeral was great, and the contortions of the body expressive of grief were remarkable. It is scarcely possible to form a correct conception of the sadness expressed in the following

WAIL FOR THE DEAD.

" Toko kai i te po.	Place the staff for the night (of death).
Te po nui !	The great night !
Te po roa !	The long night !
Te po uri uri !	The dark night !
Te po tango tango !	The gloomy night !
Te po wawa !	The intense night !
Te po te kitea !	The unseen night !
Te po te waia !	The unsearchable night !
Te na toko ka tu,	Behold the staff stands
Ko toko o	The staff of
Tane rua nuku.	Tane rua nuku."*

Not a gleam of light penetrated the thick darkness of the tomb ; it was night, night to be followed by no day. And yet the idea was entertained that the soul of man survived ; but in Po, night, a place of misery was her abode. They believed in different degrees of misery, one under the other, the lowest being the worst, and that in these places the departed spirit was confined without food or light, till she pined away into annihilation. They had therefore cause for grief at the death of their loved ones ; for they had never heard of the resurrection of the body ; reason, had they been accustomed

* Rev. R. Taylor.

to exercise that faculty on the subject, could have afforded them no real consolation ; life and immortality were brought to light by the gospel, but the gospel had not yet disturbed their slumbers ; they were sitting in the valley and the shadow of death, and hence arose the long, dismal, startling wail uttered at the grave.

Nor was their case singular : the whole heathen world was in similar delusion and distress.   Their general sentiment was expressed in the following lines :—

> " The meanest herb we trample in the field,
>   Or in the garden nurture, when its leaf
>   At winter's touch is blasted, and its place
>   Forgotten, soon its vernal bud renews,
>   And from short slumber wakes to life again.
>   Man wakes no more !   Man, valiant, glorious, wise,
>   When death once chills him, sinks in sleep profound—
>   A long, unconscious, never-ending sleep."

From a poem describing the adventures of Beowulf, who was supposed to have killed a dragon, and taken possession of a hoard of treasures which the dragon guarded, and belonging, no doubt, to the time when the Anglo-Saxon paganism prevailed in England, we learn that the same dark, sad sentiment then hung around the subject of death.   England, now so highly favoured, then sat in the valley of the shadow of death, without being able to pierce its thick darkness, and see the gleams of the Sun of Righteousness which were soon to burst upon the British isles with immortal glory. Beowulf died, and his body was burnt, according to the custom of the age, with all possible honours.   The place of his funeral pile was—

> " Hung round with helmets,
>   with boards of war [shields],
>   and with bright byrnies [coats of mail],
>   as he had requested.

Then the heroes, weeping,
laid down in the midst
the famous chieftain,
their dear lord.
Then began on the hill,
the warriors to awake
the mightiest of funeral fires ;
the wood-smoke rose aloft,
dark from the fire ;
noisily it went,
mingled with weeping."

When the body was consumed, the people proceeded to raise the memorial barrow, which the poem describes as being—

" A mound over the sea ;
it was high and broad,
by the sailors over the waves
to be seen afar.
And they built up,
during ten days,
the beacon of the war-renowned.
They surrounded it with a wall
in the most honourable manner,
that wise men
could desire.
They put into the mound
rings and bright gems,
all such ornaments
as before from the hoard
the fierce-minded men
had taken ;
they suffered the earth to hold
the treasure of warriors,
gold on the sand,
where it yet remains
as useless to men
as it was of old."

In all those ceremonies, not a hope of immortality is expressed. Earth—the hero of earth, the treasures of earth—bounded their vision. In the inscriptions on the sepulchral slabs found in various parts of Great Britain, the same absence of hope strikes our attention. In some instances touching expressions of natural affection are inscribed :—

> " To the gods of the shades.
> To Simplicia Florentina,
> a most innocent thing,
> who lived ten months.
> Her father, of the sixth legion,
> the victorious, made this." *

A slab found in Northumberland appears to have been the monument of a superior woman. The inscription is as follows :—

> " To the gods of the shades.
> To Aurelia Faia,
> a native of Salona,
> Aurelius Marcus,
> a centurion, out of affection
> for his most holy wife,
> who lived
> thirty-three years
> without any stain."†

These inscriptions, commending their loved ones to " the gods of the shades," shew us a people desirous to penetrate " that land of deepest shade, unpierced by human thought"—panting after immortality, but not knowing where to find it. On another monumental stone, belonging to the time when the Roman power

---

* " The Celt, the Roman, and the Saxon," p. 321.
† Ibid, p. 323.

prevailed in England, and before the introduction of the Gospel, the following plaintive inscription is met with :—

" Adieu, Septimia,
May the earth be light upon you !
Whoever on this tomb places a burning lamp,
May his ashes a golden soil cover."*

When we reflect upon the heathen ages through which our race has been led—when we approach the sepulchres of *our* forefathers, and hear their tremulous voices inquiring the way to eternal life—when we read the very words with which they laid their beloved ones in the dust, not daring to hope to see them again—we find ourselves standing upon the same low level with the Maories at the beginning of the present century. Both races can now, however, look through the gloom which surrounds the grave, and see a glorious world, peopled with innumerable inhabitants, who have " washed their robes, and made them white in the blood of the Lamb."

Some of the Maori customs connected with death were very shocking. In many cases, the wives of a chief strangled themselves, to accompany their husband into the unknown world ; and slaves were killed to be his attendants. Surviving relatives inflicted long and deep wounds in the paroxysms of their grief. Captain Cook tells us that he met with many women, whose husbands had been killed by their enemies, cutting themselves fearfully with shells and sharp stones, and making great lamentation. An eye witness gives the following revolting description of such a scene. A young man had been killed, and his head was brought and laid down among his friends, who gave expression to

* " The Celt, the Roman, and the Saxon," p. 310.

their grief in the most shocking manner. "One old woman, the mother of the murdered man, was a clot of blood from head to foot, and large clots of coagulated blood lay on the ground where she stood. She was uttering a dirge-like wail. In her right hand she held a piece of volcanic glass, as sharp as a razor. This she placed deliberately to her left wrist, drawing it slowly upwards to her left shoulder, the spouting blood following as it went; then from the shoulder downwards, across the breast, to the short ribs on the right side. Then, taking the rude weapon in the left hand, she proceeded to cut the other side in a similar manner. Her forehead and cheeks had been scored also."

When the Rev. J. Williams was leaving the island of Aitutaki, he saw some women who had cut themselves so that the blood was streaming from their heads, faces, breasts, arms, and legs, while their cries and shrieks were dreadful. In this manner they expressed their grief at the departure of their friends.

Having glanced at some of the customs which were observed at their entrance into life, and those, more shocking still, which were connected with their departure from this world, we will proceed to a description of the various and general features of Maori society.

The Maories were, in a certain sense, a religious people; for they never engaged in any important undertaking without first uttering a *karakia*—some sort of prayer or incantation; and it was never forgotten when they were preparing to start on a journey, or to engage in fishing, planting, or war. At the return of a war party, the tohunga, or priest, was again engaged, and various ceremonies were performed. But their religion afforded them no comfort when their heart was wrung with anguish; it provided them with no day of rest; it tormented them with witchcraft, and a thousand other fears, during life, and suggested nothing better, as we have already seen, than darkness and misery after death.

The observance of the Tapu had a very strong influence upon all classes. Sacredness was its general characteristic. A person or thing made Tapu was set apart for sacred or special purposes, which could not be violated on any account. The benefits of this singular custom were in many cases very great. A plantation of Kumaras, or any other property, was rendered safe from the hands of the dishonest if it had been made Tapu; the most daring spirits trembled at the idea of touching it. By the Tapu the sanctity of marriage was maintained, and its violation was sometimes the cause of exterminating wars. But if the Tapu was helpful in some respects, in the absence of law and order properly understood, it was an inconvenient institution in other cases. As a great chief was a tapued person, if he carried anything on his back, or if anything touched his head, it was immediately tapued—*i.e.*, made sacred for his own use. If he went into a cooking house, all the things contained in it were rendered useless; if he blew the fire with his own breath, no food could be cooked at it; and an inferior person was not permitted to light a pipe at such a sacred flame. After a long journey on a wet day, persons would weary themselves in efforts to procure a fire by rubbing two sticks together, while a large fire was burning close by them, but could not be touched, because it had been kindled by a chief. A tapued person, in many cases, could not touch food with his hands, but submitted to the ludicrous, yet necessary inconvenience, of being fed by others; and the only way by which he could slake his thirst, was by turning up his face, while an attendant poured water into his mouth out of a calabash.

Those who handled a dead body were tapued, and could not touch food with their hands. In a large pah, a person was set apart for the interment of the dead ; and to a more wretched office he could not be appointed. "Old, withered, haggard, clothed in the most miserable rags, daubed all over from head to foot with red paint— the funeral colour—made of offensive shark oil and red ochre mixed, keeping always at a distance, silent and solitary, often half insane, he might be seen sitting motionless all day at a distance, forty or fifty yards from the common path or thoroughfare of the village. . . Twice a day some food would be thrown on the ground before him, to gnaw as he best might, without the use of hands; and at night, tightening his greasy rags around him, he would crawl into some miserable lair of leaves and rubbish, there, cold, half-starved, miserable, and dirty, to pass, in fitful ghost-haunted slumbers, a wretched night, as a prelude to another wretched day."*

The inconvenience of the Tapu was felt in the commencement of the Missions, as the road between the stations was occasionally tapued, and consequently the mission families were then prevented from visiting each other. And we have known Government officers of high standing walk hundreds of miles without reaching the place whither they wished to go, on account of a portion of the country through which they wanted to pass being tapued. Such a sacred spot must not be trodden, and no inducement was sufficient to permit the Pakeha to proceed. The Tapu was fixed by a tohunga or

* "Old New Zealand." By a Pakeha Maori.

a great chief, and it could not be removed but by a person belonging to one of those classes.

Many ludicrous and unpleasant circumstances occurred among the early settlers through unintentional violation of the tapu. The singular and serious charge of "roasting his grandfather," was once preferred by a native against a pakeha, and payment was demanded. The explanation of this allegation brought out the following facts ; that the bones of the "grandfather" had been deposited upon a certain tree, that they had been removed from it ten years, that the pakeha had kindled a fire at the foot of this tree, while he was on a journey, and that the tree had caught fire and was burnt down ; and thus, by a convenient figure of speech, the "grandfather" had been roasted, and payment must be made ; and the matter was not settled till two bags of shot, two blankets, some fishhooks and tobacco, had been given to the aggrieved grandson.[*]

But the violation of the tapu, although unintentional, sometimes led to more serious consequences. In 1772, the French navigator, Marion du Fresne, anchored his two ships in the Bay of Islands, and spent a month on the most friendly terms with the natives. The friendship was suddenly closed, and without any cause which the Frenchmen could understand. An ominous silence was kept by the natives, until their plans were prepared, when the foreigners were invited to go ashore, where Marion, several of his officers, and many of his men were murdered. This sudden and shocking massacre was caused, as it has since been discovered, by some of the ship's crew having taken firewood from tapued places. Could the dark history of ships plundered, crews massa-

[*] See "Old New Zealand." By a Pakeha Maori.

cred, and the horrid orgies which followed, in different parts of New Zealand, be known, it would probably be found that the violation of the tapu was the general cause of complaint.

An instance in which the influence of the tapu operated favourably occurred recently. When the Taranaki war was commenced, several families, including the Rev. H. H. Brown and his family, chose to stay in their homes at Omata, under the impression that they were safe. But when danger became imminent, and the means of escape were cut off, all the families sought refuge in Mr. Brown's house, which was tapued, as the residence of a clergyman, and were preserved; while their neighbours were deliberately murdered, and the battle of Waireka was fought within a few hundred yards of their asylum.

The New Zealander carried the process of tattooing the face and other parts of the body as far, perhaps, as any other people in the South Sea. This kind of ornament was considered appropriate to a powerful chief, who was more profusely marked than ordinary persons. In New Zealand, as well as in other countries, pride demanded its terms of suffering. The tattooing process was so slow and painful that but little could be done at one time. The pigment prepared for this purpose was burnt Kauri gum, or the rosin of the rimu, pounded into a fine powder. The instruments used were a sharp chisel, made of bone, and a little mallet. The lines were traced with a piece of charcoal, after which the chisel was driven into the skin, and a piece of scraped flax, dipped into the pigment, was drawn over the incision. The life of the patient would have been endangered if much were attempted at one time; therefore a considerable time elapsed before the decorations were completed. The face was the principal part on which the artist displayed his skill. Beautifully curved lines were chiselled there, on the cheeks, the nose, and the chin, and care was taken to make both sides of the face alike. The thighs and other parts were ornamented also, but not so commonly as the face. The tattoo, in the case of females, was confined to the lips and chin, with a few straight lines on the chest and arms. The men plucked out their beard with muscle shells, lest it should hide the tattoo. But this custom of savage life is likely to be entirely discontinued. It is not often that a young man now submits to it; though, as a freak of fancy, he sometimes appears with his face marked with charcoal, so as to represent the tattoo. This, however, is continued only for a few hours, and many a New Zealander is seen proud of his clean-shaven face and bushy whiskers.

The early visitors to this land of the Maories invariably noticed a short, flat, stone weapon, which the natives carried everywhere, and seemed to prize very highly. Of the same material was a little uncouth ornament, representing the human figure, but greatly distorted. This was the *Hei tiki*. It was worn carefully round the neck, and probably represented one of their ancestors. Both the stone weapon, called *Meri*, and the Hei tiki were precious heir-looms. To obtain a new one, journeys of many hundreds of miles were undertaken. This was probably the chief reason why they were preserved with so much care. The following interesting account of the Poenamu—the green stone of which those heir-looms were made—is taken from the report of Charles Heaphy, Esq., who, accompanied by another gentleman, made a long and toilsome exploring tour on the west coast of

the Middle Island, in the year 1846. The small settlement of natives, where the green-stone ornaments were
made, was several hundred miles distant from any other
tribe. None of them, except a very few persons, had
then seen a white man; pigs and horses they were
equally unacquainted with. No European clothing was
found among them, nor any imported articles, besides
an axe and two iron pots. But many of their mats were
of the most beautiful and silk-like material, and of
elegant workmanship. Their chief employment was in
making Poenamu articles.

The kind of stone most valued was the Inanga—which
is rather opaque, and traversed with creamy-coloured
veins; and of this kind the best *Meris* were usually
made. The Kauairangi is of a bright green colour, with
darker shades, or mottled, and is the most translucent.
Ear ornaments were made of this kind. The Kawakawa
is of a dark olive green, and is rather dull and opaque.
Hei tikis and ear-pendants are made of this. The Maka
tangi wai is the most beautiful, being of a clear pale
green, and very transparent; but it is the least esteemed
among the natives.

The Meri was a terrible weapon in battle—one blow
with it, when the antagonist was seized by the hair,
being sufficient to cause death. As the stone is very
hard, the labour of two or three months was bestowed on
one article. In the absence of European tools, the most
difficult part of the work was to drill the hole through
the handle. To accomplish this, a piece of sharp flint
was lashed neatly in the end of a split stick, about sixteen inches long, and which formed the spindle to a large
teetotum drill. For the circular plate of this instrument,
the hardened intervertebral cartilage of a whale was

taken, a hole made through, and the stick firmly and accurately fixed in it. Two strings are then attached to the upper end of the stick, and by pulling them a rapid rotatory motion was given. This was continued till one piece of flint was blunted, when a fresh one was fixed in its place. It is pleasing to add that these ingenious and industrious people treated the gentlemen who visited them with the utmost kindness.

The Maories, compared with many of the Polynesians, are an industrious people. The neat and orderly state of their plantations of taro and kumaras attracted the attention of Captain Cook. Not only were they free from weeds, but every root was carefully surrounded with a hillock of mould or sand. Many of their gardens are perfect models of neatness in the present day, and by the care given in the selection of a properly sheltered situation, suitable soil, careful weeding, and loosening of the ground, they often secure heavier crops of maize, and some other things, than their Pakeha neighbours. The excellence of industry was proverbial, of which the following may be given as a specimen :—" He kai tangata he kai titonga, koke mahia e tona ringa ringa, tino kai tino makona "—" whosoever trusts to another man's labour for his food, will be disappointed ; but he who labours with his own hands, will have enough and to spare."

The patience with which they continued their laborious occupations before the introduction of iron tools was remarkable. Their delving implement was a stake sharpened at one end, with a piece of wood, about six inches long, lashed firmly on horizontally, about twelve inches from the point. On this piece the foot rested when the stake was forced into the ground, and by bringing the top of the stake towards the earth, the soil was loosened. We have stated in a former chapter, that some of their canoes were seventy feet long and about six feet wide; the labour expended upon a canoe of this size must have been very great. Their canoes in the North were made of the Kauri, in the South of the Totara. The principal tool used in making them was a sharp stone, strongly fastened to the end of a stick in the form of an adze. With this tool, and the careful application of fire, they felled the giant tree, cut it to its proper length, reduced it to the desired form, and hollowed out the immense log. By the same process planks were prepared, which were firmly lashed to the solid log, so as to raise the sides of the canoe. The figure-head required much labour. It was seen rising several feet above the body of the canoe, elaborately carved, and exhibiting a repulsive caricature of the human form. Two of these canoes were lashed together, and formed the celebrated double canoe. They were propelled by paddles, which were models of excellence, both in form and workmanship. The number of men and quantity of provisions which they could contain were considerable, while they were propelled with ease and rapidity. Smaller canoes, without ornament, were often made for fishing purposes, and for carrying fire-wood; these of course required much less labour.

Much ingenuity was displayed in constructing hooks and nets for catching fish. Some of these were so strong that the savage shark, and other large fishes, were secured. From these fishes they procured not only an article of food, but abundance of oil, with which they were fond of anointing their bodies. Not a little skill was shewn in building their best houses. The frame-work was made of poles firmly fixed in the ground, with cross-pieces and rafters carefully fitted, and fastened with flax. Layers of Raupo were then neatly tied on the outside of the frame-work; and on the inside, properly selected reeds and carefully trimmed fern-stalks were nicely arranged, and fastened to the frame-work with flax. The roof was thatched with a thick coating of rough grass. A small opening was left at the end to admit the light, and the door-way was low; but the interior appearance of a good house, when new, was clean and prepossessing. A neat verandah was often made to form the front; a few large stones in the centre of the house constituted the fire-place, and as there was no chimney, the smoke soon marred its beauty, and gave it a dirty appearance. Another kind of house was constructed of similar materials, but it was small, low, with no opening for the admission of light, and with a door-way only about two feet by eighteen inches in size, through which a person must creep, and admitting scarcely any circulation of air. In such a house several persons would lie down on mats, discussing topics of interest, and perspiring profusely. A fire was often burning in the centre, which fearfully increased the temperature, and so filled the house with smoke that it became scarcely supportable. This class of houses must tend to produce disease, not only from the unwholesome air which is breathed in them, but from the habit of the natives to leave them nearly, or quite naked, for the purpose of enjoying for a little time the cool fresh air of the evening.

Near their houses, sheds were built, where fire-wood was laid up in admirable order, and where their food was prepared and cooked in wet weather. The native ovens were made by scooping out the earth according to the size required; a fire was then kindled in the hole, and some stones were laid upon the fire, and made very hot; after this the fire was removed, and water was poured upon the stones to produce steam. Baskets of fish, potatoes, and other food were then placed upon the stones, and covered very carefully with kets and other things to preserve the food from dirt; more water was then poured upon the stones, and the whole was covered with earth, so as to prevent the steam from escaping. In about half an hour the earth was removed, and the food was admirably cooked. The ovens were made of whatever size was required; some of them were small enough for the use of a family, and others sufficiently large to supply a considerable number of persons. We cannot forget that in this kind of ovens human bodies have often been cooked. The remains of many of our countrymen have shared this fate; but these horrible usages have passed away in New Zealand, except under the savage excitement of war, and we trust will never be revived. Fish and birds were often roasted, by fixing them on one end of a stick before a fire, the other end being driven into the ground. Fish were dried for future use. Stages were erected on which food was kept from the rats. And notwithstanding their habit of besmearing themselves with rancid fish oil, which rendered their persons, garments, and houses offensive to a European, not a little care was taken to keep their homesteads clean and orderly.

Maori names, as suggested by any particular event, were often given to children, or appropriated in adult age. This was the case with the Hebrews, and other ancient nations, and continues to be practised in several islands of the Pacific Ocean. The original name of Pomare I., the King of Tahiti, was *Vairaatoa;* "but travelling on one occasion among the mountains, and sleeping in an exposed situation, he felt cold, and was affected with coughing. One of his companions remarked in the morning, that it had been a night of cough—Po mare; *Po,* night, and *mare,* cough. The chief was pleased with the combination, and adopted it as his name."* The Rev. R. Taylor observes, that *Heu Heu* implies, "Surprising an enemy from the brushwood;" *Tinirau,* "Slew many hundreds with his own hand;" *Rangihaeata,* "The first ray of the morning;" *Te Thi,* "The sunbeam." When Te Heu Heu was killed by a land-slip, his son assumed the name of *Horonguku,* "The sliding landslip." The Christian names of England are now commonly adopted, and others, taken from persons, offices, and things, are singularly appropriated. Hence *Kingi,* King; *Kuini,* Queen; *Kawana,* Governor; *Pihopa,* Bishop; *Kanara,* Colonel; *Wikitoria te Kuini,* Victoria the Queen; *Tikera,* Tea-kettle; *Tupeka,* Tobacco; *Kawena,* Coffin — are among the names in vogue at the present time.†

Polygamy prevailed, especially among the chiefs, and produced its natural results in the form of jealousy, quarrels, suicide, and murder. The first-born son of a chief was his successor, although the mother might be a slave. As is the case generally in heathen countries, the Maori women were much oppressed. They performed most of the field-work, as well as the more appropriate duties of cooking and making mats; they procured firewood, fetched water from the brook, and carried provisions when on a journey. These things, together with the early age at which they were often

* Ellis's "History of the London Missionary Society."
† "New Zealand and its Inhabitants." By Rev. R. Taylor.

married, contributed to rob them of their bloom before
half their days were spent. While young, the native
women are generally pleasing in appearance, and often
good looking; but they become haggard and repulsive
at an age when the men retain their freshness and vigour.
The shocking sin of infanticide was often practised.
Mothers stopped the breath of their own children, by
closing their mouth and nostrils with the hand, or by
laying a wetted cloth upon their face! The reasons
assigned for this abominable custom included jealousy,
the inconvenience of nursing when engaged in field work,
and the importance of being ready to flee without in-
cumbrances if they were surprised by an enemy. These,
and others like them, were the considerations which
dried up the stream of a mother's love, and by so robbing her of natural affection, placed her below the
monsters of the deep, and the wild beasts of the desert.
To such a state of degradation thousands of mothers,
scattered over the wide bosom of the Pacific, were
reduced. This practice has been swept away from New
Zealand, and other islands where the Gospel has been
accepted, but it is still continued in many heathen
countries.

But it must not be inferred from the preceding para-
graph that the Maories were incapable of affection.
Children were generally treated with much kindness if
they survived the state of infancy. The tangi had the
appearance of warm friendship; and no doubt, in many
cases, it was sincere. This custom, so strange to Europeans, was an expression of affection between friends
who had been for some time separated, in which they
touched each other's nose, told the events which they
had met with since they parted in a sad, whining chant,

and wept tears in abundance. This was often continued about half an hour. At a great assembly, where numerous parties from a distance met, many exhibitions of the *tangi* were seen at one time, and formed a strange and melancholy picture in the eyes of every one except a native.

The Maories are fond of public speaking, and opportunities for such an exercise often occurred. To consider an affront given by another tribe, to determine on war, to make arrangements of peace, and to discuss any other affair of general interest, a numerous meeting was convened, and their oratorical powers were freely displayed. The speaker generally roused himself into a strong passion, as he walked backwards and forwards before the audience, brandishing his weapon of war, striking his sides, and assuming a countenance so agitated and fierce, that a stranger from England would tremble for the consequences. "On these occasions," observes Sir George Grey, "according to the custom of the nation, the most effective speeches were invariably principally made up from recitations of portions of ancient poems. In this way the art of the orator was shewn by his selecting a quotation from an ancient poem, which figuratively, but dimly, shadowed forth his intentions and opinions. As he spoke, the people were pleased at the beauty of the poetry, and at his knowledge of their ancient poets, whilst their ingenuity was excited to endeavour to detect, from his figurative language, what were his intentions and designs. Quotation after quotation were rapidly and forcibly chanted, and made his meaning clearer and clearer; curiosity and attention were by degrees rivetted upon the speaker, and if his sentiments were in unison with the great mass of the assembly, and he were a man of influence, as each succeeding quotation gradually removed the doubts from the minds of the attentive group who were seated upon the ground around him, murmur of applause rose after murmur of applause, until, at some closing quotation, which left no doubt as to his real meaning, the whole assembly gave way to tumults of delight, and applauded equally the determination he had formed, his poetic knowledge, and his oratorical art, by which, under images beautiful to them, he had, for so long a time, and at last so perfectly, manifested his real opinion."

The *cannibal* propensity of the New Zealanders was very strong, and was frequently gratified; but we have no proof that they ate human flesh as common food, nor that they were induced to do so through a scarcity of provisions. Persons who were the objects of revenge, slaves who fell under the displeasure of their owners, and captives taken in war, were often killed and eaten. When a small party was surprised and killed, one or more of the bodies was devoured. The first person killed in a battle was considered sacred to the gods, and, if the body could be procured, it was baked in a separate oven, as a religious offering. Large numbers of bodies were cooked in extensive ovens at the conclusion of a battle, and the victorious party gorged themselves with the horrible repast; the remainder was then packed in baskets and carried with them on their journey, or sent as a present to their friends, and in some cases it was kept till it became putrid, and was then eaten! Females were not generally supposed to eat human flesh; but they often accompanied the war party, carried their provisions, and prepared their food.

Of the same shocking character was their custom of preserving human heads. This was done by cleaning them, and then drying them thoroughly in ovens, carefully preserving the face and scalp from being torn, so that the lines of the tattoo were distinctly retained. The heads of persons slain in battle, especially if fully tattooed, were preserved as trophies of war, and exhibited on the top of poles along the fences of a pah. It is said that this custom was in some cases the result of affection ; and that if the chief wife did not die with her husband, she would sometimes have his head dried, and sleep with it by her side ! Preserved heads were offered for sale to Captain Cook in Queen Charlotte's Sound, and a human skull was used to bail water out of a canoe. It is painful to write that, after a communication was opened between New Zealand and New South Wales, a considerable traffic was carried on in preserved heads, which commanded a high price in the Sydney market. To such a fearful extent was this horrible practice carried, that slaves were sometimes killed to complete the number of heads for which a bargain had been made with the Captain of a ship ! We blush for our countrymen ! To what a shocking state may even an Englishman fall, when he is free from the restraints of law, and is urged along in a vicious career by the demon of avarice ! This abominable traffic was continued till the Government of New South Wales put a stop to it.

The Maori was a man of war. At his birth a Karakia was offered that he might be foremost in the battle-field, and at his death his prowess while engaged in deadly strife was chanted in mournful strains. Scarcely any article was prized so highly as weapons of war. As a warrior, the darkest and basest passions were let loose, and he performed deeds of cruelty which could be hardly equalled by the fiercest beasts of prey. The perpetration of a murder, an act of adultery, the absconding of a woman to another tribe, planting upon disputed ground, or a curse denounced against an influential chief, were among the common causes of war. A young man seeing the perspiration dropping from the cheek of a chief as he was running, in great haste, remarked that "the vapour rose from his head like the steam of an oven." This expression was regarded as a great curse, and caused a war which exterminated the tribe to which the young man belonged.*

Their pahs or villages were often built upon hills, so that the approach of an enemy might be more easily perceived. A high cliff, overhanging a river or the sea, and accessible on one side only, was a favourite position, as it could be easily defended. Very strong fences, about ten feet high, in double rows, about three feet apart, were erected round the pah ; and in cases of great danger, embankments were raised, trenches were dug, and underground houses were made and stored with provisions.

The war-dance was an exhibition of terror, and was performed naked. It is thus described in Cook's voyages :—" The contortions are numerous ; their limbs are distorted and their faces agitated with strange, convulsive motions. Their tongues hang out of their mouth to an amazing length, and their eyelids are drawn so as to form a circle round the eye. At the same time they shake their darts, brandish their spears, and wave their patoo-patoos to and fro in the air. There is an admirable vigour and activity in their dancing, and in

* See Taylor's " New Zealand and its Inhabitants."

their song they keep time with such exactness that sixty or a hundred paddles, when struck against the sides of their boats at once, make only a single report." The demonstration which Captain Cook witnessed was upon the water, and although it was sufficiently energetic, full scope was not given for a complete display. We supply the following description of the war-dance as it was commonly performed :—" The whole army, after running about twenty yards, arranged itself in lines, five, ten, twenty, or even forty deep, and then all squatted down in a sitting posture. Suddenly, at a signal given by the leader, all started to their feet, having weapons in their right hands. With the regularity of a regiment at drill, each man elevated the right leg and right side of the body, then the left leg and left side, and then, like a flash of lightning, jumped two feet from the ground, brandishing and cleaving the air with his weapon, and yelling a loud chorus, which terminated with a long, deep, expressive sigh, and was accompanied with gaping mouths, inflated nostrils, distorted faces, out-hanging tongues, and fixed, starting eyes, in which nothing was seen but the dark pupil surrounded with white. Every muscle quivered. Again and again these movements were enacted, and time was marked by striking their thighs with their open left hands, so as to produce one sound."

The introduction of fire-arms followed soon after trading vessels ventured to approach their shores, and gave an unhappy impetus to their warlike movements. It is impossible to convey a correct idea of the firm grasp with which the demon of destruction held fast the soul of an old warrior. The following description of the death of an old chief of this class is given from the pen of a gentleman on whose premises the chief spent the last years of his life:—"The old man, I saw at once, was at his last hour. He had dwindled to a mere skeleton. No food of any kind had been prepared for, or offered to him, for three days: as he was dying, it was of course considered unnecessary. At his right hand lay his spear, tomahawk, and musket; over him was hanging his green-stone Mere; and at his left side, close, and touching him, sat a stout, athletic savage, with a countenance disgustingly expressive of cunning and ferocity, and who, as he stealthily marked me from the corner of his eye, I recognized as one of those limbs of Satan, a Maori tohunga. The old man was propped up in a reclining position, his face toward the assembled tribe, who were all there waiting to catch his last words. I stood before him, and I thought I perceived he recognized me. Still, all was silence, and for a full half hour we all stood there waiting patiently for the closing scene. The silence was suddenly broken, when the dying man said, 'Hide my bones quickly where the enemy may not find them—hide them at once. O my tribe, be brave, be brave! . . . I give my *mere* to my pakeha. My two old wives will hang themselves.' Delirium came on, when he imagined himself in the battle-field, and gave orders for the 'charge, and then for the rescue.' He fell back evidently dying, and murmured, 'How sweet is man's flesh!' and died. Just then the *tohunga* shook his shoulder roughly, and shouted in his ear, 'Kia kotahi ki te ao! Kia kotahi ki te po!' At a signal from the *tohunga* a roar of musketry burst forth. Thus in a din like Pandemonium, guns firing, women screaming, and the accursed *tohunga* shouting in his ear, died Lizard-skin, as good a fighting-man as ever worshipped force or trusted in the spear. During the following night his body was carried away, and laid in a cave, with his spear and tomahawk beside it, and before the next morning his two old wives hanged themselves! "

Such was the unsophisticated nature and character of people, whom the contaminating influences of civilization had not touched, according to the teachers of philosophy in the latter part of the last century, that every virtue which is pure and ennobling could be found among them. But what was their real condition? The preceding pages reveal a scene of evil, at which reason, benevolence, and honour are opposed and insulted, and from which humanity may turn away and weep on account of the degradation of our species. Yet we have not laid bare the darkest practices of their sin and wretchedness; for it is 'a shame even to speak of those things which are done of them in secret.' "

The inhabitants of other islands in the South Sea were sunk as low, and many of their most cruel and revolting customs were similar to those of the Maories. Infanticide was practised to such a shocking extent at Tahiti that "few, if any, females could be found in the entire community who had been mothers, and had not been guilty of it. By the majority of those who had been mothers it had been perpetrated more frequently than avoided; and by many to an extent which, but for the most unequivocal evidence, that of the perpetrators themselves, would be deemed incredible." It does not appear that the Tahitians were cannibals, but their savage cruelty when engaged in war led them to delight in thrusting their spears through the bodies of children, and stringing a number of infants together on a cord, and dragging them after them in triumph to their

H

encampment. Human sacrifices were frequently offered to their gods; and "the foundations of the temples were sometimes laid on the bodies of men who had been killed and offered in sacrifice to the idol for whose worship the building was reared."*

The people of the Fiji Islands were notorious cannibals. On some occasions large numbers of persons were killed, and their bodies cooked and salted for future use. In other cases the remains of a cannibal feast were kept in the ground till they became putrid, and were then exhumed and eaten with delight. More horrible still is it to relate that some instances occurred in which limbs were cut off one by one, as they were wanted for food, from a living man; and the poor mutilated wretch was compelled to be a spectator while his own limbs were cooked and roasted. These statements are made by the Rev. Walter Lawry, the late General Superintendent of the Wesleyan Missions in Polynesia, who observes that there were some circumstances in connexion with those facts which he was not able to set down: "they are before me," says he, " but a veil must cover them."†

We cannot conclude this chapter in more appropriate language than that used by the apostle Paul in describing the effects of heathenism eighteen centuries ago; only remarking that the inspired expressions were applicable to the people of New Zealand, and of Polynesia in general, in an intenser degree than they were probably applied, at least, in some respects, to the heathen of ancient times :—" God also gave them up to uncleanness through the lusts of their own hearts, to dishonour their own bodies between themselves . . . to vile affections

---

* Ellis' History of the London Missionary Society.
† Wesleyan Missionary Notices, 1848.

. . . to a reprobate mind, to do those things which
are not convenient; being filled with all unrighteousness,
fornication, wickedness, covetousness, maliciousness;
full of envy, murder, debate, deceit, malignity; whisperers,
backbiters, haters of God, despiteful, proud, boasters,
inventors of evil things, disobedient to parents, without
understanding, covenant breakers, without natural affections, implacable, unmerciful."

CHAPTER V

" There he stands ;
The mark of foreign climes is on his brow ;
He hath no power, no costly gifts to deal
Among the people, and his lore perchance
The earth-bowed worldling with his scales of gold,
Accounted folly. Yet to him is raised
Each straining eye-ball, " Tell us of the Christ."

THE establishment and progress of Christian Missions in heathen countries, form one of the most interesting features of Protestant religion in the present day. In them many of the brightest utterances of inspired men have been partly fulfilled, and an intelligent hope is given, in the success which has attended them, of the world's salvation. Not that there is anything novel in Christian missions, for the very nature of our religion is expansive, and the commission with which we are entrusted enjoins us to " go into all the world, and preach the gospel to every creature." This was properly understood by the early Christians, who " went everywhere preaching the word." Some attempts were made, even in the dark ages, to spread the truth as it is in Jesus ; and though bonds and torture and death were the penalty which a wicked world inflicted upon those devoted servants of Christ, they were not entirely prevented from pursuing their work of love and faith. Nor did they labour in vain, for the churches of the present day are their debtors, not only in the vigour and stedfastness which their example has inspired, but for the dissemination of the sacred Scriptures, whose glorious truths are the foundation of our hope and the guide of our life. The Roman Catholic Church has set us *some* praiseworthy examples of missionary zeal; the errors of their system we deeply deplore, the substitution of the saints for the Saviour, the crucifix for the cross, and the traditions of the church for the teaching of the word of God result, we fear, in the loss of multitudes of souls; nor can we look upon their efforts to overturn the labours of successful propagators of a purer faith, and so to blight the prospects of some of the fairest fields of Christian labour, without much regret; yet we cannot but admire their missionary zeal, self-denial, and incessant labours.

The earliest attempt to form a Protestant mission was made by the Church of Geneva, in the middle of the sixteenth century, when some agents were sent to America, but it does not appear to have prospered. More decisive efforts were made by the Dutch in Ceylon and Java in the early part of the next century; and a great number of nominal Christians were the result of their labours. The first British organization for missionary purposes appears to have been made in 1649, when the "the President and Society for the Propagation of the Gospel in New England" received the sanction of Parliament. In the first year of the eighteenth century the "Society for the Propagation of the Gospel in Foreign Parts" was incorporated by a charter, and included several of the most eminent persons both in the Church and in the State. Seven years after the Danish Mission in India was established on the Malabar coast. In 1731 the Moravian Brethren commenced their missionary work, and continued it in the face of trials and disappointments of no ordinary kind ; their consistent devotion and extensive labours entitle them to a high place among those whose aim is to enlighten the dark places of the earth. "The Baptist Missionary Society" struggled into existence in the latter part of the last century, under the frown of some good but mistaken men, chiefly through the indomitable energy and entire devotedness of Messrs. Carey and Thomas and a few other persons, who now enjoy the reward of their labours. Three years after the departure of Carey and Thomas to the East, the "Duff" sailed with thirty missionaries, some of whom were married, to commence their work of faith and love among the uncivilized islanders of the Pacific Ocean. This was the commencement of the "London Missionary Society." The churches of America originated the American Board of Commissioners for Foreign Missions in the early part of the present century, and other similar institutions soon after sprang up in the United States. At this time the missionary spirit largely pervaded the churches, shedding a happy influence over their immediate labours, and preparing them to take up a position in the high places of the field. In the first year of this century the attention of the Established Church of England was directed to missionary work, and soon after resulted in the formation of "the Church Missionary Society." After conducting missionary labours in the American colonies and the West Indies with success, the "Wesleyan Methodist Missionary Society" was properly organized in the year 1817, and is at present, through the characteristic energy of Methodism, one of the most influential missionary societies now in the field. So copiously has the missionary spirit been poured out upon the Protestant

churches in Great Britain and Ireland, in the European
Continent, in America, and in the British Colonies, that
many other institutions, having the same object in view,
have been formed, and are conducted with much success
in various parts of the earth. More than twenty-five
thousand agents, including ordained missionaries, native
assistants, physicians, schoolmasters, and printers, are
now engaged; all classes of talents are employed, the
gospel is preached in many languages, and a sacred
literature, including the translation of the Scriptures, is
circulated in many lands, where till lately Pagan darkness was really felt. In the support of this extensive
work about nine hundred thousand pounds sterling are
annually spent; and this goodly sum is raised, with a
few trifling exceptions, as the voluntary offerings of the
friends of missions. The effects of missionary labour
are apparent to all. More than a million of persons
now sit down to the Lord's table who have been rescued
from heathen darkness; and a million and a half of
scholars are receiving instruction in mission schools.
The temporal advantages of Christian missions are many
and great. The mariner does not tremble for the safety
of his ship as she lies in the harbour, where the church
and school-house are the most conspicuous objects; nor
are human sacrifices and cannibal feasts enacted among
a people who have placed themselves under missionary
instruction.

It is an argument strongly in favour of the divine
origin of Christianity, that it meets the social, moral,
and religious wants of all nations; none are so refined
that their habits of thought and feeling are cultivated
beyond the provision which the gospel makes for their
comfort and guidance, nor are any sunk so low in their

brutalizing customs and fierce and revengeful spirit as to render them of necessity incapable of receiving impressions of saving truth, and of becoming a part of the church of God. Several fields of missionary toil have been entered upon, with no other prospect of success than that which an unwavering confidence in God's word inspired, and in the face of the most formidable difficulties and opposition; and yet even there signal triumphs have been awarded to the faithful servants of the Most High God; illustrating the saying of the Saviour—"If I be lifted up, I will draw ALL men unto ME."

When the mission to New Zealand was undertaken, it was justly considered as being a very dangerous enterprise. Such were the savage customs and cannibal propensities of the people, that they afforded the fullest opportunity to illustrate the saying of the Apostle Paul, that the Gospel is "the power of God unto salvation, to every one that believeth." There was nothing in favour of the Gospel, but everything against it; if success could be found in this field, then we might hopefully sow the earth with Gospel seed.

Many of the Maori customs were most revolting. Murder was common, infanticide prevailed to a great extent, and cannibalism had fearfully increased during the last few years. There was no law for the protection of either property or life but that of might, except the superstitious appointment of the *tapu*. The people were ignorant of the customs of civilized life, and being confined to their own islands, with scarcely any intercourse with another race, they were prevented from rising much in the social scale. Stone, wood, the bones of fishes, and the leaves of the *raupo* and other coarse grasses, with the flax plant, formed the chief materials of which they constructed their tools, procured their food, and built their canoes and houses. They had no knowledge of metals, no means of boiling water, nor had they any vessels for holding water besides the calabash. They had no idea of any quadruped besides the rat, dog, and pig, and the last had been but recently introduced. Some sheep and goats had been landed by Captain Cook, but it does not appear that they lived. Of wholesome animal food they had none, but they had *fish* in abundance, and a *few* birds. Their clothing was made principally of flax; no covering was provided for either their feet or head, and their mats were often thrown off, so that they went about nearly nude. The glorious works of God, as they are displayed in the southern heavens, in the restless ocean, and in the rich and varied scenery of their country, had not aroused their soul to inquiry. Although conscious of a sense of restlessness, they could define only a few wants, and were desirous of nothing more than to satisfy them. The name which they gave to the North Island—*Te ika o Maui*, the fish of Maui— and the story which they told about Maui pulling up the island with his hook, when engaged on a fishing excursion, denoted their ignorance of natural science. Nor had their language been reduced to a written form, of letters and figures they were entirely ignorant. Yet their language as spoken was copious and euphonious, but before it could be made the vehicle of communication by means of the press, its sounds had to be caught, named and classified. And this was but a small part of the work to be done; for when the language was so far acquired as to enable the missionaries to converse intelligibly with the natives, and print elementary lessons, they had to communicate *new ideas* concerning God and man, the present life and the future state—ideas totally different from any which they had previously conceived. Their history as told by the *tohunga*, consisted chiefly of traditions and songs. Some of their customs were particularly dangerous to strangers; the *tapu*, for instance, might be violated by mistake or in ignorance, and lead to the most melancholy consequences. War had so raged among them during the thirty years which preceded the introduction of the Gospel, that a large part of the population was cut off; some tribes, or large divisions of tribes, had been nearly exterminated, and the survivors cherished deadly feuds. Their basest passions had been fanned into a flame, and raged with almost uncontrollable fury. Ships had approached their coasts, and the unsightly hull remained as a warning to others, while the bleached bones of the crews and passengers lay strewn around the loathsome ovens. Nor must it be forgotten that the nearest port of civilization was in New South Wales, itself a penal settlement, and more than a thousand miles distant. Dark as this picture may appear, it is a true sketch—and it is only a sketch—of New Zealand as a projected mission field.

The idea will at once suggest itself that the men who would undertake such a mission should not be common men ; that a good deal of tact to make circumstances bend to their high and holy purpose, and a determination to conduct themselves so as to win the confidence of savage men, was necessary. Undaunted courage was needed also; for dangers and death surrounded them. To be happy in their work, such men must rely upon their own efforts to a great extent for the means of domestic comfort, and conscious of their disinterested motives, must be content for a while to be misunderstood, and instead of expecting their full reward in the present world, must expect it in the world which is to come. Nor must they be cast down at the apparent want of success, for this is sometimes more apparent than real; but trusting in the promises of God, the operations of the Holy Ghost, and the efficacy of Christ's atoning blood, they must anticipate the time when the savage tribes around them shall be clothed and in their right mind, and "sitting at the feet of Jesus."

The person to whom the New Zealand Mission is most indebted is the Rev. Samuel Marsden, Senior Chaplain of New South Wales. He was born in Yorkshire, of poor parentage, and was apprenticed to learn a common trade. His earliest religious impressions were received among the Wesleyan Methodists. By means of the Elland Society, he was placed at St. John's College, Cambridge, studied for the ministry, and was ordained in the year 1793. In the same year he was appointed Chaplain to the convict settlement of New South Wales, which had been formed only five years before. He took a great interest in the enterprise of the London Missionary Society to the South Sea Islands, contributed not a little to its support, mourned in its days of adversity, and rejoiced in its success. The first vessel intended for missionary purposes was purchased by Mr. Marsden— the Active, a brig of a hundred tons burden—and was the means of communication between the colony and the mission stations. Seven times he visited New Zealand, and clung to this mission with characteristic ardour till his death. He conducted the first Christian worship and preached the first sermon among the Maories, and was permitted to see the commencement of a work of grace, on which the angels of God looked down with delight, among that people. His trials were neither few nor small; calumniated by men high in office, whose conduct he reproved, and hated by convicts, whom he had punished from the magistrates' bench—for he had served many years as a Justice of the Peace—he occasionally appealed to the courts of law for the defence of his character. He availed himself of the opportunity which those times afforded of winning extensive farms from the waste lands, by means of convict labour, and became rich; but he dispensed his wealth with a liberal hand, both in religious and benevolent channels. His name will live among the chief benefactors of the country in which most of his life was spent, and in New Zealand it will be cherished in remembrance of the first efforts which were made to introduce the blessings of civilisation and religion among a race whose deeds of cruelty and death had struck terror into the minds of hardy and adventurous seamen, who wished to approach their coast. On the 12th May, 1838, fifty-four years after his first arrival in New South Wales, this pioneer of Missionary work in New Zealand, departed to his everlasting reward.

Mr. Marsden fell into the error which affected many other good men, of supposing that an uncivilized people is not prepared to receive the Gospel, and, consequently that a course of preparatory labour, for the purpose of awakening their minds and restraining their grossest habits, must be conducted. His own words were: " The heathens in these islands are, in the strictest sense, in a state of nature. Hence it becomes the indispensable duty of the missionaries to use every means for their civilization, and not to imagine that they are already prepared to receive the blessings of divine revelation. . .

Nothing in my opinion can pave the way for the introduction of the gospel but civilization."* As the New Zealand Mission was commenced by laymen, the idea has become general that the conductors of the Church Missionary Society, fifty years ago, adopted the same sentiment, but this is perhaps not correct. If they were of opinion that the peculiar state of New Zealand required some preparatory measures, they were certainly very anxious to introduce the gospel as early as possible. Soon after the commencement of the mission, the directors wrote as follows:—" The agents employed in establishing the mission were laymen, because clergymen could not be had; and the instructions given to them necessarily correspond with their lay character. The foremost object of the mission has, from the first, been to bring the natives, by the use of all suitable means, under the saving influences of the grace of the gospel, adding indeed the communication to them of such useful arts and knowledge as might improve their social condition."†

No one can dispute the importance of civilization to a people, the error lies in making it necessary, or nearly so, to a saving appreciation of the gospel. From this error the foregoing extract rescues the Church Missionary Society. The most cultivated minds do not appear more ready to receive the gospel than the unlearned; the truth of God—the faithful saying, that " Christ Jesus came into the world to save sinners"—is placed within the reach of all classes, and the " wayfaring man, though a fool, need not err." It is an appeal to the heart as well as to the mind, for " with the heart man believeth unto righteousness." Civilization, however de-

* " Life of Rev. S. Marsden."　　　　† Ibid, p. 57.

sirable, is of slow growth ; in many of the islands, where
tens of thousands of persons, whose moral conduct and
religious efforts are satisfactory, the general advancement towards civilized life is very slow ; and is a source
of trial to the excellent men whose best days are devoted
to their temporal and spiritual welfare. But while this
is a subject of regret, we should not forget that the
tendency of the gospel is to raise a people in the social
scale, to extend the sphere of their vision, to develope
latent powers of mind, to make them conscious of new
wants, and to make them willing to use proper means
to secure both their temporal and eternal welfare.

The honoured men who were appointed to commence
the New Zealand Church Mission, Messrs. Hall, King,
and Kendall, left England in 1810 ; but on their arrival
at New South Wales, the intelligence which had just
been received from the country of the Maories, was of
such a cruel and shocking kind, that the Governor of
the colony positively refused the Rev. S. Marsden permission to visit the New Zealand coast ; and it was
deemed prudent to suspend the missionary attempt till
the general excitement in both countries should subside.
This excitement was occasioned by the massacre of the
crew and passengers of the ship Boyd, which ill-fated
vessel sailed from Sydney, and was bound for England,
having on board a number of passengers, some of whom
were children of respectable parents, who adopted this
course to secure their children a good education in the
fatherland. The Boyd called at New Zealand for the
purpose of shipping some spars, not supposing that she
was going into the jaws of destruction. The immediate
cause of the massacre lay in the improper conduct of
the captain towards a chief, who was returning to New

Zealand as a passenger; the chief refused to work on board, and was flogged as a punishment for his refusal; and as *utu* or payment for the insult inflicted upon their chief, the tribe to which he belonged formed a plan to seize the ship, and murder the crew and passengers. The captain and two boat's crews were killed in the forest where they were selecting spars, and all the persons who remained on board were murdered and eaten, except one woman and three children. "About the same time the brig Agnes, with six guns and fourteen men on board was wrecked in Poverty Bay, and all on board, save John Rutherford, were murdered and eaten. A little after this, a whale-ship was cast ashore at Whanga-nui; all the crew were immediately killed and eaten, except one European and a negro."*

It is not a subject of wonder that some difficulty was found, under such circumstances, in the attempt to convey the first missionaries to the New Zealand coast. For the accomplishment of this purpose the Active was purchased by Mr. Marsden, at the cost of two thousand pounds sterling, and a preparatory voyage was made before the families of the missionaries were committed to such a hazardous enterprise. As this voyage proved satisfactory, and the natives seemed to be favourably disposed, no time was lost in preparing for the departure of the noble-minded band, who, committing themselves and their children to the protection of God, were to lay the foundation of the future civilization and evangelization of the New Zealand Islands. During the time the mission was suspended, several natives from New Zealand found their way to Sydney; they were objects of peculiar interest to those who were anxious to devote the

* Lecture by Rev. J Warren.

remainder of their life to the temporal and spiritual welfare of the race which they represented; accordingly every means was used to secure their favour, and explain to them the object of the missionary enterprise. The company of pioneers—for such they may justly be termed —embarked on the 19th of November, 1814. In writing an account of the expedition to a friend, Mr. Marsden says:—"The number of persons on board the Active, including women and children, was thirty-five; the master, his wife and son, Messrs. Kendall, Hall, and King, with their wives and children, eight New Zealanders, two Otaheitans, and four Europeans belonging to the vessel, besides Mr. John Lydiand Nicholas and myself; there were also two sawyers, one smith, and a runaway convict, whom we afterwards found on board; a horse and two mares, one bull and two cows, with a few sheep and poultry. The bull and cows have been presented by Governor Macquarie, from his Majesty's herd."

Some narrow-minded people, whose interest in the welfare of a distant and savage race had never been developed, no doubt curled the lip in contempt as the Active spread her canvas to the breeze, and pronounced the enterprise as the outgrowth of a weak though well-meant enthusiasm. But those on board were full of hope, visions of success floated before their eye; and yet we cannot suppose that scenes of future comfort, of civilization in its various branches, of churches of various orders, of schools for the instruction of children, of colleges for the training of youth, were imagined so varied and rich as are now witnessed in different parts of both the islands. The seeds of the future colony were on board that ship. The goodly, towns and lovely homesteads which excite the admiration of the visitor in our day, are but the expansion and life-growth of the humble efforts then put forth. Nor are the results of their labours and self-denial confined to these colonial scenes, the benefits which have been conferred upon the native race are very great; their worst customs are no longer observed, they are rising in the scale of civilization, and many of them have been formed into Christian churches. How different must be the feelings with which those good men watched the coast, as the Active was steered into the harbour, from those with which they traversed the country, finding a Christian welcome everywhere, a few years afterwards—such feelings are rarely permitted to mortals.

On their arrival they found that the tribes of the Bay of Islands were at war with the people of Wangaroa, where the Boyd was plundered. The first work which Mr. Marsden attempted was to reconcile the contending parties, and the favours which he had shown to the Maories when they were in New South Wales having prepared his way, the belligerents were disposed to listen to his advice. As he approached the warriors of Wangaroa, a woman advanced waving a mat as a demonstration of welcome, and shouting, *Haere mai! Haere mai!* " The chiefs were seated on the ground, surrounded by their fighting men, leaning on their formidable spears. The warriors were dressed in their handsome native mats, and their hair was tied in a knot at the top of their heads, decorated with the long white feathers of the gannet. Some wore round their necks ornaments of green jade, some the teeth of their slaughtered enemies, while others, as if proud of their atrocious exploits, were adorned with the dollars taken from the ill-fated Boyd.

I

But what must have been the amazement and dread inspired in the mind of the European strangers, by the sights and sounds that followed. The warriors, seizing their spears, brandished them, as if in fury, against one another; yells, shrieks, and roars rent the air, while the frightful gesticulations and horrible contortions of face and limb were suggestive of the writhing of fiends. Yet this terrifying demonstration was their war-dance of welcome."*

The manner in which the night was spent at Wangaroa will be best described by Mr. Marsden's own pen: "About eleven o'clock Mr. Nicholas and I wrapped ourselves in our great coats and prepared for rest. George directed me to lie by his side. His wife and child lay on the right hand and Mr. Nicholas close by. The night was clear; the stars shone bright and the sea in our front was smooth; around us were innumerable spears stuck upright in the ground, and groups of natives lying in all directions, like a flock of sheep upon the grass, as there were neither tents nor huts to cover them. I viewed our present situation with sensations and feelings that I cannot express, surrounded by cannibals who had massacred and devoured our countrymen. I wondered much at the mysteries of Providence, and how these things could be. Never did I behold the blessed advantage of civilisation in a more grateful light than now. I did not sleep much during the night. My mind was too seriously occupied with the present scene, and the new and strange ideas it naturally excited. About three in the morning I rose and walked about the camp, surveying the different groups of natives. When the morn-

* " Sunday at Home," 1857.

ing light returned we beheld men, women, and children asleep in all directions, like the beasts of the field."*

Sunday, December 25th, 1814, was an eventful day; not only as it was set apart to commemorate the advent of Him, who was

" Born to redeem, and strong to save,"

but because it was the first Sabbath observed in New Zealand. Being in the midst of summer, nature was spread out before the Missionary company in her beautiful forms. A flag which they had brought with them floated in the breeze; and displayed a CROSS, a DOVE, an OLIVE BRANCH, and the word RONGOPAI, good tidings; contributing not a little to the interest and cheerfulness of the scene. All the ship's crew, except the master and one man, went ashore to attend divine service, which was conducted by Mr. Marsden. The worship was commenced by singing the Old Hundredth Psalm, and after the beautiful service of the Church of England had been read, the appropriate text was announced, Luke ii., 10— "Behold, I bring you good tidings of great joy," and a sermon adapted to the peculiar circumstances of the assembly was preached. The dayspring from on high had now visited the country, it was the earnest of a bright and glorious scene, in which Christ, now first named, is to fill the field of vision as the Lord of all. The poor wondering natives sat mute, being unable to comprehend the meaning of the strange scene. The angels of God looked on with delight, and the promise of the Father,—" Ask of Me, and I will give thee the heathen for thine inheritance, and the uttermost parts of the earth for thy possession," was fulfilled.

* " Life of Rev. S. Marsden."

The time came when the Active must direct her course across the sea; it was no doubt a heavy trial to the feelings of all, but especially to them who were to be left to the mercy of a savage people, with no means humanly speaking of escape from their ferocity. There was certainly room for fears unless their faith were unshaken in the divine protection. War was soon after renewed. "For months together the affrighted band kept watch night and day; their children were laid to sleep in their cots dressed, to be ready for instant flight, and the boat was always kept afloat, with its oars and sails in readiness."* In the course of time these unhappy circumstances passed away, and industrial pursuits enlivened the scene. Seeds of grain and garden vegetables were sown on a rich and virgin soil, Mr. Marsden having purchased about two hundred acres of ground for the use of the mission from a chief, who copied the tattoo of his face as his signature to the deed of sale. The natives looked on with curiosity, as different branches of industry were for the first time introduced to them. The Mission settlement soon exhibited an interesting picture; but its secular features, as might have been foreseen, were the most prominent.

But it is difficult to ascertain the anxieties which were hidden in the bosoms of the more spiritual part of the little community, and to describe the efforts they made to acquire the native language, that they might tell them of the "Lamb of God, which taketh away the sin of the world." What would they not have given for a good grammar, showing the construction of the Maori tongue, and for a dictionary in which the sounds they were

* "Life of Rev. S. Marsden."

trying to imitate, and whose meaning they were anxious to ascertain, might be exhibited in goodly columns.

The honour of introducing the gospel to New Zealand, and not the gospel only, but the nucleus of civilization, belongs to the Church Missionary Society. As the Church of England was first in the New Zealand field, has sent out the largest number of agents, and spent the most money in the enterprise, it is, and is likely to be, the most numerous and influential body of Christians in the country. This remark applies both to the colonists and to the natives; and we cheerfully give honour to whom honour is due.

Next to the Church of England, the Wesleyan Missionary Society has been most honoured in the work of grace which has been wrought in New Zealand. As early as the year 1818, the Rev. Samuel Leigh, who a little time before had commenced a successful mission in New South Wales, and whose excessive labours had seriously injured his health, was induced by the Rev. S. Marsden to visit New Zealand in the Active, which was about to sail with provisions for the mission settlement. This visit was beneficial to the infant mission, and led the way to the establishment of a Wesleyan Church. To a man of Mr. Leigh's ardent temperament and spiritual views, the scene which opened before him produced an effect which cannot be easily described. He found himself to be in the valley of the shadow of death; Satan's seat was there; few were the gleams of light which had penetrated that thick darkness. In one pah he saw twelve dried human heads exposed for sale, supposing that he would purchase them as curiosities. His whole soul was aroused to deepest sympathy, and he determined not to rest till he should see a Wesleyan mission fairly established in the country.

Mr. Leigh returned to New Zealand on February 22nd, 1822, between three and four years after his first visit. In the meantime he had sailed to England, and in the face of considerable difficulties, had succeeded in persuading the Wesleyan Missionary Society to commence a mission among the Maories, and was himself appointed to begin the work. During this visit he married a lady of suitable qualifications, with whom he soon after traversed the ocean, to the scene of his future labours.

The feelings of Mr. and Mrs. Leigh, when the New Zealand coast rose above the horizon, cannot be fully described. Hope and fear alternately took hold of their soul. What reception would they meet with from the native people? Had any exciting wars been commenced afresh, which would increase their danger, and add fresh difficulties to their work? They must commence a mission at a distance, necessarily, from their Church brethren, and Mrs. Leigh would be a lonely English-woman among an uncivilized people. Would the natives accept the glad tidings which they went to declare? Would they give their hearts to the Saviour? These were serious questions, which it were quite natural for them to indulge in the still moments of deep and anxious feeling. And then hope kindled a lamp which shed its beams through the thick darkness, and presented, in imagination, a Church gathered from the wilderness, and the people whose name was synonymous with confusion and ferocity, transformed into intelligent men, and using means to spread among others the religion which had ennobled them. " When I stepped upon deck," said Mr. Leigh, " and looked towards the shore, and then at

my wife, and reflected upon the probable consequences
of our landing, I felt as if divested of all spiritual strength.
We were running upon a nation of ferocious and blood-
thirsty heathens, where there was no power to protect,
and while the country was convulsed by war. Never
shall I forget the agony of mind I endured, until reflection brought me to feel that I was surrounded by the
Divine perfections, and that a hair could not fall from
our heads without the concurrence of God."*

The Wesleyan mission was commenced at Wangaroa,
at a convenient distance from the Church Mission, so
that, while they did not interfere with each others'
labour, a friendly and helpful correspondence could be
maintained. Not a little time was occupied in manual
labour; for their domestic comfort and their health
demanded it; but the utmost efforts were made to learn
the Maori language, and adapt their teaching to the
modes of thought to which the natives were accustomed.
Had they possessed a perfect acquaintance with the
native tongue, the difficulties lying in their way would
have been formidable; for the native mind had not been
trained to perceive, nor had they words to express, the
holiness and honour of the Divine law. Additional
labourers arrived; the fallow ground was broken up, and
the Gospel seed was sown in hope; but some time
elapsed before decisive proofs of success became apparent.

The perilous circumstances in which the mission
families at Wangaroa were placed, may be inferred from
the episode narrated in the voyages of the Rev. Daniel
Tyerman and George Bennett, Esq., who visited the
South Sea Islands as a deputation of the London Mis-

* "Life of Rev. Samuel Leigh."

sionary Society. On their way to Sydney from Tahiti, they entered the harbour of Wangaroa, in July, 1824, when the following occurrences took place :—" The ship was soon surrounded by canoes, and filled with native men, women, and children. On the following morning, so many natives crowded on board, that, to prevent confusion, the captain ordered a bar to be placed across the quarter-deck. The natives beginning to practise their pilfering habits, the captain became angry, and whilst he was endeavouring to clear the deck of the intruders, one of them, a chief, on being jostled by him, fell into the sea. This was seized instantaneously as a pretext for commencing hostilities. The natives took possession of the ship, and made the officers and the crew prisoners. Tremendous were the howlings and the screeches of the barbarians, while they stamped, and brandished their clubs and spears. The captain was surrounded with spears. Mr. Bennett's arms were pinioned to his sides, while Messrs. Tyerman and Threlkeld were in custody in another part of the ship. One of the cookies pushed off Mr. Bennett's cap, and stood with his axe, which he had sharpened on board, gleaming over him. They had handled the arms, sides, and thighs of Mr. Tyerman, who understood the meaning of those familiarities. In this condition they had remained nearly two hours, when they heard the cry, ' A boat ! a boat !' The boat contained one of the Wesleyan missionaries, and the chief George, who had come to invite the gentlemen of the deputation to Wesleydale. When the natives saw who were in the boat, they liberated the prisoners, and quitted the ship."* It is proper

* " Tyerman and Bennett's Voyages," pp. 183, 184, quoted in " Life of Rev. S. Leigh."

to add that in a conversation which the author had with the missionary who accompanied the chief George so opportunely to the ship, many years after the occurrence, the opinion was expressed that the danger was more apparent than real, as the scene was intended to intimidate the ship's crew, and to show how completely the vessel was at the mercy of the natives. Whether the natives were in earnest or not, the foregoing account sufficiently shows the perils to which the missionaries were exposed, and their continued safety can be accounted for on no other ground than that of the divine protection.

Mr. Leigh was permitted to do little more than *commence* the Wesleyan mission, as his health failed after he had laboured there one year and nine months. He returned with the Rev. S. Marsden, who had again visited the country, to Sydney ; but they had scarcely left the New Zealand waters before the ship in which they sailed ran upon some rocks, and became a total wreck. After suffering much through sickness, want of provisions, and exposure to the weather, the shipwrecked missionaries were landed in New South Wales, where Mr. Leigh spent the eight following years, and where he buried his devoted wife, in 1831. His next twenty years were devoted to the work of the ministry in England, as far as his strength would permit. Communications from the brethren who succeeded him in the mission field cheered his spirit. He sowed the seed "in weakness and fear and in much trembling," and he rejoiced in the harvest which has since been reaped. On the 2nd day of May, 1852, he closed his eyes upon all earthly things, and went to his reward. "The memory of the just is blessed."

The dangers to which the Church missionaries were

exposed were very great. The Rev. John Williams, whose praise is in all the Churches, entered the Bay of Islands in 1822, on his return from a voyage to the colony, and wrote a fearful account of the savage ferocity with which the natives were then carrying out their purposes of war. He observes :—" The large canoes are now returning from the war, some of them with human heads fixed at the head and stern. One of our seamen, when on shore, saw ten of these heads preserved, either as spoils of victory, or to *sell to Christians*, for muskets and powder, to enable them the more effectually to execute their deeds of blood." When they made the North Cape, the captain stood in for the shore for the purpose of purchasing provisions ; but such were the suspicious appearances, that guns were loaded, and every precaution taken, to prevent the ship from falling into the hands of the natives, and Mr. Williams adds— " While in this state of anxiety, expecting every moment to be attacked, I retired to my berth, and looked up to our ' present help in time of trouble.' When I returned from my berth to the cabin, to my great joy, Mr. Henry came down, and said a breeze was springing up. And so it proved ; for in less than half an hour our anxious fears were turned into songs of deliverance."*

Eleven years passed after the mission at the Bay of Islands was commenced, before any native of New Zealand made a public profession of Christianity. The first convert was an old chief, who was baptised in 1825, by the name of Christian Rangi. An improper use has been made of the fact, that so many years were spent before the Maories began to stretch out their hands towards God. The first profession of the Christian faith

* " Life of Rev. J. Williams."

was made under peculiar circumstances, a strong effort being needed to throw off the superstition which had affected their mode of thinking and the revolting customs in which their character had been formed, and not a little moral courage was involved in the profession of a new faith—a religion introduced to them by a strange race—and in the risk which the consequences of such a profession might threaten. Before the productions of spring, there is an underground movement, intensely alive and important, though unseen at the time, and whose effects are confessed in the innumerable plants and flowers with which the spring and summer perfume the air, and clothe the fields with beauty ; so, before the public acknowledgment of Christ by a native of New Zealand, for the first time, there must be deep searching of the heart, a revolving of momentous thoughts, and a fierce battle would probably be fought, to overcome the inclinations of heathenism, and to determine upon a more excellent way.

Nor must we forget the civilizing influences which were in operation in the country. Although civilization is not the chief object of the Christian missionary, it certainly is more or less the result of his labours. Proofs of this are found in Africa, in various groups of Polynesia, and in every place where the Gospel has been preached for a few years. God, in His mercy to the uncivilized portions of our race, is using both means— planting colonies as well as missions ; although, as it was in New Zealand, the missionary often precedes the mere colonist, and in addition to his spiritual labours, commences the work which the colonist successfully continues. They who still contend that the colonist should precede the missionary, and do half his work, may stand rebuked by the eloquent language of Chalmers :—" Nor are the labours of these illustrious men confined to the business of Christianizing. They are at this moment giving the arts, and industry, and civilization to the natives; they are raising a beautiful spectacle to the moral eye amid the wilderness around them; they are giving piety, and virtue, and intelligence to prowling savages, . . . and extending among the wildest of nature's children the comforts and the decencies of humanized life. O ye orators and philosophers, who make the civilization of the species your dream, look to Christian missionaries if you want to see the men who will realize it. You may deck the theme with the praises of your unsubstantial eloquence; but there are the men who are to accomplish the business! They are now risking every earthly comfort of existence in the cause; while you sit in silken security, and pour upon their holy undertaking the cruelty of your scorn."

The peculiar difficulties of the early missionaries should not be forgotten; for their meekness under insults, their constant efforts to do good, and their intense disapproval of many of the native customs, were points which the Maories could not understand. The idea that the missionaries had come from the ends of the earth to bless them was something new; they could scarcely comprehend it, as it was so contrary to every feeling of their own bosom. To root out their cruel selfishness and inspire the sentiment of gratitude among a people whose language did not contain one word expressive of such an emotion, was a great work.

There was so much to *undo*, that instead of making it a subject of wonder that many years passed away before the natives were gathered into Christian churches, and could be described as "living epistles, written not with ink, but with the finger of the living God," we should present an offering of thanksgiving to God and His servants, for the work which has been done, and the blessing which has been bestowed.

The greatest hindrances which prevented missionary success may be traced to the wars, which were renewed with unprecedented violence and destruction. The man who made himself most notorious in those exterminating expeditions, was Hongi Hika, a chief of the Ngapuhi tribe. He visited England in the year 1820, and as a New Zealand chief, was a great novelty there in those times. His presence excited a good deal of attention. His Majesty George IV. invited him to his palace, and presented him with a suit of armour, and several stands of arms. Nothing attracted his attention so much as the discipline of the army and the military stores, and his ardour was kindled by the recital of the victorious campaigns of Napoleon I. He resided for some time near the celebrated Professor Lee, of Cambridge, to enable that distinguished linguist to assist in arranging the grammar and fixing the orthography of the Maori language, for the use of the missionaries. He returned loaded with presents, and determined on war. To increase his stock of fire-arms was his great object while he stayed in Sydney, on the way to his own country; and the valuable presents of his English friends were exchanged there for muskets and ammunition.

The possession of fire-arms gave Hongi an immense advantage over other tribes. Stories, shocking to every feeling of humanity are related of his sanguinary career. As an illustration of his course of cruelty and blood, the following instance, taken from the work of the Rev. R. Taylor, may be accepted. Soon after his return to New Zealand, he formed an army of three thousand men, and attacked the pah of Hinaki. This chief received four balls, and on seeing him fall, Hongi ran up to him, and with the knife that was given to him in England, scooped out one of his eyes, and swallowed it. He then stabbed him in the neck, and drank the blood as it flowed warm from the wound. One thousand persons were killed, and three hundred bodies were cooked and eaten. The ground, which was soaked with blood—the site of this horrible carnival—now belongs to St. John's College, and forms a part of its endowment. Hongi returned to the Bay of Islands covered with savage glory, carrying with him a number of prisoners, with the stem and stern of his canoe ornamented with the heads of men whom he had slain in battle. His daughter met him at the water's edge on his arrival, and learning that her husband had been killed in the fight, she demanded *utu*. The prisoners, intended to be made slaves, were given to her, and seizing the sword which his Majesty George IV. had presented to her father, she—in the presence of a catechist of the Church mission—cut off the heads of sixteen men, who were ordered to lay their heads on the side of the canoe for this terrible purpose. Twenty other persons were also killed and eaten, and then, to complete the *utu* for her husband's death, she took a loaded musket into the bush, and shot herself; but as the bullet only wounded her, she ended her wretched life by strangling herself. For seven long years Hongi pursued his course of blood and terror, but at length he received a bullet wound at Wangaroa, and after lingering some time, he closed his eyes in death.

During these troubles, all the mission families were kept in a state of great alarm ; their property was stolen, and their lives were threatened. But the blow fell most heavily upon the Wesleyan mission. The brig Mercury was seized and plundered at Wangaroa, and the natives seemed to be ready for every evil work. It was deemed prudent to remove the women and children to one of the Church mission stations, which was then comparatively quiet. In the course of time tranquillity was restored, the separated families again met, and gave expression to their feelings by singing the following appropriate verses :—

> " And are we yet alive,
>   And see each others' face ?
> Glory and praise to Jesus give
>   For His redeeming grace.
>
> " What troubles have we seen,
>   What conflicts have we passed !
> Fightings without, and fears within,
>   Since we assembled last !
>
> " But out of all the Lord
>   Hath brought us by His love ;
> And still He does His help afford,
>   And hides our life above."

But though their lives were preserved, and the excitement for a time subsided, they were not permitted to follow their missionary work undisturbed. Battles were arranged to be fought in the immediate vicinity of the mission premises. Children were laid in bed with their clothes on, as their parents supposed that an attack would be made before the next morning. They were " in watchings oft." One of the brethren wrote in his journal: " How little do our friends in England know of the insecurity of our condition! Before daybreak we may be plundered, murdered, and eaten! O that, with the Psalmist, we may be always enabled to say: 'God is our refuge and strength, a very present help in trouble. Therefore will not we fear, though the earth be removed, and though the mountains be carried into the midst of the sea. The Lord of Hosts is with us; the God of Jacob is our refuge.'"[*] Again the storm passed over them, and left them unhurt. Their work was resumed with renewed vigour; many repairs were necessary to be made in the mission premises, as considerable damage had been done by the excited natives; and more serious injury had, no doubt, been sustained by those of whom the missionaries began to entertain a hope that they might be presented as the first-fruits of the New Zealand harvest. But their peaceful labours were again disturbed. The dark cloud was soon seen looming in the distance; onward it rolled; the storm of war shot its lightning darts, as the precursor of the terrible outbreak, and on the 10th of January, 1827, it burst upon the mission at Wangaroa in all its fury. Very narrow was the escape of the mission family from the vengeance of the savage war-party. " While the assailants were forcing their way through the back door and windows, the family escaped through the front door. They ran down the garden, made an opening in the fence, and passed over the wheat field. The party consisted of Messrs. Turner and Hobbs; Mrs. Turner, who had been confined only five weeks; Miss Davies, who was on a visit; a European servant and his wife; five native boys, and two native girls. They had before them a journey of twenty miles, over a mountainous country, and under a heavy rain.

[*] " Life of Rev. S. Leigh."

On their way they met a war party from Hokianga, about two hundred strong, who ordered the mission family to move to the side of the road, and go down upon their knees. They did so, and expected to be killed in a moment. To their inexpressible joy, the chiefs assembled around them, and then ordered the warriors to pass on."* We well remember the venerable J. Hobbs refer to this painful and yet joyful event a few years ago, at a missionary meeting in Auckland, and contrast their condition when they knelt down, as did Stephen, the first martyr for Christ, expecting to die ; and then, when their deliverance came, rising from their knees, saying : "Surely the bitterness of death is past." Here was a scene of moral grandeur, far surpassing in interest, in the estimation of the angels of God, the great points in the career of the conquerors of the world, and worthy to be represented on canvas in the best style the artist can command. Not more affectionate was the meeting of Jacob and Esau, after their long separation, than was the meeting between the brethren of the Church mission and the war-spoiled and weary company whose escape from destruction was so remarkable. Hearing at the Kiri Kiri Church Missionary station of the danger to which the Wesleyan mission was exposed, the brethren immediately started to their assistance, taking with them twenty natives to convey the children, and render other help; and meeting them twelve miles from the Kiri Kiri, they retraced their steps, and at seven o'clock in the evening all arrived safe at the station of the Church mission.

The mission premises at Wangaroa, including supplies for twelve months, were entirely destroyed, and a horrible

* "Life of Rev. S. Leigh," p. 279.

K

carnival was held in the neighbourhood. Thus to all appearance the Wesleyan mission was brought to a close. Men who counted not their life dear had laboured for five years, considerable sums of money had been spent in the enterprise, thousands of prayers had been offered up at the throne of grace; and all that was now to be seen as the results of their efforts was a solitary chimney, of rough workmanship, surrounded by the charred remains of the mission station; and a company of fugitive men, women, and children seeking a shelter under the roof of a distant mission-house. If anyone could adopt the prophet's lament—" I have laboured in vain, I have spent my strength for nought, and in vain; yet surely my judgment is with the Lord, and my work with my God "; it no doubt expressed the feelings of the perplexed and injured missionaries from Wangaroa.

But was it so in reality? Was every effort of these five years' labour destroyed when the premises were burned, and the agents were driven away? No, verily. the seed was deposited in the earth, and was germinating there, though unseen. A stranger to the operations of nature would pronounce the seed lost which is sown in the soil, but in due time it springs up a tiny tender leaflet, and rapidly rises in strength and beauty. And so was it with the gospel seed in New Zealand. But the *suspension* of the mission was complete; and the Wesleyan brethren, with their families, sailed for New South Wales on the last day of January, 1827; and so threatening were the appearances, that the church missionaries— although their stations were not immediately menaced —sent their goods to Sydney by the same ships, supposing that within a short time all the missionaries would be compelled to leave the country.

To human appearance the work of twelve years was lost ; the result seemed to confirm the prudential maxims of the men of this world ; and Christian men in their disappointment cried, " Where is the Lord God of Elijah ? " The Maories seemed to be given up to the hardness of their impenitent hearts ; and the sceptre of the Prince of Darkness was not likely to be met by the strong arm of the Prince of Peace. But there were a few persons who steadily believed God, and looked forward to a brighter and a better day ; and the following chapter will shew that they were not mistaken.

CHAPTER VI.

MISSIONARY SUCCESS.

"Onward ! onward ! men of heaven,
Rear the Gospel's banner high ;
Rest not, till its light is given,
Star of every pagan sky."

THE gracious work which we have now to describe is connected, by way of sequence, with the labours and sufferings already described ; for " they that sow in tears, shall reap in joy." It presents no new phase of human conduct and Christian effort. To a warm hearted Christian, who is ready to use every means within his reach to win the heathen to Christ, it is painful to *wait* for success ; especially as the advantages which true religion promises are so plain, so many, and so enduring. But it must not be concluded that the slow process by which a heathen people are sometimes led to the cross of Christ is the result of a want of earnestness or tact on the part of their instructors ; for many of the most flourishing missions passed through many days of despondency, and some of the men whose successful labours have filled the world with their praises, spent a large portion of their missionary life in laying the foundation of the goodly edifice which ultimately they were honoured to erect. Dr. Judson laboured arduously for about six years before even a single native of Burmah became a Christian. The mission at Tonga, in the Friendly Islands, was brought to a speedy close ; three of the missionaries being murdered, and the remainder barely escaping with their lives ; yet the Wesleyans are now conducting a flourishing mission among the same people. Nearly thirteen years after the mission to Tahiti was commenced, the discouragements were so serious, and the violence of the natives was so alarming, that all the missionaries fled to New South Wales, except two, and the mission seemed to be on the point of being abandoned. More than sixteen years passed away before a convert was made ; and when a single voice was heard in a lonely place engaged in prayer to the only true God, it cheered the hearts of the faithful men, who had long looked for a token from heaven ; and was accepted as a few drops preceding the wide-spread and gracious showers which have since fallen upon those interesting fields of Christian labour.

Contrary to their fears, the Church mission in New Zealand was not broken up ; but, although the dark and threatening clouds still hung over the land, circumstances rendered it probable that the mission station would not be molested. At the same time, a desire was expressed by some of the natives for the return of the Wesleyan missionaries, and before the expiration of the year in which they were driven from the country, they found themselves again in New Zealand, ready to commence their work anew. The men who remained at their post in the midst of such dangers, and they who returned to risk a repetition of the evils through which they had already passed, for the accomplishment of their noble purpose, were worthy of the confidence reposed in them.

> " For if a duty were to be performed,
>   Straight to the mark, like arrow from a bow,
>   They darted ; passing crowds of busy men,
>   Who turned and wondered why they went so fast,
>   And why they went at all.   But on they went ·

Mountains and rivers never checked their course:
Nothing could daunt them.

'Ah ! but I have seen
The swiftest arrow blunted at the point,
By the hard rock on which it struck.'

'You have ?
And I have seen the blunted arrow sharpened,
The metal newly tempered, and the weight
So nicely balanced, it went whizzing by
With piercing certainty, and in the mark
It quivered.' Yes ! give me the dauntless man
Who flinches not from labour or fatigue,
But moves right on, upon the path of duty.
God will stand by the man who boldly stands
By God's command ; will give him *energy
And courage now*, and AFTERWARDS SUCCESS."

In re-commencing their work, the Wesleyan Missionaries were sent to Mangungu, not far from the Hokianga,
a beautiful spot, where the Kauri grows in all its glory,
and where the rich soil is capable of producing abundance of provisions.   The river is navigable for vessels
of large size, and considerable numbers of natives resided
within a short distance; this was the spot where the
first showers of blessings fell upon the Wesleyan Mission,
and though now deserted by the native people, and consequently not continued as a distinct Mission station, it
will be held in remembrance as the site of some signal
displays of divine grace.   Much valuable time was necessarily spent in erecting houses and other buildings
suitable for Mission premises ; gardens had to be fenced
and planted ; fruit trees were introduced ; and every
thing which was likely to contribute to their health and
comfort was arranged.   This is a pleasing recollection,
and the faith of the men who were preparing for their

future comfort and work, while the demon of war was still marshalling the tribes for battle, should not be overlooked. The missionaries belonging to the different stations witnessed many a *taua*, fighting party, depart determined on revenge; and saw it return flushed with victory and cruelty, or broken by defeat, ashamed and irritable. Reports still reached them of ships being seized and plundered, but strong in the promises of God, and firmly believing in the efficacy of the gospel, they fainted not.

The utility of a printing press, which was soon after set up in each mission, was very great. Before the people could be expected to learn to read, lessons in their own tongue must be prepared. Considerable attention appears to have been paid to this important point, and the results were soon seen in a general desire to acquire the art of reading. The first printed page in the Maori language was an era in their national character; the natives looked at it with pride and pleasure, and the men who had risked so much for their welfare, saw in it the precursor of a useful and sacred literature. The orthography then adopted was cumbrous and defective, and compared with the principles of spelling the native language now in general use, can be in some instances scarcely understood. General attention was aroused, thought was awakened, and a new course of influences, both attracting and reclaiming, was operating among them. Many persons among both old and young began to learn to read. The *raupo whare* often presented a scene of interest; there sat the warrior, whose hands had often been dyed in blood, there lay the old man who had watched with trembling limbs the approach of the first British ship to his shores, the youth and the child were there, all engaged in one pursuit; and the object which had drawn together the old and the young, and which so completely absorbed their attention was the effort to put vowels and consonants together, in the form of intelligible words. In another place might be seen the mother who had with her own hands stopped the breath of her infant children, regretting the course which she had taken, and wishing she could restore them to life, to partake of the blessings which began to fall upon her people. These were to a certain extent decisive results, and were accepted as the commencement of a greater work. But the missionaries were not satisfied, results of a more spiritual kind were earnestly desired, and formed the burden of their prayers; and with something of sadness they wrote about this time,—"The higher objects of this mission are, as yet, but imperfectly understood."

But before the missionaries were distinctly aware of it, the Holy Spirit was awakening the conscience, and softening the heart of these children of superstition and cruelty. They began to see more clearly the difference between a course of rectitude and a course of sin, the reasonableness of divine law became more apparent, and the fruits of sin in their unhappy experience was quite in accordance with the teaching to which they had lately listened with attention. The work of grace is often begun before those who are the most interested in it are aware; so it was in the commencement of native conversions. The death of some, before a profession was publicly made by the people who had received spiritual good, was not without hope that they exchanged a scene of trouble and sin, for a place of holiness and joy; and their remains were interred in the hope of the resurrection to eternal life, through our Lord Jesus Christ; instead of the long dismal wail of *te po roa*, the long night, to which they had become accustomed to commit their departed ones.

Unmistakable signs of prosperity were perceived about the year 1831. Distant tribes were desirous that a missionary should reside in their midst; they became dissatisfied with the customs in which their fathers lived and died, and a new moral and mental world was opening before them, causing their instructors to say, " This is the Lord's doing, and it is marvellous in our eyes." The churches in Great Britain being aware that these tokens of spiritual success called upon them for increased help, sent out a reinforcement of labourers, strong in health, devoted in spirit, and joyous in anticipation of winning to Christ the tribes that had so long resisted the offers of divine mercy, and had filled the world with the report of their atrocious deeds. New fields of labour were entered, remote parts of the country were visited, and houses were erected in the best native style for the worship of God. The first Wesleyan class meeting composed of Maories was held in 1831; it comprised five members, one of whom, having received the Spirit of adoption, enjoyed the peace which passeth understanding, and the others were striving to enter in at the strait gate. Then the devoted missionaries and their equally devoted wives, who had submitted to a home in the wilderness, and had laboured so many years without seeing the fruit of their toils, could joyfully sing :—

" When the Lord turned again the captivity of Zion,
We were like them that dream.
Then was our mouth filled with laughter,
And our tongue with singing :

Then said they among the heathen,—
' The Lord hath done great things for them,'
The Lord hath done great things for us ;
Whereof we are glad."*

The attention of the brethren was seriously directed
to the translation of the New Testament into the native
language ; but in making the attempt, it was found to
be a work of no little difficulty, as the Maories had no
words which could convey many of the ideas expressed
in the sacred Scriptures.   The Divine character, the
Atonement, the operations of the Holy Spirit, the fruits
of the Spirit, Scriptural worship, and the purity of
heaven, were among the subjects with which the native
mind had never, till lately, come in contact.   The
habits of animals of which the Maories had never heard,
geographical descriptions to which they were entire
strangers, and the records of ancient nations, increased
the difficulties of the translation.   To those already
named, must be added the arts and sciences of the
civilized world, with the manners and customs of the
East ; the schools of heathen philosophers, and the
sectaries of Jewish worship ; the working of miracles,
and the errors of some of the early Christians.   All
things considered, the work of translating the sacred
Scriptures into the Maori tongue was an extraordinary
undertaking, even in these days of translations, requiring
much thought, and the special assistance of the Divine
Spirit.

In executing the translation, it was deemed best, after
much deliberation, to use as many of the native words
to express Christian ideas as was possible, although for
a time many persons might be in danger of attaching

* Psalm cxxvi.

a mistaken meaning to them; but this danger was
expected gradually to become less, and after a few years
to be entirely removed. Thus, *Atua*, a god, was used
for GOD; *Karakia*, an incantation, was retained for
prayer, divine worship; tapu, a superstitious sacredness,
was used for *holy*. Thus, *te ra tapu*, the holy day, *i.e.*,
the Sabbath; *te Wairua Tapu*, the Holy Spirit. Many
words were transferred from other languages : as *repeneta*,
being the English word repent; and *nakahu* is the Hebrew word for *nachish*, a serpent. Difficulties were found
also arising from the various dialects which prevailed
among different tribes, not only in a singular pronun-
ciation, but, in some cases, words were in use among
certain tribes which were unknown in other parts of the
country ; and in other cases, where the same words were
used, different meanings were attached to them. Before
the language was reduced to a written form, these
variations were seldom of much consequence, as the
tone of voice, or an explanatory clause, was sufficient to
indicate the speaker's meaning, when a word of this
kind was used ; but the printed page required precision,
and especially so when that page was employed to express a portion of the oracles of God. The event towards
which many persons in New Zealand looked with ardent
feelings—the printing of the New Testament—took place
in the year 1835, when an edition was issued by the
British and Foreign Bible Society, and divided for
distribution between the Church of England and the
Wesleyan missions.

The importance of the sacred Scriptures to the well-
being of society in general, as well as constituting a
religious guide, and an object of undoubted appeal,
makes it very desirable that all people among whom a

Christian mission is established should read the sacred
records in their own tongue. In many instances—as
the Baptist brethren at Serampore ; Judson, in Burmah ;
and Morrison, in China—the translation of the Bible
was the chief object to which they directed their attention during the first years of their missionary life; and
in other missions, where more active labours were required, the necessity of the vernacular Bible was not
only acknowledged, but deeply felt. This was the case
with the New Zealand missionaries; and when this
object was gained, although it was confined to the New
Testament, except some detached portions of the Old
Testament, they were placed in a new position, and an
era of increased light and favour was realized by the
native people.

The large edition placed at the disposal of the missionaries, was absorbed in a short time. To possess a
copy of the *Kawanata Hou*—the New Testament—was
the most desirable object in the estimation of many, and
no toil was spared to accomplish it. "One thing only
do I desire," said a native. "It is not a blanket; it is
not anything that will pass away; but this, this is my
great desire—the Word of God." In some instances,
persons travelled to mission stations, two hundred and
fifty miles distant from their home, and then cheerfully
waited several months for the arrival of a ship with
books, to secure a copy of the Scriptures. A missionary
writing in the year 1840, says : "The Scriptures are
with us almost as scarce and as valuable as they were
in England in the days of Henry VIII. The demand for
them and Prayer Books is much greater than we can
supply; and many a person have we been obliged to
send away disappointed, after he had spent a good part

of a day, and much importunity, in seeking for a copy."
Nor was the mere possession of the Scriptures sufficient;
they attentively studied the Word of God, and became
wise unto salvation. Kaitupeka, the wife of a chief, took
her worn copy of the New Testament to her minister,
tied up in a neat little bag, lamenting that it was so
broken, and requesting to have it repaired. He could
not, of course, repair the book, nor was he able to procure her another copy. An edition of twenty thousand
copies of the New Testament was issued by the British
and Foreign Bible Society, and proved a great blessing,
but was far from being sufficient to supply the demand.

The mission presses were also fully engaged in printing the Book of Common Prayer, Hymns, Catechisms,
and the Book of Psalms. The Rev. Mr. Williams (now
Bishop of Waiapu) wrote, in 1840: "A commencement
was made to print four thousand copies of the Prayer
Book entire; but when it was advanced to the end of
the Evening Service, it was deemed expedient to put
into immediate circulation the four thousand copies,
with the addition of the Hymns, and to strike off three
thousand more for the entire work. But the three
thousand were required as soon as printed. Then six
thousand copies of the entire work were commenced;
but before the type of the first half-sheets is distributed,
we have found it necessary to have twenty thousand
more of the smaller book, which will make a total of
thirty-three thousand." *

Circumstances equally encouraging were witnessed in
the Wesleyan mission. On the last Sunday of August,
1837, one hundred and twenty adults, who had been
for some time under instruction, were publicly baptized

* " Report of the British and Foreign Bible Society, 1841."

at Mangungu ; and soon after, one hundred and thirty-eight adults, and forty-six children, were presented to Christ through the ordinance of Baptism ; and among the latter were several persons who took a part in expelling the missionaries from Wangaroa, and destroying the mission premises. They were anxious to search the Scriptures, and looked forward to the time when they should possess so precious a treasure with great delight. Their language was: "Our hearts are sick for the Word of God ; we desire it more than axes, hatchets, or blankets." Nor were these the only expressions of success. Clear and scriptural statements were made by some who were deeply convinced of their low estate, and of their need of salvation, while others rejoiced in the overflowing feelings of their first love to Jesus.*

The conversion of many persons among the Maories was remarkably clear and satisfactory ; and as an illustration, we quote the following instance from the pen of the Rev. John Warren, of the Wesleyan mission:—"I choose this example, because the man was immeasurably the worst native I ever knew; and I assure you that is saying a great deal. He was such a compound of arrogance and meanness, such an arrant liar, and such an incorrigible thief—such a *tangata kino, wakaharahara*—that even the natives did not respect him. He took the lead in a cannibal feast which was held near the place on which the station was formed, only a little time before I went there, and pointed out to me, with a horrid laugh of satisfaction, that would have well become the devil himself, the skulls of the persons they had eaten, sticking up on poles, and the teeth, which they had in derision driven into the trees. This man was for some

* See "Life of Rev. S. Leigh."

time a most terrible nuisance to us—who then knew nothing of the language or customs of the people. He would march into the house, and take the butter from our table, and anoint his head with it, and appropriate anything which he desired to have, at the same time pretending to be our patron and friend. He attended Divine Worship—for some time, I think, because it gave him consequence to be considered the protector of the *pakeha*. By degrees, however, he came under the influence of Divine truth, became greatly distressed on account of his wickedness, and found the pardoning mercy of God in Christ. Though he could not be far from fifty years of age, he soon learned to read the Word of God. He was for several years a consistent Christian man ; endured his last affliction, which was severe and protracted, with the most exemplary patience ; and I saw him die full of peace and joy, and committed his remains to the grave in sure and certain hope of a glorious resurrection." *

When the work of grace began to be displayed, there were many strange and inconsistent scenes, in which Christianity and heathenism were placed side by side, so as to show the true character of each very distinctly. In the description of a scene of this kind, which was witnessed by the Rev. S. Marsden, in 1830, the following statement was made :—" The contrast between the state of the east and west side of the bay was very striking. Though only two miles distant, the east shore was crowded with different tribes of fighting men in a wild, savage state, many of them nearly naked, and, when exercising, entirely naked ; nothing was to be heard but the firing of muskets, the noise, din, and commotion of

* Lecture by the Rev. J. Warren, delivered in New Zealand.

a savage military camp; some mourning the death of their friends, others suffering from their wounds, and not one but whose mind was involved in heathen darkness, without one ray of Divine knowledge. On the west side was the pleasant sound of the Church-going bell— the natives assembling together for Divine Worship, clean, orderly, and decently dressed, most of them in European clothing. They were carrying the Litany and the greatest part of the Church Service, written in their own language, in their hands with their hymns." *

The Gospel gradually produced salutary restraints and changes among those who did not heartily receive it. Many were married according to acknowledged rites, and polygamy became less common. The last act of cannibalism was perpetrated in 1843. † Infanticide was no longer practised. The arts of reading and writing became commonly known, and after the establishment of the colony, the Post-office was the common medium of communication between distant friends. A few young men wrote a fluent hand, and were acquainted with the elements of arithmetic. An improvement was seen in their industrial habits, European clothing was in demand, and a desire was felt to place their children under instruction. These, as fruits of missionary labour, were apparent to all, and formed a rich reward for the toil, self-denial, and money by which, among other means, this great change had been wrought.

But a more spiritual work was in progress; this often stood out in fair proportions, but at other times it was marred by their narrow and defective views of the Gospel, and the outbursts of their own nature. "A mis-

* "Life of Rev. S. Marsden," p. 221.
† It has been renewed under the excitement of war.

sionary in Waikato met with two large bodies of men, fully armed, fiercely contending over a piece of fencing, and using the most violent language to one another. At the ringing of the bell for evening prayers, both parties, each in their position of defence and attack, with their guns lying beside them, joined in worship, while the men of God addressed them from Ephesians iv., 26, and pointing to the setting sun urged the text, " Let not the sun go down upon your wrath." Many persons became living witnesses of saving grace, and adorned their religious profession by a holy life and a triumphant death. The number of churches increased, native labourers were employed in the Church Missions as catechists, and in the Wesleyan Missions as local preachers ; and within the last few years several promising young men have been ordained to the regular work of the Christian ministry.

The Church Mission received a new impetus in 1842, by the arrival of the Right Rev. Dr. Selwyn, as Bishop of New Zealand, with a strong staff of assistants; and the enthusiasm with which his lordship entered into the native work was felt in all directions. In February of the following year, he wrote ; —" I held my first confirmation, at which three hundred and twenty-five natives were confirmed ; and a more orderly, and, I hope, impressive ceremony, could not have been conducted in any Church in England : the natives coming up in parties to the communion table, and audibly repeating the answer, *Ewakoatia ana e ahau*, I do confess. On the following Sunday, three hundred native communicants assembled at the Lord's table, though the rain was increasing, and some of them came two days' journey for this purpose." We regret to state that the Christian

L

intimacy which had been so helpful to both the Church and Wesleyan Missionaries in the hour of danger, and which had been honourably maintained, was discontinued, except in particular cases, after the arrival of the Bishop ; as the narrow views—or High Church principles—of his lordship prevented him from recognizing in the labours of the Wesleyan Missionaries anything beyond the efforts of devoted laymen ; and, therefore, the Christian rites performed by them were improper and invalid, according to the teaching of those who adopted the Bishop's principles. As might have been expected. the controversy which this course of proceedings introduced among the natives produced, for a time, considerable injury, and is to be deeply regretted.

The native converts were not ashamed of their Christian profession ; but regularly observed the morning and evening worship, whether they were at home or abroad, whether they were journeying by land or by water. It was interesting to see them assemble upon deck, when they were passengers on board a coasting vessel, regardless of remarks which might be made by the crew or other passengers, and go through the order of evening worship with reverence : the chanting of a hymn of praise, the offering of a prayer, in which the ship's company were not forgotten, and the reading of a chapter of God's holy Word, while all listened with devout attention—a lovely scene—the very counterpart of the orgies which had been practised a few years before on the decks of British ships. Grace was always said before and after their meals. No little annoyance was sometimes given to gentlemen when engaged on a coasting tour, by finding their journey suddenly stopped on a Saturday evening ; the natives whom they had engaged as guides and servants being determined to remember the Sabbath day, and keep it holy: in this manner a reproof was practically administered to Englishmen, who, with all their superior privileges, would have desecrated the Sabbath by travelling, had they not been prevented by men who had recently been rescued from heathen darkness. The following anecdote places a chief of the Bay of Plenty in an interesting position :—" An Englishman was applied to by the captain of a vessel then lying at anchor, to use his influence with the chief and his tribe to permit the captain to put out to sea on a Sunday. Accordingly, when divine service was over, the chief was requested to allow the captain to avail himself of the fair breeze and leave the bay. In reply to this request the chief arose, and, looking steadily into the face of the Englishman, repeated slowly and emphatically the fourth commandment,—' Remember the Sabbath day, to keep it holy. Six days shalt thou labour, and do all thy work.' And when he came to the clause, '*nor the stranger that is within thy gates,*' he repeated the words very slowly, and sat down."

Another instance of this work of grace shall be given, as well for the glory of God as to show that it was not effected without some severe trials to the mission families. An old chief woman hired out her slave—a man who was imbruted by hardship—as a servant to the Rev. J. Warren for twelve months, but when the planting season came she wished for the services of the slave, which were refused by the missionary, at the urgent request of the poor man. A quarrel ensued, and a *taua*, fighting party, was assembled to maintain the rights of the chieftess, who determined that the slave should be taken from the mission-house, and in all probability slain. "At sunset a company of about thirty men came rushing up the path in front of the house, like so many roaring lions, headed by the old woman, with her tongue protruded to the utmost extent, and her eyes as if they were standing upon her cheek-bones, calling the slave by name at the top of her voice." The excitement continued all night. Sometimes they procured firebrands for the purpose of burning down the house, at other times they shouted *Murua, murua, murua!* plunder, plunder, plunder! One man rushed into the house with his tomahawk uplifted, threatening to smash the bedroom door, but soon after said *Ka he ahau*, I am wrong; and then addressing himself to the old chieftess said, "You are the root of bitterness spoken of in the Scriptures as springing up to trouble the people. *Ko Hatana pu Koe*—you are Satan, the woman of the large mouth and unruly tongue. When you are dead we may hope for a little peace and quietude, but never before. Did we not all promise that if we could get a missionary we would give up all our Maori habits? And did we not especially promise that we would never shed blood on the mission station?" A proposal was then made to redeem the life and liberty of the slave by paying about £10 in blankets, calico, print, and axes—a proposal which the old lady at first refused, saying, "Did I not run after him and catch him when he was not longer than my arm, when we killed and ate his father and mother on the Waikato? Did I not bring him part of the way home on my own sacred back? and ever since, whenever I fed my pig, did I not always throw him a potato at the same time?" But at length the affair was settled, the payment was accepted, the slave was free, and the mission premises were safe.*

The whole of the Old Testament was not translated

* See Lecture by the Rev. John Warren, 1863.

and prepared for the press till a few years ago. The translator is the venerable Archdeacon Maunsell; he laboured at this great work through severe domestic affliction and bereavement, and in the midst of active missionary labours; and his translation was finally revised by a committee of brethren, selected from the Church and the Wesleyan missions. The devout and grateful feelings with which a misssionary writes the last sentence of a translation of God's word cannot be described. " I could have died when I had finished the translation of the Bible," said Dr. Morrison, in reference to the first version of the Scriptures which was made in the Chinese language. When Dr. Judson had completed his translation of the Old Testament into the Burman language he wrote as follows :—" Thanks be to God I can *now* say that I have attained. I have knelt down before him, with the last leaf in my hand, and imploring his forgiveness for all the sins which have polluted my labours in this department, and his aid in future efforts to remove the errors and imperfections which necessarily cleave to the work. I have commended it to his mercy and grace; I have dedicated it to his glory. May he make his own inspired Word, now complete in the Burman tongue, the grand instrument of filling all Burmah with songs of praise to our great God and Saviour Jesus Christ. Amen." And though the translation of Archdeacon Maunsell will be read by a less number of persons than those which we have referred to, the effects which may be expected to flow from the Maori Bible, with God's blessing, are such that the translator may contemplate them with strong feelings cf joy and gratitude.

Attempts were made about twenty years ago to establish missions among the natives by other Christian denominations without much success. Among these was a Presbyterian mission, which was commenced at Manawatu, and a Lutheran mission, which was conducted near Cape Egmont for some years, but was swept away by the unhappy collision which has taken place between the natives and the Government. It would not be difficult to state the causes of failure which affected the labours of the excellent men who were appointed to this work; among other things, the excitement and novelty connected with colonization, and the unhappy, but unfounded jealousy of the intentions of the Government towards the native race may be mentioned; but they who were not permitted to share largely in the honour of preparing the Maories for the service of Christ bear their willing testimony to the work which others have been enabled to accomplish.

In the year 1836, the Right Reverend Dr. Pompallier was appointed Roman Catholic Bishop of New Zealand, who accordingly arrived at the Bay of Islands, with a strong staff of priests, in 1838. With the usual zeal which that Church displays in Protestant countries, the labours of the priests were spread among several tribes; in the course of a few years the results of their teaching were seen in the crucifix suspended from the neck, and the missal, translated into Maori, as the manual of their devotions, instead of the Prayer Book and Hymns and Catechism—not to mention the New Testament—which had been instrumental in their deliverance from heathen night.

It is possible that some persons who may read these pages, and who have recently arrived in the colony, will suppose that the account which we have given of missionary success in New Zealand is presented in too bright a light. Associating in their own minds an advanced state of civilization with religious sincerity and growth, they are ready to suppose that because the former is not the case, the latter can have no existence in reality, or, at farthest, that their religion must be elementary and overstated. But this is not sound reasoning. The Rev. Walter Lawry observes in reference to the natives of Polynesia, "Nations do not readily change their ways. Very little progress has hitherto been made in the civilization of the South Sea Tribes, in the Friendly Isles, and Fiji; nor are the signs at all encouraging in this matter. The expectations entertained in England are by no means realized on the spot, at least, not with the rapidity which hope had painted, but left experience to correct." But who has the temerity to assert that the Spirit of the Lord has not been copiously poured out in those islands; or that the proofs of regenerating grace are not clear and scriptural in the conduct maintained by thousands of native Christians? It is just the same in New Zealand; with much that is revolting to the tastes and habits of a European, and with much that is earthly, sensual, and devilish among large numbers of the natives, a great and gracious change has passed over the race. A missionary writes in reference to the past, "Two mothers lived near our station, and each lost her only child. One mother was a Christian, the other was a heathen; the Christian mother came to weep and pray with my wife, the heathen mother went and hanged herself." Numerous facts, pointing out in the clearest manner the change which has passed over the native people, and which must be acknowledged, might be stated.

Nor should it be forgotten that the advantages of the

Maories are less than those with which the colonists are favoured. They have very few books beside the Bible, and this precious volume in its completeness has only lately been placed in their hands. Not a little injury is also done to their Christian character through ignorance of their customs and language ; many of their proceedings being condemned because they are misunderstood, and their motives suspected simply because they are not known. We say nothing here on the unhappy position in which many of the native tribes have placed themselves in reference to the British Government, as this subject will be found discussed in a future part of this volume.

Some persons may be disposed to raise objections to the character which we claim for the missionaries, who were the principal agents under God in accomplishing the work described in this chapter. We admit that some who filled the honourable position of a Christian missionary, both among the Church of England and the Wesleyans, proved unfaithful to their engagements ; and after a proper course of reproof, were removed from the cause which they had dishonoured. Others, fearing the effects of confining their children to native society, left the mission work, and entered upon the pursuits of secular life. But many of those who entered into the mission work in its darkest days, and many also of those who are now in the field, belonging to both the Churches which God has so remarkably honoured in this country, are worthy of all confidence and esteem.

During the unhappy war, which has dragged its slow length along for more than ten years, the missionaries have been the faithful servants of the churches ; their property has been made a prey, they have ventured among infuriated natives, where few white men could have gone, on messages of mercy; and both the Church of England and the Wesleyan Church can point to their missionary martyr, whose blood has reddened the New Zealand soil, and whose faithfulness unto death—death in horrible forms—will long live in the religious history of the country.

CHAPTER VII.

" Just then, within the thicket rude,
A log-rear'd cabin's roof they view'd,
And its low shelter bless'd.
On the rough floor, their simple bed,
In weariness and haste they spread,
And laid them down to rest."

GOD intends, as we have attempted to show, the whole earth, so far as it is suitable, to become the dwelling place of man. Probably the tracts of land which lie at both the poles will never be trod by human feet, and there are comparatively extensive deserts covered with sand and bare of vegetation, which are incapable of affording either human accommodation or food, and mountain ranges, some of them being hard, bare rocks, and others the sites of glaziers and avalanches, having their altitudes above the line of perpetual snow, forbid the thought of making them our home. But with such exceptions, the earth is prepared for the human race. The abundant vegetation of ages long passed by is compressed and turned into coal ; myriads of living creatures built up the coral rocks from the bottom of the ocean, and others contributed to form the masses of limestone, which is found so useful in the advancement and comfort of our race. As the soil of many countries newly discovered is found rich in all the qualities required for the production of food, the climate suitable to preserve the health of body and vigour of mind, as streams of refreshing water, clear as crystal, flow musically along, and larger streams, capable of bearing on their bosom richly laden ships, may be traced far into the interior of their respective countries, and as the coasts are indented with goodly harbours, it is impossible to deny that God has prepared these lands for the habitation of man. Nor are we to suppose that the Divine purpose is accomplished in the peopling of such portions of the earth with a race that is incapable of appreciating its conveniences, and making use of its treasures. A hunting ground may cover an area of several thousands of square miles, and support only a few families; and that support may be afforded in the crudest form; while, in the hands of another race, the same area of country may furnish sites for populous towns and cities, where may be found the mart of commerce and the rewards of industry; and other parts of the same tract may bloom with beautiful gardens, and wave with richly covered cornfields. None among us can determine the number of centuries through which human feet trod the plains of Australia, without having the smallest idea of the wealth which lay hidden in their soil; nor is there any reason to conclude that the rich mines of gold would have been discovered by that race in any future time. The conclusion to which we are led, therefore, is that God intended to introduce another portion of the human family to those extensive countries—a race capable of discovering the treasures which He had laid up, and of using them in accordance with His purposes.

A similar remark may be made concerning New Zealand and the Maori race. Far superior to the people who roamed the Australian country, ingenious in converting bones into fish-hooks and tools for labour—in weaving the green leaves of the flax plant into baskets and mats, and in constructing warm and comfortable houses with the long grass of their swamps—yet they knew nothing of the metals laid up in their soil, nor could they cultivate the rich plains covered with fern or dense forests, except in a few small patches. Looking upon the future character of races which are sunk so low as are the tribes inhabiting the islands of the South Sea in the light of acknowledged history, and supposing that no influence reaches them from without, there is nothing to relieve the melancholy reflection that they will probably sink gradually lower, and still lower, until it is impossible to imagine a picture so dark and wretched as their condition might become. Instead of improving in comfort and number, the general testimony of their past history shews that the reverse is the fact; for their wars—almost exterminating in their design and management—the abominable practices of infanticide and self-murder, not to mention many other things of fearful import, prevents us from supposing that the natives of the Pacific isles would have risen above the condition in which they were found when ships from the civilized world first visited their coasts.

It is confessedly an important object, and agreeable to the will of God, that the natural beauties and treasures of countries lying, till recently, beyond the pale of the enterprising world, should be laid under contribution to the general welfare of mankind; but it is a nobler object still to raise the races inhabiting those countries to a place in the civilized world, and to lead them to our common Saviour, and so to give them a glorious hope of everlasting life. The difficulties lying in the way of the elevation of a people, so far and so long sunk, are many and great; but they should not prevent the enterprising and enlightened race, which seek a home in their country, from using patiently the means which are most likely to effect their improvement. There is not a little danger that, although some attempts may be made of this kind, the mass of aborigines may remain uncared for and unblest, while hundreds of thousands live in comfort and plenty on the soil which was the dwelling place of the tribes who make the wilderness their home. A dark page may be written on this subject. The Spaniards are verily guilty, and the English colonists have not always been free from blame. A better spirit and more enlightened views of colonization have characterized our younger colonies ; and notwithstanding the cloud through which we are now* passing in New Zealand, and the obloquy which has been, in some instances, heaped upon us without hesitation, and without properly understanding our position and our doings, we hope to prove to the world that the colonization of New Zealand was commenced on Christian principles, and that, while the British race are endeavouring to reproduce, on a small scale, their bright and beautiful native land, they are trying to elevate the Maori race to a participation of the advantages which they have received as their birth-right.

The present is especially a colonizing age. Means have been contrived by which long voyages may be accomplished with comfort, safety, and despatch. Distant countries are now connected by telegraphic wires ; and such are the improvements made in the common arts and in commercial management, that the comforts of England may be enjoyed, to a great extent, at the ends of the earth. The extensive use of machinery is of great

* In 1864.

importance to a new country, where labour is always costly, and often, when most needed, hardly to be obtained at any price. Many branches of science are now so well understood, and are taught with so much clearness, that an intelligent and influential nation may rapidly grow up in a country which, a little time before, was known only as the land of ignorance and cruelty. Christian missions, of the Protestant stamp, have developed their power as a civilizing, as well as a religious institution, chiefly in the present century; and the amount of influence which they have contributed, not only towards the mental, moral, and social improvement of uncivilized tribes, but in the formation of the character and in the prosperity of British colonies, cannot be easily calculated. The free circulation of the Word of God must have a great effect upon colonial settlements ; for being issued at a price which places the sacred volume within the reach of all classes of persons, it finds its way into nearly every house, is appealed to as the highest authority of morality and religion, and is the source of consolation, through Jesus Christ our Lord, to thousands in the chamber of affliction and in the hour of death. The Bible also throws its restraints over the inclinations of the vicious; its principles are respected in legislative enactments; and the framework of colonial society is constructed, professedly, in accordance with its design. Religious and political liberty was never so well understood, nor so freely conceded, as it is at the present time ; and from this advantage many benefits may be experienced in the colonies which we are planting.

Great Britain is appointed, in the providence of God, to take the lead in peopling the waste places of the earth with an enterprising and intelligent race, and in raising the uncivilized tribes to a place of respectability and usefulness. No other nation, perhaps, has equal opportunities to confer these advantages. The pre-eminent position of that famed island has been secured, and is maintained, to a very great extent, by its religion. This contributes not a little, together with the virtuous and admirable character of the present Royal Family, to maintain the throne on the firmest foundation—the love of all classes of the people. To this, also, we owe the extensive liberties which are the boast of the British subject, and the motives which affect the industry and honesty, the morality and honour of the nation. The construction of her polity, by which the Crown enjoys its prerogatives, and the people their freedom—by which every man has an opportunity to rise in the social scale, and to exercise the talents with which he may be entrusted, either in the mother country or in her distant dependencies—is of immense importance. The philanthropic institutions which were begun by our fathers, as the expression of honourable sympathy towards the ignorant, afflicted, and unfortunate, and which have been continued with wisdom and experience, have not only conferred inestimable blessings on the classes whose welfare they were designed to meet, but have prepared the way for the establishment of similar institutions in the colonial settlements. The manufactures of Great Britain are known everywhere; they supply garments to screen the hardy inhabitants from the piercing cold of a polar winter, and furnish the light dress worn in tropical countries; and the tradesman of almost every country purchases the tools, and the farmer the implements of his industry, which were constructed in English workshops. No nation possesses a richer or more varied literature than our own, nor are we aware that any country places the choicest works on every branch of sound learning before the public at a lower price. The limited extent of their home territory indicates the colonizing work to which God has called the British race. A vast stream of emigration has been flowing out for many years, and yet the country is full of inhabitants. This stream will probably continue to flow on, to people other lands, and plant the virtues of England in the soil of far distant countries. Would that this could be done without planting her vices too! The general improvement in the customs of society must not be forgotten. Many of the gross vices which belonged to former years —not to say ages—have given way to sober, refined, and decorous conversation and manners among all who are not lost to self-respect; and this happy improvement is, perhaps, nowhere more plainly seen than in the respectable portions of colonial life.

The merest glance of the colonial course which our Anglo-Saxon race has run excites our wonder, and in many respects our admiration too. They laid the foundation of the United States of America, giving that mighty people their language, their literature, and their religion; and the extensive tracts of rich soil and goodly forests lying northward of those states are still a part of our Empire. The West Indian Islands are British too. Large portions of Africa are the scenes of English habits and industry; and the Queen of England rules many millions of the inhabitants of India. British influence does not now merely skirt the Chinese Empire, but is felt through the length and breadth of the land. The Southern world is undergoing the process of being moulded into British form. At the call of her industry

Australia is opening her treasures of gold, and promising a home for millions of her descendants. Tasmania and New Zealand are already English, and bid fair to reproduce many of the best and most interesting features of the fatherland. The work which she has done, and the peculiar qualifications for carrying on her colonial engagements, cause us to rejoice with trembling at the position of our native country. We rejoice that she is doing so much for the good of man, and the gracious purposes of God ; and we tremble at the amount of vice which is incidentally spread by her influence, and lest she should, in any case, lose sight of her great mission.

The early colonization of New Zealand possesses some peculiar features. Captain Cook recommended these islands as a suitable site for a penal settlement ; but the Government did not entertain the idea of such a course, and it is probably well that they did not ; for a colony so commenced would likely have inflicted untold evils upon the native people. It has often been said, and with some justice, too, that the missions established here won the country for the British crown. But other influences, and some of them much to be deplored when considered by themselves, contributed not a little to the erection of the colony. Not a few of the first settlers, who ventured to live among the natives on different parts of the coast, were convicts who had escaped from New South Wales and Van Dieman's Land ; others were seamen, who had absconded from their ships ; and a few were young men of better principles, but of an adventurous spirit, and who wished to see life in some of its most strange and stirring forms. As might have been supposed, the immoral practices of many of those men had an injurious effect upon the

natives, and tended to counteract the influences which
the mission stations were calculated to effect. Yet they
were, in some respects, beneficial; for their habits,
although rough, gave the natives some idea of civilized
life, as their clothing was contrasted with the flax mat,
and their cultivations enlarged the natives' acquaintance
with different kinds of vegetables, and the manner of
cultivating them. Some of them were industrious men,
and took delight in securing a comfortable homestead,
the effects of which were seen at least among the natives
who lived with them. Many of those adventurers were
engaged as sealers on several parts of the coast, and at
other places whaling companies were established. The
exciting and hazardous employment of the latter attracted
the attention of the natives, many of whom were proud
to take their place among the crews of the whale boats,
and soon became efficient in that dangerous and profitable enterprise.

But while these civilizing proceedings were carried
on, and the influence of the Pakeha was widely felt, the
rough, cruel, and ferocious spirit of the natives was
shockingly displayed. The year 1827 was a crisis in
the history of New Zealand. Events then trembled in
the balance. Would the influence of the white man be
for good or for evil, or would it be entirely swept away?
In that year, the agents of one missionary society left
the country, and those of the other were prepared to go.
But in that time of extreme danger, God stretched forth
His arm of defence. Before the close of that eventful
year, the missionary band returned, and tokens of happier times were given. European intercourse increased,
trade was encouraged, more white men arrived, and
orderly settlements were deemed desirable. As early as

the year 1825, and again in 1828, efforts were made to form settlements in the North Island; but without success. The exports shipped from New Zealand in those times of lawlessness, when every man did that which was right in his own eyes. is truly astonishing. The exports of the year 1829, consisting of whale-oil, wood, flax, pigs, and potatoes, amounted to the large sum of one hundred and thirty-five thousand four hundred and eighty-six pounds sterling, and goods had been imported for the previous fourteen years averaging the annual value of thirty thousand pounds sterling, besides the trade carried on by many whalers, of which no account was kept.*

Much of the payment which the Maories received for their labour and exports, consisted of fire-arms and ammunition; and this contributed largely, no doubt, to the exterminating wars which raged so fiercely for some years. The chief Rauparaha—of unhappy notoriety, on account of his connection with the Wairau massacre in 1843, and still later as a prisoner on board H.M.S. Calliope—purchased a large stock of muskets. powder, and shot, and made his name terrible. In those days, some of the commanders of British vessels were guilty of the vilest practices for purposes of gain, as the following narrative will show:—In the year 1829, Te Pahe, a chief, was murdered by the natives at Banks' Peninsula, during a friendly visit to purchase green-stone. Rauparaha and Rangihaeata, his nearest relations, determined to avenge his death. For this purpose, Captain Stewart, of the brig Elizabeth, on the promise of a cargo of flax, conveyed Rauparaha and eighty warriors from Kapiti, in Cook's Strait, to Banks' Peninsula, in the Middle Island. Rauparaha's party hid themselves when

Dr. Thomson, "Story of New Zealand."

the ship dropped her anchor, and the unsuspecting natives came on board, to whom the captain represented himself as a purchaser of flax. When the chief, named Tamaiharanui, accompanied by his wife and children, with other persons belonging to the tribe, came on board, Rauparaha and his men left their hiding-place, and falling suddenly upon them, murdered every native, except Tamaiharanui, his wife, and daughter—the latter being about sixteen years of age—who were made prisoners, and intended to honour their return to Kapiti. Rauparaha and his warriors then landed, and killed every native whom they could reach. Ovens were prepared, and many human bodies were cooked, which were then packed in native baskets, and taken on board the brig. When their work was done, the anchor was weighed, and the ship stood out to sea on her return voyage. But who can describe the horrible orgies which were practised during that voyage on the deck of an English ship! Obscene songs, the war-dance, and cannibal feasting were the type of their disgusting enjoyment, and were conducted in the presence of their humbled prisoners, who were compelled to look on while the bodies of their friends were devoured. We cannot write this without blushing for the dishonour done to the name of our country, and of our race. The cool fortitude of Tamaiharanui, as he lay bound hand and foot, without shewing a sign of terror, was remarkable. By his order the mother strangled their daughter, to put an end to her disgrace. The loss of this girl so enraged Rauparaha, that he sucked the blood of Tamaiharanui as it flowed from a vein ; then, after heating a ramrod red hot, he thrust it through his body, and endeavoured to aggravate his sufferings with bitter jests. The chief died in these tortures, but without disclosing a sign of fear, and his wife some time afterwards was killed at Otaki.* It will be some relief to know that the captain of this dishonoured and blood-stained vessel could not obtain the cargo of flax which he expected, and that, on his arrival in Sydney, he was tried by the Supreme Court for the part which he had taken in these abominable affairs; but, as a matter of course, almost, for want of sufficient evidence to convict him, the case could not be sustained, and he escaped punishment. Not long after, however, as the same ship was doubling Cape Horn, the wretched man, then in a state of drunkenness, fell down dead, and was thrown overboard by his own crew.†

The anxiety of the Maories to increase their commercial connexions with the traders of the neighbouring colonies, led them to sell large tracts of land at little more than a nominal price. It is not probable that they understood the importance of those transactions; the idea of land being an article which might be bought and sold by persons who never trod their country, was not likely to be comprehended. But many persons in Sydney determined to avail themselves of this opportunity to become extensive landowners in New Zealand. To facilitate their intended purchases, deeds were drawn up in English, leaving blank spaces for the insertion of names, boundaries, and dates, according to the common form; and with these preparations they sought to invest

---

* Eighteen years afterwards, Tamihana, Rauparaha's son, with his cousin Matini Te Whiwhi, and other Christian friends, introduced the Gospel, as the best reparation he could make for the wrongs which his father had done them.

† Extracted from Dr. Thomson's "Story of New Zealand," pp. 264—266.

a small amount of merchandise—and some of it of a very questionable character—in large purchases of land. A few of the missionaries fell into the same temptation, which raised for a time an evil report of the whole missionary band — some of whom purchased no land, and others secured only a moderate quantity for the use of their children, and at a fair price. These early purchases became a subject of careful enquiry after the colony was erected. Land Commissioners were appointed, by whom more than twelve hundred claims for land, said to have been bought before the commencement of the colony, not including the claims of the New Zealand Company, were examined. Some of these claims were very large; three of them exceeded a million of acres each, more than half a million of acres each were claimed by three others, three more claims exceeded a quarter of a million of acres each, and upwards of thirty of the claims comprised more than twenty thousand acres each;* and before the colony was formed, no less than twenty millions of acres were claimed by white men, as having been bought of the natives.†

The reader will observe that, while such a flood of British influence was rolling in upon the country, especially upon the North Island, no measures were used to prevent the evils which might be expected from such a course of things. No one can imagine to what extent those evils might extend in such a country as New Zealand, and among such a susceptible and excitable people as the Maories. The happy influences which the mission stations had produced were in danger of being superseded by others, in which the natives were likely to suffer much injury. It is not surprising, therefore, that

---

* Swainson, p. 90. † Thomson's "Story of New Zealand."

a letter was written by thirteen chiefs of the Bay of Islands to William IV., asking his protection. This was followed by the appointment of Mr. Busby as British Resident, who arrived at the Bay of Islands in 1833. In this appointment the independency of the country was acknowledged, and a political position attributed to the chiefs who requested the protection of Great Britain which they did not really possess. At Mr. Busby's suggestion, a New Zealand flag was prepared, acknowledging the Maories as an independent nation; and H.M.'s ship Alligator was dispatched to inaugurate the flag by a Royal salute, and orders were issued by the Lords of the Admiralty, that the New Zealand flag should be respected. This very flag has recently been hoisted in the Waikato district, with the words "Potatau, King of New Zealand," inscribed upon it. It will be seen at once that this act of the British Government gave up their claim upon New Zealand—at least upon the North Island—founded upon the discoveries of Captain Cook, and, without intending to do so, increased the difficulties connected with the colonization of the country. The appointment of a British Resident was not of much use. He was compared to a man-of-war without guns. He might issue orders, but had no power to enforce them. A small sum was placed at his disposal, to be distributed among the natives; but it was sufficient only to excite their cupidity, without doing them much good. We doubt whether this appointment was of any real value, except as it was a step—but contrary to the intentions of the British Government—in the providence of God, towards the erection of the colony.

It is not easy to describe the state of things which

existed at the Bay of Islands at the time of which we write. More than a thousand persons are said to have been located there in the year 1838, and the number of vessels which entered the harbour in the preceding year is given as follows:—American, fifty-six; English, twenty-three; French, twenty-one; Bremen, one; New South Wales, twenty-four; coasting vessels, six—shewing that, in the year 1837, no less than one hundred and thirty-one vessels, and many of them ships of large size, entered into the Bay of Islands for purposes of trade. Many were the evils and dangers to which such a people were exposed by ships' crews, at the end of long sea voyages, gathered together from different countries, and being without the restraints of wholesome laws. Numbers of native girls were kept by chiefs for the worst purposes, and were distributed temporarily among the seamen for gain. Neither property nor life was safe. Desperate efforts were sometimes made to preserve something like order. Persons who figured in that singular state of society, and who are now respectably settled in Auckland, speak of a company which was formed to preserve order, each member having to provide himself with a musket, bayonet, brace of pistols, cutlass, and twenty rounds of ammunition. Sometimes persons of more than ordinary trouble were visited with a ludicrous and inconvenient form of punishment, of which the following description may be accepted as a specimen:—"The culprit, a white man, already nearly suffocated from being secured all night in a sea-chest, was first denuded of his garments, then smeared thickly over with tar, and covered with the white feathery flowers of the *raupo* plant, for want of true feathers. He was then marched along the beach, preceded by a fife and drum playing the 'Rogue's March,' and accompanied by drunken white men and astonished natives to its termination. Then the criminal was put into a canoe with the musicians, and landed on the opposite side of the bay."*

It is easy to see that this state of things could not continue long—a properly formed colony must be its result; and if Great Britain determined not to colonize the country, some other nation would make the attempt. A French ship was fitted out for this purpose, and several families came from France to form a settlement in New Zealand, under the protection of their national flag; and it was not until the emigrants from France were off the New Zealand coast, that the British flag was unfurled, and the right of Great Britain to these islands tacitly asserted. A delay of a few days only would have been followed by the loss of the colony to the English, and the establishment of French authority.

The New Zealand Company, no doubt, contributed not a little to hasten the jurisdiction of England, by its zealous, and, in some respects, imprudent proceedings. This language will not be deemed too strong if we remember that, while the Government was refusing to erect these islands into a British colony, a preliminary expedition was sent by the Company to purchase land, and to determine the sites of the respective settlements; and assuming that there would be no difficulty in procuring land, they proceeded to offer it for sale in England, with the right of selection when the purchasers, or their agents, should arrive in New Zealand. Purchases of this kind were made to the amount of a hundred thousand pounds sterling;

* Swainson.

and several ships, full of emigrants, were sent off before the Company heard of the proceedings and success of the preliminary expedition.* Being aware of the anomalous position in which they were placed before the establishment of British authority, the emigrants entered into an agreement among themselves, whereby a Council of Government was formed, and provisions were made by which any offender should be punished in the same manner as he would have been if the crime of which he might have been convicted had been committed within the realm of England. We can hardly conceive how a body of emigrants could proceed to plant a colony in a distant land, where there was no legal appeal, without some provision of this kind: and the cheerful manner in which they arranged for their common safety and honour, under very singular circumstances, shews their fitness for the arduous work which lay before them as the pioneers of a great colony. But it must not be forgotten that *their Provisional Government was illegal;* and that soon after their arrival in New Zealand they were officially warned that, if their self-imposed authority were exercised, they would be liable to a prosecution for usurping the functions of the Crown and Parliament, and that it was the intention of the Government to enforce the strict letter of the law.†

The precipate purchases of land, and the immediate commencement of surveys, led to frequent misunderstandings with the natives, and prevented many of the best class of settlers from taking possession of the sections which they had paid for before they left England. But while those immature measures, and especially the sufferings and losses among the first settlers, are deeply re-

* See Swainson, p. 77.   † Idem, pp. 102, 103.

gretted, they were overruled for good. A better class of emigrants could not have been selected; they were industrious and healthy, they possessed a good share of common sense, which is often invaluable to an emigrant, and many of them were fairly educated, and respected for a high-toned moral character. Such were the men who laid the foundation of the southern provinces of the North Island; and, irregular as their proceedings, no doubt, were, they were perhaps necessary to induce Great Britain to commence the work of colonization in New Zealand—a work to which the providence of God had so plainly called her people.

The position in which those early colonists were placed on their arrival in Cook's Strait was such as is seldom experienced. At the distance of sixteen thousand miles from their native country, and not knowing before their arrival that an acre of land had been purchased which they were to call their own, and on the coasts of a country whose native population were known till very lately as ferocious cannibals when excited, and whose natural susceptibility might any time kindle the flames of angry passions, they would naturally have feelings both peculiar and painful, as they looked upon the uncultivated hills and plains from the deck of the ship. Nor was their condition very favourable when they landed. Mothers and helpless children looked around upon the barren hills of Wellington from the beach. Houses there were none. Crops could not be obtained for many months; all the necessaries of life must be imported. Some were cast down for a while, and wished themselves in England again; but this feeling soon passed away, temporary houses were erected, plots of ground were planted, and the blessing of the Most High rested upon them. Many of those pioneers can now look back upon that season of trial without regret, they now enjoy the reward of their industry, and feel an honest pride in the thought that they were the founders of the goodly colony which they see growing up around them. These remarks may be applied with equal fitness to the first settlers of Nelson and New Plymouth, who commenced their colonial life under very serious difficulties, but many of whom, after a few years' labour, found their reward in a cheerful competence.

It was on the 12th of May, 1839, that the first expedition sailed, and on the 16th of the following September —four months after—three ships full of emigrants left Gravesend, and reached Wellington in the early part of 1840. The English Government now saw that decisive steps must be taken. Accordingly, Captain Hobson, R.N., was commissioned as Consul and Lieutenant-Governor on the 14th day of August, 1839, *providing that he could obtain the cession of some part of the country to the British Crown.* He arrived in the Bay of Islands early in the year 1840, with a staff of officers, which he had obtained in New South Wales, of which colony New Zealand was to be a dependency.

In the instructions furnished to Captain Hobson by the Most Honourable the Marquis of Normanby New Zealand was recognized as an Independent State. "We acknowledge New Zealand," says his lordship, "as a Sovereign and Independent State, so far, at least, as it is possible to make that acknowledgment in favour of a people composed of numerous, dispersed, and petty tribes, who possess few political relations to each other, and are incompetent to act, or even to deliberate in concert." On the cession of sovereignty by the natives, his lordship says, "Her Majesty's Government have resolved to authorize you to treat with the aborigines of New Zealand for the recognition of her Majesty's sovereign authority over the whole or any part of those islands which they may be willing to place under her Majesty's dominion." And to prevent, as it was supposed, a wild and injurious land speculation, the document provides as follows :—" It is further necessary that the chiefs should be induced, if possible, to contract with you, as representing her Majesty, that henceforward no lands shall be ceded, either gratuitously or otherwise, except to the Crown of Great Britain." It should be observed that in an explanatory letter of the Marquis of Normanby, addressed to Captain Hobson, August 15th, the newly appointed Consul was informed that his instructions, so far as the independence of New Zealand was concerned, strictly applied only to the North Island, and that if the British sovereignty could not be established in the Middle Island by treaty, it might be done on the ground of discovery.

The trust reposed in Captain Hobson was a very important affair, requiring great judgment, much forbearance, and considerable tact ; a false step might give rise to a thousand jealous feelings, and prevent a friendly and safe commencement of the colony. And who can imagine the dangers which hung over the settlers in the north, if the proceedings of the Lieutenant-Governor were not successful; and who can tell the difficulties lying in the way of the projected settlements in the southern part of the island, which might arise from the same cause ? It is not often that a man is placed in such delicate circumstances ; when such a case occurs an opportunity is afforded to lay unborn generations under a tribute of gratitude ; such a debt is owing to Captain Hobson, and will be cheerfully acknowledged. His career in New Zealand was short, but the work which he accomplished was great. He wisely sought the assistance of the missionaries, who were almost the only white persons in the country that had acquired a knowledge of the Maori language and customs, and possessed their confidence. This course of procedure stamped a missionary character upon the early movements of the colony ; the natives looked at the subject through a missionary medium, and signed the treaty of cession more in confidence of the missionaries, whom they knew well, than of the British Government, of which they knew but little.

The Bay of Islands was the first place where the native chiefs were invited to transfer the sovereignty of the country to the Crown of Great Britain. It was most desirable to establish the strong arm of the law there without delay, on account of the character and number of the people who had made that neighbourhood their home. Only a few weeks passed after the arrival of the Consul and his staff before a meeting was convened at Waitangi, and the treaty of cession laid before the chiefs for their discussion and signature. As this treaty has been called the Magna Charta of the Maories, and was really the foundation upon which the colony was founded, and has been the object of appeal in our colonial history, we will give our readers an opportunity to examine it.

TREATY OF WAITANGI.

" Her Majesty, Victoria, Queen of the United Kingdom of Great Britain and Ireland, regarding with her royal favour the native chiefs and tribes of New Zealand, and

anxious to protect their just rights and property, and to secure to them the enjoyment of peace and good order, has
deemed it necessary, in consequence of the great number
of her Majesty's subjects who have already settled in
New Zealand, and the rapid extension of emigration,
both from Europe and Australia, which is still in progress, to constitute and appoint a functionary properly
authorized to treat with the aborigines of New Zealand
for the recognition of her Majesty's sovereign authority
over the whole or any part of those islands. Her Majesty,
therefore, being desirous to establish a settled form of
civil government, with a view to avert the evil consequences which must result from the absence of the necessary laws and institutions, alike to the native population
and to her subjects, has been graciously pleased to em-
power and authorize me, William Hobson, a captain in
her Majesty's Royal Navy, Consul and Lieutenant-
Governor over such parts of New Zealand as may be, or
hereafter shall be, ceded to her Majesty, to invite the
confederated and independent chiefs of New Zealand to
concur in the following articles and conditions :—

"Article the First.—The Chiefs of the Confederation of the United Tribes of New Zealand, and the
separate and independent chiefs who have not become
members of the Confederation, cede to her Majesty
the Queen of England absolutely, and without reservation, all the rights and powers of sovereignty which
the said confederation or individual chiefs respectively
exercise or possess, or may be supposed to exercise or
possess, over their respective territories, as the sole
sovereigns thereof.

"Article the Second.—Her Majesty the Queen of
England confirms and guarantees to the chiefs and

tribes of New Zealand, and to the respective families and individuals thereof, the full, exclusive, and undisturbed possession of their lands and estates, forests, fisheries, and other properties which they may collectively or individually possess, so long as it is their wish and desire to retain the same in their possession. But the chiefs of the united tribes, and the individual chiefs, yield to her Majesty the exclusive right of preemption over such lands as the proprietors thereof may be disposed to alienate, at such prices as may be agreed upon between the respective proprietors and persons appointed by her Majesty to treat with them on that behalf.

"Article the Third.—In consideration thereof her Majesty the Queen of England extends her royal protection, and imparts to them all the rights and privileges of British subjects.

"(Signed)   W. HOBSON.

"Now, therefore, we, the chiefs of the Confederation of the United Tribes of New Zealand, being assembled in Congress, at Victoria, in Waitangi, and we, the separate and independent chiefs of New Zealand, claiming authority over the tribes and territories which are specified after our respective names, having been made fully to understand the provisions of the foregoing treaty, accept and enter into the same in the full spirit and meaning thereof.

"In witness whereof we have attached our signatures or marks at the places and dates respectively specified.

"Done at Waitangi this 5th of February, in the year of our Lord 1840."

A careful examination of this Treaty, especially in the light which has been thrown upon it by a better knowledge of native customs, and by the unhappy events which have recently taken place, will enable us to point out several important defects. The words "We, the Chiefs of the Confederation of the United Tribes of New Zealand, being assembled in Congress,"— suggest a political status which did not really exist. The idea no doubt grew out of the letter sent by thirteen chiefs to William IV., imploring protection from the lawlessness that threatened the peace and safety of the country. But allowing that this could be satisfactorily explained, so that no cause of jealousy was likely to be sown in the minds of neighbouring chiefs, a still greater mistake was made in ceding to the Crown the exclusive right of pre-emption over all lands which the natives might be disposed to alienate. This article constituted the Governor the great land purchaser, and no doubt, in many cases lessened his influence, and gave rise to jealousy concerning his intentions. If exorbitant prices were demanded for their land, it was the duty of the Governor to negociate through his agent till a fair price might be accepted; and if a block of land was sold beneath the supposed value, the Governor was liable to be charged with displaying the low motives of a mercenary trader. In some places a track of land was of great importance to the neighbouring colony, and of little use to the native people, and it was quite natural that the Governor should be requested to purchase it; and then his attempt to do so would perhaps lessen the respect of the natives, and make them suspicious of the designs of the Government. It were no easy task to point out all the evils

N

which were likely to flow from this source, and which have really flowed from it. It is in one view probable, that much of the dissatisfaction which so unhappily prevails over large portions of this island, may be traced to this mistake. Yet the motives of the Government demand our respect; a great evil lay before them, in the loose and extensive land purchases which had been made; and in the innumerable purchases of a similar kind, with which different parts of the country were threatened; and this system of "pre-emption" appeared the best which could be devised, to put a stop to those dangerous proceedings.

By this Treaty "all the rights and privileges of British subjects" were conferred upon the Maories. But much of this must in the nature of things be merely nominal. British law could not reach a large portion of the people; robberies were committed and murders were perpetrated, without the possibility of bringing the criminals to justice; and some of the native customs were directly contrary to both the letter and spirit of English law, and yet they could not be expected to be laid aside, except in a gradual manner. The peculiar circumstances of the Maories, which were the result of the lawlessness in which they were trained, made it difficult if not impossible to apply well known laws, or to prepare others which should meet their case. Some things, for instance, might be sold by the individual proprietor, others could not be alienated without the consent of the chief, and in some cases the consent of the whole tribe, or the division of the tribe to which the party belonged, was necessary to the validity of the sale. We mention these things to show the dangers and difficulties attending the colonization of this country; but while we point out some of the fundamental mistakes which were made, before that valuable article—experience —could be obtained, we would express our admiration of the honourable conduct of the British Government, and especially of the officers to whom the Government entrusted these onerous transactions.

The meeting which was convened at Waitangi, as has been related, was numerously attended, and a similar meeting was held at Hokianga five days afterwards. The Missionaries of both the Church of England and the Wesleyan Societies attended, and acted as interpreters. To them the Maories applied for explanations and advice, and it was owing to their influence that the Treaty was accepted and numerously signed. It has been lately stated that the Maories were deceived, that they had no correct idea of conceding the sovereignty to the Crown, and, consequently, that they affixed their signature to a document which was not morally binding. But in reply to this it may be stated, that several of the missionaries now in the field, and whose love for the natives and anxiety for their well-being no men doubt, assert that the Treaty was fully explained, and well understood by the numerous chiefs who signed it.

On the 21st of May, a little more than three months after the meeting of Waitangi was held, and after the signatures of many chiefs residing in distant parts of the country had been obtained to the Treaty, the Queen's Sovereignty was proclaimed in the following form :—

PROCLAMATION.

" In the name of Her Majesty, Victoria, Queen of the United Kingdom of Great Britain and Ireland.

By William Hobson, Esquire, a Captain in the
Royal Navy, Lieutenant-Governor of New Zealand :—

" WHEREAS, by a Treaty, bearing date the 5th day of
February, 1840, made and executed by me, William Hobson, a Captain in the Royal Navy, Consul and Lieutenant-
Governor in New Zealand, vested for this purpose with
full powers by Her Britannic Majesty, of the one part,
and the chiefs of the Confederation of the United Tribes
of New Zealand, and the separate and independent
chiefs of New Zealand, not members of the Confederation, of the other, and further ratified and confirmed by
the adherence of the principal chiefs of this island of New
Zealand, commonly called 'The Northern Island,' all
rights and powers of sovereignty over the said Northern
Island, absolutely and without reservation :—

" Now, therefore, I, William Hobson, Lieutenant-
Governor of New Zealand, in the name and on the
behalf of Her Majesty, do hereby proclaim and declare
to all men, that from and after the date of the above-
mentioned Treaty, the full Sovereignty of the Northern
Island of New Zealand vests in Her Majesty Queen
Victoria, her heirs, and successors, for ever.

" Given under my hand at Government-House,
Russell, Bay of Islands, this 21st day of May,
in the year of our Lord, 1840.
" (Signed,)
" WILLIAM HOBSON, Lieutenant-Governor."

On the same day, Governor Hobson proclaimed the
Queen's sovereignty over the Middle and Southern
Islands, principally on the ground of discovery. But
Major Bunbury, of H.M. 80th Regiment, who visited the

chiefs of the Middle and Southern Islands and obtained their signatures to the Treaty of Waitangi, issued a proclamation with the usual ceremonies in the following June, on the ground of the sovereignty having been ceded by the principal chiefs.

The colony was then fairly launched, although it remained for a little time as a dependency of New South Wales. The Sovereignty of the entire country was vested in the Crown of Great Britain, and all classes looked forward hopefully. That a fierce and warlike people should transfer their *mana*, their sovereign right, to a foreign nation, was remarkable; and when the manner in which it was done is considered, the influence of the Christian missions,—which had been established for twenty-six years in the country, among the tribes whose signatures were among the first affixed to the Treaty, whose agents, as we have seen, took an active part in the business, and whose word formed the principal ground of confidence among the native chiefs,—challenges our grateful acknowledgment and support.

The land which was so lately polluted with blood, and the scene of the most horrible orgies, was now fairly opened to the influence of the Anglo-Saxon race; henceforward their language is to be heard from the North Cape to the Southern Coast of Stewart's Island, their arts are to be taught and their knowledge is to be spread over the plains of New Zealand, where the virtue and happiness of England are to find a home, and, we regret to add, where her vices and miseries will be found also. The hand of God may be fairly traced in the history which we have sketched. With a determination not to colonize New Zealand, an irresistible influence compelled

ˈthe Government of England to undertake the work; and the experience of a quarter of a century, notwithstanding the interruptions of war, shows that her Majesty did not mistake her mission.

Cities in embryo—towns of real importance—have grown up in different parts of both the principal islands, and smiling villages, with hundreds of happy homes, are found in various directions. Many and great are the advantages which the natives have reaped from the colonization of the country. Being well dressed in European clothing, and possessing considerable property, many of them are rejoicing in circumstances of comfort of which their race had no idea only half a century ago. The New Zealand Colonist may cherish an honest pride in the fair-dealing with which the Maori race has been treated, as being the counterpart of the general dealings of the white race towards the aborigines, whose lands they wished to appropriate to themselves. We have been particular in our remarks on this subject, on account of the misapprehensions which have been entertained, and, in some cases, the undeserved obloquy which has been heaped upon the settlers.

CHAPTER VIII.

IT is not easy to describe the disadvantages under which the first settlements in this country were formed ; for, in addition to the inconveniences arising from a wilderness, which produced no food for man, and but little for cattle, without cultivation, the number of aboriginal inhabitants, and the jealousy with which they regarded the influx of the white race—especially as many of the pahs and cultivations of the natives were either upon the land, or adjacent to the ground which the settlers expected to call their own—supplied causes of anxiety and alarm. The Maories at this time were the dominant race in respect of numbers and physical force, and the settlers felt that they were really under their power. Yet, while these things continued, the danger was not considered to be great ; for the natives were alive to the superior skill and industry of the Pakehas, and to the advantages which were supplied through them. In some instances, the plantations of the Maories supplied the newly-arrived settlers with food, at fair prices, till their own crops were ripe ; and in others, where their Pakeha neighbours were without money, in the commencement of their country life, the native chiefs have supplied them with the necessaries of life *on credit*, expecting to be paid when their crops should be ready for the market. But while such benefits were sometimes obtained from a neighbouring pah, the injuries which were done to the crops of the settlers by the pigs, and to their fowls by the dogs of the pah, were numerous and irritating.

The busy scene which a newly-formed settlement presented, was a strange and interesting object to the Maori people. Everything about the farm, the yard, and the house, was an object for examination, and a subject of conversation. Innumerable questions, prompted by curiosity, were asked, but answered with difficulty, on account of the little knowledge which each had of the language of the other. Not setting much value on their own time, they were regardless of the time of the settlers, to whom they gave no little inconvenience and discomfort by lounging in their houses and premises in considerable numbers. These annoyances, however, were not likely to continue long, except on the arrival of strangers, as their curiosity would be gradually satisfied, and the benefits of civilized life would excite among themselves the industry necessary to procure them. This was the case with many persons who, instead of being indolent, dirty, and troublesome, soon became industrious and respectable.

But troubles of a serious kind awaited the infant colony, and fell heavily, and in a distinct form, upon each of the wide-spread settlements. A collision with the native people was most to be feared, both on their own account and on ours ; for it would militate against the benefits which the former might enjoy from the example and trade of the settlers, and, in the defenceless condition of the colony, it might inflict untold miseries upon the settlers. Yet such a collision was extremely probable. The naturally proud, suspicious, and defiant spirit of the Maori—the misunderstandings which were likely to occur through ignorance of each others' language and customs—the careless expressions, and, in some instances, the wanton treatment of which the white man had been guilty towards the Maories—their want of patience during the slow process of English law—and, more than all others, the vexed land question, which had been a source of trouble among the native tribes from time immemorial—might at any time disturb the peace of the country.

One of the greatest blessings which could be conferred upon the Maori people would be, without doubt, an appropriate code of laws; but we know, from repeated failures, that this is beset with difficulties. Many of the principles of justice were so distorted in the native mind, that they demanded blood for blood, without regard to the guilt or innocency of the persons devoted to destruction. Large numbers of their own race, in every part of the country, have fallen from this perversion of justice; and they have sometimes been restrained with difficulty from inflicting similar punishment on innocent persons of the white race who have settled amongst them. An event, however, occurred in the early history of the colony, in which an appeal was made to the Maori sense of justice, under the extreme penalty of the law; and their conduct through the heavy trial was worthy of all praise. As this was the first case of capital punishment executed in the colony, a further account of it may be narrated.

Maketu, a native youth, seventeen years of age, murdered a family of five persons with whom he had been living at the Bay of Islands. From his own confession, and other evidence, his guilt was proved, and on the 7th March, 1842, he was hanged at Auckland. The natives gave him up to justice, watched with anxiety the process of his trial, and saw him die upon the gallows. When more than three-quarters of a year had passed away, the father of this unhappy youth asked permission to remove the bones of his child to the family burial place. This being granted, the bones were carefully scraped, and removed to the Bay of Islands for interment. And the affection of the parent further manifested itself in the following pathetic lamentation, which was translated by Mr. C. O. Davis :— *

"O, my son !
I may ne'er forget thee. Thou art gone
Far hence, for the deep springs of fatherly
Affection are bubbling now, and the mind
Seems all bewildered—o'ertaken by a storm.
I fed thee with the fish which line the rocks
Along the ocean shore, and taught thee how to meet the enemy.
O, my son, I used to press thee to my breast.
Yes, Maketu, that child whom priests
Baptized in the fast flowing stream.†
Stay, my son. It was a day of life
When the people came in companies,
When the birds and other dainties were set out
Before them. How now ?
Ah ! do not look upon my bird with scorn ;
Lo, it is newly-fledged, and comes from
That noble one, Whara Whara the Great.
And when its death is known, the grandsons
Of famed Taingahue will come from
Distant places. Here are thy lines,
O'er those I weep, and then I place
Thy hooks within a basket, as a memorial
Of my lost one.
My son, thy name was scarcely known.

* "Maori Mementos," 1855.
† A Heathen rite called Iriiri.

Thou wert but a stripling, and yet
Thy hands have touched another's treasures.
Thy sires, Pehi and Te Ngatata, were great
And wise ; then how hast thou become
Acquainted with Whiro, the god of plunder ?"

In the year 1844, about four years from the commencement of the colony, the town and neighbourhood
of Russell, at the Bay of Islands—the first town formed
in the colony—became the scene of alarm and.disorder
through the turbulent proceedings of armed natives.
Two causes were assigned for this breach of the peace,
by a chief named Hone Heke—abusive language, which
had been uttered against him by a native woman, the
wife of a settler, and the strangely mistaken design of
the Government flag-staff, which was supposed to be
used to prevent American vessels from coming into the
harbour, and, consequently, to prevent the natives from
enjoying the advantages of the American trade. In July
of that year, Hone Heke assembled his fighting men,
entered the town in a defiant manner, resolving to have
compensation, according to native customs, for the
insult offered to the chief, and to cut down the flag-
staff. All that could be done by the Government officers
and influential chiefs to appease their wrath, was
attempted ; but without much effect ; for they danced
the war-dance, threatened to violate some of the females,
and plundered several houses ; and then, having cut
down the flag-staff, they deliberately burnt some parts
of it, and carried other parts away. Alarmed at the
defenceless state of the infant colony amidst these proceedings, his Excellency the Governor requested troops
from the colonies of New South Wales and Hobart Town,
and in the month of August a considerable body of

soldiers were landed. H. M. S. Hazard, with the Governor on board, visited the Bay of Islands at the same
time, and took the steps which were deemed most
prudent to prevent the collision from spreading, and to
point out the evils which were likely to flow from such a
cause. At a meeting of the principal chiefs, on the 2nd
of September, the Bishop of New Zealand and several
missionaries being present, his Excellency spoke at
length, and with precision, on the course which had
been taken by Heke and his adherents. He reminded
them that thirty years before they were " wild barbarians,
utterly unlike Christians, utterly uncivilized ;" and that
to reclaim them from that state the missionaries had
denied themselves many of the comforts of life, and
exposed themselves to many dangers. The probability
that New Zealand would become a colony of some European nation, which induced the British Government to
protect him by its flag; the unhappy effects which
were produced at Tahiti and the Marquesan Islands ;
the benefits which they might derive through their
connexion with the English race ; and the large sums
of money which were spent in support of the missions,
whose object it was to raise them as a people in things
both temporal and spiritual—were clearly pointed out.
His Excellency further stated that Hone Heke had
written him a letter, apologising for cutting down the
flag-staff, and offering to put up another, and, consequently, all that he should insist on more was, that ten
guns should be given us "as an atonement," and as
marking the offence by a public acknowledgment. A
number of tomahawks and twenty guns were immediately
laid at the Governor's feet, and an offer was made to
give up more, if his Excellency required them. The

object of the Governor having been secured, he returned the guns to their former owners, and the meeting ended. The services of the troops not being needed, and their presence being likely to produce suspicion, they returned to the neighbouring colonies without delay, in the same ships which conveyed them to New Zealand.

The letter which was sent by Hone Heke to his Excellency may be deemed interesting. The following is a translation of it :—

" FRIEND GOVERNOR,—

" This is my speech to you. My disobedience and rudeness is no new thing. I inherit it from my parents, from my ancestors ; do not imagine that it is a new feature in my character. But I am thinking of leaving off my rude conduct to Europeans. Now I say that I will prepare another pole inland at Waimate, and I will erect it at its proper place at Kororarika, in order to put a stop to our quarrel ; let your soldiers remain beyond sea, and at Auckland ; do not send them here. The Pole that was cut down belonged to me ; I made it for the native flag, and it was never paid for by the Europeans.

" From your Friend,

" HONE HEKE POKAI."

Concerning the charge alleged against the Government, of not paying for the flag-staff, we can say nothing, only that it is not likely to be correct.

Although the breach was repaired, and the settlers breathed freely again, the source of disaffection was not dried up. Before the end of the year, native customs again clashed with English law, and the property of

Europeans was taken as compensation for injuries said to have been inflicted upon the Maories ; but the persons from whom the property was taken had no connection with the individuals by whom the provocation had been given. And in the early part of the ensuing year, several cottages were plundered of all they contained, and personal violence was offered at Matakana, twenty-five miles from Auckland. These acts of violence were supposed to be committed in consequence of the disaffection which had been shewn at the Bay of Islands. This led the Governor to issue a proclamation, in which the sum of fifty pounds sterling was offered for the apprehension of each of the chiefs who were principally concerned in the robbery. At the same time the flames of rebellion burst out afresh at the Bay of Islands, and on the 10th of January, 1845, Hone Heke and his warriors again cut down the Government flag-staff at Russell. A temporary flag-staff was soon after erected, but within two days Heke went and cut that down also, in the presence of the few friendly Maories who were placed there to guard it. A hundred pounds sterling were then offered for the apprehension of Hone Heke ; but with no other effect than to cause the roots of disaffection to strike deeper. Kawiti, a chief of much influence, belonging to the Kawakawa tribe, having joined the insurgents with a great number of men, they were prepared for further demonstrations, to which they were excited still more by the presence of a small reinforcement of troops. An attack upon the town was threatened ; consequently the fears of the inhabitants were aroused. In this state of things the Lord's Day was spent. On the Monday, the Rev. Mr. Williams assured the people that there was no immediate danger,

forming his opinion on the positive statements of the
natives. But on Tuesday morning, March 11th, 1845,
an attack was made in different directions, by strong
bodies of natives. The women and children sought
places of refuge. The small military force—consisting
of a detachment of H.M.'s 69th Regiment, about thirty
men from H.M.S. Hazard, and the men who were residents in the town—met the attack with much spirit, but
could not prevent the advancement of such superior
numbers. The magazine exploded, and left us almost
without ammunition. Nothing remained now but to
flee, or to make a stand with the mere show of muskets.
In this singular dilemma the British troops were placed,
when it was determined to embark all the Europeans
on board the ships lying in the harbour. This was
done. The town was evacuated; the Maories gained a
complete victory; and the prestige connected with the
British name was completely fallen. In the evening,
the insurgents deliberately plundered the houses, kindled
fires, and reduced the town to ashes. The church and
the houses of the missionaries, however, were respected,
and remained as melancholy monuments of the fallen
capital of New Zealand. Five days after, the inhabitants
of the ill-fated town of Russell arrived in Auckland harbour, in H.M.S. Hazard, the U.S. corvette St. Louis,
the Matilda whaler, the Government brig Victoria, and
the Dolphin schooner. The Bay of Islands. has not
gained its former influence, nor is it likely to do so.
It remains as a part of the province of Auckland, to
which port the general trade of the northern part of the
colony is attracted, and the goodly harbour at the Bay
—once the chief resort of ships visiting New Zealand—
is consequently almost deserted.

The object of the insurgent Maories seemed to be gained, for the Europeans were really driven away; but this dishonour the British name could not lie under long. In the latter part of April, a comparatively strong expedition, composed of troops and naval forces, arrived at the Bay of Islands; the Union Jack was hoisted under a salute of twenty-one guns from H.M.S. North Star, and martial law was proclaimed. An attack was made upon several pahs; much fatigue and suffering, by exposure to the weather and want of provisions, were borne by the expedition, and severe losses from the fire of the enemy were experienced. The officers in command in the various attacks, were surprised at the extraordinary strength of some of the pahs. In a description of one of Hone Heke's pahs, Colonel Despard, 99th Regiment, says:—"The strength of this place has struck me with astonishment, and I feel convinced that some European has had the direction of it. Independent of the double stockade, many of the timbers of which were twelve inches broad from from four to twelve inches thick, and sunk three feet in the ground—there was a ditch within the inner stockade, about five feet deep, and the same broad, which was crossed by traverses every five or six feet, with a narrow communication between each, and would admit of only one man passing at a time. Deep holes were sunk in various parts of the interior of the place, thick embankments of earth were thrown up around them, and some of them were strongly blockaded besides with heavy timber, which enabled the garrison to remain in them without being endangered by our shot." It will not surprise the reader to learn that many a brave heart ceased to beat in an attempt to scale these strongholds, particularly as some of the attacks were made without the aid of artillery, as it was a very difficult undertaking to convey field-pieces over many miles of rough country, where a foot-path constituted the only road. In the official despatches, describing an unsuccessful attack made upon Heke's pah on July 1st, 1845, a melancholy list of names is presented. Thirty-nine men, including two officers, were killed, and seventy-three were wounded, some of whom died soon after of their wounds. Thus fell one hundred and twelve men, all disabled for some time, and many of them to rise no more till the voice of the Archangel and the trump of God shall restore them to life, leaving the Maories in possession of their fortress, and strengthening the idea of their own superiority. But in the course of time, the British arms, in conjunction with Tamati Waka Nene, a faithful and valuable Maori ally, were successful. Heke, when wounded and threatened with increasing reverses, sued for peace, and offered land as an atonement for his rebellion; and Kawiti, when driven from his strongholds, and reduced to wretchedness for want of food, offered his unconditional submission to the Governor, and expressed his willingness to give up any land which his Excellency might demand, as a compensation for his hostility. But before the course of events had arrived at this point, Governor Fitzroy had been recalled, and Captain Grey*—the present Sir George Grey—had been appointed as his successor, and a different line of policy was adopted. Governor Fitzroy had pointed out several places to be ceded to the Crown, as a memorial that no man can take up arms against the Queen with impunity. But this course was turned aside, and Governor Grey, on receiv-

* Governor Grey arrived in Auckland November 13th, 1845.

ing Kawiti's submission, granted a free pardon to all who had joined in the rebellion, and immediately proclaimed peace. The design was to secure the hearts of the native people by this act of clemency, and it furnishes us with an argument of some value against the charges which have been alleged against the New Zealand settlers, and against the Government also, by the press and the platform of Great Britain. But as recent events have thrown light upon that line of policy, we may venture to suggest that a different course would have been best. This was the opinion of many intelligent natives also, and was consistent with the general usages of the Maories. In an address to Governor Grey, a little before that time, Tamati Waka Nene said :— " There is no chance of making peace, unless Kawiti and Heke agree to give the land mentioned in the terms proposed by Governor Fitzroy. Unless they did so, peace would not remain. What I say are not my thoughts only, but the thoughts of all. There is no chance of peace until the lands are given up to the Queen."

Considerable prosperity has marked the progress of the colony in several parts of the country; but, as we have before stated, the Bay of Islands never recovered its former position. It became for some years after a military post, and still possesses but a small number of settlers. The flag-staff, which had been the object of so much contention, was not erected again. A Wesleyan missionary, while passing it many years after, in company with a native, was reminded of its humiliating position in these words :—" Ko Wikitoria tena, e moe ana i te puehu, i rote i te wahi i tura kina ai ia e Hone Heke " — (" There is Victoria sleeping in the dust, in the place into which she was thrown by Hone Heke.'')

The unhappy struggle which has been described shed a considerable influence upon Auckland. This town had been made the seat of Government, and was rapidly increasing in trade and interest. But Heke's threatened attack produced a panic. Many persons sold valuable property in the principal streets of the city, for a very small sum, and left the country; trade became dull, and workmen were engaged on the roads at one shilling and sixpence a day. The entire destruction of Russell, and the presence of its inhabitants—whose life had just been given them for a prey—were calculated to confirm the terror which the threat of the insurgent chief had inspired. Heke was, no doubt, in earnest. Flushed with victory—having driven the white men, the military as well as the civilians, into the sea—in the north, he presumed on the same success at Auckland. Accordingly he applied to the Kaipara tribes for permission to go through their territory, and invited them to join the expedition; but his design was checked by the positive refusal of the Kaipara chief, Tirarau, to allow the war party to pass over his land. The militia force was called out, a commencement was made to throw up defences, the town and neighbourhood were guarded by night, and orders were issued for the safety of the women and children, and for the general defence of the town in case of a sudden attack. The loyalty and energy of Tamiti Waka Nene and his men contributed much to the safety of Auckland, and was acknowledged by the pension of £100 a year being settled upon this excellent chief during his life, and by the respect

with which he was always treated when he visited the
city.   In those days it was deemed the best policy
to allay the native irritation by every possible means,
and as the payment of the customs' duty for goods
brought into the colony was a source of unpleasantness
among the Maories, a bill was introduced by his Excellency Governor Fitzroy into the Legislative Council, in
September, 1844, the object of which was to abolish
the Customs throughout the colony.   This bill was
passed, although the colonial chest was empty, and all
the settlements were proclaimed free ports.   Instead of
the usual way of raising the necessary revenue, a
graduated Income-tax was instituted ; but it was extremely unpopular, and in some parts of the colony the
greatest difficulties were experienced in collecting it.
Specie became very scarce, and debentures were issued,
some of them as low as two shillings and sixpence, to
the amount of £37,000.   The Act by which these debentures were authorized was disallowed by the Queen, to
the consternation of the settlers ; but, by a special effort,
the case was met, and the losses threatened were prevented.   The public feeling against the debentures was
very strong, especially as they were made legal tender.
It was the cloudy and dark day through which the
colony was destined to pass on its way to the sunshine
of prosperity.

The settlement of Nelson was seriously disturbed in
the year 1843 by a collision with the natives of that
neighbourhood, and originating in a land dispute.   The
position occupied by the Agents of the New Zealand
Company was one which required extraordinary knowledge and tact.   Of this they were not, probably, aware ;

and hence the loose way in which their purchases of land were conducted. Their ignorance of the native land-tenure, customs, and language, led them into serious mistakes, which being published, and generally acted on, were followed by many evils. We look back, also, with regret upon some of the articles in which payment for the land was made, and see an unhappy connexion between them and the disasters which followed. We sowed the wind, and have reaped the whirlwind. The following is a list of the articles given to the natives at different places in the land purchases :—

300 Red Blankets
200 Muskets
 10 Single-barrelled Guns
  8 Double-barrelled Guns
  2 Tierces Tobacco
 15 Cwt. Tobacco
148 Iron Pots
  6 Cases of Soap
 15 Fowling-pieces
 81 Kegs of Gunpowder
  2 Casks of Ball Cartridge
  4 Kegs of Lead Slates
200 Cartouch Boxes
 60 Tomahawks
200 Yards Calico
300 Yards Check
200 Yards Print
480 Pocket Handkerchiefs
 72 Writing Slates
600 Pencils
204 Looking Glasses

   2 Cases of Pipes
  10 Gross of Pipes
  72 Spades
 100 Steel Axes
  20 Axes
  46 Adzes
3200 Fish Hooks
  24 Bullet Moulds
1500 Flints
 276 Shirts
  92 Jackets
  92 Trousers
  60 Red Night Caps
 300 Yards of Cotton Duck
  12 Hair Umbrellas
 100 Yards Ribbon
 144 Jews' Harps
  36 Razors
 180 Dressing Combs
  72 Hoes
   2 Suits Superfine Clothes

276 Pocket Knives   36 Shaving Boxes
204 Pairs Scissors   12 Shaving Brushes
12 Pairs Shoes   12 Sticks Sealing Wax
12 Hats   11 Quires Cartridge Paper
6 lbs. Beads   12 Flushing Coats
24 Combs.*

It may seem to persons who have the history of the colony before them, very strange that a large portion of the articles forming the payments for land should consist in arms and ammunition—particularly as it might have been foreseen, by their eagerness to procure them, and the sad use to which they had been devoted in their inter-tribal quarrels, that the Maories might turn these very arms against the settlers. But while we condemn this as a serious mistake, we must not forget that the Sydney traders executed their payments in similar articles, and that, in some instances, the mission stations had been dishonoured by the same traffic ; nor is it likely that other articles of equal cost would have commanded the same value in the eyes of the natives. But no explanation can justify the course taken ; it was an error, and speedily brought forth its bitter fruits, as the following account will show.

The Wairau plains, connected with the settlement of Nelson, were among the lands alleged to have been purchased of the natives. Accordingly, a company of surveyors were sent to lay out that block into sections, for farming purposes. When some *raupo* huts had been constructed for the convenience of the surveyors, and the natives saw what was intended, Rauparaha, who had distinguished himself by his cannibal ferocity at

* Dr. Thomson, Vol. II., p. 16.

Banks' Peninsula, related in a former chapter, and Rangihaeata, who had married the daughter of Rauparaha,—the principal chiefs of their tribe, and the former owners of the soil—disputed the validity of the purchase, determined to prevent the survey, and, after removing to a place of safety the surveyor's instruments, burnt the huts. The argument in their defence is this : The land was not properly purchased, and the huts were constructed of raupo which was gathered from the swamps belonging to the natives. But the settlers considered this to be an act which should be promptly met by the strong arm of the law; arguing that, if it were passed over, a precedent of rebellion would be formed, which might result in much injury to the infant settlements. A warrant was therefore issued by the bench of magistrates for the apprehension of Rauparaha, on a charge of robbery and arson. This was a bold and spirited stroke ; but the difficulty lay in executing the warrant. To accomplish this, nearly fifty men volunteered their services, among whom were several of the principal gentlemen of the settlement, the whole force being led by the police magistrate. To send such an armed force to arrest a chief of high standing, and thus to risk a war with a numerous and well-armed foe, whose delight had always been in deeds of cruelty and blood, especially at a time when there was but a small force in the country to protect the newly-formed settlements, was a great mistake. It is easy to say that, had the Maories suffered the course of war to run smoothly, justice would have been done them, and that they might have learnt lessons of moderation and order, which would have been of advantage to them in after-life. But for this course they were not prepared ; all their habits were contrary to it. To imprison a chief was to reduce him to the position of a slave, and so to affix a brand of infamy to his name till his dying day. The consequences of their mistake were written among the settlers in deeds of blood. The settlers and the Maories met on the disputed land, both parties being under arms. A recriminatory conversation followed, and explanations were attempted, in the midst of which a shot was fired, —whether by design or accidentally is not known, but this was a signal for an attack on both sides, and several persons fell. Then an effort of reconciliation was made. A chief, named Puaha, appealed to the New Testament, which he significantly held up before them as the only gun which he should use, and urged its spirit and teaching as being contrary to war. Several persons of both parties advanced towards each other with open arms, and the melancholy affair seemed to be near its close. But, unhappily, the eye of Rangihaeata just at that time fell upon his wife, who had been shot ; and immediately after his voice was heard above the general confusion in the ominous words—"Rauparaha, remember your daughter !" This awoke every feeling of revenge in the native breast, and the fearful surge of battle swept over the contending parties with deadly effect. Several of the settlers submitted to Rauparaha, hoping that their lives would be spared; but this being a refinement of war to which this infuriated chief was a stranger, they were all brutally massacred. In this miserable struggle twenty-two men were killed and five were wounded. Among the former were several of the principal gentlemen of Nelson, in the prime of life, of good character, and deeply interested in the welfare of the colony. They were interred on the spot by the Rev. S. Ironside, a

Wesleyan minister, belonging to a neighbouring mission station. By their untimely death the Nelson settlement was thrown into mourning, many persons lamenting the loss of a husband or father, a son, a brother, or a friend. Nor could they tell how soon the natives might resolve on a further attack, under the excitement of their victory; for such they had cause to consider it, as their loss was much less than that of the settlers.

This was a gloomy day for the Company's settlements, for in all of them there were serious disputes about the land, and at any time an appeal might be made to arms. Every eye was turned to the Government, anxious to know what course would be taken. Governor Fitzroy soon after visited the settlement of Nelson, and, instead of sympathizing with its stricken inhabitants, coolly laid the blame on them: then, crossing the straits, he talked with the sullen chiefs who had so fearfully massacred his countrymen, pointed out the wrong they had done, forgave them, and so healed the breach. Had his Excellency taken such a course as would have kindled afresh the flames of war, the consequences would have been most lamentable; as it was, his policy indicated weakness in the eyes of the natives, who would have looked upon him with more respect had he taken the Wairau plain as *utu* for the white men who had fallen there, instead of giving them additional payment to conclude the purchase of the disputed land. But whatever opinion may be formed of the Governor's policy towards the natives, nothing can justify the coldness and pettishness with which it is alleged he treated the survivors of his mistaken and fallen countrymen. More than a quarter of a century has passed since this unhappy episode occurred; but it is still fresh in the memory of many, and will always be considered as a dark page in our colonial history, and the graves of our countrymen, now surrounded by a rude fence, will be pointed out to coming generations as a sad memorial of a mistaken policy.

The district of Taranaki, in which the New Plymouth settlement was planted, had been a very populous part of the country, and figures prominently in many of the most fierce and desolating wars recorded among the traditions of the native people. Numerous pahs meet the eye of the traveller, and in many of them may be seen the remains of defences, which were their chief protection against the invader, when every man did that which was right in his own eyes. The settlers are annoyed with the "Maori pits," choked up with fern, so that the unwary cattle sometimes fall into them and perish. These pits, we suppose, were used both as hiding-places and as storehouses during the native wars. The latest and most destructive of these wars occurred about the year 1830. It was conducted by Te Whero Whero—the same as Potatau, the first Maori King—in the most approved style of Maori warfare. Neither age nor sex was spared. At Puteorangiora, Te Whero Whero is said to have slain two hundred persons with his own hand. Horrible stories have been related to us by the persons who took their part in those orgies of death—cloven skulls, mutilated bodies, and cannibal feasts being the common events in those times of heathen darkness, perpetrated within forty years of the present time, and near the spot on which we now write.

During the struggle, many persons found shelter in the dense forest, and effected their escape by the east side of Mount Egmont to the southern part of the island, where they were suffered to remain unmolested. Numbers were taken to Waikato as slaves, and a few persons were permitted to remain in the district. While the country along this coast was lying desolate, under the curse of the Waikato war, the agents of the New Zealand Company made their purchases, and commenced the settlement of New Plymouth. Assuming that their purchases were valid, notwithstanding the small number of persons who appeared upon the soil, and not supposing that claimants would be found at a distance, the township of New Plymouth was surveyed, with suburban and rural sections; then lines were cut, roads were made, bridges were thrown across streams, and houses were built. A map of the settlement was made, in which the beauty of both town and country sections was exhibited. Land being offered for sale in England, intending emigrants bought their farms in London, and paid for them there, with an arrangement that a right of selection should be given them on their arrival in New Zealand. The first settlers had scarcely broken up the virgin soil, and cast into it their first sowings, before ominous tokens were apparent. The Waikato people liberated their slaves, who immediately returned as freemen to inhabit the land of their birth. No sooner was this known, than the refugees from the south came back also. It was not surprising that the natives of the district should disallow the authority of the few persons with whom the agents of the Company effected their purchases, nor that they should make an effort to secure the entire district for themselves. The case was a peculiar one. We can scarcely conceive of a more complicated and difficult question in the history of the colony; but it was made much worse by the unhappy manner in which it was treated.

When the unsatisfactory character of the Company's purchases was made known in England, Mr. Spain was sent to the colony by the Government as a Commissioner, to enquire into the alleged purchases, and report accordingly. In 1843 his report was rendered, stating that the quantity of land which he considered as having been fairly bought of the natives by the agents of the New Zealand Company, amounted to two hundred and eighty-two thousand acres—seventy-one thousand acres belonging to Wellington, one hundred and fifty-one thousand acres belonging to Nelson, and sixty thousand acres belonging to New Plymouth. Governor Fitzroy disallowed the award of the Commissioner, and declared that the quantity of land belonging to New Plymouth, as having been fairly purchased of the Maories, was no more than three thousand five hundred acres, comprising the town and immediate neighbourhood! The Governor's declaration fell upon the settlers with paralysing effect. Many of them had been prevented from taking possession of the farms, which they had bought and paid for in England, until they had spent most of their remaining money; and now that they had built houses and planted their crops, they found themselves on the land of the natives, and completely at their mercy. Under these circumstances, it was natural for the Maories to determine on the settlers' removal as soon as their growing crops could be reaped. At the appointed time, the families were removed unto the land whose purchase his Excellency approved, and which, by a special arrangement, was given in compensation for the sections they formerly occupied.

By this course the foundation was laid, as we believe, for the native quarrels, the disputes with the settlers, and the war which afterwards followed. Had Mr. Spain's award been maintained, there would have been sufficient land for the colonial purposes of the time, the Maori people would have possessed large tracts which they could never cultivate, and which they would have been at liberty to sell or otherwise, at their pleasure, and the feuds, in which many lives have been lost—feuds originating in the disputed land—would have been prevented.

Wellington, the principal settlement planted by the Company, had its full share of early trials. Scarcely were the houses and stores completed, so as to give the appearance of a town, before a terrible fire swept away the property and the hopes of many. The noble-hearted pioneers soon recovered their spirits, and regained their position; but upon a few persons the blow fell so unexpectedly and so heavily, that their heart sunk under it, and to this day they drag along a miserable and useless life. Such persons—we know of whom we write —are quite unfit for colonists, and should not have left their native land.

Other difficulties, peculiar to those times, lay before the Wellington people, arising out of the vexed land question. The reported fertility of the Hutt Valley made it a desirable spot for agricultural purposes; but the native owners contended that it had not been sold, and resolved that the Pakeha should not possess it. After much ill-feeling, the crisis came in 1846, and the Hutt became the scene of war. Men were murdered while they were at their work without arms; military detachments were surprised with fatal effects; and the inhabitants in general were alarmed. As a sufficient force was at that time in the colony, and prompt measures were taken to meet the insurgents, the town remained safe. The leader of this demonstration on the native side was Rangihaeata, of Wairau notoriety. His father-in-law, Rauparaha, still more notorious, ventured to play the dangerous game of siding with both parties. When this became sufficiently plain, his Excellency Captain Grey — the present Sir George Grey—who had a little time before succeeded Captain Fitzroy in the government of the colony, determined to surprise the chief, and send him on board a ship of war. This was certainly a bold undertaking. The friends of Rauparaha seemed to wince before the decisive spirit of the Governor, and instead of shewing his distress in a more objectionable form, Rangihaeata composed the following Lament for his friend Rauparaha :—

" My brave canoe !
In lordly decoration lordliest far.
My proud canoe !
Amid the fleet that fleetest flew ;
How wert thou shattered by the surge of war !
'Tis but the fragments of the wreck
Of my renowned canoe
That lie, all crushed, on yonder war-ship's deck.
Raha ! my chief, my friend,
Thy lonely journey wend—
Stand with thy wrongs before the god of battle's face :
Let him thy fate requite.
　　Ah me ! Te Raukawa's foul desertion and disgrace !
　　Ah me ! the English Ruler's might.
Raha ! my chief of chiefs,
Ascend with all thy grief
Up to the land of peace ; there stand before his face :
Let him thy fate requite.

Ah me ! Te Toa's sad defection and disgrace ;
Ah me ! the English Ruler's might.
One counsel more, the first I gave :
' Break up thy forces, comrade brave ;
Scatter them all about the land,
In many a predatory band.'
But Porirua's forest dense—
Ah ! thou would'st never stir from thence.
' There,' saidst thou, ' lies my' best defence.'
Now, now, of such design ill-starred,
How grievously thou reap'st thy full reward !
Hence, vain lamentings – hence, away !
Hence all the brood of sorrow born !
There will be time enough to mourn
In the long days of summer, ere the food
Is cropped abundant for the work of blood.
Now I must martial in compact array
Great thoughts, that crowding come of an avenging day."*

After being kept on board Her Majesty's Ship Calliope many months, the war being over, and several
influential chiefs being willing to answer for his future
conduct, Rauparaha was set at liberty. He did not
recover his wonted spirits, but sank down into a sullen
gloom. After he had been at liberty about eighteen
months, he died, at Otaki, in the midst of his friends.
Fifteen hundred persons are said to have attended his
funeral, the obsequies of which were composed of a mix-
ture of Christian and heathen rites.

Another calamity, differing from those which we have
mentioned, awaited the town and neighbourhood of
Wellington—one in which the power of God, and the
impotence of man, are sufficiently apparent. A considerable portion of the brick buildings were thrown down

* Thomson, Vol. II., pp. 135, 136.

by an earthquake. Of all the calamities to which we are liable, none are more terrible than the earthquake. In war, force meets force, and something may be done to mitigate its horrors ; but the shaking of the earth is so sudden—the area over which the motion is felt is commonly so broad—the upheavings and depressions, the motions of other kinds, the chasms which suddenly open and sometimes as quickly close—the eruptions of gases, water, and other materials—are so completely beyond the control and calculations of man, that the most hardened sinner instinctively seeks for refuge at such a time under the shadow of Divine mercy. Many persons have gone down alive into the pit, both in ancient and modern times ; nor can we hope that these dreadful events will not occur again. Earthquakes are common among the islands of the Pacific ; but as the buildings are not often constructed of stone, we do not hear of much injury being done. It is probable that New Zealand has always been the scene of such convulsions. Many parts of the country are covered with the unmistakable proofs of volcanic agency of terrible magnitude.* But there are reasons for concluding that these occurrences are becoming fewer and less severe. The northern parts of the colony are nearly free from them already, and we believe that the same statement may be made of the extreme southern part ; for although the vibrations of the earth have been felt there, the motion was so slight that no damage was done. It

* Dr. Hochstetter states that within a radius of only ten miles from Auckland, not less than sixty-three separate points of eruption may be traced. These have long been extinct, but the lava which flowed from them remains, as an object of interest to the stranger, and an article of annoyance to the settler.

seems that the neighbourhoods of Cook's Strait are most liable to disturbances of this kind, and certainly the town of Wellington has been the greatest sufferer. The first severe series of shocks took the colony by surprise; the alarm excited was great, and the damage done was considerable. As descriptions of such events are cal-·culated to teach us important lessons, we supply the following account :—

It was on the 16th October, 1848, at two o'clock in the morning, that the first severe shock occurred. The inhabitants were aroused from their sleep by the moving earth and falling chimneys; an inspection of the cracked and shaken walls which were yet standing increased their terror, for another shock might occur in a moment, and bury them in its ruins: The houses were, therefore, immediately abandoned, some persons taking refuge as they imagined in the neighbouring hills, and others remaining on the level ground, beyond the reach of the trembling buildings—and all wishing earnestly for the morning light. From a despatch written to the governor-in-chief by Lieutenant-Governor Eyre*—who was in Wellington at the time—we subjoin the following extracts :—

" During the whole of Monday shocks and tremblings of the earth were from time to time experienced, but of a slighter character than the first. On Tuesday, the 17th October, about four o'clock a.m., another rather smart shock was felt, and again at eight o'clock. Lighter ones continued at intervals during the day, until about twenty minutes to four o'clock in the afternoon, when a sudden and much more violent shock took place ; by this chimneys remaining up were, for .the most part,

* The late Governor of Jamaica.

P

thrown down. The native hospital, the gaols, many of the large brick stores, and the high brick walls were then cast down; immense destruction of property took place, and, I regret to add, a melancholy loss of life.

"Barrack Serjeant Lovell and two of his children were thrown down and buried by falling ruins. Upon being extricated, one of the children was found dead, and the other so seriously injured that it died in a few hours afterwards. The serjeant himself was much hurt, and now lies in a precarious state.

"During the remainder of Tuesday and the succeeding night slight shocks only were felt; but about five o'clock on Wednesday morning a stronger one occurred, and another about eight o'clock a.m. Minor shocks continued at intervals during the remainder of the day and evening, until the morning of Thursday, the 19th, at ten minutes past five o'clock, when a most violent and awful shock took place; every building was rocked to and fro in a fearful manner, and, with the exception of the wooden buildings, most of the houses and stores were seriously shattered or fell in. The whole population were in the utmost consternation and alarm, and the destruction of property was immense; but most providentially, up to the present time, no further loss of life has ensued.

"Numbers of persons are, however, ruined; many left houseless and homeless, excepting such temporary shelter as can be afforded by the new church, Te Aro, by Government House (where the hospital patients and some others are taken in), and by the wooden buildings of their friends.

"Many persons are afraid of remaining in any of the houses at night, and return to the bush, among the hills, in the hope of being more secure, notwithstanding the wild and inclement weather by which the earthquake has been accompanied.

" A blow has been struck at the prosperity, almost at the very existence of the settlement, from which it may not readily recover. Terror and dismay reign everywhere : for the last four days no business of any kind has been transacted. The energies of all seemed paralyzed, and during that period no one has been able to feel for a moment that even life itself is secure. . . .

" The sad ravages which have already occurred, and the terror which so frightful a visitation naturally produces in most men's minds, will, I apprehend, drive from the colony all who can find means to get away. The few ships now in port waiting for moderate weather to sail are crowded with colonists abandoning the country, and numbers are unable to obtain passages.

" Under this awful visitation I deemed it my duty at once to summon my executive council, and, with their approval, to proclaim a day of public and solemn fast, prayer, and humiliation, in order that supplication may be offered up to Almighty God to avert the recurrence of any similar visitation, and Friday, the 20th October, was appointed for this purpose."

Wellington was visited by another earthquake in some respects more severely than in that which has been described. It was felt from Auckland to Otago. At Wanganui the shock was very heavy ; chimneys were thrown down in Nelson and New Plymouth ; eruptions of gas burst forth in various places, mounds several yards in height were thrown up, the ground was intersected with deep ravines, and the sea beach was raised several feet. This occurred in January, 1855 ; from which time there have been no shocks sufficiently strong to do any damage, or to cause any serious alarm.

The terror occasioned by these awful events soon passed away, and with their fears the religious impressions to which the earthquake gave rise among many of the people were obliterated; showing that while they " feared the Lord," like the ancient Samaritans, they " served their own gods." Damages were speedily repaired, houses were constructed upon principles which were more likely to resist the vibrations of the earth, and the current of business soon flowed along in its usual channel. As an expression of honourable sympathy subscriptions were raised in other parts of the colony and sent to Wellington, to meet, in some measure, the losses which had been sustained; this assistance was, however, respectfully declined, the noble-minded sufferers choosing rather to depend on their own energies, with God's blessing, than on assistance which might reach them from other sources. As future years pass over them, and substantial forms of prosperity increase, the inhabitants of Wellington will review the peculiar difficulties through which they have passed with gratitude to God, and derive from the retrospection fresh motives for thankfulness and perseverance.

The promising settlement of Wanganui passed through a series of early struggles, the effects of which continued for many years. The threatening aspect of affairs led to the appointment of a detachment of troops, and their presence, no doubt, still further irritated the discontented natives. In the year 1847 the crisis came; this was occasioned by the folly of a midshipman, who, pointing a loaded pistol at an old chief, playfully threatened to shoot him; unhappily the pistol went off, by accident, and wounded the chief in the face. The " accident "

was not admitted by the natives, but was made a cause
of war. The campaign was opened in the barbarous
style of the Maories, by the murder of a soldier and of
an unoffending family of settlers, residing a few miles
from the town. The immediate actors were five native
youths, sent to the work of destruction by their seniors.
Through the efforts of influential Maories the murderers
were soon after apprehended, and delivered up to the
jurisdiction of a court martial, by which they were convicted and sentenced to be hanged. Four were executed,
and one, on account of his extreme youth, was pardoned.
But it was more easy to deal with the murderers than
to put down the spirit of rebellion. On the 19th of May
the insurgents attacked the town in considerable force;
but as the settlers and troops kept under cover, no personal injury was sustained. Much of the property was
of course, swept away. In the early part of the war the
natives possessed many advantages; for they could move
up and down their beautiful river with canoes at pleasure.
An extensive country opened before them where they
were safe, they could easily visit the powerful tribes residing inland, and had every opportunity to grow large
quantities of provisions. Yet they soon began to feel
the loss of comforts, to which they had for a few years
been accustomed; they could obtain no English clothing,
tobacco could not be purchased, and no market was
open for their produce. This led them to reason soberly
on their condition, and determined them eventually to
sue for peace, which was restored in February, 1848.

The settlers were so dispirited by the losses they had
sustained and other dangers which had surrounded them
and not knowing how soon they might witness a repetition of these evils, that most of them left the place, to
seek a home where the prospects of peace were brighter.

After some time a few families returned; but for many years wide plains of excellent land lay unoccupied, and apparently uncared for. At present Wanganui constitutes a part of the province of Wellington, and notwithstanding the part which it has been called to take in the war that is scarcely closed, its population is rapidly increasing, its grazing lands support large numbers of sheep and cattle, and other signs of prosperity are apparent.

Later settlements have met with difficulties, for, however wisely planned and carefully conducted, circumstances will arise which will more or less detract from the amount of prosperity anticipated. Persons who come into the colony at the present time, and are located at a distance from any other settlement, find many inconveniences in their earlier colonial life; but their difficulties are hardly to be compared to those of the pioneers of whom we have written. A market is now open for as much produce as can be grown, although the state of the roads, in some seasons of the year, makes carting a serious undertaking. The proper seasons for seed time and harvest, and the best mode of cultivating the ground, have been ascertained. Not a few mistakes were made in earlier days in the kinds of wood used in building, fencing, and for other purposes. Cattle, sheep, and horses were introduced at some risk, and a high price, from Australia; and when landed, were in danger from the New Zealand herbage. Those provinces which were planted subsequently to the struggles which we have described, and which have attained to a position of great prosperity, will not forget the honour which is due to those who were first in the field, and whose fortitude and perseverance were conspicuous in the cloudy and dark day.

CHAPTER IX.

GROWTH OF THE COLONY.

AFTER the lapse of thirty years from the foundation of the colony, the population, excluding the Maories, has risen to nearly a quarter of a million. A corresponding increase has been maintained in its industrial pursuits, and signs of vigorous growth are apparent in all directions. A few remarks on each province may prepare for a more intelligent view of the advancement which has been made. In such remarks the province of Auckland claims the first place, as the colony was planted there, and by far the greatest amount of territory lies within its boundaries. The city of Auckland is well situated for trade, as it commands two seas in connection with Onehunga. The natural scenery around the city cannot be called beautiful, although it is deeply interesting, on account of its extinct volcanoes. Some of these were at one time in terrible operation, as is evident from the masses of stone which cover the land around them, in sheets of various thickness. Some of the channels through which the lava flowed are now the water courses, at which the traveller refreshes himself. The Scoriæ may be seen piled up in heaps by the settlers to clear the ground, or formed into fences, and it is often used in the city for mason work. The " Scoriæ ground " found near the extinct volcanoes, within a few miles of the city, has to be cleared of stone, just as other parts of the country must be cleared of bush and fern, before it is fit for the settlers' use. Chasms in these masses of stone were the burial places of the Maories. And we know some farmers who were annoyed at the quantity of human skulls and other bones which such mounds contained. The Scoriæ soil is very light, and water percolates so easily through it that in dry seasons every plant withers. But it is admirably suited to early crops, and bears grass plentifully. Water is obtained with difficulty in this ground, or perhaps not at all; so that in dry seasons much distress has been caused by want of water for domestic purposes, as well as for the sustenance of cattle. Within a few yards of the Scoriæ ground there is an entirely different soil, which in some cases is little better than common brick earth, and in others strong and rich, capable of bearing the heaviest crops, both of roots and cereals. In the extensive province of Auckland land of every description may be found; mountainous, plains, and swamps, of the poorest and richest description, covered with the heaviest forest, or with fern and *ti* tree. The gold-field at the Thames is the scene of a busy community; some of whom have been made rich by their findings, while a greater number have reaped little more than disappointment.

The Taranaki province has always been noted for the salubrity of its climate, and the richness of its soil. It presents the most promising materials for the agriculturist. But there is no harbour; an open roadstead, with good anchorage, is the only accommodation for ships.

Wellington possesses a good harbour, and its situation is in the centre of the colony; so that a steam-ship can reach any of its ports within a few hours. On this account the seat of Government has been fixed here. The scenery around the harbour is not inviting. Along the Hutt valley there is good land, which produces heavy crops, but it is subject to serious floods. Beyond the Hutt are the Wairarapa plains, with a thriving community. Along the west coast the rich and valuable land is becoming the sites of flourishing townships, and the homesteads of our most substantial farmers. Wanganui, which makes a part of the Wellington province, has a port and trade of its own; and from its rich pastures a great number of cattle have been shipped, for consumption in the gold-fields.

Hawke's Bay province lies on the east coast of the North Island. In extent it cannot bear comparison with those of Auckland and Wellington, and is not much larger than that of Taranaki. It is less humid than most parts of New Zealand, yet much of its land is well watered by streams which flow from the mountains. Large sheep runs are found here. The capital is the town of Napier. It has a small harbour, but is not suitable for large vessels. A happy and flourishing future, no doubt, lies before its community, who have for some years suffered much from the native insurrection.

The provinces of the Middle Island have made rapid progress in everything which is of substantial value. Nelson has long gained celebrity for its orchards, whose produce is shipped to less favoured parts of the colony. Its sheep and cattle runs have enriched many of their proprietors. Its farming operations have been remunerative. But these have been eclipsed by the productions of its gold-fields. Nelson is a pretty little town, with a good harbour, but requiring much caution on account of the tide current and the narrowness of its entrance.

Canterbury is a fine province. The plains stretching from the sea to the foot of the Alpine mountains, furnishing natural pasturage for flocks, and proving suitable for all the purposes of the agricultural settler, have become a beautiful scene of happy thriving industry. The first settlers comprised both capitalists and labouring classes, each deriving advantages from the other. The energy of the Canterbury people has enabled them to carry a railway through the mountain, which intervenes between the seaboard and the plains ; while the road across the Alps, connecting Christchurch and Hokitika —on the east and west coasts—is an honour to the country. Canterbury is singularly destitute of bush, which makes fencing and firing more expensive articles here than they are in other parts of the country. A very heavy amount of gold has been exported from this province ; particularly before the county of Westland was formed.

Otago rose slowly to the proud pre-eminence which it now commands. Founded by the sturdy sons of Scotland, who were prepared for patient toil, much was expected from this southern province. Several things were found in its favour. The native title had been extinguished, so that there was no fear of a Maori war. A Crown grant was obtained for the land on which the settlement was formed. The natural advantages were considerable. In a description of the settlement published during its early stage, we read of " a noble harbour, abundance of untimbered fertile land and open grassy pasturage, interspersed with adjacent supply of wood ; a navigable water communication running up to the centre of the block for nearly its entire length, and the richest land lying on either side of it, remarkably well watered ; with an ample supply of coal; and to the west, and stretching away to the foot of the strong mountains, an unbounded sheep-walk open to the farmer and the flock owner." But notwithstanding these advantages, Otago remained for many years an almost insignificant part of the colony in the estimation of the people in the north. The discovery of its rich gold-fields made it famous at a bound. The village of Dunedin became a beautiful and busy city. The population of the province rivalled that of Auckland, while in the splendour of its buildings, the beauty of its situation, and the energy of its inhabitants, the city of Dunedin is an improvement on the capital of the north. While we write accounts reach us of heavy and disastrous floods on the Otago plains, sweeping away the effects of long months of toil; by which some will probably be ruined, while others will replace their losses with difficulty.

The province of Southland* lies at the extreme south of the Middle Island, and includes Stewart Island. It possesses much fertile land; but its principal exports have been wood and gold. Some good harbours are found on its coasts. The capital is Invercargill; and the Bluff harbour is known as the first place at which the Melbourne steamers touch on the New Zealand coast, and from which telegrams are sent into various parts of the colony.

Marlborough was made a province from that of Nelson in 1859, and lies at the northern part of the Middle Island. Picton—a little town at the foot of the hills in Queen Charlotte's Sound—is the principal port, but the seat of the local Government is Blenheim. There is fertile land in the Wairau, and some other plains; but the general character of the province is mountainous, intersected by deep sounds, which are surrounded by

* This province was made a part of the province of Otago in 1870.

picturesque scenery. For some time an amount of gold was found sufficient to excite hopes so bright that public works of an expensive kind were commenced; but, instead of being a benefit, they have done injury to the community. Among the principal exports from this province, we may name timber, which is cut by saw-mills, some of which are worked by steam.

The county of Westland was a part of the Canterbury province till 1867. But little was known of this coast till gold was discovered in 1865; yet within three years of this discovery it became one of the most populous districts of the colony, and by an Act of the General Assembly it was constituted a separate county, with a local Government of its own. The scenery is bold and rugged, and some parts are heavily timbered. Spurs from the mountain ranges come down to the sea, in some instances forming inaccessible cliffs. Gold is found almost everywhere. It is the staple export, and is likely to continue so. Hokitika is the principal town, and the seat of the local Government; but its shipping accommodations are very defective, and the town itself seems liable to be swept away by the action of the sea and the river.

We have seen it stated that a mistake was made in planting so many settlements, and so far from each other, in the commencement of the colony, the argument being, that it was impossible to unite their strength for defence, if menaced by an enemy, and that the cost of transit hindered the exchange of local productions. But whatever opinions may be entertained on this subject at present, it will be readily admitted that from these settlements an enterprising spirit has gone forth, and the patience and industry of the people have been rewarded. In illustration of this, we lay before the reader some statistics from the official returns made to the Government. In the year 1858, the population of European descent in the entire colony was 59,413 ; at the end of the next three years, it shewed an increase of 39,608 ; by the close of 1864, the population had risen to 172,158 ; three years later, it numbered 218,668 ; and the estimated population of the colony in December, 1869, was 237,249—shewing an increase for the last eleven years, of 177,836 persons. These numbers include 184 persons who reside in the Chatham Islands, but they do not include the military nor their families.

The population of the several provinces and chief towns will be found in the following table, according to the last general Census, taken in December, 1867 :—*

PROVINCES.			CHIEF TOWN IN EACH PROVINCE.		
Auckland	... ...	48,321	Auckland	... ...	11,153
Taranaki	... ...	4,359	New Plymouth	...	2,180
Wellington	... ...	21,950	Wellington	... ...	7,460
Hawke's Bay	...	5,283	Napier	... ...	1,827
Nelson	... ...	23,814	Nelson	... ...	5,652
Marlborough	...	4,371	Picton	... ...	506
Canterbury	...	53,866	Christchurch	...	6,647
Otago	... ...	48,577	Dunedin	... ...	12,777
Southland	... ...	7,943	Invercargill	...	2,006
Chatham Islands		184			
Total	... ...	218,668	Total	... ...	50,208

It will easily be seen that a population amounting to 168,460 must be looked for outside the chief towns.

* The Population Census of the colony was taken again in December, 1870, by which we learn that the population had risen to 256,000.

Many of these are gathered into towns of considerable importance, as the subjoined list will shew :—

Province of Auckland—	
Parnell	3,226
Newton...	3,227
Onehunga	2,177
Otahuhu	552
Panmure	349
Howick...	640
Province of Canterbury—	
Lyttleton	2,510
Kaiapoi...	708
Rangiora	1,042
Timaru	1,027
Ross	855
Hokitika	4,866
Greymouth	1,607
Province of Wellington—	
Wanganui	2,157

Province of Nelson—	
Westport	1,500
Charleston	1,800
Brighton	1,000
Cobden	727
Addison's Flat ...	1,500
Province of Otago—	
Port Chalmers ...	1,347
Milton	527
Oamaru	1,377
Hawkesbury... ...	481
Province of Hawke's Bay—	
Clive	146
Havelock	120
Province of Southland—	
Campbell Town ...	316
Riverton	383

The foregoing list of towns, with their population, as taken in December, 1867, will probably show considerable variation, in some instances, when compared with their present number of inhabitants.

It does not necessarily follow that the large increase which our colony has realized must contribute, in all cases, its proportionate share to the general prosperity; for there are classes in the colony which are an injury to society, as well as a burden to themselves. The following table, however, will shew that the majority of our population belong to the right classes :—

DISTRIBUTION OF OCCUPATIONS.

Trade, Commerce, and Manufactures	10,194
Agricultural and Pastoral	18,863
Mechanics and Skilled Workers	13,695
Mining	20,372
Clerical Profession	292
Legal Profession	161
Medical Profession	280
Teachers	928
Surveyors	305
Other Educated Professions	244
Labourers	13,025
Domestic and General Servants	7,259
Miscellaneous	6,883
Mariners	3,537
No Occupation stated (principally Women and Children)	122,630

The war in which the colony has been unhappily engaged for more than ten years, has considerably hindered the agricultural pursuits of all the provinces in the North Island, and a large number of men in the South Island are engaged in mining; yet the returns show no inconsiderable quantity of land won from the wilderness. According to the returns prepared for the Government, and taken in February, 1870, the quantity of land under crop, including that which has been sown with grass seed, was 900,504 acres, each province presenting its portion according to the following table :—

PROVINCES.	ACRES.	PROVINCES.	ACRES.
Auckland ...	142,996	Marlborough ...	24,003
Taranaki ...	24,714	Canterbury	217,527½
Wellington ...	184,274¾	Otago	172,003
Hawke's Bay	51,946	Southland	36,675½
Nelson	45,333½	Westland, County	1,030¾

According to the General Census, taken in December, 1867,—the last returns which have been made—there were in the colony 65,715 horses; 312,835 cattle; 8,418,579 sheep; and 115,104 pigs. The number of threshing machines driven by steam, water, and horse power was 579, with twelve steam ploughs and 28 steam harrows. Our colonial dairies produced in that year 3,834,252 lbs. of butter, and 1,300,028 lbs. of cheese.

A visit to the nearest settlement was for some years a serious undertaking, often performed on foot, as the only means of locomotion; and as there were no proper roads the traveller had to ford rivers, climb mountains, wade through swamps, and depend upon the Maories for his food and lodgings. Several weeks of valuable time were spent on such occasions, in the accomplishment of purposes for which a few days are now sufficient. So late as the year 1850, the author had to charter a small vessel to convey his family from New Plymouth to Auckland, after waiting some weeks for a more favourable opportunity to remove. It is interesting to the old colonists to recall the excitement occasioned by the sight of a large ship entering our harbours; and then to remember that in 1867 the number of vessels which entered was 944, with a burden of 309,568 tons.

The conveyance of mails was very defective. Respectable settlers, whose presence was required in distant townships, were often entrusted with a mail bag; and missionaries were requested to convey mails when on their journeys, and to act as postmasters at their stations. Merchants could not reckon upon answers to their letters, posted for England, under nearly twelve months;

and communication with the Australian colonies was very irregular. But such are the improvements in our postal arrangements, that we are now supplied with European intelligence within six weeks of its publication in England; while a summary of English news flies over one half of the globe, by the help of the submarine cable, in a single month.

It is amusing to compare the accommodation provided for the early settlers, by those who had arrived a few months earlier still, with the conveniences and comfortable houses which are prepared for strangers of the present time. The author was sitting in the company of some of these pioneers very recently, listening to reliable descriptions, of which the following is a specimen :—On learning that Mr. B and family—respectable farmers in England—were coming to the colony, Mr. G., who had been here some little time, met his friend on the beach, and offered him a house for ten shillings a week ; being a lower rent than many were charging. When the family entered the house, they found that the walls and roof were constructed of raupo and grass, tied to a framework of poles ; it was minus one end, there was a doorway, but no door, and window places, but no windows ; no chimney had been built, and the floor consisted of common earth, strewn over with grass. The house was accepted, and the blessing of God rested upon the family ; the mother now sleeps among the dead, while the father and his family occupy a respectable position. This class of houses is rarely or never seen now in the towns; handsome and substantial residences have taken their place. At the close of 1867 the number of houses built of wood was 38,844 ; stone and brick were the materials of which 1,182 were

Q

formed; while a large number in the country districts were constructed of less substantial matter. Many of the houses built of wood, as well as those of brick and stone, are large, elegant, and costly, and the ground around them is laid out with much taste, and planted with the choicest shrubs and flowers.

The improvements in commercial stores are very great. It was common to find groceries, drapery, iron-mongery, and stationers' goods in the same shop, to which drugs were added; and in some that we can call to mind, butchers' meat was sold in addition to the articles which we have enumerated, besides furnishing accommodation for the family. But these departments of business are now kept separate in the principal towns, and are carried on with all the order and respectability which are found connected with them in England. Our principal merchants' stores are heavily stocked with all the necessaries of life, and with many of its luxuries too.

The number of letters received in the year 1867 was 2,404,788, and those despatched amounted to 2,402,909. Newspapers to the number of 1,670,520 were received, while those sent from our colonial Post-offices reached 1,390,368. Joint Stock Companies had been formed up to the end of December, 1867, to the number of ninety-one, with a nominal capital varying from £500 to £150,000 each. The banking houses are doing extensive business, and secure for their shareholders large profits; and Savings' Banks have been opened by the Government, in connection with all the principal Post-offices.

The total value of imports for 1867 was £5,344,607, while the exports amounted to £4,644,678; the balance being evidently on the wrong side for the continued prosperity of the colony, unless some measures can be adopted to increase our exports, in addition to providing for our own consumption from Colonial productions. That this can be done no one can reasonably doubt, that it will be done is equally certain. The Maori war has prevented much that would have been done in agricultural pursuits, but this complaint will soon be a thing of the past.

In describing the principal articles of export, the first place must be given to gold. In the year 1867, the total value of gold exported by each province was as follows: —Auckland, £20,700 ; Nelson, (including Westland North) £894,728 ; Marlborough, £1,978 ; Canterbury, (including Westland South) £1,159,326 ; Otago, £587,426 ; and Southland, £36,117 ; in all amounting to £2,700,275. The total value of gold which has been exported up to the end of December, 1867, amounts to no less than £14,540,573.

As the exportation of wool was carried on in all the provinces, we will show the comparative value of each province in this respect by the following table :—

Comparative Table, shewing the Quantity and Value of Wool Exported in 1867.

PROVINCE.	QUANTITY. lbs.	VALUE. £
Auckland	477.338	... 37,822
Taranaki	9,279	... 495
Wellington	2,824,437	... 182,158
Hawke's Bay	1,156,819	... 71,926
Nelson	534,297	... 28,590
Marlborough	1,058,965	... 46,803
Canterbury	11,232,948	... 627.678
Otago	8,317,079	... 479,927
Southland	1,541,804	... 105,209
Total... ...	27,152,966	... 1,580,608

In the large sum of more than five millions sterling paid in 1867 for goods imported into the colony, no less than £355,994 was required for spirits, wine, and beer; and for tobacco, cigars, and snuff £90,008, not including that used in sheep-wash and similar ways. Large as these sums are, they were considerably exceeded in 1864, when £614,699 was paid for intoxicating drinks, and £213,670 for tobacco, cigars, and snuff; but these amounts were greatly increased that year by the presence of the troops.

That such large sums are spent in intoxicating drinks is a serious and dangerous mistake, and many of the best and most enlightened colonists are alarmed at it; the natural consequences are disease, wretchedness, and premature death. The provincial councils have passed various acts for lessening these evils; temperance societies are lifting up their voice against them, but they are scarcely checked. Both the Maori people and the colonists are drawn into the vortex, and the effects upon both races are alike injurious.

This chapter would not be complete without special attention were invited to the facilities which are afforded for education, compared with those of former years. Schools abound—the best class being much more expensive than similar institutions are in England—and according to the General Census, to which we are largely indebted, the number of young persons and children attending day-schools, private or public, amounted to nearly 20,000, and nearly 18,000 were receiving Sunday-school instruction. Some years ago it was almost impossible to educate our children well, without sending them out of the colony; and the result of that defect is felt now by many young persons, whose natural talents and steady attention to business have placed them in a respectable position. But the children of the present day are favoured with opportunities—when the cash can be afforded—to acquire a sound commercial education, and such an acquaintance with the Greek and Roman classics as may be followed by University honours.

It were easy to illustrate the growth of the colony by reference to many branches of industry which we have not named, to an increasing revenue, to wealth which has been acquired, to fresh tracts of country which have been surveyed for settlements; but we hope that enough has been said to show that Anglo-Saxon mind and muscles have not been exercised in vain. Yet various opinions are formed by persons on their arrival of the advancement which the colony has made; the bright dreams of some not being realized, while others are surprised that within the short space of thirty years the wilderness has been changed into a scene so much resembling their native land. But it is really difficult to form an estimate of the change which has passed over the country. Those only who have grappled with the facts can understand them. The first settlers had formed no pictures of busy towns, solid wharves and elegant villas, except as the results of years of earnest toil; they expected to find a wilderness, whose soil was fertile, and whose climate was salubrious; they knew that all beside, under God's blessing, depended upon themselves. As a community, we have not been disappointed, for more satisfactory effects than the most hopeful imagined have been accomplished.

Immigrants may find it difficult to believe that the very families who now occupy houses equal in comfort and elegance to those inhabited by the middle classes in

England, once occupied a raupo whare, or a rough weather-boarded house. Many a house have we seen, with no other floor than the common earth made smooth, with no chimney, a piece of calico stretched across a rough frame forming the window, and sleeping apartments screened off by a piece of carpet. Those who aspired to luxuries covered their floors with fern clipped into short pieces. Boxes served for tables and sofas, stools were used instead of chairs, and bedsteads were formed of poles driven into the floor, with sundry pieces laid crosswise, and secured with nails or native flax. It is amusing to compare these dwellings with the elegant houses, well furnished, presenting verandahs and flower gardens which invite attention and challenge the approval of the most fastidious among the immigrants of the present day.

Instead of the unsightly general store, which retailed all kinds of provisions, our shopkeepers are proud of their handsome plate-glass windows. Where the tangled fern made it difficult to walk, we have our solid macadamized streets, with paved foot-paths; and so much has land increased in value, that a building site in our principal towns would probably command a higher price than a similar site would do in the provincial towns of Great Britain.

Before steam-ships anchored in our harbours no little curiosity was excited among the children as their parents described the effects of steam power; and that large vessels could move swiftly along the sea, without either sails or oars, was almost too much for the Maories to believe. The first appearance of a steamer was the signal for a holiday. Every one went to look at the strange object; among colonists and Maories she was the subject of general conversation. The arrival of the English mail was an affair of deepest interest—it was a rare occurrence. Hearts throbbed with hope and fear, and eyes overflowed with sincere affection, as a well-known hand-writing revealed the thoughts and feelings, the purposes and doings of loved ones on the other side of the globe. Without losing any of our regard for those we left in the fatherland, we are not conscious of such deep emotion at the arrival of the English mail in the present time, as the regularity with which the mails are brought, and the short time which elapses between them, together with the few weeks required for the transit, make the mail day a mere ordinary affair.

In reviewing the advancement which the colony has made we can distinctly trace the hand of God. The treasures lay hidden in the earth, and in greatest quantity in the most rugged parts of the country, where none were likely to fix their home till the colony was in a sufficiently advanced state to meet the excitement which a disclosure of these treasures would create. Within thirty years a company of lawless adventurers have been replaced by nearly a quarter of a million of persons, respecting wholesome laws, and cherishing institutions which must give them a place among the most enlightened countries of the earth. The soil was not cultivated except in small patches by the natives, but it is now producing wide-spread and abundant crops. In distant settlements a few families were gathered together, inviting the smile of the visitor at their loneliness and pretensions; but these settlements have become cities, respected in both hemispheres. To become a New Zealand settler in the early days of our colonial life was to bid adieu to the comforts of a happy English home;

but homes quite as happy, and as full of comfort are found here now in large numbers. We have had our trials, and severe some of them have been; the seedling colony has been exposed to wintry blasts, but our trials have not discouraged us, and the seedling planted by the providence of God, and watered by his care, has already become a large and sheltering tree.

The advancement which the colony has made in providing churches and schools, and in supporting ministers and teachers, is not described here, as we have devoted a separate chapter to this subject.

CHAPTER X

THE cultivation of the soil will probably be the staple support of large parts of the colony, notwithstanding its extensive gold fields and sheep runs. Both the climate and soil are adapted to almost every kind of English produce. Hitherto we have not been troubled with the droughts which sometimes prevail in Australia ; but in some cases, as on the Otago and Canterbury plains, floods have occurred, threatening to sweep away, within a few hours, the entire crops of a season. This, however, is the exception rather than the rule, and in large portions of the country the farmer has no reason to dread such a calamity. The sealing adventurers have finished their work, and the whaling companies have scarcely an existence. The falling away of the latter is a thing to be regretted, as the fish continue to approach our coast, where they are met by American crews, and turned to a satisfactory account. The past history of the colony shews farming to have been the most steady and certain form of prosperity. In our opinion it will continue so, although the other departments of industry may yield large profits ; we may therefore devote a few pages to New Zealand farming.

This is the more necessary, as serious mistakes are often made on this subject, many persons supposing, while in England, that the virgin soil is so rich and strong, that the heaviest crops may be anywhere grown with the smallest amount of labour. This delusion generally vanishes within a few days after their arrival ;

but it is sometimes followed by an unfair depreciation
of the real value of the land, without a proper discrimi-
nation of the several kinds which are sometimes met
with within the range of a few miles. Some immigrants,
of a hopeful temperament, resolve at once to grapple with
the difficulties of a new sphere, and generally succeed ;
while others, of a desponding bias, wish they had not
left their fatherland, and commence their colonial life
with tears and indecision.

The most obvious division of the land for the purposes
of the farmer, is that of the open country and the bush.
Each requires a proper treatment, and each is selected
according to the taste and object of the proprietor, and
the capital which he can command. The open country
is generally preferred, on account of the facility with
which the plough may be introduced, and the first wide-
spread crops be raised. But other distinctions should
be kept in view, and some of them are very important ;
for many thousands of acres, in some districts, are
scarcely worth cultivating, and other extensive tracts
still worse are to be found, which would certainly ruin
the persons who are unfortunate enough to settle upon
them, with a hope of supporting their families by agriculture. A few such cases have occurred, producing
loud complaints and heavy losses. This subject deserves
the special attention of farmers on their arrival, some
of whom are likely to act upon the advice of persons
whose object may be to dispose of land 'which they know
cannot be sold to experienced settlers. The labouring
man should embrace the first opportunity to obtain work
with fair wages, without binding himself for any considerable term, except in particular cases ; but the farmer
who has some capital at command, should visit the

districts recommended to him, examine the state of the farms in the neighbourhood, and inquire into the value of the crops which they have produced.. We will quote a description of soils found in the Auckland province, and recommend it to the attention of the immigrant :—

"Nearly the whole of the open lands of this province have been, at no very great distance of time, covered with forests, which have been destroyed by fire. It depended much on the nature of the woods so destroyed whether the action of that fire was detrimental or otherwise to the soil on which they were grown. Accordingly, wherever trees of the Kauri species are indicated in the open soil, either by the presence of the gum, or the remains of the tree itself, above or below the top soil— or by those small raised mounds of hard, impervious soil, which point out the spot where the tree stood at the time of its upheavement—there we shall find the soil to be inferior in quality, varying, we believe, for better and worse, in exact proportion as the original forest was more or less heavy, and the action of the fire, consequently, more or less intense. . . . We have the 'brick dust soil.' This is a light grey-coloured soil, close and compact, and when pulverised between the fingers, comes down to a fine dust, of the same consistency as a powdered Bath brick. . . . Again, we have another description of soil equally worthless, which for three successive years we have, by experience, found to be incapable of producing even grass. This is a friable brown soil, of light texture, overlying a porous subsoil of a similar nature, only more closely cemented, and on which the action of fire is apparent. Kauri has been the prevailing timber on such land." It should be further stated that, in some instances, good crops have been produced on land whose general features resemble those just described; but in such places the action of the fire was probably less intense.

We must not hastily conclude that those districts will never become valuable. The soil of many of the "commons" of England were so poor, half a century ago, that they produced nothing of any value; but by a well-conducted course of labour, and the application of proper manure, they rank now among the fair fields and well-conditioned farms of Great Britain. But such a course will not be followed in the treatment of barren soils in New Zealand, at least for many years to come, on account of the high price of labour, and the difficulty of procuring suitable manures. The rich lands found in extensive tracts would, if properly cultivated, employ the labour and afford support for a large population, and will be naturally occupied first, as far as the native title may be extinguished. Strangers should be very careful of the site which they select for a home, and on which their capital and labour are to be expended; and not only is carefulness necessary in fixing upon a supposed tract of good land, but also in the selection of the particular spot which he intends to make his own; for the soil of some parcels of land lying contiguous to each other, is, in some instances, found to vary exceedingly, from a rich deposit of good vegetable matter, to a kind such as has been described, or, if it has other properties, it may, notwithstanding, be destitute of the qualities necessary for the farmer.

When a farm is secured in the open country, whose soil is good, abundant crops, both of grain and other things, may be generally produced. From forty to sixty bushels of wheat per acre have often been grown, where

the land was properly cultivated, and that without
manure. But in the early days of the colony, the most
slovenly mode of farming was generally followed. Wheat
was sown year after year, with no other preparation of
the ground than a light ploughing; or in small fields,
the seed was merely covered with a hoe. The straw
was thrown in a heap to rot, in some cases, and in others
it was burnt as a nuisance. The English farmer may
smile at this; and the New Zealand farmer of the present
day acknowledges it as being a mistaken course. A better
system is now generally followed, the necessity of suitable manure is admitted, and the ordinary means to
secure it are used. The farmers are now saying, that,
"as a general rule, one-fourth of the portion of the farm
which is devoted to agriculture, should be sown or
planted with crops to be consumed upon the farm, and
to be returned again to the land as manure; another
fourth in the production of green crops, such as potatoes,
beans, &c., intended for use or sale; and only one-half,
at the very most, should be used for the growth of white
crops, such as wheat, oats, or barley." Manure is now
admitted to be of such importance that, for the growth
of turnips, one hundred weight of guano, and from three
to seven hundred weight of bone dust per acre, are
recommended. The nature of the crops which it may
be desirable to produce, must, of course, be regulated
—partly, at least—by the distance of the farm from the
nearest market, and the facilities and cost of conveyance.
On this account, corn growing, dairy produce, and the
breeding of cattle and sheep, will be the chief objects of
the farmer whose land is at a considerable distance from
the chief towns; while potatoes, hay, and other heavy
and bulky produce, will probably be found more remunerative near the centres of population.

Some of our best farmers contend that the partial failure of crops on many farms is owing to a want of underdraining. While labour is so expensive, it is not likely that much will be done in this direction; but where it has been properly tried, the advantages are said to be so great, that underdraining is strongly recommended for all wet lands. The usual way of doing this has been by cutting a deep trench, filling the bottom with brushwood, and then covering it with earth. But the plan recommended by a practical farmer for draining grass or fern lands, where the roots of the fern are matted together into a solid sod, is the following :—The drain, if intended to be three feet in depth, must be cut to the full width as far as the first three spits, which will be about thirty inches deep; the bottom is then to be cleaned out, and will be about fourteen inches wide. A narrow gutter, in the shape of the letter V, six inches wide at the top, must then be cut to the depth of six or eight inches along the bottom of the drain, leaving, of course, a shelf on each side of four inches in width, for the sides of the sod or turf to rest upon. The gutter can be best cleaned out with a tool called the draw-scoop, which is made for the purpose. The top sod, which the workmen carefully laid on one side of the drain, the loose earth having been thrown on the opposite side, is to be laid over the gutter, taking care that it rests on the four-inch ledge on each side. By this means the gutter will remain quite free for the escape of the water. This kind of drainage has been found more successful than that in which brushwood is used ; it will be less expensive, and the drains will be less liable to be choked.

Mismanagement has been, without doubt, a common cause of failure among New Zealand farmers. In many cases there has been an entire want of system; and in others, respect has been almost entirely paid to the kind of crops which were likely to sell at a high price, without regarding the poverty of the soil which must follow by exhausting crops of a similar kind being grown from the same soil in many successive years. The result has often been, as might have been expected, that the farm became unproductive, and the farmer became poor. Other causes of failure may be observed, and may be traced to mismanagement. In some instances, the settler erects an expensive fence of posts and rails round his farm, before any, or scarcely any, of his land is broken up. After this heavy outlay, he finds that he cannot cultivate above one-fourth part of his land at present, and by the time that all the soil can be broken up, the costly fence has become rotten. Many persons have attempted to cover their fern land with grass, at scarcely any expense. Making use of a favourable breeze, at the season of the year when the fern is quite dry, and when some showers are likely to fall, a fire is conducted over the land, leaving a crop of blackened, bristling fern-stalks in every direction. The clover and grass seeds are then sown, and good pasturage is expected. We have seen this plan succeed in some cases, where the soil is light and rich; but in the majority of instances it fails, and we would recommend that it be very rarely tried, except on light, rich soil, and where success is not of much importance. The inexperienced settler, who wishes to get his farm into a good state as soon as possible, may take it for granted that defective measures are not advisable.

The open country, too, certainly secures advantages which cannot be obtained in the bush. If cattle and implements are at hand, a large farm may be won from the open waste lands in a short time. Large fields of grain may be seen waving in the breeze, with extensive meadows, looking green and beautiful, stocked with goodly herds and flocks. Broad acres, covered with turnips and mangold-wurtzel for winter use, may be produced, with proper care in the selection and management of the soil. On such land, hedges may be raised of the goodly hawthorn, rivalling the beautiful fences of the fatherland in the month of May. Many such spots are now witnessed in different parts of the colony, recalling some of the sweetest associations of country life in England. On these lovely spots, beautiful houses have been built—less substantial, it may be, than the English farmhouses, but convenient, and often quite as picturesque. This class of homesteads, of course, belongs to the capitalists—in some cases to those who have lately come to the colony; but in many other cases, they are the property of the old colonists, who worked their way up from the labouring classes of Great Britain by steady and well conducted industry.

The bush lands have their peculiar advantages also. There, firing, fencing, and timber for building purposes, may be cut on the spot, and the heavy expense of carting is consequently saved. Much of the bush land is very strong, being a rich vegetable soil, composed of the decayed leaves of many years' growth. Very heavy crops may be produced here; but care must be taken to prevent them from growing too rank, or they may be bowed down by their own weight, and rot before they become ripe. As bullocks, ploughs, and other heavy implements, are of little use in the first course of bush farming, a strong, industrious man, with but a small capital, can soon carve for himself, chiefly by his own labour, a pleasant homestead among the thick trees. Some of the prettiest rural homesteads which we have seen are found among the forest openings. We have visited places in the dense bush so entangled with the luxuriant undergrowth, that a bill-hook was necessary to cut our way along; and returning to the same spot some years afterward, have found the trees cut down, leaving their roots and about six feet of their massy trunks gradually to decay. Fields of delight spread out in different directions invited our admiration; pleasant cottages, with flowery gardens blooming before them, added to the beauty of the scene, and families of healthy happy children, intent upon their pastime, completed the picture, and deeply impressed our mind with the contrast which may be produced in a New Zealand forest within a few years.

The removal of a family into the country is a serious event, unless the provision necessary for their comfort has been properly arranged; yet there is much which is exciting and hopeful in country life. Where the proper spirit is found, and the inconveniences and difficulties have been fairly considered—where there is a resolution to meet the new state of things with a cheerful heart— and where the presence and blessing of Almighty God is consistently sought and enjoyed—there is not much room to fear, providing that the natural quality of the land, and the situation of the farm, are what they should be. By the well-conducted labour of such a family, the wilderness will soon " rejoice, and blossom as the rose."

It is well to fence in a suitable piece of ground for a garden, and to plant fruit trees, as soon as this can be done without infringing on more important duties—

R

those of growing the necessary family provisions as
quickly as possible. The best kind of fruit trees may be
obtained in the colony, and if planted in a sheltered
situation, they will bear fruit in a few years. English
gooseberries, currants, raspberries, and strawberries
will produce plentifully in a short time, with proper
culture. Apple trees are very subject to the American
blight, and we fear that their culture, on this account,
will not be very extensive ; yet the orchard would not
be complete without a few apple trees of the best kinds.
Peaches may be produced in great quantities in a little
time, and if the trees be carefully selected, the flavour
of the fruit will be found very good. A good kitchen
garden will, of course, be found desirable, as it will yield
a considerable quantity of food, and supply a wholesome
variety of diet. The common garden vegetables of
England may be grown here with little trouble—some of
them with less trouble than in England, owing to the
mildness and humidity of the climate. In addition to a
well-stocked kitchen garden, we have often seen small
flower gardens, laid out with much taste, and planted
with many of the choicest specimens of English
floral culture. There is an advantage here, especially
in the Northern provinces, over the climate of England,
in the fact that many of the plants which require to be
kept in greenhouses there, flourish luxuriantly here in
the open air, and some of the bulbs which the frosts of
an English winter would destroy, remain safe with us in
the ground, and grow vigorously when the proper season
returns.

The farmer in New Zealand, as in other countries,
meets with evils against which it is often difficult, and
sometimes impossible, to provide a remedy. He may

prepare his ground in the best manner, sow it with the most approved seeds, and watch it with great interest; but may, after all, be disappointed in its results. Grasshoppers, crickets, slugs, caterpillars, and swarms of little creatures generally included in the term *insects*, may destroy his hopes. Some of these injure the tender germ while it is under the surface; others eat off the blade as soon as it appears above the ground. Similar enemies are ready to attack it in all the stages of its growth, and caterpillars often bite through the ear of corn when it begins to ripen. The potato is frequently exposed to danger from a small moth, which flies about in the summer evenings, seeking a suitable place where to deposit its eggs. The tubers of the potato plant are among the favourite resorts of those little winged enemies. On these they will, if possible, lay their eggs, from which small worms will soon be hatched. These worms will eat their way into the potato, and make it unfit for human food. To prevent this kind of injury, the plants should be carefully earthed up while growing, so that none of the tubers are exposed; and when they are taken out of the ground, they should be covered from the moths before sunset. These annoyances are probably increased by the mildness of our winter, the frost not being sufficiently sharp to destroy the myriads of little foes, which " abide their time " to commence their attacks.

The wheat plant is subject to some diseases here of a serious kind, two of which may be mentioned—the mildew (*Puccinia graminis*), and the smut (*uredo segetum*). Such has been the prevalence of these diseases in many cases, that the crop has been entirely destroyed; and in other cases, the injury has been so great that the quantity of grain obtained has been scarcely sufficient to pay the cost of cutting. Experienced farmers suppose that much may be done towards preventing these injuries. On land subject to mildew, they say that only the early kinds of wheat should be sown, and in a smaller quantity than usual. No manure should be applied immediately before sowing the seed; the land should be well drained, and kept free from weeds. The smut is, perhaps, most common. Various means have been used to prevent the destruction of crops by this disease, and of them the following is particularly recommended:— " Wash the seed in a tub of hot, but not boiling water, stir it about well, then strain it, and spread the wet grain over the floor about two inches deep. Sprinkle this layer over lightly with new dry lime, not too much slaked; add other layers of wheat and other sprinklings of lime ; then turn over the wheat with a wooden shovel, until every grain has received a slight coating of lime. The moisture will be absorbed by the lime, so that the wheat will be dry enough for sowing in a few hours. The action of the lime will entirely destroy the vegetable power in the sporules of the smut. But care must be taken that the seed be not subjected to a fresh contagion by being put into sacks in which smutty grain has been kept, or sown on land where a diseased crop has been grown." Turnips and cabbages have lately been destroyed by innumerable parasitical little creatures, and almost all kinds of vegetables have their enemies here, as well as in other parts of the world. With the hope of remedying these evils, at least in some degree, sparrows and other insect-eating birds have been brought from England. The farmer who, when in the fatherland, paid for the destruction of those useful little birds, would here willingly give them a few grains from his harvest for the part which they might take in preventing his crops from being destroyed by insects.

The inexperienced farmer should be careful in the selection of his stock, and distinctly keep in view the object for which he purchases them. If he intends his stock to run on the waste lands around his homestead, he should secure cattle which have been used to a similar run; for cattle reared in rich pastures would pine away on the wide and scanty waste lands, where others, bred in similar places, would probably thrive and fatten. Keeping this fact in view, the very best stock suitable for his purpose should be procured, as the cost of their maintenance would not be more, and the profit arising from them would be considerably larger, than from stock of an inferior quality.

Dairy farming has been followed by many with much success. But it must not be forgotten, that this line of industry requires a good deal of time, both morning and evening, of every day; that it is not always easy to procure the necessary assistance, even at high wages, without the farmer's own family can supply it; that much labour will be necessary to provide a good supply of winter food. If, however, all these wants can be properly met, a good dairy farm, where both butter and cheese can be made of a superior quality, will very probably be found satisfactorily remunerative.

One of the most profitable investments, particularly in the southern part of the colony, is, perhaps, found in sheep farming. This requires a considerable outlay; but the abundance of wool produced from well-selected flocks, and the high price which it has lately made, together with the great natural increase which has been obtained, have secured large profits. Occasionally diseases are introduced among the flocks, causing much trouble and expense, and serious losses may be the result. Sheep farming, on a large scale is, of course, beyond the means of small capitalists ; but a small flock is often found attached to a common farm, and where it is properly managed, the profits are found considerable.

The remarks of the "Wool Supply Association of the Bradford and Halifax Chamber of Commerce," concerning the New Zealand produce, may be quoted as an interesting statement :—" Large supplies of this wool have already come to England, and we believe the country is peculiarly adapted to produce the long combing wools required, from its soil and climate ; and an unlimited market is open here for such wools." For some years past, wool has formed one of the chief exports of the colony. The Middle Island is generally considered more suitable for extensive sheep farming than the North Island, on account of the coarse grass which covers the waste lands of the former, and which supply food for large flocks at small cost ; while the waste lands of the latter island, as is well known, are covered principally with fern. *

The following " Hints on Farming and Gardening," taken chiefly from the *New Zealander*, are quoted, supposing that they may be of use to the newly-arrived settler, and may be interesting also to some who have no intention to leave the shores of Great Britain :—

* Since the above was written, the price of wool in the English market has been so seriously lessened, that many of our sheep-farmers, after suffering severe losses, have turned their attention to other pursuits. Wool will probably continue to be a valuable export, but the high prices occasioned by the American war must not be anticipated.

" The land recommended for a homestead should be, if possible, partly bush and partly open country, having streams of water running through it, but neither swampy nor very hilly. The first business may be to erect a house for the family, with two or more rooms according to the number of persons who are to inhabit it. A house ten feet wide and twenty feet long for two rooms, or thirty feet long for three rooms, may be built according to the following directions :—Cut straight posts of hard wood, eight feet long and six inches in diameter, sawing the top ends level. After levelling the ground, dig the corner holes two feet deep ; put in the posts, and ram them well, taking care that they are at the same level at the top. Put in other posts two feet apart, leaving proper openings for doors, windows, and chimney. Let the posts for the centre of the gables be fourteen feet long, and be firmly fixed in the ground. Cut long, straight pieces for wall-plates ; square the part which rests on the posts, and fasten it to them with nails. A straight pole, the length of the house, and two or three inches in diameter, should be cut for a ridge pole, and nailed to the central posts. Rafters must be provided, straight, with a diameter of three inches, and fastened to the side posts and to the ridge pole. Nail small poles, split in halves, horizontally along the wall-posts and rafters, about ten inches apart. Cut *raupo* from a neighbouring swamp, and expose it to the sun and wind a few days to dry ; then tie it to the framework with strips of flax leaves, as the Maories do. Build a chimney with clay, in which chopped grass is well mixed, to make it adhere ; but take care to line the front of the chimney inside with stones, if they can be procured, to prevent the fire from causing the clay to

moulder away. A few boards should be obtained for
doors and floors, but glazed window sashes may be best
procured from the nearest town. Carefully thatch the
roof with a good coating of long rough grass, which may
generally be found near a water-course; or cover the
roof with shingles, if they can be easily procured. A
house of this description will last five years, with a little
repairing. When this time has expired, the industrious
settler will probably be enabled to erect a more comfortable residence, and the original dwelling-place will
still be useful as an out-house, if a little attention be
paid to repairs. We have seen many happy families in
such houses, and not a few of the most influential
farmers in the country commenced their colonial life
with a residence of no greater pretensions than that
which we have here described. We may further remark,
that it is important to select a site for a house sufficiently distant from trees, so as not to be endangered
by the fires which occasionally, in the dry season, rage
in the bush, and in trees formerly charred, for weeks
together. We have known houses burnt down through
the bush fires, much valuable property destroyed, and
even human life sacrificed to their uncontrollable fury."

In the selection of a situation for your garden, take
care that the spot be well sheltered from the prevailing
winds, and let it be open to the north. In preparing
and cropping the ground, making fences, and building
out-houses, the following directions may be of value;
for each month has its particular claims, which may be
so met as to make the labour, and its results, with God's
blessing, both easy and satisfactory.

FEBRUARY.

Plant different kinds of cabbage for winter use, in

rows two feet wide each way, and sow turnips in drills twenty inches apart. Let the fern be burnt off your waste land, and the bush which was cut down in the preceding winter should now be burnt. The harvest is generally ended by the latter end of this month, and the early crops of potatoes may be taken up.

MARCH.

Finish burning off all fallen bush and heaps of roots which may be dry. Break up fresh ground. Cut drains, so as to keep your house and premises dry during winter. Sow grass seeds on bush-land as soon as the ashes are cool and well spread about, and on fern-land after the ground has been ploughed and well harrowed. It is important to procure grass seed of different sorts, and to mix them well, so that, when one kind dies off, others may continue green. Two bushels of mixed grass seed, and eight pounds of clover, per acre, should be sown on fern-land; but a smaller quantity will suffice on bush-land. Finish taking up potatoes this month.

APRIL.

Sow grass seed, if prevented from doing so in the last month. Continue to break up fresh ground, and burn any bush which has been cut down and dried.

MAY.

Continue to break up new ground, and burn off roots. Sow cabbage, cauliflower, and brocoli seed at the end of this month. Winter wheat is sometimes sown at the latter part of the present month, the quantity of seed being a bushel and a half per acre.

JUNE.

Prepare ground for fruit trees, which should be transplanted this month. Procure the best varieties of apple, pear, peach, plum, and cherry trees, from a respectable nurseryman, rather than depend on those raised by persons who do not understand them. Plant them in a circular hole, large enough to let their roots lie in their natural order, after having cut off their ends. Then fill in the earth carefully, so that the roots are six inches below the surface, and tread the soil firmly round the tree. Plant out gooseberry bushes and strawberries. Prune fruit trees this month. Continue to break up fresh ground, and cut down bush.

JULY.

Plant fruit trees and gooseberry bushes, if they could not be planted in the preceding month. Oats may be sown on fern land, and continue to cut down bush, to be burnt in the following autumn. A few early potatoes may now be planted in a light, dry soil.

AUGUST.

Plant out cabbages, cauliflower, and brocoli, and put in early potatoes. Sow carrots, in a good light soil, in drills fifteen inches apart. Spring wheat may·be sown, at the rate of two bushels per acre. Onions should now be sown in drills, eight inches from each other, on good soil, well prepared; also peas, broad beans, reddish, and cress.

SEPTEMBER.

The general crop of potatoes should now be planted. By sowing two hundred weight of guano per acre in the drills with the potatoes, upon fern land, the crop will be considerably improved. Let the early potatoes be earthed up. Shut up grass paddocks, which are intended to produce hay. Finish sowing all kinds of garden seeds. Lucern and sainfoin may now be sown in drills; they will form a valuable green crop.

OCTOBER.

Finish planting potatoes. Sow maize, by dropping five or six seeds in holes three feet apart each way, and cover them lightly with mould. But let it be remembered that the growth of maize is confined to the northern part of the colony, where large quantities are produced by the Maories. In the southern provinces, it may not ripen; yet it will be found profitable to raise a green crop of maize as food for cattle and pigs. Sow turnips and mangold-wurtzel on good land, well prepared.

NOVEMBER.

Sow cucumber, melon, and pumpkin seeds in a rich soil. Cucumber plants, raised under a frame, may now be planted out. In the early part of the month, let different kinds of kidney beans and scarlet runners be sown. More cabbage may be planted out. Thin out turnips, mangold-wurtzel—which may be transplanted in moist weather—and onions. Hoe between the rows of growing crops, to destroy the weeds. Prepare fern land to lie fallow for a few months, by mowing and burning off the fern, and ploughing it four inches deep.

DECEMBER.

Sow cabbage, cauliflower, and Savoy seeds, taking care to water them properly. By sowing at this time and in May, and planting out as has been directed, a good supply of these useful and wholesome vegetables may be secured for the whole year, unless the blight which has lately attacked them be very abundant. Grass seeds will ripen the latter end of this month. Where these seeds could be obtained free from weeds, they have been a very profitable crop for some years past, and are likely to continue to be so, as the country will be more extensively cultivated. Colonial seeds are often preferred to English seeds, as the latter have often lost their vitality before they reached the colony, owing, probably to a want of care in packing. But valuable as the crop of grass seeds may appear, the farmer will not forget that his pastures will soon be impoverished if these crops be often repeated. The hay season will commence in the latter part of this month.

JANUARY.

Harvest may now be expected, if the crops have been put in at the time we have directed; but if the crops were sown later, as is often the case, the corn will not be ripe till the next month. The harvest is as busy and as interesting a season, in those parts of the colony where a good deal of grain is grown, as it is in England. The early planted potato crops, on light soil, will be found ripe, and may be prepared for the market. Let the hay harvest be completed this month.

It may be useful to add the following list of tools, which will be required for the work described :—Two American axes, a grindstone, a six-feet cross-cut saw, files for sharpening saw, a set of wedges, some maul rings, a hand-saw, hammer and gimlets, a strong spoke-shave, a small bench axe, an inch-and-half augur, a smoothing plane, a foot-rule, a strong line, garden spades, grubbing rake with six teeth fixed three inches apart, some billhooks, a fern hook, a scythe and stone to sharpen it, sickles, wooden rakes, and hay-forks. And if working bullocks be employed, a strong cart, bows, yokes, chains, plough, and harrows will be needed. It should be observed, that some of the articles mentioned above can be best obtained in the colony, where they are properly understood, although they will cost more than they would do if purchased in England.

From the pages just quoted it may be inferred that farming in New Zealand is not such easy work that persons who have never been occupied in manual labour will always be found quite prepared for it. Nor must the hard-working man, well acquainted with farm work in Great Britain and Ireland, suppose that he can succeed in the cultivation of the colonial soil without expending on it a proper amount of labour. Many persons, who were brought up as clerks and shopkeepers, have been bitterly disappointed at finding their romantic ideas of New Zealand farming vanishing at the very time they stood in most need of their support; and the indolent man—for indolence is occasionally seen in the colonies—finds that, without industry, he must continue poor and wretched. But the cases are very many in which sober, industrious, labouring men, from the agricultural districts of the mother-country, who arrived in the colony without twenty shillings of their own property, are now among the most thriving men in the country, respected by all who know them; some of them now fill a place on the magistrates' bench, or have been elected to take an important part in the legislature of their adopted country.

But other persons, who have spent many years in the colony, and whose advantages were equal to those of their prosperous neighbours, remain poor and comfortless. In some instances, this has doubtless been ordered, in the providence in God, for the accomplishment of a wise and gracious purpose, which may be more fully made known in a future state; but in other cases, it is not difficult to discover the causes of continued poverty. We have seen some men bestow their principal time in cultivating a garden—perhaps a flower garden—while their wide acres lay waste, and their family could scarcely get bread. Some persons, the subjects of misfortune in their native land, emigrated with the thought that they could more easily fall into the ranks of working men where they were not known; but, unfortunately, they brought with them some notions of respectability, and those false ones, that they could not consent to cultivate their farms with their own hands, and having no capital with which to employ others, they sank into misery, and are wearing out their days unknown, unblest, and un-loved. We could mention the names of persons, were it right to do so, in whose colonial career we have often observed examples of all the classes mentioned above. Intending emigrants would do well to ponder carefully their objects in seeking a home in a distant part of the world, and they should, by all means, guard against the hope of finding plenty without labour of some kind or another—unless they are prepared to bring the means of support for their families with them, and are resolved to be judicious in the expending of those means.

Those who select a farm in the thinly-peopled part of the country, should keep distinctly in view the opportu-nity of securing the means of public worship for the religious welfare of themselves and their families, and a day-school for the instruction of their children. In many country districts, this is very difficult; in some places, it may be almost impossible. But much may be done where there is a willing mind. A Christian family has an opportunity of being a shining light in such circumstances. If no other place is open, their rural cottage should be made the "house of God" every Lord's Day, where neighbours, whose residence may be at a considerable distance from the sanctuary, should

be invited; and if there be no ordained minister, nor
any one whose labours as a lay agent are recognized by
a respectable body of Christians, the master of the
house in which they are assembled, or some other Christian brother, should conduct Divine worship in the most
profitable manner that he can. Suitable books may be
obtained as helps in such cases, and the Scriptures may
be devoutly read. Sermons, full of Gospel matter are
published in the present day, and will be found very
suitable for such secluded districts. The hymn of praise,
and the voice of prayer, may be heard in the midst of
the thick trees, with peculiar solemnity and pleasure;
and by means like these, with the blessing of God, the
moral, as the natural, desert " may rejoice, and blossom
as the rose." We have not supposed a mere imaginary
case; for in different parts of the country such meetings
have been convened, the religious life of the settlers
has been preserved, and the Divine blessing has been
largely enjoyed.

Yet let no one forget the superior advantages which
are to be obtained in places where the inhabitants are
more numerous, and the public means of grace are properly maintained. In such circumstances, the honoured
and hallowed means by which young and old are brought
before God, " to hear of heaven and learn the way," in
the most privileged parts of the world, may be found,
though possibly on a small scale. The Sabbath school,
with its happy throng, and busy classes, and songs of
delight; the preaching of the Word, which is able to
make us " wise unto salvation;" the meetings convened
for prayer and praise; the pastoral visits of men of God,
through whose faithful labours the Church in the wilderness is an object of joy to the angels of heaven;—

present such social, moral, and religious advantages, that, where it is possible to select a home within their reach, it should be done. But let it be borne in mind, that in occupying a distant part of the country as colonial pioneers, much may be done of a social and religious kind, if a few Christian families were to select their farms in the same locality, and carefully avail themselves of every opportunity of Divine worship and social improvement. By such a course they will prepare the way of the Lord, and themselves become the nucleus of a Church, which, after a few years, may become a power in the colony.

It is possible that this book may fall into the hands of some family whose colonial residence completely isolates them from their countrymen. In such a case they are dependent on themselves, under God, for the sources of improvement and pleasure which they enjoy; and much will depend upon the course they resolve to take, in determining their future well-being of body and soul. The following advice to such may be observed with benefit :—Remember that you are as completely under the eye of God in your solitary situation as they are who dwell in the populous city; you are as much the objects of His care and love; He is as willing to accept your worship, and to save your souls. Your prayers may be as distinctly heard, and as completely answered ; and, both in sickness and in health, in the midst of life and in the hour of death, Jesus may be as near and as precious. Therefore, let the Sabbath be kept holy ; let the family be as decently clothed on that day as they would be if you were in the midst of neighbours, and let the whole family be convened for Divine worship. You will then often find that your lonely cottage is "the house of God, and the gate of heaven." Every morning and evening let the family altar be set up, upon which the sacrifice of thanksgiving is daily laid, and at which prayers are offered for present and future blessings.

It has often been observed that some persons—and we fear many—who are observant of religious duties while they mingled with society, throw off religious restraints, and perhaps moral restraints too, when they take up a residence in the wilderness. Such a course may justly be denounced as unmanly, unreasonable, and dangerous—unmanly, as it displays a total want of principle and honourable character; unreasonable, as if religion had no reference to God, or as if He were confined to populous districts; dangerous, for the evil spirit will urge such persons on in this course of ungodliness, unless they quickly repent, until their eternal condemnation be sealed.

The country life of New Zealand has many charms, and to a romantic spirit it may appear very inviting. The happiness which is found in it by many is considerable, and the advantages in certain respects may be great; but, as it has been shewn, there are dangers also, both to the young and to the old. Persons, therefore, who intend to occupy a homestead far away from the settled parts of the colony, should well weigh the circumstances which are likely to affect them, ask counsel of God, and resolve, wherever they go, that God shall be in all their thoughts.

CHAPTER XI.

UNREASONABLE expectations of the cities and towns of this colony are indulged in by some persons who find their way thither that are necessarily doomed to disappointment on their arrival. The fervid ones forget that the well-paved and beautiful cities of Europe are the growth of many centuries ; and that we may not go far back in the history of our native country to see its principal cities with muddy streets, the houses thatched with straw, the long, dark nights of winter without a single lamp to relieve the pedestrian from his perplexity, and the crowded, ill-ventilated, and undrained lanes and alleys, the dreaded nursery of the plague. Other persons, who remember that thirty years ago there was neither village nor town in New Zealand, except the Maori pahs ; no law in the country but that of might ; no vestiges of civilization but in connection with the missionary stations, and here and there marking the dwelling places of the whalers and a few other adventurous Pakeha Maories ; are pleased with the unmistakeable evidences of progress which the first sight of a colonial settlement affords. Here the spire of a church is seen, and there the sails of a wind-mill, while cottages with glistening windows, and ranges of buildings which evidently mark the principal thoroughfares, form a beautiful and pleasing picture as seen from the deck of a ship after several months spent upon the restless ocean. The town and country life are as distinct from each other here as they are elsewhere. Each has its pleasures and its advantages, and, it may be added, its dangers and its miseries. We have sketched the country life of New Zealand ; we will now depict its town life.

The cities of this colony must not be confounded in imagination with the extraordinary towns which have grown up in Australia within the last few years. Yet as they are steadily—and in some instances rapidly— growing into importance, increasing in population and commercial influence, they will probably soon rival the present cities in the neighbouring colonies. Several of the provinces already boast of their capitals ; where there are substantial buildings, well-formed streets, beautiful shops, stocked with all that is necessary for life and comfort, and much that is merely ornamental. Handsome buildings have been erected for the worship of God. Halls for public meetings, and buildings for legislative and other purposes of the Government, are now in the course of erection, which would be ornamental to any town in England. Mechanics' institutions and other means of improvement are found here. The sins which disgrace European town life generally are found here too ; the mind is sharpened both for good and evil, character is perhaps more fully developed ; the incentives to goodness and the temptations to sin are stronger in towns than they are in the thinly peopled country.

The mortality of our towns is greater than that of the country districts ; this, we presume, does not arise so much from the number of persons who are brought to-gether as from the want of proper sanitary regulations being carried into practice. So deficient is the drainage in some places that no amount of cleanliness can pre-vent fevers and other diseases. This subject is now re-ceiving the attention it demands, and town boards are engaged to remedy this and other evils; so that before these pages are in print proper means will be used to secure wholesome air and water in most of the principal towns.

Our towns are particularly exposed to the ravages of fire, as they were originally built of wood; and although in some provinces the Government has determined that no more wooden structures shall be erected in the most populous parts of their towns, yet the large number of old timber houses endanger the substantial edifices which have recently been erected, with much taste and at great expense. Some fearful fires have occurred, particularly in Auckland and Dunedin; but though the damage done involved a heavy loss, it is surprising that it was not more extensive. As in some of the old cities in Europe, those fires have been the means of removing a mass of injurious matter, and prepared the way for more substantial houses and a better circulation of air.

Strangers are generally surprised at the high price of land in the principal parts of our towns. It is easier to secure a freehold in a good business street in many a provincial town in England than it is in the chief towns of New Zealand. This indicates, we suppose, commercial prosperity; but it operates against the small tradesman, who expected, before his arrival, to carry on his business on his own property. The high price of town land, and the present high prices of building materials and labour cause the rents of houses to be very high. A decent cottage of four rooms can be scarcely obtained under twenty shillings a week,* and for premises sufficient to carry on a respectable business, the rent may amount to several hundred pounds sterling per annum.

* House rent is lower now than it was when this chapter was written.

But as the time of which we now write is that in which
the Maori war is raging, it is possible that the present
rate at which houses are rented will not be long continued. The high price which town land commands
will be the occasion of ill-constructed cottages being
built on every foot of ground which can be appropriated
to such a purpose, to the danger of the public health,
and increasing the liability of destructive fires. This
has already attracted the attention of the town boards ;
and as soon as proper regulations can be applied to
prevent such close packing of families, the better it will
be found both for health and morals.

Our colonial towns are troubled with persons who
obtain a livelihood by pandering to the pleasures and
vices of the public. In these ways large sums are often
spent, and the results are seen in the heart being hardened, the mind dissipated, and the morals of many
corrupted. One of the most dangerous forms in which
these amusements are now presented, is that in which
virtue and vice are mingled ; instruction is given, but it
is accompanied by sensuality of some kind, so that the
good derived from the one is more than counterbalanced
by the evils of the other. The theatre is here ; not in
the perfection of its trappings and song and eloquence,
which may be occasionally seen and heard in the principal play-houses of Great Britain, but though of lower
pretensions, the attractions are strong, and we fear that
the harm done is great.

The prevailing sin of the colony is drunkenness. Wages
are so high that working men earn considerable sums,
and thousands of them spend every spare shilling at the
public house. Large numbers of young men are imitating their seniors in this pernicious habit, and will grow

up, we fear, confirmed drunkards. Our heart shrinks from writing it, but honesty obliges us to confess that some—we had almost written many—of our females, of low caste of course, are addicted to this degrading habit. Among them we have witnessed scenes in some of the public streets, and in the open daylight, which we dare not describe. Some of our provincial papers contain almost daily, statements of fines and imprisonments, inflicted upon men and women for the oft-repeated and disgusting sin of drunkenness.

In the years 1859 and 1860, the quantity of strong drink imported amounted to 1,143,003 gallons, the declared value of which was £327,080 sterling; the ordinary revenue of the colony for those years was £441,552 sterling, of which the sum of £211,765 sterling was paid into the customs' house as duty on strong drink, making 46 per cent. of the whole revenue of the colony. The public house and its victims form the chief blot on our colonial character, and is the greatest hindrance to our social, moral, and religious welfare; but—we blush to write it —it has been among the chief sources of our public revenue.* How cutting—and cutting because they are true—are the lines of our national bard in reference to our public houses.

> " 'Tis here they learn
> The road that leads from competence and peace
> To indigence and rapine : till at last
> Society, grown weary of the load,
> Shakes her encumbered lap, and casts them out.

* Since this chapter was written the importation of strong drinks has been fearfully increased, as may be seen in the chapter on the growth of the colony. In the year 1864 the Customs' Revenue was £592,346, of which £337,942 was paid as duty on strong drink.

But censure profits little.   Vain the attempt
To advertise in verse a public pest,
That, like the filth with which the peasant feeds
His hungry acres, stinks and is of use.
Th' Excise is fattened with the rich result
Of all this riot ; and ten thousand casks,
For ever dribbling out their base contents,
Touch'd by the Midas fingers of the state,
Bleed gold for Ministers to sport away.
Drink and be mad then ; 'tis your country bids!
Gloriously drunk, obey the important call,
Her case demands the assistance of your throats ;—
Ye all can swallow, and she asks no more."

The sum expended by the working population in strong drink is very large ; but the amount of money which is spent is the least evil ; the health, character and eternal welfare of the soul, are sold for strong drink.   The home of the drunkard is made miserable, his wife is wretched, and his children, uneducated and unblest, seek a home elsewhere, as soon as they are able, and deem themselves happy if they can forget the persons whom in other circumstances they would have delighted to honour.   This vice is not confined to town life exclusively, for some fearful scenes of Bacchanalian revelry are witnessed in the country.   Port wine and other expensive drinks are sometimes dispensed there in common buckets, and drunk by companies of bush men out of tin mugs.   Casks of spirituous liquors are tapped and made common property.   If this book falls into the hand of any persons who have been overcome by this vice, let the affectionate and earnest entreaty of the writer prevail that they do not in future touch, taste, or handle the unclean thing ; and let all persons who think of seeking a home in the colonies remember that it is only the sober man who is likely to succeed.

As the result of drunkenness, a number of ragged, dirty, un-cared-for children are found in our towns, and when hunger has made them urgent for food, their unnatural parents have beaten them, and ordered the miserable little creatures to steal to allay their hunger. We have known children burnt to death while their parents were lying in the same room, too drunk to attempt to quench the flames which were consuming the flesh of their own offspring! Scenes almost as revolting as are found in the dens of London have been witnessed in some of the crowded lanes and alleys of our New Zealand towns. We dare not describe those which have met our own eyes in some of our attempts to rescue these sons and daughters of dissipation and misery. From such objects it was most natural to turn away and weep. Praiseworthy efforts have been made in several places to gather the outcast children of such parents into ragged schools, and in others, to bestow upon them the care, and provide for them the necessaries of life, so that they may grow up to fill places of honour and respectability. In some instances the parents also have been rescued from their vice and misery, have entered upon a career of industry and respectability, which their education and natural abilities had fitted them to fill, and have been admitted into the Church of Christ, examples of the power of divine grace.

But our town life has its lights as well as its shadows, its pleasant scenes as well as its painful ones. Means have been used to deliver them who all their lifetime had been subject to evil. Society is seen in many pleasing, helpful, and holy forms. The crying evil of the day is met by praiseworthy efforts to arrest its course, by establishing Temperance Societies and Bands of Hope. By their aid, many adults have become sober, and many young people prevented from acquiring a vicious taste. To make the Band of Hope more interesting, to communicate useful knowledge, and to foster the best feelings of our nature, instructive lectures, suitable to the juvenile mind, have been delivered, the curiosities of the magic lantern displayed, and occasional festivals have been held. On these joyous occasions, it is difficult to repress a feeling of admiration and pride as the procession, formed of several hundreds of happy children, the hope of the colony, preceded by a band of music playing temperance melodies, and banners floating in the breeze, march out of town for a few hours' appropriate recreation.

The lovers of music and song form themselves into societies for both instrumental and vocal exercises. Young persons are admitted into classes, which are conducted by efficient teachers, and proceed from the first efforts by which the notes are distinguished through the several pleasing gradations, till they can take their part in the rehearsals of the masterpieces of the age. The evenings devoted to these rehearsals are generally joyous ones, and the occasional concerts—chiefly for sacred music—are very attractive.

The religious societies which are the moral glory of Great Britain, are found here, breathing the same spirit, and doing similar work. Among these, the auxiliaries of the British and Foreign Bible Society may be mentioned first, as their object is to spread abroad through the colony—as into other lands, when opportunities may be offered—the sacred Scriptures, as the foundation of our Christian hope. Colporteurs are engaged, by whom the Word of God has been introduced into hundreds of the darkest and most wretched families. Annual meetings, at which his Excellency the Governor sometimes presides, are held, and interesting reports of the circula-

tion of the Word of God are read. This colony is spe-
cially indebted to the Bible Society of London. They
supplied the natives of New Zealand with the Scriptures;
from them not a few grants were made of the same precious book to the struggling colonists in their early days;
and it is therefore with a peculiar pleasure that we can
now join our hands with our fathers and brethren in the
opposite hemisphere in spreading more widely the first
Book which was written and the last that will be read.

Hallowing seasons are occasionally enjoyed, when
brethren from distant lands relate the great things which
God has done by them among the heathen. Sometimes
natives of this country, men who are intrusted with a
place in the Christian ministry, address an attentive
assembly, composed of the white race—their language
being interpreted by a missionary—on the great change
which has passed over their race through the influence
of the Gospel. To such converts from heathen darkness
and vice, the men of God who risked their lives on the
high places of the field can point with holy and grateful
feelings, and say—"These are our epistles, known and
read of all men; written, not with ink, but by the
Spirit of the living God." The state of the islands
studding the bosom of the wide Pacific ocean is often
considered, and a strong desire is felt to carry to their
people the bread of life. Something has been already
done in this direction, not only in providing funds, but
in supplying missionaries; for the high honour of occupying a place in the noble missionary band—whose
labours are to be followed, we trust, by the overthrow
of idols through every group of islands, and by multitudes of converted souls—belongs to some Christian
men and women who were lately numbered among the
colonists of New Zealand. Missionary ships sail from

our ports, and after a long cruise among the Polynesian and Melanesian Islands, return with tidings of trials and success.

The union of Christian Churches, without uniformity in the *modus operandi*, is a pleasing feature in our town life. From a paper now lying before us, we quote the following advertisement of meetings for special prayer, and addresses on important subjects, the objects being —" The attainment of a higher standard of holiness by the people of God.—A large increase of true conversions, especially in the families of believers.—The speedy overthrow of all false religions, and the full accomplishment of the prayer ' Thy kingdom come.'—A large outpouring of the Holy Spirit upon all pastors and Churches, upon all seminaries of Christian learning, upon all Protestant missionaries among Jews and Gentiles, and upon their fields of labour.—Thanksgiving for past revivals, and the solemn responsibility resting on every Christian to spend and be spent in making known the name of the Lord Jesus at home and abroad." In those truly devout and admirable exercises, the Presbyterian, Baptist, Independent, Wesleyan, and Primitive Methodist Churches were united; and at the close of the services the members of these Churches sat down together at the Table of the Lord, recalling to mind the prayer of Christ—" That they all may be one; and that the world may believe that Thou hast sent Me."

Additional interest is occasionally felt when a young man, who has previously given himself to the Lord, is ordained to the work of the Christian ministry. The statement of his conversion to God, his early efforts in the Sabbath school and tract distribution, his desire of further usefulness and fear of unfitness, the anxious feelings with which he devotes himself to the service of the Church, under the impression that he is called by the Holy Ghost to preach the gospel; followed by the laying on of the hands of the Presbytery, and the ordination charge, given by one who understands the devices of Satan, the consolations of the Holy Spirit, and the means by which the work of God is wrought; and the prayer, in which the congregation heartily join, for the divine blessing to rest upon the young minister, to keep him from evil, to guide him into all truth, and to grant him much success in the conversion of souls to Christ, and in building up the Church of God; make deep and gracious impressions, that are not likely soon to be defaced. Sometimes the religious interest is excited by the consecration of one who has been tried and found faithful to the responsibilities and honour of a bishop. And if anything can add to the interest of such proceedings it is when the person who is to be received into the gospel ministry belongs to the Maori race; presenting in a striking manner the contrast between the savage cruelty and heathen darkness of his fathers and the decided and satisfactory results which have in many instances followed the labours of the devoted missionary.

Sabbath-schools are common in New Zealand. They were commenced in the earliest days of the colony, the *raupo whare*, the humble cottage, and, if I mistake not, the open air, were the places where they were first held. Such is the value attached to them that it may not be easy to find a village where they are not conducted. Groups of children are seen every Sunday pursuing the path among the thick trees, listening with delight to the deep-toned notes of the Tui-tui and other birds on their way to the school-house, and in the open country the scene is not less interesting; but it is in the towns that the Sunday-school becomes most efficient, that the knowledge communicated is most varied, and that the success which has attended such an institution has been most marked. Not only are large numbers of *children* convened in the school, but Bible classes are established for *young men* and *young women*; the object of which is to impart instruction of a superior order, relating to the contents of the sacred Scriptures, the persons who wrote them, the character, circumstances, and influence of the people to whom each portion was originally given, together with the doctrines revealed, and the effects which they are to produce upon the world. In these exercises hundreds of persons are earnestly engaged, some of whom are advanced in life and deeply experienced in the things of God, others are young, buoyant with hope, and delighting in their work. The anniversary gatherings of these youthful bands are generally days of rejoicing; but times of joy are often times of danger, and it must be confessed that the boundaries of decorum have been sometimes overstepped on these occasions. Such things, however, have rarely occurred, but pleasure and profit have been found by both parents and children. As an illustration of the interest which is felt in this department of Christian labour, it may be stated that large sums of money are annually raised at the anniversaries, to be expended in conducting the schools, providing libraries, and other things to increase their efficiency. At the last anniversary of the Sunday School in charge of the writer, by no means among the largest in the colony, upwards of forty pounds sterling were raised.

Beautiful and substantial churches, belonging to various denominations, have been built; and some now in the course of erection are still more valuable. They vary in size, and style, and cost; some being erected for a few hundred pounds, and others costing as many thousands. Those which were erected some years since are undergoing enlargement, and many noble expressions of liberality are made in connection with them; yet it is found difficult to keep up with the growth of the colony, so as to find church accommodation for all the community.

Bazaars are held to provide funds for church extension, or some philanthropic object. The spare hours of many months being spent by ladies in preparing materials for sale, and the time for admitting the public to inspect their handiwork, is anticipated with pleasure. The most convenient places are tastefully fitted up, useful articles and products of refined taste are arranged for sale, choice specimens of fruits and flowers are presented, in some instances views of foreign cities and other places have been arranged with consummate art, and stalls loaded with the most enticing articles of the pastrycook secure attention. There may be some things connected with them to which a fastidious taste might demur; but they have secured general favour, and resulted in profits varying from one hundred to seven hundred pounds sterling.

The soirée is a common form of social intercourse. It is occasionally suffered to degenerate into objectionable proceedings; but, generally, it is so conducted as to afford both pleasure and profit. At many of them, addresses are delivered on subjects of social, benevolent, and religious interest; instrumental and vocal music is introduced; prayer and praise are offered to God; and under the influence of such gatherings, many find the best feelings of their nature improved.

The Young Men's Christian Association, conducted after the manner of the noble institutions bearing its name in England, has been successfully tried in several parts of the colony. In connection with, or rather as a part of it, Reading Rooms have been provided, the nucleus of a good library formed, and the leading journals and reviews of the day procured. In some of them, arrangements are made to supply refreshments at a small cost, so that the young men who are strangers in the place may have as few reasons as possible to visit the public house. These institutions have been made a blessing to many young men on their arrival in the colony, and have called forth the grateful expressions of their parents from the other side of the earth. Not the least important feature is the Discussion Class, in which the mind is sharpened, and the intelligent youth enabled to prepare himself for the place which he may soon be called, by the providence of God, to fill. The courses of lectures which have been delivered in several successive years, by clerical and literary gentlemen, have been the means of directing the attention of the community to subjects of importance and interest; and to meet the wants of all classes of youth, the means of instruction in many branches of science have been gratuitously provided during several evenings of the week. In our description of the working of these excellent associations, we have had principally in view the one which was established in Auckland some years ago, simply because it was best known to us. We learn, with much regret, that it has lately met with some serious reverses. The buildings in which its operations were carried on have been destroyed by fire, involving, we believe, considerable loss to the Society; and perhaps a still heavier blow was given to it by the present New Zealand war, by which large numbers of young men have been drawn from the town, their habits injured, and their minds dissipated. But we hope that, before long, this useful institution will be found again in working order.

Of the formation of Ragged Schools we have already spoken. Their necessity, in some of our towns, none can dispute, and their usefulness, where they have been fairly tried, none can deny. Ladies' Benevolent Societies, whose object is to search out and relieve persons whom affliction and misfortune have placed in circumstances of want, have done much good. In connection with them, medical dispensaries have been provided, and visits of physicians have been gratuitously and cheerfully made.

Mechanics' Institutes, which have been found of great use in England, among the means by which the mind of inquiring youth has been instructed, and the phenomena of nature explained, have been introduced, with various success, into the colonies. In connection with them, lectures are delivered, chemical experiments made, libraries formed, and reading-rooms provided. Where they do not secure the support of the public, and accomplish the purposes which they are designed to do, it is probably owing to the want of a few leading minds, of sufficient leisure, earnestness and tact, to turn circumstances in their favour, and present the desired benefits in their most improved form.

We are sorry to add that dancing classes, balls, and similar scenes of gaiety, are too prevalent. Young men and girls, who can scarcely write their names—some of them, we suppose, really not able to do so—are spending their evenings, and paying their money, to learn to dance ! Balls are given by both the gentry and the working-classes, till the dissipation of mind is fearful, and health is injured. In some cases, death has been induced by the sudden change from the heated ball-room to the cold and piercing night air; and in others, the mind has been turned from sober, useful studies, to the exciting and dangerous exercises which we unhesitatingly condemn.

The preceding pages show that both good and evil influences are at work in the nascent towns and cities of New Zealand; but it is satisfactory to know that, however powerful the influences of evil are, those which proceed from God and lead to Him are more mighty. The former must decrease ; their days are numbered, although they may flourish awhile ; but the influences of sobriety, truth, and holiness will become brighter and wax stronger, till our race shall be regenerated, and the kingdom of Christ shall come in all its glory. Much of the grosser forms of dissipation in our principal seaports are occasioned by the loose habits of many seamen, who seek enjoyment, after a long voyage, in the forbidden paths of revelry. The Church of Christ owe much to this class of men, for by them we are supplied with all the luxuries and many of the necessaries of life, and more attention should be paid to their spiritual welfare than is generally done. In some of our ports, the Bethel flag is hoisted, and the Gospel is preached. Some of our ships regard the Sabbath with propriety, but others contrive to make it a day of common work. The public means of grace are much prized by seamen who fear

God, after being prevented, by a long voyage, from join-
ing in such hallowing exercises.   May the time come
when every ship shall be a Bethel, and every sailor a
Christian.

The *moral character* of some of our towns is not a little
affected by the newly-arrived persons, who intend to find
their way into the country after a few weeks' enjoyment
of town life.   Means of gratifying their inclinations are
not wanting, if vice is their object; for it must be confessed, that those who pander to the lovers of pleasure
are more in earnest, and manifest more tact and wisdom
than are usually shewn by people who advocate an
honourable and holy course of life.   Were Christians
more careful to seek the welfare of strangers, they might
be more useful.   Forgetting that " some have entertained
angels unawares," we act as though a free and loving
spirit is constantly in danger of imposition.   But this
is observed chiefly in our towns.   In country life it is
the reverse; there a social and genial heart is thrown
open to the stranger, and forms one of the refreshing
and happy features of rural life.

It must not be forgotten, that our towns have arisen
from the wilderness in our own day.   Their promising
institutions are only in their infancy, and have been
formed under the pressure which every one has felt while
seeking to gain his proper place.   To profess the order,
and strength, and wisdom of maturity were preposterous ;
for our plans and efforts are but buds of promise, which
we hope will in due time break forth into bloom, and
bear goodly fruit.   We do not forget that sin is hydra-
headed, and that a strong arm is needed to break its
power.   Of this we are reminded by the numbers that
are confined in our prisons, by some of the patients who

fill our lunatic asylums, and by the gallows which ends the earthly career of a few of our criminals. Possibly, these things may increase, but much may undoubtedly be done to prevent that increase, by the use of judicious means. The call to action is loud, and should be answered by every one who feels an interest in his brother's welfare.

Town life is proverbial for sharpening the business faculties. This is often carried too far in the colonies, so that a stranger mingling for a short time only with many of our merchants and tradesmen would be ready to conclude that every man is a supplanter. Thrown upon their own resources, surrounded by new objects, and cherishing a hope that they may raise themselves to competence, and perhaps to wealth, give our men of business the air of haste and impetuosity. Some of them become the leaders of our social and political progress, and earn for themselves a good degree. The political constitution of the colony gives every man who possesses a freehold, or is a householder, a share in its management. Any man of parts and influence may be elected to serve his country in the House of Representatives, or in the Legislative Council. Further still, he may find his way into the Cabinet of the Governor, and sustain the office of Prime Minister. It need not, therefore, be a subject of wonder that our political elections are accompanied by disorderly proceedings. Our towns, as the principal polling places, then exhibit scenes of excitement, which the plain and homely speeches from the hustings may tend to increase. These are often followed by political dinners, at which loyal toasts are given, and much is done towards healing the wounds which have been recently inflicted.

In the town life of New Zealand there is much to praise, and not a little to condemn ; it might be both much better and much worse. We have tried to give the emigrant reader such a view of it, that he may not be mistaken on his arrival, that he may be on his guard against the seductive invitations of vice, that he may seek out places of safety and profit, and that he may find among the Churches of New Zealand the peace which passeth understanding. It is probable that neither the evils nor the honours are to be found in every town of the colony to the extent of our description ; but they exist as we have shewn them in some of our cities —they exceed our description in others, and are found more or less in all.

CHAPTER XII.

THE religious features of the colony of New Zealand is, in some respects, the most important; as the religion of a people, underlying the general current of their thought and actions, determines their moral character, and forms an object of appeal in everything affecting their conscience. The religious doctrines and practices prevailing here have not had to work their way up from the errors of heathenism, and through the difficult and dangerous courses which marked the early progress of religion in the mother country. For the heathenism which dishonoured these islands, in the practices of the Maories, could not, of course, affect the character and the conduct of the settlers, except in an indirect and limited manner. With the commencement of the first settlements, the Christian religion was introduced; with their spread, it has increased; and as they cover the land with the effects of civilization, foremost and prominent in every respect will be the religion of their judgment, their conscience, and their heart. Some persons may affect to see no necessary connexion between the religion of a country, and the happiness and progress of its inhabitants; but we think that it does not require an extraordinary faculty of penetration to see that, where religion is most free, and the Bible unfettered, society is most fully developed, the land is better cultivated, commercial enterprise is better sustained, education is more general, and the political institutions are more liberal.   It were easy to point out portions of the earth, possessing every natural advantage—a fruitful soil and lovely scenery, sunny skies and a salubrious climate, noble rivers and goodly harbours—whose inhabitants are withered by forms of false religion, in consequence of which their industry is checked, and poverty and wretchedness are their portion.   And in other countries, where Christianity is professedly maintained, but so maintained that the traditions and superstitions of men really supersede the commandments of God, the effects are traced in the moral character and political disquietude of the people.   Wealth, pleasure, and fame may appear to have made their home there; but beneath these smoulders the fire of national dissatisfaction, ready to burst into a flame at any time, and involve the people in the horrors of a civil war.

The quietude of Great Britain while almost all the continent of Europe was shaken by political convulsions a few years ago, was owing, we presume, in no small measure, to her religion.   On this account, principally, the great work of colonizing the waste and distant places of the earth may have been committed to our race, in the providence of God; so that, wherever a British colony may be erected, there, not only the advantages of civilization may be introduced, but also an enlightened literature, and religion in its power and freedom fully enjoyed.

The importance of true religion to the prosperity of a people is not invalidated by a reference to the fearful, protracted, and unnatural war which has been lately maintained in the United States of America; for the foul blot of slavery there—that unhappy institution, which lay like an incubus upon all that was fair and promising in their industrial and political pursuits, was seen in darker features still as it spread its influence over their religion.

The colonies which we are planting at the present day must be religious, to correspond with the laws, customs, and character of the parent country; and their religion must be of the Protestant stamp, to echo back the great truths for which our fathers died, and which we are appointed to maintain. Our religion must be a living power, operating in the heart and in the life, so as to move in accordance with the strong pulsations of the religious life of our native land. In this respect, we have many advantages over the colonies which were planted by powerful, but heathen nations. The legions of Rome carried their gods with them into Britain; and remains of altars, with inscriptions to Jupiter, Mars, Apollo, Mercury, among many others, are still found in different parts of the country. *We*, as colonists, carry *our* religion with us. It is indicated by our churches and chapels, it moulds the character of our children and enlightens their minds, it is our safeguard in this life, and our hope for the life which is to come.

But in her colonizing efforts, England is not free from reproach; for, notwithstanding her religious professions and advantages, much remains to be done before the majority of her people, either in the parent country or in the colonies, can be referred to as satisfactory examples of spiritual religion. Yet the restraining influence of Christianity permeates all classes of society; it forms a fair and useful character in numberless instances, where the heart remains unchanged; it gives rise to innumerable efforts of a benevolent kind, which lessen the misery of the poor and afflicted; it controls the Parliament, and guides the magistracy in the execution of the laws; it rescues the fallen ones from the streets, enters the cell of the felon, and may accompany the criminal to the gallows; its influence is felt in the nursery, the schoolroom, the farm, and the workshop; it is found in festive scenes, in the house of mourning, and on the bed of death. True religion produces righteousness, peace, and joy in the Holy Ghost; furnishes fresh motives for the pursuit of all that is lovely and of good report, and prepares the soul for a higher and holier state in the world to come.

The foremost place in the religious history, and in the present efforts of the colony to reach all classes, is due to the Church of England. The first missionary settlers, who risked their lives in their arduous undertaking, belonged to its communion. When the colonial settlements were formed, clergymen were appointed to administer the ordinances of religion, and both their labours and self-denial are worthy of all praise. Being first in the field, and having gained extensive influence among the native tribes, the missionaries of the Church of England rendered important assistance to the Government in the commencement of the colony; and in all the changes which have taken place, its ministers have been ready to act their part, and have won the esteem of all classes. In addition to the towns, clergymen of the English Church are located in villages and country districts, and cheerfully conform to the circumstances of the people among whom they labour. Many of them have acted as schoolmasters for several hours in the day, and cases we could name in which the usefulness of others has been lessened by the insufficient stipend allowed for the support of their families.

During the administration of Dr. Selwyn as Bishop of New Zealand, the Church made rapid progress. It is now divided into several dioceses, presided over by as many Bishops, with a Metropolitan at their head. Among the clergymen, some intelligent and tried Maories have found a place ; but the natives forming their charge have been scattered in the late war, and, worse still, have dishonoured their race by the adoption of a cruel, and base, and most revolting form of heathenism. Visiting clergymen have been suggested, as the best means of reaching the scattered population in some parts of the country ; but we fear that the want of funds will prevent the object from being efficiently carried out. In some places, Lay Readers have been appointed to conduct public worship, and we have seen a happy influence stealing over the people as the result of such labours.

As the status of the Church of England in the colonies is the same as that of other religious denominations—there being no Church Establishment—special provisions have been made for its support and management. Under the title of " The Church of New Zealand "—which is little regarded among the people—dioceses have been formed, Bishops have been consecrated, and Synods have been held. But no alteration has been made in the order of Divine worship, as prescribed in the Book of Common Prayer, its refreshing Litany,·its Services for Baptism, Marriages, and Deaths. Some of the clergy are supposed to hold High Church sentiments ; but we know of none who have copied the ritualism which has been practised in some churches in England, and very recently Dr. J., nominated to the See of Dunedin, was refused on ritualistic grounds.

While we cheerfully accord to the clergy our meed of praise, and admire the energy and usefulness of their first Bishop, we regret that his lordship's views on ecclesiastical matters should be so exclusive as to ignore the labours of other ministers, as being only those of laymen. This, however, is not the case with all the clergy, for, throwing the notion of the Apostolical succession, as held by ultra-Churchmen, to the winds, they are ready at all times to unite with their brethren of other Churches in every good enterprise and work.

Next in order is the Wesleyan Church, which sprang out of the mission which had been commenced and carried on among the Maori people. The senior ministers did much to secure the good-will of the natives towards the Government in its infancy, and many long and toilsome journeys, and, we may add, dangerous ones too, have they cheerfully undertaken to act as interpreters, or as the mediators of peace, when the newly-formed settlements were completely within the power of the Maories. No one doubted their helpful influence in those early days, and it ought not to be forgotten now. To the Wesleyan Church the early settlements were indebted for soul-refreshing services, especially by those who were not accustomed to the Church of England, before ministers of other denominations had commenced their labours. Being in the field when the first immigrants arrived, they had the opportunity of laying a good foundation, and of building up their church as the colony enlarged its borders. Nor have they neglected these opportunities, but the same energy which distinguishes the Wesleyan Church in England, has resulted in the appointment of their ministers to the most important places in the colony.

Some of their senior ministers, after labouring many years among the natives, have entered into the colonial work, owing to the effects of the war, or to a wish to place their families in English society; and others, who have laboured long and faithfully, and risked much, have fallen back into the superannuated class, to work according to their strength, while they watch the onward movements of younger men, and give them the advantage of their experience. Several day-schools, of the Wesleyan order, have been admirably conducted, and young men trained in them have entered upon a successful missionary career. Other schools, of lower pretensions, are placed within reach of the poorer classes, and their Sunday Schools are a power in the colony.

The Presbyterian Church has struck its roots deep into the colony, particularly in the Auckland and Otago provinces. A few congregations belong to the Church of Scotland, but the great body of Presbyterians are in connexion with the Free Church. Many of the most enterprising merchants belong to this communion, and their wealth and influence have contributed to place the Church of their earliest associations in its present prominent position. For some years, a difficulty was felt in the fact that many persons, who had been members of different Presbyterian Churches in the fatherland, were unwilling to ignore their respective peculiarities; but this difficulty has been, to a great extent, overcome in the hearty, earnest manner in which their high and holy calling is pursued. The Presbyterian Church has made the colony its debtor for the educational establishments which gather in the children of the working classes, and secure a collegiate training for the youth of the refined and opulent classes.

Congregational Churches have been planted in most
of the provinces. They are earnest, respectable, and
influential, and are true to the enlightened voluntary
principles which have won for them a high place in
Great Britain. But, so far as we know, these Churches
are not fairly distributed. Within seven miles of Auckland, there were lately five Independent Churches, while
in other populous parts of the colony there are none. A
few Baptist Churches have been formed; but they are
not numerous, although members of the Baptist denomination are found everywhere.

The Primitive Methodist Connexion has had three
stations in the North Island for many years, and their
labours have been followed by numerous converts,
brought from the service of Satan to that of the living
God. Large and handsome chapels have been erected
in the towns, and a number of smaller ones in country
places. Hundreds of children are taught in their Sunday-schools, and day-schools have been formed for the
most neglected and needy. Influential congregations
have been gathered, from which some young men have
gone forth into the ministerial field, and others are
preparing to follow. Requests have been frequently
made for ministers of the Primitive Methodist body in
other parts of the colony, and we know of none where
their labours would not be thankfully received.

Within the last few years, the United Methodist Free
Churches have planted missions in Canterbury, Westland,
and Hawke's Bay, where a fair prospect of usefulness is
opening out before them. The angles of separation,
which are less acute in England than they were, are
hardly discernible here. But although they have no
distinctive principles to maintain in New Zealand, the

still greater work of preaching the Gospel to a perishing world invites their characteristic energy and faithfulness.

A large body of persons, calling themselves " Christians," and repudiating every other distinctive name, are found in most parts of the colony. Some truly excellent and highly respectable families are numbered among them. We admire their devotedness, and bear cheerful testimony to their usefulness, which would have been much greater, in our estimation, if their labours had been directed chiefly to the unconverted, instead of disturbing the minds of members of other Churches on controverted and minor points.

In some of our towns, institutions of the Ragged School kind have been tried with some success. Open-air services have been conducted in the most public places, by ministers of various Churches, for the purpose of attracting the careless and profane, and Divine Service has often been held on board ships lying in our harbours, with the hope of doing good to a class of men to whom our colonies are so largely indebted.

The religious denominations which we have mentioned are the principal Protestant churches now labouring in the colony. Some ministers of other churches, both from Great Britain and Germany, commenced their labours here many years ago; but some of them not meeting with the success which they had anticipated, and a door being open to them into other denominations, they became enrolled as ministers in the churches already named. It will be acknowledged that if the churches now engaged in New Zealand were brought into a holy alliance, with funds and agents necessary to reach all other classes, in every part of the colony, to follow the woodman into the bush, the gold-seeker in the diggings, the shepherd on his extensive plains, and to fix their residence in the midst of the new towns and villages, which the sons and daughters of enterprise are occupying, the religious prospect of the colony would be very encouraging. It is to be regretted that the distribution of religious agency cannot be more equally determined. Most of the towns are well supplied, a few of them are more favoured with ministerial labour than some towns having a similar population are in England; while many of the country places are destitute of regular public worship. We admit the importance of taking hold of the centres of population by every denomination, but we deprecate the little attention which is paid to the sparsely peopled districts. For this work the itinerant system is probably the best; we cannot see how the wants of the scattered community can be supplied by a different course. Men of robust health, capable of sustaining much fatigue, abounding in zeal for the salvation of souls, and being full of faith and of the Holy Ghost, would, with God's blessing, be of unspeakable benefit to the colony. Praiseworthy efforts have been made in districts, with encouraging success; but others are so far lying waste, that some families do not see a Christian minister for many months together. Nor can the great want of the country be supplied by the ministers whose chief work lies in the towns, without neglecting the souls which form their special charge.

The importance of a much larger supply of Christian agency will be apparent if we consider the sad effects which result from the want of the means of grace. We are sorry to state that in many instances of this kind the Sabbath is not religiously observed, the heart becomes hard, the pleasures of sense absorb the attention, and

God is forgotten, Many families, who were respectable members of churches in their native country, lose their reverence for the house of God, the children are brought up without proper training, and while God in His mercy blesses them with temporal favours, and all the appearances of nature around them are delightful, their moral condition is truly lamentable. It has often caused us both sorrow and wonder that some persons so easily throw off their religious profession, when they enter upon their colonial life ; their object is to be rich, and whether they accomplish their purpose or not, "they that will be rich fall into a temptation and a snare." There is much of this to be seen in the towns, but still more in the country, especially in those parts where the worship of God is not publicly maintained. We have seen men reaping in their fields, or otherwise employed, on the Lord's day ; but our approach had so much disconcerted them, that they hid themselves till we had passed by.

Our remarks have been confined to the Protestant churches labouring in the colony ; we must now mention the Roman Catholic Church. A large portion of the population in some of our provinces belong to this communion ; they came principally from Ireland, but both England and Scotland have furnished a small number. The Roman Catholic mission was formed before the erection of the colony, therefore the priests were ready to welcome the members of their community on their arrival, and to provide for them the means of public worship. The exclusiveness which characterizes the clergymen of the Romish Church in other Protestant countries is seen here, and the same care is taken to prevent books bearing the Protestant stamp—even common school books—from falling into the hands of their children. The head of the Roman Catholic Church in New Zealand is the Right Rev. Bishop Pompallier; after spending many years in active service in this hemisphere, he visited Europe, for the purpose of stirring up attention towards New Zealand. In February, 1861, he returned to Auckland with an additional staff of seventeen priests and four persons to assist the Sisters of Mercy, who had been for some years engaged in the colony. A public demonstration in honour of the Bishop was attempted. Numbers walked in procession to St. Patrick's Cathedral, where the choir sang the antiphon *Ecce Sacerdos Magnus* and the usual genuflexions were performed.

The activity of the Roman Catholic Church is admirable. The priests are found in the wards of the hospital, in the cell of the felon, in the cottages of the poor, and in the houses of the rich. Their children are taught in schools conducted by Sisters of Mercy. Some of their clergy are stationed in the towns, some in country places, and others travel about over extensive portions of the provinces. There are two Bishops, four vicars-general, and thirty-three priests engaged in the country, partly among the Maories and partly among the colonists. More than half the number of priests are we believe Frenchmen, and many of them speak English with difficulty; yet their influence among their own people is considerable, and will no doubt make a deep impression upon the future character of the colony. Not that we suppose many Protestant families will go to their communion—we have known some to do so—but the number of Catholic immigrants will probably be considerable, furnishing sufficient materials for the peculiarities of Roman Catholicism.

In concluding this description of the religious aspect of the colony we wish to express our gratitude for the amount of Christian influence which has been diffused over the country, and the increase of spiritual life which is apparent in some places, but at the same time we deeply deplore the fact that large numbers of the people are not careful to improve their gracious advantages—and we earnestly pray for an out-pouring of the Holy Spirit, that through His influences the desert may blossom as the garden of the Lord.

An excellent staff of ministers is already in the field, but as the number of immigrants is likely to increase very largely in future years, special means being used to accomplish this purpose, the number of Gospel ministers must be increased also, or the spiritual condition of the colony will be sad. But in saying this it must not be inferred that we confine our views and hopes of Christian agency to regularly appointed ministers; for there are hundreds of men and women engaged, each class in its proper sphere, in doing a great and glorious work. Numbers of laymen, of approved character and abilities, preach the Gospel to devout assemblies. Sunday School Teachers are happy in their blessed and successful work. Tracts are distributed from house to house by others ; and the man of God, though aspiring to office in the Church, is often found at the bedside of affliction and death. So important are the exercises of the office-bearers and members of the churches, that we wish those exercises were speedily increased and rightly directed, both on account of the churches already instituted and of the world which is still "lying in wickedness." But as we generally find that the lay-agency loses its power, if it be not, more or less, connected with the regularly appointed ministry, our prayer should be, that God may speedily send forth more ministerial labourers into the colonial field.   U

WE now enter upon a subject which recent events have made painfully interesting—the discontentment of the natives at the increase of the colony. A few shrewd men, it is said, had their fears from the first that the Pakehas would become the dominant race, and that the native people would melt away before them, as the natives of other colonial lands had done. At the same time, so many advantages were perceived in connection with the settlements of the white race, that the latter became a desirable acquisition; for their settlements provided a market for native produce, and supplied the newly-found wants of the people. So great was the confidence reposed in the Maories, that many of the houses of the settlers had no locks or bolts to their doors in lonely places. Their property was then rarely stolen, and their persons still more rarely assaulted. After some years, suspicions spread among the tribes, almost imperceptibly, as the white people increased in number, new townships were laid out, and extensive districts became covered with the results of industry. Some looked on with silent misgivings, and others expressed their regret that their chiefs had invited settlements among their respective tribes. But no one among the colonists thought that these discontented feelings would result in any serious consequences, nor that they would continue long. The Maories had made rapid progress in the common usages of civilization. Their food and raiment had undergone a great change; in cattle and horses many of them had become rich; their produce was generally conveyed to town in bullock carts, instead of being carried on their backs; and some of them adopted the dress and air of colonial gentlemen—their boots shining with Day and Martin's blacking, their hands covered with kid gloves, and either a cane or umbrella under their arm. The female natives were equally attentive to dress, purchasing hats and dresses of the newest fashions, and wearing veils, crinolines, and jewellery to correspond with those worn by the English ladies around them. It was not easy to suppose that these marks of civilization and comfort would be laid aside for the sword, their old habits, and coarse fare; and conscious of our benevolent feeling towards the native race, of the abundant room for a numerous colonial population, without curtailing the Maories of any comforts, but rather increasing them, and adding greatly to the value of their lands and of their produce, it was supposed that the last New Zealand war was ended, and that a course of peace and prosperity lay before both races.

But a more careful examination of the new circumstances into which the Maori people were brought, might have awakened our fears that discontent would follow. In the impartial administration of justice, which is the boast of our country, the natives found a cause of complaint. The chief was placed upon a level with the least man of his tribe, when his case was brought into our courts of law. It was of little use that we explained to them that justice demanded the prince and the peasant to be treated alike; this was so unlike the usages in which they had been trained, that they could not accept the custom. In some instances, they rescued their chiefs from the hands of the policemen ; and in others, their feelings were so much aroused at the idea of their chiefs being sentenced to imprisonment, that they took them by force from the bar of the Supreme Court, and set them at liberty. The reason why these strange proceedings were determined on, was to prevent the degradation which must otherwise rest upon a chief, in the eyes of all his tribe, on account of his imprisonment. These outrageous doings were overlooked by the colonial authorities, in view of the peculiar circumstances of the people, and with the hope that a better acquaintance with the principles of law and order would induce them not only to comply with our mode of administering justice, but to see the advantages of our impartial administration.

A source of discontentment was found in the treatment which some of the native females met with among a few of the colonists. The improper *liaisons* to which we refer were often formed, not only with the consent, but with the full approval of the girls' parents—who were proud of the attentions of the *pakeha*, and of the altered appearance of their daughters. But thoughtful men of their respective tribes saw many evils in this course, as the females were gradually weaned from their families and tribes, and their course of life was a direct violation of the law of God. Sometimes criminal connexions were formed with married women, and were followed by summary and severe punishments—the injured party taking away various articles of considerable value, blankets, prints, furniture, horses, &c., as *utu*. Such dishonourable conduct on the part of a few of our countrymen, did much at one time to disturb the peace of the two races ; but these things, in their worst form, are now, we hope, comparatively rare, and are condemned by all classes.

The chief subject of contention is the land. From the commencement of the colony this has caused wars and sullen contempt among the native tribes, and lies at the bottom of their surmises concerning the intentions of the Government. Before the colony was formed, the land was freely sold—very often for a small portion of merchandise. But whether the sellers were distinctly aware of the true nature of the bargain is disputed. Many contend that the idea of alienating their land from themselves and their children for ever, never entered their minds; but that they meant by it little more than a right to its occupation by the contracting parties. The idea of a right to land in New Zealand, as an article of property, by persons living in Sydney, was, no doubt, new to them. It was difficult to be comprehended; but, when understood, it became the subject of discontentment. We have no doubt that the whole question was explained, as far as possible, by the earlier missionaries, among whom were found some of the largest purchasers ; but we are not sure whether any explanation could meet the case. So completely had the land been appropriated among the tribes, before the introduction of the missionaries, that it is said by some, whose opinion is entitled to respect, that there was not an acre in the Northern Island, however barren and useless it might seem, but was held as the property of some person or tribe.

The grounds on which their claims to land were founded were often very ludicrous. They had spent a portion of their life there; their family had once a small plantation on the spot; a chief had walked over the land, and tapued it; perhaps, some years ago, a relative had died there, or a burial-ground had been made in the neighbourhood. It is easy to see that such claims to land must cause continual broils among the natives themselves, and when the land passed into the hands of the Government, the difficulties were likely to increase. The high price at which the Government sold the land to the settlers, compared with the amount which the Maories had received for it, produced dissatisfaction, the natives not taking into consideration the cost of surveys, roads, bridges, and other expenses incident to the settlement. Nor did they consider the comparative uselessness of considerable portions of some tracts which were purchased by the Government—tracts which consisted of swamps, hills, and broken ground, which no settler was likely to purchase, except at a very low price. The Act which secured to the Crown the right of pre-emption, was, we think, a mistake. The object of this policy was morally good—to prevent the natives from being wronged by interested persons; but it placed the Government in a false position, and brought forth bitter fruit. This is now acknowledged, and the Pre-emption Act is rescinded.

The causes of misunderstanding and complaint were so numerous, between people whose manners and customs were very dissimilar, that we need not be surprised at them. Neither party understood the language of the other sufficiently to explain their intentions, and many acts, which were simply national customs, were supposed to be insults. But in the nature of things, these mistakes would gradually cease, as the parties became better known to each other. In numerous instances, the differences in manners and language became the source of much merriment among the Maories. The pah often presented a lively scene on a summer evening, when the inhabitants, old and young, were squatted upon their heels, listening to the talk of a few persons who had spent most of the day in disposing of their produce among the settlers. The salesman described his journey, giving a comic account of any particular incident which had occurred, the persons of the settlers, particularly of the women, their tone of voice, their attempt to speak Maori, and the gesticulations which were called to their assistance, were so treated as to cause abundance of enjoyment.

The Maories saw the colony gradually advancing under the constant industry and skill of the settlers, whose homesteads were increasing yearly in value, beauty, and comfort. The former looked on with astonishment and delight, and often brought their friends from a distance to see the improvements of their industrious neighbours. But while the results of the *pakeha's* industry were applauded, his continual toil was deprecated. The plan of the Maori was to work hard for several weeks, or perhaps months; and then lose as much time in disputing the merits of some trifling case, or in attending a distant market, accompanied by his wife and children, to dispose of the surplus of his crops. The settlers found it necessary to keep their fences in good repair, and that pigs, especially, should be restricted in their range. This was so unlike the customs of the natives—except in the case of their most valued plantations, and during a small portion of the year only— that trespasses gave rise to much unpleasantness.

Notwithstanding the increase which has been lately made to the colonial population, the ground which is really in a state of cultivation forms but a small part of the country; yet the additional tracts which were yearly brought under the plough, or covered with herds or flocks, were sufficient to rouse the jealousy of the Maories. They revolved the idea that the white race would continue to increase, so that not a foot of land would be left for their children, until, in their imagination, no other prospect arose before them. In vain were they assured of the honest intentions of the Government; they were reminded that not one foot of land had been taken from them by force; that in every case in which their title had been extinguished they had been a willing party—for they could have kept their land had they chosen to do so; appeals were made to them on the treatment which individuals of their race had received when they visited England; and they were aware that in courts of law no favour was shewn to the pakeha; but nothing could turn their attention from the idea that they were a doomed race, if the enlargement of the colony were suffered to proceed unchecked.

The very means which the Government used to increase their knowledge, and to prepare them for a higher state of civilization, were misunderstood, and had a contrary effect. The history of England was translated and circulated among them, shewing the state of Britain at the Roman invasion, and the turbulent proceedings through which the nation passed, as they fell a prey to the Angles and Saxons, the Danes and the Normans, on their way to the high and influential position which they now occupy. The design was to breathe into the Maories a resolution to improve the superior advantages which were thrown around them. But the contrary effect, as we have said, was produced; for to their imagination the influx of a foreign people into England resembled the colony of their own country ; the warlike exploits of the ancient Britons were models of patriotism, which they would do well to imitate ; and the escape of the natural owners of the soil to the mountains of Wales and the Highlands of Scotland, while their conquerors settled down upon the rich and well-watered plains, formed a picture, in their view, of the destitute condition of the Maori people at no great distance of time, unless the progress of the colony could be stopped. A sketch of the history of Russia was translated also for their improvement, shewing particularly the steps taken by Peter the Great to raise his people in the scale of civilization, but without producing much effect. It is easy now to see that such translations were not judicious; but none could condemn while the object was praiseworthy, and no one could foresee the wrong use which would be made of them.

The native mind is very retentive of grievances, and acts of revenge, though committed many years after the cause occurred, are often marked by the darkest atrocities. This has always been one of the worst features of Maori character, and has been the occasion of numerous murders and wars. We fear that this feeling has shed its influence on the late disasters which have fallen upon the North Island; for the wars which we have briefly described were suffered to die out, instead of being brought to a proper close, leaving the native mind to subside into a sullen dislike of his pakeha neighbour, and wishing for an opportunity to avenge the wrongs which he imagined had been done to him or his race. It were difficult to end the unhappy wars in a different manner. We would not write words of blame, but that does not prevent the unhappy circumstances which followed. The avenging spirit did not die with the death of the principal actors in the early troubles, but continued to work, silently but surely, in the bosoms of their sons, who were glad of an opportunity to repay with interest the supposed wrongs which their fathers had suffered at the hands of the white race.

The real position of the native race was certainly a singular one. Called British subjects, and having the national flag waving over all their tribes, our courts of justice being open to redress their grievances, immature efforts being used to regulate their desire for law and for the general improvement of their people; there were many things which were left to the management of the respective tribes, not only things of a trivial kind, but matters of the greatest moment also; for property was appropriated, murders were committed, and inter-tribal wars were carried on, without the interference of the Government. This anomalous position was in reality provided for by the Treaty of Waitangi, by which the sovereignty of the country was transferred to Her Britannic Majesty, while the government of the native people was to remain in their own hands. This singular position of the Maories affords room for endless caveats, explanations and abuse. It includes so many points from which observations may be made, that writers of the most upright principles, men whose anxiety for the welfare of the native race no one can doubt, have arrived at opposite conclusions on some of the most important points affecting the honour of the colonial government, and the rights of the Maories. In such a complicated state of affairs, it is no wonder that errors have been committed, that a line of policy should be occasionally changed, and that a Governor should hesitate to carry out the arrangements made by his predecessor.

When Governor Grey arrived in 1846, the native mind was probably more plastic than it has been for many years since. It is true that some tribes were in a turbulent state, and that a costly war was on the eve of conclusion, but the general state of the native mind was we think in a hopeful condition. His Excellency applied himself entirely to his mission, sparing neither personal fatigue nor inconveniences; and after a short time he saw the Maori race considerably improved and the colony rising into substantial prosperity. Among the means which Govenor Grey was anxious to try, in order to introduce intelligence and a desire for skilled labour among the tribes, was the establishment of industrial schools. In this attempt advantage was taken of the influence of the mission stations, by inducing the missionaries to undertake the superintendency of these institutions, and as much as possible to become the teachers; the Government finding a considerable portion of the necessary funds, as well as supplying valuable grants of land for the purpose. Some of these institutions have been admirably conducted, and a few native youths have received the elements of a good education; but as a whole, we think that the expectation of their founders has not been answered. This is to be attributed partly to the difficulty of confining the attention of the Maori to one subject, except for a short time; so that his interest is likely to decrease, and he soon longs for the loose habits and the society to which he has been accustomed. And even if the persons brought into the industrial schools, had been aware of the advantages which were afforded, only a small number in each tribe

could have been largely benefited. The most promising
way of introducing among the native people generally,
the blessings of skilled labour and superior education,
must be by stirring up among them a strong desire to
learn, and by attaching them to the settlers for this
purpose. We know of some who have done so with
success, but the number is small, nor is there much
prospect of its being largely increased for many years
to come. It is a subject of regret that some of the young
men who have enjoyed the advantages of the schools
afore mentioned, and excited hopes of their future
superiority and influence in their tribes, were among the
foremost to oppose the Government on the breaking out
of the war ; and as the consequences of their rebellion
and ingratitude, some have been wounded or killed in
battle, and others still maintain their hostile position
against the hand that administered to their well being,
and sought to give them pre-eminence among their
people.

For some years those who watched the signs of progress
developed by the growing intelligence, industry and comfort of the native race had much cause to rejoice. The
amount of produce brought into the market was large,
they were throwing off many of their former customs
and adopting those of the colonists. In some instances
good houses, built of wood, with chimneys, windows and
doors complete, were substituted for the raupo whares,
in which they had been bred. A still greater number
dressed well in English clothing, and accustomed themselves to the use of many articles such as are in domestic
use among Europeans. Not a few of them became rich
in cattle, horses and pigs. Large fields were covered
with wheat, which was ground into excellent flour at

their own mills, and sold to the settlers at market price. The plough and the sickle were managed by themselves. No working oxen in the country were superior to theirs; not many saddle horses were better than those which they rode. Hundreds of carts were in daily use. Canoes often gave place to cutters and schooners, manned and commanded by themselves. In many persons we have observed the easy and respectful manners in which lies true politeness, the very reverse of their condition but a few years before.

Religion was prospering among the people; places of worship were erected of substantial materials, and at a considerable cost; children were gathered into schools conducted by native teachers; a few young men made such improvement in education and religious knowledge, and were so satisfactory in their conduct, that they were admitted into the Christian ministry. We by no means assert that this promising state was seen among the people generally, it was not so, but there were specimens of such improvement in different parts of the country—supplying proofs of the moral power of missionary instruction, and showing that the divine blessing had largely attended the labours of His servants.

Not supposing that the people who had manifested such signs of advancement would retrograde, the colonists looked forward to the gradual improvement of the whole race. No one had the slightest thought that war would ever disturb the happy connexion of the two races again; not that there were no indications of dissatisfaction on the part of the Maories, nor do we deny that there was cause for dissatisfaction, in the want of law and order, which our relations to them and the want of a proper system of government made it most difficult to supply;

but it was fully supposed that the benefits which they enjoyed would be a sufficient safeguard against any approach to insurrection.

This pleasing state of things was the result of the united influence of missionary and colonial society; the one was not able to accomplish it without the other, although persons belonging to each claimed the honour of having brought it about. A great mistake was made by many persons in the colony, and it is no wonder that the people of England were misled, by supposing that the leaven of order and happiness was working in every part of the country ; the contrary was the case, for fears were excited, especially among thinking men, who saw that the introduction of disease, drunkenness, and other evils, were counteracting much of the good that had been done among the tribes. It was easy to draw a lively and pleasing picture of the glorious changes which had taken place among the natives, and to exhibit the Maori as standing far above some of the colonists in many of the moralities of life. Such a picture was often drawn with much effect, and copied into valuable books, as evidence of the change which had been produced in a people so lately rescued from the horrible rites of cannibalism. The error lay in attaching the idea of such improvement to the people generally, or at least to large portions of them, when it ought in truth to have been confined to a comparative few ; and in contrasting the conduct of persons belonging to each race, for the purpose of shewing the superiority of the Christian native, the Maori was probably far in advance of many of his own people in general intelligence, and as a Christian, while the white men with whom he was compared might have been far below the common English character, or at least might have made no decided profession of religion. We yield to no man in our love for the Maori people, and the joy with which we see their advancement in knowledge, industry and religion; but we wish to correct an error which has done injury to the native people, and to the holy cause of Christian missions, by an unfair—unintentionally no doubt—exhibition of their character.

The interest which Sir George Grey took in their welfare was appreciated by many of the tribes. In their letters to him he was often called their Father, and they described themselves as his children. He came to govern the country just as it was rising out of the peculiar difficulties that had crushed it, means were placed at his disposal to attempt new measures for their good, and the prosperity which rested upon the colony shed its influences in many respects favourably upon the native race. His travels among the people, through journeys of hundreds of miles, and his knowledge of the Maori language, increased their regard for him. Not knowing anything personally of a new Governor, nor of the line of policy which he might pursue, their minds were naturally disturbed by the departure of Governor Grey, as soon as they heard that he was to leave them. Very pleasing signs of friendship were shewn by many of the chiefs and people in the latter part of the year 1853, while his Excellency was preparing to give up the seals of office, and return to England.

Deputations from various and distant parts of the country waited on the Governor, addresses were delivered, valuable heir-looms were presented, and verses were chanted. "On your arrival in this island," said a Waikato deputation, "the rain was beating, and the wind blowing fiercely; and then you lifted up your voice to calm the raging elements. Go, O father, to England, and may the Divine Being preserve you while you are voyaging on the great sea! When you go into the presence of Queen Victoria, and inquiries are made by her, say that we are blessed with peace, owing to the good Governors she has sent us." The Maories delight in mingling prose and poetry in their addresses; accordingly the deputation chanted the following verses, but of course in their own language :—

> " Cease from your strife, ye wintry blasts,
>   And let our isle be free ;
>   Then western airs shall fan the land,
>   And southern airs the sea.
>
> " And darkness shall be seen no more
>   To lift its gloomy form ;
>   And light-winged clouds shall gild the sky,
>   And calm succeed the storm."

From Rotorua, situated far inland, a goodly number of the principal men, well dressed in European costume, paid their respects also. In their address to his Excellency, they observed —" When the Missionaries first came to this land, there was little industry, and little good was visible; but there was much indolence and much wickedness, and all lived in ignorance. Then God kindled His light, and, lo! it became as day. Your efforts on behalf of God's cause were seen in the establishment of schools, and the erection of houses of prayer, thus following the footsteps of the Church; you encouraged industry in the cultivation of the soil, you pointed out the means of acquiring property, and raised this island to its present state of prosperity." Verses were then chanted in Maori style, and the following translation of some of them will be read with pleasure :—

" This pining heart the live-long day,
  O Governor, is turned to thee ;
And who will bring thee back the way
  From yonder land across the sea !

" O Grey, I'll patiently await
  Thy wish'd return, from Britain's Queen ;
Perchance I may again relate,
  That thou upon our isle art seen.

" May nought be here to give thee pain,
  O friend, in yonder sacred land ;
Since thou art not allowed to reign
  O'er Zealand's isles and Zealand's band."

   " Go, while the sun is shining,
     Great shelter of our land ;
   Go, while the hearts are pining
     Of this once savage band.

   " Go, while the winds are playing
     In gusts above our head ;
   The while our hearts are saying,
     ' He's now to us as dead.'

   " Go, and before the morrow,
     Gaze on the dark, deep sea ;
   And then these hearts, in sorrow,
     Shall whisper, ' Where is he ?' " *

To introduce the above extracts into a chapter on
Native Suspicions, may appear as a misnomer; but we
know that those expressions did not represent the state
of the native mind generally. The seeds which have
borne such bitter fruit were already sown. As early as
the year 1849, the idea of the famous Land League may
be traced ; for in that year the Ngatiruanui tribe dis-

* Extracted from the " Leisure Hour," 1860.

cussed the proposition, that no one should be allowed to sell land, except by the permission of the whole tribe. Nothing was decided at that time, except to convene a meeting of all the tribes between New Plymouth and Wellington, and the departure of a zealous Land League advocate, to visit all the people along the west coast, in order to secure their consent and assistance.

The general meeting of the tribes was held in 1854, at Manawapou, where great preparations were made. A house was built, one hundred and twenty feet long, and thirty-five feet wide—at least, such is the description given of it—for their accommodation. They boasted that this was the largest house ever built in New Zealand. It was certainly significant of their zeal, and of their intention to unite the tribes in a general cause. About one thousand persons constituted the assembly. After the usual amount of talk, they resolved :—

" I. That from this time forward, no more land shall be alienated to Europeans, without the general consent of this confederation.

" II. That in reference to the Taranaki and Ngati-ruanui tribes, the boundaries of the Pakeha shall be Kai Iwi, on the south side, and a place within a short distance of New Plymouth, on the north side.

" III. That no European magistrate shall have jurisdiction within native boundaries ; but all disputes shall be settled by the *runaga* [native Council] ."

A New Testament was then solemnly buried on the spot, and a heap of stones raised over it, to give the act the sacredness of an oath, which was to be further confirmed by appointing persons to beat the ground at stated times, so as to preserve the boundaries between the two races.*

The arguments urged on this occasion were these: That the land which their fathers occupied, should be handed down to their children as a sacred deposit; that a colonial settlement would result in the seduction of many of their young women, and lead their young men into habits of drunkenness; that the Governor would give them but a low price for their land, compared with the price at which it would be sold to the settlers; and that the Maories would sink into an inferior position, if they allowed a settlement of white men to be formed among them.

It must be confessed that some value is to be attached to these arguments. To our dishonour, let it be stated, that some of the evils dreaded by sober and thoughtful natives have almost always accompanied our colonial progress; it is, therefore, not surprising that means were taken to prevent the planting of settlements in fresh parts of the country. Nothing appears to have been said concerning the benefits which a settlement of white men would confer upon the Maories, in the increased value of the land which might be kept in their own hands, the ready market which would be provided for all their produce, the habits of cleanliness and order which their young people might acquire, and the general improvement which would eventually be the result of their connexion with a superior race. They looked at the subject from one point only, and saw but one side. Had they looked on both sides, the advantages as well as the evils would have been considered; and, while taking care to prevent the injuries dreaded, they might have been desirous to secure the benefits of colonization.

* "The Maori King Movement," by the Rev. T. Buddle, pp. 5, 6.

However much we may be disposed to sympathise with the tribes in the endeavour to preserve their young people from the vices of our settlements, our fears for their safety are aroused when we see them deliberately decline the advantages of a mission station, and of an industrial school, rather than give or sell a few acres of land for these purposes. The Ngatiruanui tribe adopted this course, in the same year that the Manawapou meeting was held. An offer was made them by the Wesleyan Missionary Society, to erect buildings for a Training Institution, if they would give or sell land for the purpose. About seventy acres were at first offered; but when an attempt was made to survey the ground, the offer was withdrawn. As the result of this, the mission was given up. This step was, we think, unhappily taken; for no one can tell how much evil might have been prevented by continuing the Ngatiruanui mission. Six years before, this mission was in a flourishing state, having five hundred and fifty accredited Church members, eight hundred and seventy week-day and Sabbath scholars, and one thousand six hundred and fifty persons attending public worship. In the annual report of the station, the resident missionary wrote as follows:—"A gracious influence has rested upon the people, in the public means of grace, at the different settlements. Those who have believed, and found peace, are encouraged to go forward, and are adorning their profession by an upright walk and conversation. Religion is the theme in the house, in the field, and in the way; and their leisure time is employed in searching the Scriptures, which they delight to understand." * The excellent missionary who wrote this

* "Wesleyan Missionary Report, 1848," p. 56.

pleasing account sleeps in the grave, undisturbed by the present insurrection and troubles of the people among whom he laboured with such promise of success; but before his removal, the signs of religious defection were very apparent. They probably deepened his affliction, and hastened his death. Not only among the Ngati-ruanui tribe did the Land League operate against the missions; but at Kawhia and Otawhao an effort was made to take back the land which had been given for the purposes of the Church and Wesleyan Missionary Societies.

Within a few months of the great meeting at Mana-wapou, when the Land League may be said to be formed, an opportunity was offered to test its reality. Rawiri Waiaua, a chief of excellent character, a true friend to the settlers, and holding an office under Government at New Plymouth, offered to sell a block of land near that town. Not belonging to the Land League, Rawiri and his men did not consider their tribe bound by the decisions of the Manawapou meeting. They disregarded, therefore, the threats of a neighbouring chief and his followers, to shoot any man who might attempt to cut a line marking the boundaries of the land intended to be sold. Rawiri and his men went to the disputed spot, with tools, to cut the boundary line. Katatore, the opposing chief, and his men, met them there, under arms. The threat was firmly repeated by the one party, and the instruments of the workmen were as coolly applied by the other party. A volley was fired into the ground, to signify their determination to prevent the cutting of the line; but, being assured in their conscience that they had a right to dispose of their own land as they pleased, the working party continued to mark the

boundary. The guns were then pointed at the unarmed
men, and a volley was fired. Rawiri and six men fell
dead, and ten others were wounded. These were the
first fruits of the Land League. The harvest, as far as
it has been reaped, has been tares instead of wheat—
disorder, ruin, and blood, instead of the blessings which
were expected from it.

The settlers became alarmed, not knowing to what
extent this unhappy feud might be carried. The natives
of the injured party flew to arms; pahs were put in
fighting order, and shots were exchanged. The Government authorities were taken by surprise, and scarcely
knew what course to take. Sir George Grey had left,
and his successor had not arrived. The Government
was administered by Colonel Wynyard, Commander of
the Forces, who shrank from carrying out a line of
policy which a Governor fully appointed might have
ventured upon. Supposing that the provisions in the
Treaty of Waitangi shielded the natives from the operation of British law in all feuds which might arise among
themselves, no steps were taken to apprehend Katatore
and his party. This was a mistake, and was followed
by very serious consequences. There were so many
circumstances of a peculiar kind in this case, that it
would, no doubt, have been right to place Katatore at
the bar of the Supreme Court, giving him the advantage
of whatever could have been said in his favour. As the
case was passed over by the Government, the natives
were confirmed in their idea, that they were British
subjects in name only, that their lives could not be
protected by the British law, and, in consequence of
this, their property was not safe. If one party might
deliberately murder another in open day, near the

principal town of the province, and surrounded by the homesteads of the settlers, and no means be used to punish the murderers, then the deed may be repeated by the friends of the deceased, without any fear of the consequences. It was natural that the natives should argue thus, and knowing their thirst for revenge, it is not surprising that a resolution was formed to murder Katatore. An opportunity was soon after afforded, and Katatore was murdered in the Queen's highway, at Bell Block, within a few yards of the settlers' houses. The authorities were now in a dilemma. To let this state of things continue was both dishonourable and dangerous, and to assert the voice of the law, and apprehend the murderers of Katatore, was a difficult thing, as it was generally known that he was killed in consequence of the Government taking no notice of the death of Rawiri, who was a Government officer when he was shot.

To protect the settlers, a detachment of the 58th Regiment was sent to New Plymouth, with orders to take no part in the native quarrel, while it was confined to the Maori people. This miserable state of affairs continued for a long time, and many men were killed, and more still were wounded, in numerous skirmishes. That this was permitted within ten miles of a garrisoned town, containing four hundred and fifty men, with two 24-pounder guns, may appear strange; but rather than risk a war between the two races, the feud was allowed to work its own destructive course. When hostilities ceased, a sullen hatred settled in the bosom of each party—and rankles there still. It has contributed not a little to the bitter feelings indulged and expressed by one tribe against another, and unless God remarkably interferes by a communication of His grace, a long time will likely pass away before the remains of this Land League quarrel in Taranaki be entirely removed.

Some of the natives have watched the advancement of the colony till in the excitement of a morbid imagination their lands were all passing into the hands of the Pakeha, while their own children were likely to be left without the necessary means of support. Statements of this kind have sometimes been made in England by respectable clergymen and others on platforms and in magazines; the colonists have been unfairly represented as overlooking the well-being of the natives, and as having nearly all their lands at this time in their possession; and it is deeply to be regretted that some persons in New Zealand, excellent men in their own sphere, have shut themselves up to the native view of the land question till they have mistaken the intentions of their fellow colonists, and have written hard things against them. To enable the reader to form a correct opinion on this subject, we will supply the following extracts from a paper which was prepared for the Government in 1861 by Charles Heaphy, Esq. :—

" The area of the Northern Island of New Zealand, the seat of three-quarters of the Maori population, is about twenty-nine million six hundred and eighty-eight thousand four hundred and eighty acres; and of this area about seven million sixty-four thousand six hundred and sixty acres are in the hands of the British, while twenty-two million six hundred and twenty-three thousand eight hundred and twenty acres remain to the natives; the latter then have an extent of land nearly equal in area to three times that which they have alienated. The numbers of each race by the last census (1861) were, of Maories fifty-three thousand and fifty-six, and of Europeans thirty-nine thousand four hundred and eighty-four. If a pressure had existed, its effects might have been looked for amongst the natives who had sold the largest proportional share of their territory, and of those the Ngatikahungunu, the Rarawa, and the Ngatiwhatua tribes are most conspicuous.

"The Ngatikahungunu tribe, of the East Coast, with a population of six thousand three hundred and thirty-nine souls, out of a territory of five million five hundred and thirty thousand two hundred and forty acres, have retained but three million twenty-five thousand four hundred and forty acres. The Rarawa tribe, at the North Cape, numbering one hundred and seven souls, has retained but two hundred and sixty-four thousand acres; and the Ngatiwhatua, in the vicinity of Auckland, with five hundred and five souls, has kept but one hundred and seven thousand five hundred and twenty acres. These tribes are friendly to the Government; they are industrious and prosperous.

"The Ngatiawa, Wirimu Kingi's tribe, hold about four hundred and sixty thousand eight hundred acres, with a population of one thousand four hundred and sixty-six souls. . . . The Taranaki and Ngatiruanui tribes inhabit the fertile and almost plain country, extending southward from the New Plymouth settlement along about ninety-seven miles of coast, from the Hauranga stream to within a few miles of Wanganui. Their population is about two thousand and forty-nine; and of a territory which comprises one million two hundred and thirty-six thousand four hundred and eighty acres, they have sold one hundred and fifty-two thousand three hundred and twenty acres; leaving themselves one million eighty-four thousand one hundred and sixty acres.

"Few tribes in New Zealand had less cause to fear the encroachment of the Pakeha than the Ngatimaniapoto at Kawhia. Out of a territory of nine hundred and forty-four thousand acres, not more than fifty-three thousand six hundred and five acres have been alienated; leaving nine hundred thousand three hundred and ninety-five acres, with a good harbour, and fifty miles of coast, to a Maori population of two thousand five hundred and eighty-five persons. . . . . The interior land of the Waikato, Waipa, and Taupo—particularly fertile and attractive, and accessible by means of rivers—is exclusively in the hands of the natives. The chiefs of the Taupo country had, at the commencement of the king movement, urged that the Europeans should be expelled the country. They and the Upper Wanganui natives afforded assistance in men, arms, and ammunition to the rebels. The Taupo and Upper Wanganui country comprises two millions eight hundred and eighty thousand acres—the white people held but two acres."

By a careful consideration of the above statement, which, we suppose, approximates very nearly to the real numbers both of persons and acres, it will be seen that the land in possession of the natives was very much more than they could possibly cultivate. Allowing that a considerable portion of their land is unfit for tillage, consisting of hills and swamps, and supposing their race to become twice its present number—of which there is no ground for hope—there will then remain a far greater quantity than could be brought under cultivation by their labour. We have been amused to see an argument built up in favour of the Maories by English speakers and writers, founded on the idea that large tracts of land were necessary to be preserved by the natives as

hunting grounds. Such persons forget that the only
quadrupeds that are found on those extensive tracts are
rats, which will hardly pay for hunting; on some other
lands there are wild pigs and cattle—the offspring of a
few which wandered from the settlements—but to argue
that large plains are to be preserved, that these animals
may roam at large, and occasionally be hunted, rather
as field sport than to procure means of support we will
suppose, as abundant provisions may be procured as the
result of labour, is to display considerable ignorance of
the habits and wants of the Maori people.

But whatever view may be entertained, the fact that
the natives have been for some years before the opening
of hostilities suspicious of the intentions of their white
neighbours cannot be ignored. We have certainly given
room for such fears, not in our real intentions, but in
our neglect to provide a government for them ; we saw
the difficulties lying in the way, and suffered them to
deter us from making the attempt ; and the consequence
is, that the Maori people, supposing we were careless of
their welfare, and that we wished to build the colony on
the ruins of their race, resolved to stop our proceedings,
and declare themselves an independent nation.

CHAPTER XIV.

APPOINTMENT OF A KING.

" Talks of a shred and patchwork King ;
But for a deed—Good Heavens forlorn !
There's not the trace of such a thing !"

FERDINAND FREILIGRATH.

THE idea of a king possessing authority over the whole
country of New Zealand is not natural to the Maori
mind ; nothing like it existed before their intercourse with
a foreign race, not is there any probability that they
would have attempted such a deed as this notion has
given rise to, if they had not been aroused by new circumstances. The race is divided into a number of tribes,
some being much more numerous and powerful than
others ; and a few tribes have ceased to exist, through
disease or exterminating native wars. The tribes are
divided into branches, with their respective chiefs of inferior order. The principal chiefs exercised much influence in their heathen state, not only among the members of their own tribe, but through the tribes generally,
especially in the time of war ; and any strong-minded
man, who was successful in the field of battle, might
rise to a very prominent place, and cause his voice to
be heard on all subjects of general interest. It was their
constant object to preserve their tribes distinct, by preventing inter-tribal marriages, except to a small extent ;
to this cause Dr. Thompson, in his excellent " Story of
New Zealand," attributes in part the present decrease
of the native race ; blood relations having inter-married
so long, that the physical consequences are seen in the

number of sterile marriages of the present day, one fifth of the married women having no children, or none that reach the years of maturity. As the tribes kept so much apart, many of them never meeting but as hostile parties, and as the smouldering fires of revenge were continued in all directions, the probability of a general effort for any political purpose was extremely small.

The notion of a Maori King is said to have originated by the visit of some natives to England. This is not unlikely, for they would learn that all the people of Great Britain bow to one sovereign, and the thought might occur, that to this fact some of their superiority was to be traced. Hongi Hiki, a chief whose name will always be mentioned in connection with the introduction of fire-arms into this country, and on account of the terrible and exterminating wars which he conducted, spent some time in England in the year 1820. A native of New Zealand was a novelty in England in those times ; and the curiosity which was awakened by his presence, received additional interest from the superiority of his natural abilities. All classes shewed him respect, and were desirous to raise his countrymen through his instrumentality. Accordingly every means was used to direct his mind, by giving him an opportunity to examine the results of industry and skill. He was taken to the principal places of interest which London contained. George the Fourth invited him to Carlton Palace, and presented him with a suit of armour, besides guns and ammunition. Hongi had numerous presents, but he esteemed none so much as he did his fire-arms ; he saw many splendid sights, but none excited so much delight as the military stores, and the discipline of the troops ; and of all the information which he gathered none was so much to his taste as the career of Napoleon Bonaparte. Under these influences he resolved, that as there was but one king in England, there should be but one chief or king in New Zealand, and that he would win the royal position for himself, by imitating the extraordinary career of Napoleon I.

On his return the work of slaughter was commenced without delay, and being in possession of fire-arms he had an immense advantage over the other tribes, among whom those destructive weapons were not found. He pursued his work of cruelty and blood, accompanied by many very shocking displays of cannibal ferocity, through the Thames and Waikato districts, and along the coasts as far as Taranaki; by this course he has gained an unenviable name, but did not succeed in establishing himself as the King of New Zealand.

It does not appear that the idea of a Maori king was entertained again till the year 1852, when the suggestion was made by Matini Te Whiwhi. With the design, it is supposed, of gaining the honours of royalty for himself, he sought the co-operation of several chiefs; having succeeded in this attempt, a deputation visited Rotorua, Maketu, and Waikato, to invite a convention of all the tribes for the purpose of appointing a chief to be their King. But instead of falling in with the new proposal, the chiefs of those tribes wrote to the natives of Wanganui and Taranaki as follows:—" We salute you all. This is our word to you : New Zealand is the house, the Europeans are the rafters on one side, the Maories are the rafters on the other side, God is the ridgepole against which all lean, and the house is one."

But although the idea of placing themselves in an independent position does not appear to have influenced them for many years, there were loud complaints, as we have shown in the preceding chapter, occasioned by the changes which our institutions had caused, and the want of sufficient authority to repress the evils which were increasingly felt. On this subject a letter was written in 1848, to Sir George Grey, by Tamati Ngapora, an intelligent and influential chief of Waikato, which was printed among the parliamentary papers for that year. That letter clearly expresses the state of the native mind, under the changes which our institutions have caused; and shows that the chiefs had been humbled, and the lower orders had been raised; the course of vice had been turned, and in some respects vicious conduct had been increased, without the appointment of laws to restrain it. This was not our intention, but it is a change which has grown up through us, and which we should have been prepared to meet. A heavy expenditure would have been necessary to have met their case as far as we could possibly do so, and it must be confessed that it were impossible to provide a remedy for all their serious complaints. If we could have arranged a code of laws adapted to their condition, with proper courts in every native district for their execution; if we could have devised a scheme of education, sufficiently attractive and extensive to benefit the youth of every tribe; and if we could have provided a wholesome literature, instead of confining it to a few numbers of a news-paper, containing articles of doubtful value, and the translation of two or three books, such as " Robinson Crusoe," in which they took but little interest, we should, no doubt, have conferred upon the people important benefits. But two things stood in our way—the expense on the one hand, and the Treaty of Waitangi on the other. The latter might perhaps have been found less difficult than was supposed, and the former would have involved only a fraction of the expenditure which our present troubles have already cost us. Tamati Ngapora, the writer of the letter referred to, · has been one of the most active in the appointment of a king. What he sought of the governor without being able to obtain it he has since tried to secure by the force of arms; his case is not singular, it may be accepted as a fair specimen of the difficulties which lay in the way of the Government, and the resolution of the Maories to redress their own wrongs.

The principal person who sought a remedy for the social evils of his race in the appointment of a king is Wiremu Tamihana Tarapipipi, commonly called William Thomson. His father was a great warrior of the Ngatihaua tribe, of which Tamihana is now the principal chief. He was born about the year 1820, and in early life was brought under the direct influence of the Church Mission. Being inclined towards peace, the excitements of the battle-field had few attractions for him, and as he was naturally of a thoughtful, enquiring disposition his chief pleasure was found in study and other means of self-improvement. He had carefully read those portions of the sacred Scriptures which had been translated into the Maori language, and was able to make some use of the English Bible. He is said to be a very intelligent man, and to be well acquainted with the circumstances and wishes of his people.

For some time after the Taranaki war was commenced Tamihana refused to express an opinion on the merits of the regal case, but he afterwards took the side of Wirimu Kingi. Several men belonging to his tribe went to the Waitara, and fell there. Weteni Taiporutu, who was killed at Mahoetahi, was his relation and intimate friend, whom he restrained for some time from going to the war, and at last parted with him in displeasure, saying, " Then go, and stay there." Weteni went, was killed, and his body lies in the burial-ground of New Plymouth. Tamihana himself afterwards went to the Waitara, which was then the seat of war, but chiefly with the intention of making peace ; his object was gained, for within a few days after his arrival a truce was obtained, arrangements were made on both sides, and hostilities ceased for more than two years. But he determined to support the Maori king with all his influence, and no longer acknowledge the supremacy of the Queen. He steadfastly resisted every endeavour made by Sir George Grey, on his return to the colony, to conciliate him, and when the Waikato campaign was commenced he took a prominent place in the conduct of the war. His attitude at this time is perhaps little better than that of a conquered enemy ; for although it were possible to fall back upon the bush for a refuge, and to harass the British troops and settlers for some years to come, his plans are disconcerted, his king is a fugitive, the very spot—Ngaruawhahia—which was selected as the royal residence and the seat of power, has been surveyed and sold as a colonial township ; many of his firmest friends, the principal chiefs of his own and other tribes, have been killed, and he has been obliged to seek a place of safety on land which he never called his own. Under these circumstances Tamihana is, no doubt, desirous of peace, and willing to acknowledge himself a subject of her Britannic Majesty.

We confess to a strong feeling in favour of Wiremu

Y

Tamihana ; he has made a very great mistake in stirring up the King movement, and defending it by force ; but his influence has been exerted to prevent the atrocities which many of his people were inclined to commit. On more than one occasion he has sent food to the troops, with an expression of good-will. To Sir Duncan Cameron, Commander of the Forces, he sent two milch goats, three turkeys, and five fowls, with a note, quoting Romans xii. 20, " If thine enemy hunger, feed him ; if he thirst, give him drink." Tamihana is still in middle life, many years may yet be his portion ; while he can never repair the injuries his mistaken career has caused, much may be done by him to reconcile his people to the Government, and to encourage their industrial pursuits. He may yet occupy the post of honour and usefulness which his candour, intelligence, and influence may fit him to discharge.*

The old chief who was the first Maori upon whom the honours of royalty were conferred, was an extraordinary character. Had we the materials at hand to sketch his life, an interesting view of him might be given. Trained amidst the customs and influences of a past generation, before the gospel had been preached, or any ideas of civilization had been introduced among his race, he was a Maori in his thoughts, habits, and feelings. Familiar with the horrid cruelties connected with cannibalism, he shrunk not from taking his part in some of the most revolting scenes which disgraced the East and West coasts, before the erection of the colony. He had been a noted warrior ; being wise in the council and brave in the field

* Since the above was written we learn that Wiremu Tamihana is dead ; he died worn out with troubles resulting from his unhappy opposition to the Government.

he was both feared and esteemed. Forty years ago he fled before the victorious Hongi Hika, whose newly-imported fire-arms gave him such a terrible pre-eminence over his contemporaries. After that storm of war passed away, he prepared for the expeditions of slaughter, which will long be remembered by many tribes. He was then called Te Whero Whero, a name which for many years suggested the ideas of blood and victory.

When the colony was established, and missionary influences were felt in Waikato, Te Whero Whero became a man of peace; he respected the Europeans, became their firm friend, and would have remained so without giving any one reason to doubt the sincerity of his friendship, had not younger and determined men led him into trouble in his dotage. His name was changed to Potatau, by which he will in future be best known out of New Zealand, on account of the pseudo-royal honours connected with it. He was desirous to preserve peace and friendship with the white race after he was made king, and retained a firm hold of the Christian religion, as may be seen by the following Proclamation which he addressed to all the tribes in the country: —" Hold fast Christianity, hold fast love, hold fast law; what is the worth or advantage of all other work? Christianity is not a wealth we have purchased; it is a wealth that has been freely given to us, and wealth for which we have made no adequate return. Maories, your former god was Uenuku, the man eater. You have a different God now, the great God of heaven; therefore, let war cease in New Zealand, among both Maories and Pakehas."

Potatau was selected on account of his rank, the prestige of his name and his relation to several large tribes, rather on account of what he had been than what he then was; they did not, and could not, expect much from him but his name served better than the name of any other man to draw around it the interests of various and distant tribes. He was not happy in his honours; other men were busy while he lay in his whare asleep, or sat there smoking his pipe; he excused himself from attending to the affairs of government, by saying "What can I do, who am but a bundle of bones?" When he was informed of the evils which were likely to follow the appointment of a King, Potatau complained of others :— "They came and dragged me away from Mangere," said he, "and brought me here to be King, with three things to guide me, and now they have added a fourth and a fifth, and what next? Let me return whence I came. If I were young and strong as once, they should not do such things with impunity; but a bundle of bones just held together with a cord, what can I do?" Then quoting a Maori legend to illustrate his position, he remarked: "I am like Ouenuku (a Maori god). Ouenuku sat under a tree that shaded him from the sun, and gave him fruit to eat. He was happy beneath the shade and enjoyed the fruits, till Tama-te-Kapua envied him, and destroyed his resting-place. Tama came out in open daylight, but came on stilts, ate the fruit and destroyed the tree. Ouenuku was ignorant of what was going on, for the thief was on stilts, and nothing but wood was visible, till by and bye his food and shelter both were gone. I am Ouenuku!"

Potatau never really lost his friendship for the Government; nor did the Government forsake him, for a pension was paid to him till within three months of his death. He died on the 25th June, 1860, and was buried at

Mangere, within a few miles of Auckland. In the account of money expended by the Government for native purposes, during the year 1860, the sum of £1 17s. is mentioned as having been paid for Potatau's coffin and furniture.

The first great meeting convened for the appointment of a king was held at Taupo, in December, 1856. That meeting determined that a king should be elected, that no roads should be made within a very extensive native district, and that no public prayers should be offered for the Queen. This was followed by the expunging of the petitions for her Majesty the Queen from many copies of the Book of Common Prayer. Another meeting was held at Paetai the next year. About two thousand persons attended it, divided into two parties—Wiremu Tamihara being the leader of one party, and William Naylor (Te Awaitaia) being at the head of the other. The last-mentioned chief was a superior man. In his early years he took a prominent place as a warrior, and his eloquence in Maori councils was very commanding. He had united with the Wesleyan mission nearly twenty years before this meeting was held ; his allegiance to the Queen was a sacred thing, and his friendship to the white race was indisputable. The settlers at Wangaroa, Raglan, have been safe through the year in which the tribes were driven out of Waikato—their safety being attributable, in no small degree, to the influence and efforts of William Naylor. In alliance with this chief, at the Paetai meeting, were all the tribes of Lower Waikato. They then opposed the appointment of a king; but, unhappily, they afterwards changed sides, allied themselves to the king party, joined in the war against the Queen, and were driven out of the wide plains which their fathers cultivated, and in which they might have remained unmolested. William Naylor, and the people under his immediate control, remain our steadfast friends, and will reap the reward of their fidelity.* At the Paetai meeting, Naylor hoisted the Union Jack, and Thomson unfurled the flag which had been presented to the Confederate Tribes at the Bay of Islands, by William IV., but now bearing the words, "Potatau, King of New Zealand."

At this meeting, many speeches were made by both parties. William Thomson argued that law and order were necessary to prevent bloodshed and murder; Te Heuheu, the principal chief of Taupo, pointed out the evils which they then suffered from the Pakehas, in the prostitution of their women, the drunkenness of their men, and the dishonour offered to their chiefs, and urged the necessity of expelling the white race from the country; Paora, a man of better spirit, endeavoured to shew the people, that as Israel had a king, and the Gospel does not command people to have no king, the Queen of England ought not to be angry at the appointment of a Maori king, who would be in alliance with her Majesty, and that the benefits of such an appointment would be seen in the advancement of the Maori race to the position now occupied by the white people, instead of their being swept from the country. The speech of William Naylor was so appropriate, and displayed such a friendly spirit, that the following extract from it will be read with pleasure :—"Ngatihaua, do not be dark! Waikato, hear! Taupo, attend! I speak as a father, and my word is this. I promised the first Governor,

* William Naylor died lately, maintaining his Christian profession and his friendship for the white people to the last.

when he came to see me, and I promised all the rest, that I would adhere to him, and be a subject of the Queen. I intend to keep my promise, for they have kept theirs. They have taken no land. The desire to sell was mine, and they gave me money. Why do you bring that flag here ? There is trouble in it. I cannot see my way clear; but I know that there is trouble in that flag. I am content with the old one. It is seen all over the world, and it belongs to me—I get some of its honour. What honour can I get from your flag? It is like a fountain without water. Do not trouble me. You say that we are slaves. If acknowledging that flag makes me a slave, I am a slave. Let me alone—do not bring trouble upon us. Go back to the mountains : let us live in peace. I and the Governor will take our own course." *

Being aware of the value of continual efforts to secure the attention and assistance of various tribes which were slow to perceive the benefits that would result from the proposed revolution, many zealous advocates left their industrial pursuits, travelled long journeys, and worked incessantly at the accomplishment of their project. So important did their national status appear, with a king at their head, that it absorbed every other subject. This object filled the field of vision, so that they could speak and think of nothing else. Letters were sent by post to different parts of the country. In some of these the most glowing descriptions of their doings were given ; in others, urgent calls for help were made, joined with absurd statements of the benefits which should flow from the kingdom. Of the latter kind, the following may be taken as a specimen :—" Do ye hearken, O ye

* "The Maori King Movement," by the Rev. T. Buddle, p. 10.

tribes, both small and great, even all people of all places. Let your call for a king be carried into practice, and let the king be placed upon his seat of honour. Then the ministers of all the Churches, and the assemblies of the Europeans, will pay their respects to this our great king. Be strong to perform this. Will you? Yes, you will. Your call for the establishment of a kingdom is just; the necessity of this step has been seen by those who look at the law of the Europeans and natives. All the people will protect [us]. Do not suppose that the Europeans will stand aloof from this great king of New Zealand. Five thousand of them [the Europeans] will adhere to this cause, and there will be six thousands of millions of Maories! Let the king be placed upon his kingly throne, and after him let governors be sought out for each district, and councils for the whole. The money [to defray the expenses] is easily procured. If you are unsuccessful, the Europeans will taunt you, and laugh at you. When the king is elected, we shall be a sacred people, and our former greatness will return unto us."

But while some saw only good in the results of the kingdom, others foresaw many evils. These were pointed out at their great *runangas*, in private conversation, and in social evening hours. An interesting anecdote is related, illustrating the latter:—"An evening party were enjoying themselves in a house lighted with candles. The subject of conversation was the proposed king, whose cause was warmly advocated by a zealous partisan. While he was in the midst of his speech, a man, named Tarahawaiki, quietly walked round, and put out the lights. The speaker, surprised by sudden darkness, just as he was urging that the Governor, missionaries, and settlers should all be sent out of the country, and not perceiving the significancy of the act, said, ' Would it not be better to light up the candles again ?' ' Most certainly,' replied Tarahawaiki ; ' it was very foolish to extinguish them.' ' *

The meeting at which Potatau was installed king was held on the 2nd of June, 1858. Only about two thousand persons were present, although numerous invitations had been sent to near and distant tribes. Those who were present did not agree concerning the honours which were to be conferred upon the chief-elect. In the course of the proceedings, Wiremu Tamihana asked the people, in reference to Potatau, "Will you have this man for a king?" They replied, "Yes." "Will you give all the power and all the land to the king?" They replied again, "Yes." Potatau was then asked, "Will you be a father to us?" He answered, "Yes;" when a salute was fired, and three cheers were given. The following instructions were laid before the king, in a written form, on the next day:—"The laws for the king are these : The power he is to exercise over men and land, is the power of protecting them against quarrels, wars, and murders—a power which shall extend to all the chiefs and councils of all the tribes. Every man is to live upon his own land, and the king is to defend him against all aggressions against his land or person."

Another display awaited the new-made monarch fourteen days after, when he rode in state into Rangiaohia. The king rode on horseback ; one, bearing a flag, went before him, and an honourable company followed. The inhabitants of the village walked in procession to meet him, an address was presented, musketry was fired, and

* Rev. T. Buddle.

a guard of honour was formed. All uncovered their heads, and paid their humble respects, at the signal being given to "honour the king." A native teacher then conducted Divine Service, in which the Scriptures were read, prayer was offered, and a hymn was sung. More chanting and firing followed, with the further presentation of lowly respects, and the ceremonies were ended.*

The appointment of a Maori king had now become a fact. To ignore it, were impossible; to guide the movement, were difficult. Various opinions were formed of the danger or value of this strange appointment. Most people smiled at the absurdity of the thing, and supposed that it would die out after the excitement was over. His Excellency Governor Browne and his ministers seem to have thought the same, and therefore took no steps towards opposing it. A few persons, among whom were some very influential gentlemen, saw in it the seed of future excellence—the pathway to the improvement of the entire people. There were others, however, who foresaw the cloud which was gathering, and which has since broken with terrible violence over both the races. The appointment of a king and the Land League had no necessary connexion; but the one greatly accelerated the other. Many were attracted much more strongly to the one than to the other; but, eventually, the two objects became co-efficient. The fact that each had a distinct origin, and was for some time maintained separately, has given rise to many mistakes among our countrymen, both in England and in the colony. To this may be traced much of the false reasoning which has been published, and the suspicions

* See "The Maori King Movement," pp. 13, 14.

which are entertained against the colonists by a certain class of respectable men in our fatherland. Different views were taken by the principal persons belonging to the king movement. Some wished his majesty to have the full powers of a king; others considered that he should act simply as a governor. By one party, the allegiance to the Queen was to be entirely cast off; another supposed that it could, to some extent, be continued. The removal of all the white people from the island was deemed necessary by a few; while the majority were disposed to let us remain in possession of the land we had already occupied.

Not long after the movement had become a serious fact, signs of unpleasantness and danger were apparent. Laws were made for the districts over which the king's power was supposed to extend, and applied to the Europeans residing there as well as to the natives.

For some time, however, the path was not only smooth but strewn with roses; the success of the kingdom could not be doubted, distant tribes sent deputations of their best men to present their profound respects, and place all their land in the hands of the king. Old feuds were forgotten, unity and love were words used by everybody. Native teachers rose in the estimation of the people, and English missionaries were less desired. Schools were established in some places, taught by natives, and maintained by chiefs. Places of worship were built of substantial materials, the Scriptures were read, and order was preserved. A few Europeans, who looked only at this pleasing picture, were surprised and delighted; in their view the lever was applied which would lift up the race into a new life of honour and usefulness, and expressions of good will were neither few nor small.

A good deal of shrewdness was displayed in selecting places for particular purposes, and men for various offices. The chief residence of the king was to be at Ngaruawahia, the spot where the rivers Waikato and Waipa meet on their course to the sea. It is a beautiful place, and the land is fertile. Water carriage into the Upper Waikato and Waipa districts add greatly to its value, and bridle roads to Auckland and to other parts of the country branched off from this meeting of the waters. A large town was intended to be built here, native surveyors were employed to lay out the place in one acre allotments, with wide streets crossing each other at right angles, and named after chiefs both living and dead; and a map of the town was made. Since then Ngaruawahia has fallen into the hands of General Cameron, and after this into the hands of the provincial authorities; a colonial town has been surveyed, and named Queen's Town; and will probably become a place of great commercial importance to the interior parts of the country.

While the natives were preparing to throw off their allegiance to the Government, though unconsciously on the part of some, an infatuation seized the General Assembly of the colony. The Act prohibiting the sale of arms and ammunition to the natives was rescinded. Many persons, among whom were some of the members of the Assembly, saw the danger of this step; not on account of the king-movement only, but in the support which it would give to native quarrels; and used every effort to prevent the alteration of the law. The arguments for the rescinding of the Act were these : That as the Maories were British subjects, they had a right to all the privileges which the colonists enjoyed; and to prevent merchants from selling to them the articles which were sold to the Europeans was an infringement of this right; that it was impolitic, and tended to raise suspicions among the natives, to prevent the sale of fire-arms; that in some cases it might be a hardship, as fowling-pieces were often useful to shoot pigeons and other game, to procure a variety of diet; that no laws which we could make were likely to prevent a great number of arms and a large quantity of ammunition from being smuggled ashore, from American whalers and other vessels, as the extent of coast was extremely favourable for such purposes; and that to expose the Maori people to such nefarious traffic, by withholding from them the rights of British subjects, was to demoralize them. But no sooner was the Act of Prohibition rescinded than its effects were seen. The money which had been spent in wholesome food and suitable clothing was now devoted to the purchase of guns; their families were allowed to be half-starved and covered with rags, rather than they would forego the privilege of purchasing ammunition. Industry was interrupted, and long journeys were taken to the places where these coveted articles might be obtained. Within nine months about eight thousand pounds' weight of gunpowder, three hundred double-barrelled guns, and five hundred single-barrelled guns were sold to natives. The Auckland merchants imported, it is said, not less than a thousand stand of arms for native trade. This was sowing the "dragon's teeth," and it is no wonder that we have reaped accordingly.

That this Legislative blunder greatly increased the facilities for carrying out the violent measures which were afterwards adopted does not admit of a doubt; the

discontentment existed before, the effort to govern themselves from a central point might have been attempted,
but we can hardly suppose that they could have organized
such a prolonged opposition to the Government if they
had not been encouraged by a great addition to their
means of defence.

Being able to arm themselves *ad libitum*, by both
purchases and manufactures, we need not be surprised
that the king's cause prospered. Tribes living hundreds
of miles away from the seat of Maori government, became
zealous partisans, chiefly because they supposed that
this was the best way to prevent the increase of the
colony. The writer saw a numerous deputation from
the Ngatiruanui tribe pass through New Plymouth, on
their way to Waikato, to present the land and allegiance
of their tribe to the Maori king. They were fine-looking
men, very clean, and well dressed in European clothing
—a proof that they had been prosperous while under
the government of her Majesty the Queen. They all
wore good cloth caps, such as are generally worn in the
colony, but covered with white muslin, to distinguish
the wearers as subjects of the Maori king. On the 10th
April, 1860, they arrived at Ngaruawahia, in the company of several other tribes. The ceremony of pledging
their allegiance we will quote from the pen of the Rev.
T. Buddle, who, we believe, was present:—" They
marched up to the flag-staff, three abreast, wearing
favours to distinguish the respective tribes. On reaching
it, one stepped forward, and with a clear, distinct voice,
said : ' Honour all men ; love the brotherhood. Fear
God ; honour the king.' Then, turning to the train, he
said, ' Honour the king.' All responded, by uncovering
and kneeling. The leader of the Ngatiruanui then read

from a memorandum-book an address, beginning, ' O king, live for ever! Thou art bone of our bone, and flesh of our flesh ; thou art a saviour for us, our wives, our children,' &c., and went on to pledge their allegiance. The leader of the Ngatiawa then read a similar address. ' Honour the king,' was again commanded, and a low salaam, with a general cry of ' hear, hear, hear,' was the response. A native teacher then stepped out of the ranks, and gave out the following verse of a hymn :—

> " ' Ka mahue Ihipa,
>   Te kainga o te he,
> He kainga hou te rapua nei
>   Hei okiokinga.
>   Hariruia !
> Arahina ki t' Atua.'

Which is the translation of a verse in one of Kelly's hymns—

> " ' From Egypt lately come,
>   Where death and darkness reign,
> We seek our new, our better home,
>   Where we our rest shall gain.
> Hallelujah ! We are on our way to God.'

After singing the verse, the Divine blessing was implored for the king and people. They then retired, facing towards the royal presence, wheeled round, and marched off."

A great meeting was held at Ngaruawahia in the latter part of the following month, attended by men, women, and children, to the number of about three thousand persons, for whom the following articles of food were provided :—

Potatoes, 2,000 baskets
Eels, 36,000
Pigs, 84
Bullocks, 3
Flour, 31 tons and 8 bags

Fresh Eels, 580
Bags of Sugar, 9
Baskets of dried small Fish, 16
Sharks, 20
Chest of Tea, 1

Pumpkins and Vegetable Marrow, without number.*

As the tribes arrived, the scene became deeply interesting. War canoes, with flags streaming in the breeze, were filled with excited men, singing appropriate verses. Two hundred women, gaily dressed, chanted the song of welcome; and the king, thoroughly aroused by the scene, shouted—"Come, my fathers! come, my brothers! come on the waters over which your ancestors pulled their canoes! Come on the Waikato. Welcome! welcome!" This was followed by a war-dance, the firing of muskets, and other demonstrations of joy. A few days afterwards, the flag-staff was fixed in the ground, amidst the further firing of muskets and demonstrations of the war dance. A man standing on the cross-trees cried—"The top of this flag-staff signifies the king, the centre is for the chiefs; these four ropes represent the tribes east, west, north, and south; the name of this flag-staff is Pane."

In their excitement, they seem to have been at a loss for words sufficiently strong to express their loyalty: for one man addressed Potatau thus: "O king, live for ever! Thou art not a man, but a spirit. Thou didst not spring from earth, but came down from heaven. Thou art a god. Thou art like Melchizedek, without father, without mother, without descent—having neither

* See " Maori King Movement," p. 53.

beginning of days nor end of life!" It is no wonder that the war-spirit was displayed in the speeches which were made at this meeting, especially as news of the Taranaki disturbance had just reached them. Some, advocating a vigorous policy, wished for an expedition to start at once to the conflict. The same persons went soon after to Taranaki, and were killed in action. Others were less violent; and there were some who advocated pacific measures. Among the latter, a blind man, named Solomon, distinguished himself by chanting the following *waiata :—*

> " The wind blows keenly ;
> Its blast has sorely pierced me.
> The stars are hidden from me ;
> And I tremble, like the birds
> That flutter when the dark clouds
> Fly across their path.
> Who has created this night of sorrow
> That now o'erspreads the land ?
> Who is he that conceived
> This thought of war ?
> Why does he not return
> By the same plebeian path
> That brought him here,
> Nor dare to tread on sacred ground ?
> From the councils of the great ones
> Hast thou come
> To break our long repose ?
> Whither would'st thou lead us ?
> End now thy strife,
> And leave us pure,
> That we may rest in peace.
> Who is the evil spirit
> That prompts to war ?
> Bid him keep at a distance,

z

Lest, maddened by his wiles,
We fall into the snare of Rongo—
The man who came to fetch us.
Withdraw thy stretched-out hand ;
Return it to thy bosom undefiled—
Pollute it not ! "

The intelligence that several of their friends had fallen
in the battle of Waireka, gave a stronger *animus* to their
speeches. Loud complaints were uttered against the
Pakeha, and missionaries were denounced as having led
the way to the loss of their land. The propriety of
permitting mails to be carried across native districts
was doubted, and it was resolved that no roads should
be made across their land. Touching expressions of
grief for friends recently fallen in battle, were uttered.
" Alas for me !" cried one ; " my affliction is great. I
have talked about land till I am weary. Now I sit in
grief ; my very vitals move. I shake like the leaves of
the weeping fern tree for my children !" and concluded
his mournful speech with the following chant :—

" The clouds are coming up from the sea.
I am here, sympathising with and weeping for my children—
Am I not a man ?
The very fountain of blood in the heart will burst
With the depth of my feeling within me."

The principles on which the new kingdom was professedly founded, were three—Te Whakapono, Te Aroha,
Te Ture ; *i.e.*, the Gospel, Love, and Law. Potatau
was, we believe, sincere in his wish to carry out these
principles. " Should the Pakehas," said he, " come
and kill me, never mind ; let it be so ; do not avenge
my death." Many persons supposed that, with the new
order of things, they would be able to spread the Gospel

more effectually; and efforts of this kind were made in
the erection of places of worship, and the establishment
of schools. The unity displayed among tribes who had
been for many generations decided enemies, was considered to be an expression of love—love covering old
offences, love exciting to deeds for their common welfare.
Law was the object after which most of them panted—
the great need of the people. We had drawn them away
from their former customs, without supplying them properly with a code suited to the changes through which
they had passed. Attempts were made to supply this
defect, when the restless and dangerous spirit of the
people alarmed us. It should have been done before,
and done as effectually as the circumstances of the case
would have permitted. In establishing a *Kingitanga*—a
kingdom—upon those bases, many supposed that they
were acting an honourable part; others, no doubt, made
these a mere subterfuge, to draw their people into
opposition against a race which they saw to be greatly
increasing in numbers, and whose superiority in all
matters of knowledge and handicraft they were ready
to acknowledge; and many younger men, whose superior
intelligence prepared them to take a prominent place in
public proceedings, saw in the new establishment a fair
chance of securing an honourable position. They endeavoured to create a literature—we may smile at the
word, and at the puny character of the work produced—
but, as might have been supposed, without much success.
Yet, the mere fact that a printing apparatus was purchased, at the cost of several hundred pounds sterling,
and a newspaper commenced, shew their desire for
improvement, and their resolution to help themselves.
There were, however, so many things affecting the

government of a people—not to say, affecting their safety from foreign powers, supposing their independency to have been gained—of which they appear to have had little or no knowledge, that, under the most favourable circumstances, there was little prospect of lasting success. But when we add to those the evils which lurked around the movement, in some instances, and which were at the root of it in others, we cannot see that any good fruit could have been brought to perfection. Our worst fears, excited at the time when these events were transpiring, have been more than realised, in the effects which have taken place, involving a long and sanguinary war, in which a very large sum of money has been expended, and the lives of hundreds of our countrymen, and large numbers of the natives, including many of their principal chiefs, have been sacrificed.

We have been particular in describing the steps by which this singular event has been accomplished, as it must always be considered an interesting chapter in Maori history. We are not aware that any event similar to this has been achieved in any other country—an event in which a half-civilized people, divided into many tribes, kept apart for ages through deep-seated revenge, and extremely jealous of giving any power or honour to an equal, asserting their independency against a race vastly superior, in every respect, to themselves, and from whom they have derived the tools with which they work, and the arms with which they defend themselves. Could they have succeeded, many a voice would have been loud in their praises; the noblest patriotism would have been ascribed to them, and they would have taken a high place in the estimation of the world. But, as the case really was, there was room for unmingled regret.

A very large sum has been spent in restoring order, and a heavy debt will remain on the colony for our children to pay. Yet this may be overcome in a few years; and though we have lost many valuable lives, and the graves of our countrymen will long be pointed out as melancholy memorials, the colony will outgrow the evils which have fallen upon it. But it is otherwise with the Maori people. They were decreasing before, by the silent operation of natural causes; and the infatuation which led them to appoint a king, urged them on to a war, which many of their chief men have been laid in the dust, and numbers of men of lower rank, who might have been made a blessing to their race, have been cut off in the prime of life. By these events, the Maori race have been reduced in numbers; but we would hope, and do earnestly pray, that God will lead them into the spirit of peace and satisfaction, that the missionary labour bestowed upon them through more than half a century, may yet produce its choicest fruits, and that, with increasing numbers, the Maori race may be continued, and be made a blessing in the land.

CHAPTER XV.

THE TARANAKI WAR.

"The war-club rang upon the threshold stone,
And heavy feet of savage men came trampling fiercely on."

THE Taranaki war, which commenced in the early part of the year 1860, will always form a painfully interesting event in the history both of the colony and the native people. Little in itself compared with the widespread and devastating wars of many countries, and in our own times, it has proved the beginning of a course of hostilities, involving a very heavy expense, and the loss of many lives; and will result in the modification of the colony, especially in its relations to the native tribes. Not like the wars which prevailed in the Bay of Islands and in the province of Wellington nearly twenty years ago, and which were confined to a few tribes within a limited district, the present rebellion is spread over a large portion of the Northern Island, unsettling many tribes, and fostering a deep hatred of the Pakeha race.

It were difficult to name a district where the native mind was more unsettled than it was in the Taranaki province, and had been for many years previous to the commencement of hostilities. There the principles of the Land League were accepted and strongly defended, resulting in the murderous feuds described in a previous chapter. Persons belonging to the same tribe became deadly enemies, according to their opposition or adherence to the British Government; each party lying in wait to murder, or threatening to roast the other over a slow fire. This state of feeling was publicly avowed, and corresponding proceedings were carried out within a few miles of New Plymouth, endangering the cattle and persons of the settlers by the shots which were fired across their farms. Pahs were fortified by the side of the Queen's highway, so as to render travelling unsafe. The most noted person who figured in these sorties was Wiremu Kingi—William King—whose name has since been rendered famous by the opening out of the war. This man possessed considerable influence, and, had he not been so doggedly opposed to the Government, might have been wealthy, respected, and happy. In the early wars of the colony, he was our ally, and it is with much regret that we have now to describe him as our enemy. For some years before the Taranaki war was commenced, repeated efforts were made by the natives to bury their mutual animosities ; but without success, on account of the refusal of Wiremu Kingi, so that he was called "the troubler of the people."

A proper opinion cannot be formed of the circumstances which led to hostilities, without a knowledge of the unhappy spirit which had .been for years fostered among the Maories. This, of course, made it necessary that the utmost prudence should be used in an appeal to force, and, at the same time, it rendered some measures necessary to prevent the continuance of the native quarrels. His Excellency Governor Browne stated to the General Assembly, that, in the policy which he pursued at Taranaki, his object was "to secure peace, by putting an end to the constantly recurring land feuds, which for years had maintained barbarism among the natives of that district." The general opinion was, that the natives would not maintain their defiant tone, if they saw the Governor in earnest to maintain the honour of the

Crown. A few days before the troops were marched to the Waitara, his Excellency wrote to his Grace the Duke of Newcastle, the Secretary of State for the Colonies, as follows:—" I do not anticipate any real opposition, when the chief, William King, sees that I am determined not to permit him to defy her Majesty's Government." And in another despatch, written about the same time, the Governor assured his Grace that every care should be taken to avert a collision between the races, and that every forbearance, compatible with the honour of the Crown, should be shown in dealing with the natives. It is now generally admitted that a great mistake was made in resorting to force with only about two hundred troops for disposal. Had a large force been available, the natives might have considered submission as the better part of courage; as it was, they found no difficulty in mustering a larger force, and determined to risk their chances in a war. We say that such *might* have been the case ; but we think that the feeling of a large portion of the native people was in favour of war. It was the theme on which they delighted to dwell. They had secured a large stock of guns and ammunition; their young men had never seen war, but had been much excited by the stories of battles fought and won, which were told by the old men ; a morbid feeling was entertained against the white race, as being intruders upon their soil—the disturbers of their ancient customs ; and a strong desire was cherished to limit the influence of the Pakehas, if not to expel them from the Northern Island. A great change had passed over the native mind in reference to the prestige of British troops ; but we think Mr. Busby, the British Resident at the Bay of Islands before the commencement of the colony, was mistaken, when he expressed his opinion that one hundred soldiers would be more than a match for the martial force of all the tribes.

It became quite common in England to denounce the settlers as being the real cause of the New Zealand war. The accusation is easily made, and as easily repeated; and any denial given by the colonists to such reports was often treated with contempt by one class, and ignored by another. The secular press, from the *Times* downward, was stout in its accusations against the settlers. The religious press joined in the same cry, and, as might have been foreseen, their strong partisanship damaged the object which they sought to establish —the cupidity of the colonists, and the wrong done to natives. The platform was called in to reiterate the charges, with all the influence which warmth of feeling and eloquence of language could convey. Dignitaries of the Established Church so far forgot themselves as to express, in no measured terms, the supposed injuries which were done to the Maori people. Imaginary wrongs were insisted on, equal in atrocity to those perpetrated in the worst forms on the American continent, implying that a voyage to the antipodes changed the peace-loving and humane Englishman into the burly savage, who could cut down his fellow-man for no other cause than that he was of a less privileged race, and held in his possession the land which the newly-arrived immigrant wished to call his own. Military officers contributed, by their letters, to maintain this unfair sentiment. They were engaged in a campaign in which they could not expect to earn unfading laurels; for their enemy was a half-civilized people, few in number, ill-supplied with arms, and maintaining an undignified mode of warfare, and it was not unnatural for them to accept the statements which they read in some of the colonial newspapers, and to confirm those statements without taking the trouble to inquire into their correctness. Gentlemen who had spent many years in the colony, lent their influence—and in a few cases that influence was considerable—to denounce their fellow settlers, and sustain the natives in their defiant position, on the principle that it is not easy to writhe with elegance and groan with melody. And we deeply regret to write that some excellent men, who had laboured long and successfully on the New Zealand mission field, looking only at the great injury that their mission-churches and schools had sustained for some years, so far forgot themselves as to write statements of the usages and intentions of the Colonial Government, especially as it is administered by the provincial authorities, equal in bitterness to almost anything which was expressed by mistaken persons in England. These statements have been publicly and repeatedly contradicted, both from the press and from the pulpit, by many clergymen of the Church of England, including some of their Bishops, as well as by the clergy of other denominations. Some who read these pages may probably call to mind expressions in some of the colonial newspapers which would justify the most serious charges that have been preferred against the settlers. These expressions, we admit, have repeatedly appeared; but it is as unfair to make them the standard by which the colonial feeling towards the native race is measured, as it would be unfair to estimate the moral and loyal feeling of the people of Great Britain and Ireland by the occasional expressions of indecency and doubtful loyalty which are sometimes seen in the pages of their newspapers.

We do not insinuate that the New Plymouth people did not wish for more land. They addressed a memorial to the Governor, praying that proper steps might be taken to purchase an additional block from the native owners. In this memorial there was nothing unfair, if the circumstances of the case be properly considered. Large tracts of land were purchased in other provinces, while the waste lands of the Taranaki province were very extensive. With a coast line of more than a hundred miles, and embracing two millions one hundred and seventy-six thousand acres, the province of Taranaki is larger than the English counties of Kent, Surrey, Middlesex, and Hertford.* The number of Maori inhabitants does not exceed two thousand, including men, women, and children, so that the average quantity of land in the possession of each person was more than a thousand acres, while they could not possibly cultivate, or occupy even as grazing grounds, one-tenth of it. The comparatively small quantity of land in the hands of the farmers was not sufficient for their increasing herds and flocks ; their sons were desirous of securing farms of their own, but they could not do so without leaving the province or locating themselves in the thick forest ; and there were no inducements for the enlargement of the population by immigration—it was not strange, therefore, that a desire was cherished to purchase some of the neighbouring waste land.

In the month of March, 1859, his Excellency Governor Browne visited New Plymouth, and the subject of purchasing additional land of the natives was brought before him. Some of the Maories were desirous to sell a portion of their land, but were intimidated by others

* F. A. Carrington, Esq., Government Surveyor.

who determined to prevent it. Native meetings were
convened in the presence of the Governor, and many
speeches of but little importance were made. It was at
one of these gatherings that a Maori chief named Teira
—Taylor—offered to sell six hundred acres, situated at
the mouth of the Waitara, laying down a handsome mat
at the feet of the Governor to confirm his offer, according
to Maori custom. This was done in the open air, and
in the presence of a considerable number both of Europeans and natives. Wiremu Kingi was present and
objected to the sale of the land, not by removing the
mat, as it is said he should have done according to
native usage, but by peremptorily stating that he would
not permit the land to be alienated; concluding his
speech with these words, "*Ekore, Ekore, Ekore*," "I will
not, I will not, I will not;" and not wishing for any explanation on the subject he arose, the men belonging to
him following his example, and immediately left. The
Governor then stated that he was willing to purchase
land in all cases where the Maori owners could show a
good title, but that he would not purchase land whose
title was disputed, and that this principle must be applied to the six hundred acres now offered by Teira. No
one, we think, could doubt the fairness of the course
then taken, considered apart from the unhappy events
which followed. Nor was any haste shown in the investigation of the title; for nine months passed away before
decisive steps were taken to complete the purchase;
both settlers and natives looked on with surprise at this
apparently unnecessary delay, the farmers because they
wanted to enlarge their farms, and the latter because
they wished to dispose of their useless land for immediate
benefit, if they could break through the trammels of the
Land League.

Much has been written and printed about the alleged injustice of this purchase by gentlemen whose colonial position has given them an opportunity to form a correct opinion; but who have notwithstanding made serious mistakes in applying rules which the customs of the Maories will not at present admit, and in overlooking the usages which have been observed for many years past. The institution of a land court would be undoubtedly the most satisfactory way to determine the value of native claims, *if the Maori people would have submitted to its decisions;* but no such tribunal had then been established, all the land purchases having been conducted by officers appointed by the general Government. The natives' view of the case has been argued most strongly by Sir William Martin, who filled the office of Chief Justice in the colony for many years; but it should not be forgotten that Sir William raised no protest against this usage while he presided over the administration of justice, although nearly thirty millions of acres had been purchased in a similar manner, and most of it during the time of his judicial position. No person would have raised a doubt on the subject of injustice in the Waitara transaction if subsequent events had not given it an extraordinary importance, the two points on which the question turned being these: The right of Teira to sell his land, *if he could show a clear title to it;* and the incompetency of Wiremu Kingi to forbid its sale, on the ground that no land should be alienated in the Waitara district.

No decisive steps were further taken till January 25th, 1860, when Governor Browne suggested to his Executive Council the propriety of completing the purchase. After carefully examining the subject, the Council advised that Mr. Parris, the land commissioner at New Plymouth, should have the six hundred acres surveyed. The general feeling of Wiremu Kingi remained unaltered and some opposition from him was anticipated, for Mr. Parris was directed to arrange the time and circumstances of the survey in such a manner that he might be aware of it, without being officially informed. The course of action which the Governor in Council determined on, if the survey should be prevented, was this —To protect the surveyors by a military force, to call out the volunteers and militia for active service, to proclaim martial law, to maintain possession of the land after the survey by force if necessary, and to request the civil authorities of New Plymouth to co-operate with the military in carrying out those measures; and the necessary instructions were sent to Lieut.-Colonel Murrey, the military commander at New Plymouth, to execute these decisions.

Nearly a month passed by after these preparations before further decisive proceedings were taken. But on February 20th the native officer, two gentlemen of the Survey Department, and a policeman rode to the Waitara to survey the disputed block of land. Parties of natives met them in various places on the way, but nothing unpleasant occurred. When they arrived on the disputed ground a considerable number of Maories —men, women, and children—were ready to oppose them; yet there were no signs of disturbance further than a settled resolution that the land should not be surveyed. No sooner was the chain drawn out than it was taken up by the *Maori women* and thrown aside, the men standing by approving of the deed, and apparently ready to act in like manner. Repeated efforts were made with no better success; and, as it seemed plain that the survey could not be completed at that time, the instruments were gathered up, and the Government officers returned to New Plymouth. No person was surprised at the defeat, but many trembled to contemplate the state of things which might follow. A letter was then sent to Wiremu Kingi, offering him twenty-four hours to offer an apology on behalf of his people for having obstructed the work of the Government officers, and to promise that he would not again oppose the survey of the disputed land. The chief replied, stating that he did not wish for war; that he loved the white people very much; but that he would not permit the land to be surveyed.

On the 22nd of February martial law was proclaimed. The proclamation· was signed by Governor Browne, and countersigned by the Colonial Secretary on the 25th of January, ready to be published at the discretion of the officer commanding the troops. It was translated into the Maori language, and copies of it, both in English and Maori, were posted in all public places. Exception was taken by some influential parties to the terms used in the translation, on the ground that the natives would understand by the words " fighting law " that a challenge was given to arm themselves, and stand up in a fair fight for their object. But this was a strained view of the proclamation, and was maintained rather to oppose the Government than to describe the real effect of martial law on the native mind. When the struggle was carried on between the troops and Maories in the province of Wellington, in 1846, that district was placed under martial law, so that the natives had not now to inquire for the first time what it meant. Many of the settlers knew not what might be implied in the new form of power which was to be exercised over them, nor could anyone explain it; for martial law is nothing more than an arbitrary assumption of authority, without any sanction from the civil law until an Act of Indemnification has been passed by the legislative powers of the realm. It is clear that such a suspension of civil authority—or if that is not suspended, its action being *permitted* only by the military authority—should not be attempted except on occasions of extreme danger. In its operation among the settlers of New Plymouth the bullocks and carts of the farmers were unceremoniously taken for military purposes, their houses were used as temporary barracks, without any care being taken in some instances of the furniture which was turned out to make way for the troops, and block-houses were placed on their farms. After some time the rougher forms of authority gave way to the general usages of civil law; but yet we could never forget the strict military rule which was kept in abeyance, and which might any moment be let loose against us. Some of the friendly natives, whose houses and plantations were situated in or near the town of New Plymouth, were exposed to similar inconveniences, their lands being found necessary for the purposes of the war; we do not know that any real suffering ensued, except temporarily, as compensation was fairly given to them in such instances.

The time selected for the enforcement of the survey was unseasonable, as the harvest was not over, consequently the country settlers suffered very heavy losses. Placards were issued by the Colonel Commanding, promising to give sufficient notice of danger to the farmers, and recommending them to pursue their work without alarm. Such advice, however, was not of much value while the plainest preparations for war were going forward, and it was not known whether the Maories would be so complaisant as to wait till the troops were quite prepared. Without overlooking the value of their crops, the farmers considered the lives of their wives and children as being of the most importance, and therefore the time which should otherwise have been spent in gathering in their harvests, was employed in removing their families into the town. In some cases, fields of corn were hurriedly reaped, and then immediately half-threshed, it being deemed better policy to secure only a portion, than, by attempting to gain the whole, run the risk of losing all. Extensive fields of potatoes were growing, but not sufficiently advanced to be taken up. Hundreds of tons were therefore left in the ground, and large quantities of an earlier crop, which could not be removed for want of carts, were laid in heaps, and soon after fell into the hands of the insurgent natives. In most cases, household furniture was left, because means of conveyance were not to be found; and much that was removed was broken in the journey, or destroyed by exposure to the sun and rain. Stoves, ploughs, and other large iron goods, were, of course, left, and soon after were either taken away, or broken by the natives. Crockery, glass ware, and other things admitting such treatment, were put into cases, and buried in the earth. Feather beds, and such other articles as could be removed, were generally taken into town; but some ventured to leave them in their deserted houses. The consequence was, that the natives ripped them open, and scattered the feathers to the winds. Valuable books were treated in the same manner, or taken away to be

A*

used as cartridge paper. It was a common but pitiable sight to see a long train of carts, laden with baggage, on the top of which were seated women and children, wending their way to New Plymouth, while the beautiful weather which had ripened their harvests invited them to gather together the proceeds of their industry, no one knowing whether they should soon return in safety to their pleasant homes, or whether they had left them for ever.

Events soon transpired which showed that the fears of the settlers were not without foundation, and that, in the early removal of their families, instead of harvesting their crops, they were pursuing the better policy. The men were called into active service as a body of militia; stockades were erected in different directions by the militia, under military orders; bullocks and carts were summarily employed—the goods of the settlers, in some instances, being thrown out of the carts into the street—by military officers; and there is much reason to fear that, had the families remained in their homesteads after the troops had been set in motion, many would have fallen beneath the fearful tomahawk. Yet we think that the removal of the families from the country produced an injurious effect upon the Maories. Wonder, alarm, and defiance seemed depicted in their countenances. They seemed to read in such hurried movements that war was determined on. Accordingly, they hastily threshed out their corn, and took up their potato crops. Large quantities of produce were brought into New Plymouth for sale, and a stock of clothing, groceries, and tobacco was bought. Spades, axes, tomahawks, and other tools, were purchased in considerable numbers, until an order was issued by the

Government prohibiting their further sale—and every effort was used to secure ammunition. Some of the Maories, more open-minded than their neighbours, kept their intentions no secret, but told the settlers, in broken English, that they were preparing "to make a fight." So excited did some of them become, that they acknowledged to us, in our own house, that in the following year they should put in no crops beyond what might be necessary for their own support, but should direct all their energies to the coming war.

The country settlers had great difficulty in securing even the poorest accommodation in the town. None of the houses were large; nearly all of them were small, with no other accommodations than were necessary for the comfort of the families inhabiting them. Yet in some of these as many as forty persons were temporarily lodged. Churches and chapels were filled; piles of bedding were lying in them during Divine Service on Sundays. Out-houses, without chimneys, windows, or floors, were tenanted by unhappy families. Disease soon made its appearance, the consequence of excitement, a change of diet, and overcrowding. English cholera, fever, diphtheria, hurried many into the grave; consumption wasted others.

" Woes clustered, rare are solitary woes."

The melancholy scene which met the eye in every direction, was the more to be regretted from the fact that many of the sufferers had spent nearly twenty years in the province ; some of them were among the first occupants of the soil; they had passed through a course of rough and laborious life ; their youth and early manhood had been spent in laying the foundation of a civil community on the very site of the most shocking heathen orgies, practised only a few years before their arrival. Their industry had brought its natural reward; plenty and loveliness were found in their rural homes, and, so far as appearances went, their declining years were likely to be spent in comfort. When, from the top of their loads of baggage, they looked a last farewell to their "home," the peach trees were loaded with unripe fruit, the flower gardens perfumed the air, the cattle, sheep, and horses were quietly grazing, and the cows, with heavy, distended udders, had been milked for the last time. Such was the state of society in New Plymouth, when arrangements were made to march the troops to the Waitara.

On the 1st of March, his Excellency the Governor arrived at New Plymouth, accompanied by Colonel Gold, Commander of the Forces, his staff officers, about two hundred rank and file, and a great quantity of military stores; and a few hours after, H.M.S. S. Niger came to anchor in the roadstead, conveying artillery, including several field-pieces, and nine thousand rounds of ammunition. Everyone saw in these movements a preparation for war. Conciliatory proclamations were issued by the Governor in the Maori language, and posted in all public thoroughfares; and other proclamations were published in English, directing the settlers to use the utmost civility to the friendly and neutral natives. The militia had been under drill for some time, and ammunition was now served out to them. By this time, affairs had assumed such a serious aspect that it was evident that an appeal to force must be made, or the honour of the Government must be given up. Letters addressed to Wiremu Kingi were treated with disdain. A safe conduct was offered him if he would come into town, and discuss the subject of complaint with the Governor; but, although he did not doubt his safety, ·according to his own statement, the offer was declined. The fact is, that the Governor determined to have the disputed land surveyed, and the defiant natives resolved that it should not be done; and as neither party would yield, the consequence was war.

The order to move the troops to the Waitara was given on Sunday, March 4th, the time for starting being fixed at a very early hour, long before daylight, the next morning; causing the Sabbath to be spent in excitement and military preparation. Blacksmiths and others were at work all day, bullock-carts were driven about and loaded with stores, and but few persons seemed to be at liberty to attend divine worship. The next morning about four o'clock the line of march was formed, headed by Colonel Gold, who was accompanied by mounted orderlies; skirmishers were thrown out, and every precaution taken to prevent a surprise from the natives; a long line of carts filled with ammunition and military stores, and field-pieces drawn by bullocks and attended by artillery, figured in the scene; it was our first display of the pomp and circumstance of war—with which we were destined to become familiar—and was, therefore, the more imposing. Within a few hours the intended position was gained, *nem. con.*, the natives in sullen defiance remaining in a pah situated on the disputed land, and which Wiremu Kingi had some years before built with the consent of Teira's father. The survey was commenced under the protection of the troops, but was not completed. The Maories appear to have spent the day in forming their plans, and at night they proceeded in an energetic manner to execute them;

for by daylight one morning a pah was seen built across
the road, on the borders of the contested block. This
spirited movement convinced the governor, who was
with the troops, that the Maories meant to display their
prowess in the field; on a further examination it was
found that they had pulled up the surveyor's stakes and
burnt them, so that the position of his Excellency
became increasingly unpleasant, being compelled either
to commence hostilities or to retire beaten from the
field. On March 17th, 1860, the artillery opened fire
by throwing a rocket and then a shell, to which the
Maories replied with their small arms. The firing
continued till daylight was past, when the troops were
ordered to cease firing, but to keep their position till the
morning; an occasional shell was, however, thrown into
the pah during the night, and a few bullets were heard
striking the ground near the men outside; and when
the morning came, which was to have witnessed the
capture of the rebels, the pah was found empty. The
first shot was fired by Lieutenant McNaughton, R.A., a
young man highly esteemed for his private conduct and
military abilities; and on the same day of the following
year, as he was laying a Cohorn mortar in front of
Hapurona's pah, a ball passed through his wrist, entered
his bosom and laid him down dead. Although the
natives had fled, there were proofs left sufficient to show
that some terrible wounds had been inflicted, but it is
not certain that they suffered more than ourselves; for
we had one man killed and several others wounded, and
some who escaped without physical injury had their
clothes perforated by bullets. This was the first fight,
and like many others which followed led to no definite
results; the Maories leaving the pahs not with the

understanding that they were beaten, but in accordance with their mode of warfare; and the soldiers, after spending many hours in the post of danger, and seeing their comrades shot down by their side, finding no other occupants of the pahs when, with the shout of triumph, they successfully rushed in, but a poor bewildered solitary dog.

For ten days direct hostilities were confined to the banks of the Waitara. The south side of New Plymouth was certainly menaced by the arrival of natives from distant Kaingas, or villages; yet the settlers put the fairest construction upon their movements, and went about unarmed, conscious that the Governor wished to confine his operations to Wiremu Kingi's people. The farmers did not see it probable that other tribes would interfere; this was a fatal mistake, and soon led to very sad consequences. The author was looking at a body of militia drawn up in the centre of the town of New Plymouth, on March 27th, when some horsemen rode in at full speed, with the melancholy news that three white men were lying dead in the public road at Omata, a village four miles distant. None of these men were armed. They were well known, and had been on very friendly terms with their murderers; yet they were cruelly shot down under cover of a furze hedge, and then shockingly hacked with the tomahawk. One of these men was a trader, who left town a little while before to inspect a flock of sheep; the other two were farmers, residing near the spot where they fell—one being on his way to milk his cows, and the other was driving a bullock-cart, loaded with wood; and not content with taking the lives of the men, the bullocks were shot dead in the yoke. All these men left widows, and

two of them were snatched away from children who
were too young to understand their loss. The next
morning, the bodies of two lads were found on the edge
of the bush, not far from their homes, which they were
visiting without arms. They were terribly chopped with
tomakawks. We looked at their mutilated remains with
painful feelings. These lads were quiet and industrious;
they belonged to the Sabbath-school connected with our
own Church, and it was our melancholy duty to inter
their remains, together with those of two of the men
above mentioned, in one funeral service. We have
been more particular in giving an account of *these* murders, because they proved to be the first fruits of a
plenteous harvest of cruelty and death.

The battle of Waireka was fought on the following
day. The occasion of it was found in the injudicious
determination of a few families to stay in their homes
at Omata, after their neighbours had come into town.
Among them were the Rev. H. H. Brown, of the Church
of England, and his family; and, so far as we can see,
the safety of all the Europeans in the neighbourhood
depended on his presence. He had not been long in the
colony, knew but little of the Maori language, and was
not known personally to many of the natives; but they
were aware of his clerical profession, and on this account
tapued his house, which became an asylum—and, through
the influence of the tapu, a safe one too — for the
alarmed families. Considerable anxiety was felt in
town concerning them, as Omata was filled with excited
rebels, and the excitement was, of course, increased after
the murders had been committed. An expedition was
therefore sent to their relief on the 28th, and as a fight
was very probable, the disposition of the force was

arranged accordingly. A detachment of the 65th Regiment, under the command of Lieutenant-Colonel Murrey, and a strong body of Volunteers and Militia, under the command of Captain Stapp, marched by different roads. The civilian force met with the natives, quite prepared for battle, as the former left the beach, a little south of the Sugar Loaves, and a determined struggle was begun. The troops hastened to the scene, and took part in the engagement till the evening, when the bugle sounded a retreat, Lieut.-Colonel Murrey having received orders to return to town by dark. The Militia and Volunteers were left in the field, with their ammunition expended, and their retreat rendered very difficult. Late in the afternoon, Captain Cracroft, and a detachment of men from H.M.S.S. Niger, then lying in the roadstead, arrived in the field, and soon made their influence felt. They rushed into a temporary pah, containing a number of natives, and dealt out the work of destruction with a strong hand. The Maori flag had floated from the palisading of this pah, on seeing which Captain Cracroft promised £10 to any of his men who could secure it. The attempt was soon made, the flag secured, and the prize obtained. The Militia and Volunteers were left, after all their companions in arms had returned to New Plymouth, causing much anxiety and sorrow among the people, whose husbands, sons, and brothers were exposed unaided to the casualties of the field. After much loss of time, another expedition was formed to relieve the civilian force, and started a little while before midnight; but they had scarcely left the town before we heard the mingled hurrahs of both parties, and a few minutes after they came into town, and met with the warmest reception. A touching inspection was then commenced by the women — wives seeking their husbands, and mothers their sons. Some were still missing who were known to be wounded, but not removed from the field. A company of volunteers went in search of them in vain. They were found early the next morning, exhausted by fatigue and loss of blood. We had some men killed, and many wounded. What the natives suffered, we do not definitely know, as their accounts vary much; but we know that several of their principal chiefs, as well as men less famous, were killed, and that many cartloads of dead and wounded were removed the next day.

Much as this battle was regretted by the humane and Christian settlers, it was very probably the means of preventing an attack upon the town of New Plymouth; and had such an attack been made—according to the avowed intentions of the Taranaki and Ngatiruamui tribes—the slaughter of women and children must, we think, have been great. The highest opinion was expressed by the friendly natives of the prowess of our men, and the boasted pride of the enemy was, for once, laid in the dust. It is the opinion of many, that, had Colonel Gold followed up the victory of Waireka, taking advantage of the crest-fallen state of the southern tribes, the war might have been crushed at once, and hundreds of lives been spared. Without expressing an opinion on this point, we do say that it was dangerous policy to allow them to take away their wounded, when we might have taken them as prisoners of war, and treated them humanely; and still worse to let them gather up their guns and ammunition, to be used against us at a future day. As this was the first engagement in which the Volunteers—whose training has caused a considerable

stir both in Great Britain and the colonies—had been
engaged as a body, and as it was the commencement of
a series of contests which were likely to become numerous, a demonstration was made in Auckland by the
gallant captain of the Niger, in which the young men
of Taranaki were spoken of in the highest terms.

This course of action prevented the immediate relief
of the Rev. Mr. Brown and his refugees. They saw the
natives pass on to the scene of action, whose eyes
sparkled with pleasure, and their countenances beamed
with hope. The firing was heard, and the flashing of
the powder was seen by them, not knowing what effects
were then produced, or what consequences might follow.
A night of terror followed ; and it was a great relief when,
late the next day, they watched the progress of the cartloads of dead and wounded along the southern road.
Soon after this the hour of their deliverance came, and
great was their joy when they found themselves under
the protection of their countrymen, without a person
having received any injury, beyond the natural effect
which the peculiar circumstances through which they
had passed must produce. And sincere was their gratitude to Almighty God, to whom they owed their safety,
through the means of a heathen custom. Thus ended
an episode in the history of the Taranaki war, which
will be remembered as long as the present generation
shall live.

That a mistake was made in permitting the southern
tribes to remove down the coast at leisure, to bury their
dead, to mourn over their losses, and recount their
supposed wrongs to their countrymen, soon became
apparent. To lie under the thought that the Pakeha
had beaten them in battle, was chafing to the native

mind ; and another effort must be made to regain their status as men of war. To allow the death of their relatives, especially of their principal chiefs, to remain unavenged, was contrary to all their ancient customs. So strong was the feeling of some of their old men— whose forefathers, for several generations, had died on the battle-field—that they were intensely desirous of a death equally honourable ; and as the English did not seem disposed to fight again, the fear of meeting the Maories in another action was supposed to be the cause. The result was, that a resolution was formed to retrace their steps, and revenge their dead upon the ground where they fell. The valley of the Waireka and the adjacent hills were again covered with hostile Maories, anxious to fight ; and because the troops did not move, the natives took up a position there, and held it without disturbance for about three months. They could occa- sionally be seen from the town, and were constantly within sight, if not within rifle range, of the men shut up in the Omata blockhouse. From this position they sallied out at pleasure, to kill sheep and oxen, or drive them, together with a considerable number of horses, down the coast to their own country. We often saw houses on fire in the country, from the Barrack Hill. In a word, the natives were permitted to do what they pleased during these three months, provided only they kept from the town, and from the immediate precincts of the blockhouses. But as their challenge to fight was not accepted, after waiting about three months, the war- party moved homeward, taking with them a goodly amount of spoil, to the no little relief of the Colonel commanding, who constantly dreaded an attack would be made upon the town.

A melancholy reverse attended our arms on the 27th day of June. The natives had built a strong pah at Puketakauere, not far from the Waitara river, and it was deemed necessary to drive them from their position. A report was current in New Plymouth, that Major Nelson, of the 40th Regiment, commanding at the Waitara, was to meet a force from the town, and attack the pah. On the morning above stated, the gallant Major marched his men to the front of the pah, wondered that his expected assistance from New Plymouth had not arrived, and commenced the attack. The troops were exposed to a fearful fire, while the Maories were defended by strong rows of palisading, besides their rifle-pits. It soon became probable that, instead of getting possession of the pah, the troops would all be cut off. The retreat was therefore sounded, and the dead and wounded were left lying in front of the pah. Some of the wounded men lay still till the curtains of darkness were drawn around them; they then silently crept towards their camp, which a few succeeded in reaching. Others were unable to drag themselves through a shallow stream which crossed their path, and were drowned in a few inches of water. Those who yet lived, but had not strength to move, were tomahawked, it is said, by Maori boys. A printed account was posted in the principal places of the town, signed by the Colonel commanding, stating that twenty-nine men were killed, and thirty-three wounded. Among the former was Lieut. Brooke, 40th Regiment, who, being attacked in a swamp and wounded, surrendered his sword; but instead of being taken as a prisoner of war, was immediately despatched with savage delight. A strong indignation was felt in the town at the loss of so many brave men, and Colonel Gold found it necessary for his own honour to contradict the report that he had ordered the attack, or engaged to reinforce Major Nelson. Very little value, however, was attached to this contradiction, as Colonel Gold led out a strong detachment, with field-pieces, up to the Waiongana river that morning, and some of the Volunteers, understanding that the Puketakauere pah was to be attacked, went with the troops, without being ordered to do so, to share in the events of the day. When the river was reached— within little more than half an hour's march of the pah —the retreat was sounded, and the men retraced their steps to the town. The reasons assigned were, that the river was not fordable—it was narrow, and about four feet deep—and that an attack upon New Plymouth was imminent.

It was our pleasing and yet painful duty to visit the men who were wounded in this unhappy attack, and to administer to them the consolations of religion. Some months afterwards, when visiting the Waitara camp, we witnessed a strange spectacle. Some men of the 40th Regiment were cleaning and drying a few human skulls —the relics of their comrades who fell at the front of Puketakauere, intending to preserve them as a memorial of that unhappy event. A melancholy interest attaches itself to the circumstances under which those skulls came into their possession. When a search was made around the pah, after it fell into our hands, a heap of human skeletons, eleven in number, was discovered. All of them were tomahawked, the skulls of the greater part being fearfully smashed. Those that were less broken were taken away, and preserved as we have stated. We looked with sorrowful interest at two large coffins, in which the bones of our countrymen were placed, and longed for the time when peace should be restored to the earth.

An attack upon New Plymouth was, no doubt, often meditated by the insurgents, though we do not believe that it was ever seriously planned. The number of armed Maories lying in the bush was occasionally considerable; but the reports concerning them were often exaggerated. Yet, as they went about at pleasure within an hour's walk of the town, a feeling of danger was natural. Garrison orders were issued, appointing places of safety for women and children. The principal buildings selected for this purpose were the soldiers' barracks, and the places of worship. These were sometimes filled by night; babes were unexpectedly born there, and other things transpired quite different from the purposes for which they were erected. Subsequently, the orders were changed, the women and children being directed to remain in their houses in case the town was attacked, and to place a candle at every window, so that the streets might be clear and light for the operations of the troops. After this, iron bars were seen in some windows, sufficient to prevent the sudden ingress of an enemy, and candles were placed ready to be lighted at the given signal. In July, it was resolved to intrench the town, and on as small a scale as possible, so that the trenches might be the more easily manned. About thirty acres, including the centre of the town, were speedily surrounded with a ditch and bank, the entrances being defended by strong gates. A stranger would have pronounced these intrenchments of little value, as in some places cattle could climb to the top, and at others a palisading, which a man could easily pull down, was substituted for the ditch and bank. Broken bottles were strewn along the trench, and sentries were carefully placed within a few yards of each other. Several times in the week the trenches were manned, so that everyone might know his proper place. Allowing the necessity of the entrenchments, and the propriety of the orders for their regulation, it must be admitted that a serious mistake was made in excluding a populous part of the town, thereby exposing many families to the risk of a crossfire, or obliging them to come within the entrenchments, where there were not places to afford the poorest shelter. Observing a great number of dogs about the town, the thought was suggested to Colonel Gold that they might be kennelled, so as to give notice of the insurgents, if they should pay us a nightly visit. The statement which he had read in his school-days, that Rome was once saved by the cackling of geese, confirmed the idea, and orders were issued for the capture, kennelling, and feeding of dogs, to act as extra sentries. It is cheerfully admitted that great care was taken to preserve the town from an attack; but it must be said that no measures were used to prevent the destruction of property in the suburbs. We have stood on the Barrack Hill, within the entrenchments, and with painful feelings looked at the destruction of costly and beautiful homesteads by fire, in the middle of the day, within one mile of the town, while their owners and their neighbours could easily have driven off the incendiaries, had they been permitted to move. Murders were repeatedly committed within the same distance of the garrison. Through a mistaken policy, or a dishonourable fear, the suburbs of New Plymouth were open to marauding parties; and we have heard the alarm sounded in the middle of the day, while the shops were closed by request of military

officers, the trenches manned, and the streets lined with
troops, cannon pointed, and the gunners standing by to
fire them at a momentary signal ; while a company of a
hundred men could with ease have driven off all the
rebels whose presence and practices caused so much
immediate disturbance. It will scarcely be credited, yet
it is true, that the Maories deliberately yoked the bullocks at the suburban farmsteads, loaded the carts with
articles most valuable to them, and drove them to their
Kaingas ; and we must further state, that one night they
burnt an extensive range of raupo buildings, erected by
the troops as temporary barracks, *within the precincts of
the town,* though at a little distance from the most populous part, *nemine contradicente.* If these things are fairly
considered, it will not be thought surprising that the
inhabitants of New Plymouth felt a relief when, on
August 3rd, Colonel Gold was superseded by the arrival
of General Pratt, to take the command of the war.

Not many days passed before the settlers learned that
General Pratt intended to carry out the purposes of his
predecessor, the most unpopular of which was to send
the women and children away to the Middle Island.
Nelson was determined on as the place of refuge ; and
a hearty welcome was given to them by the Nelson
people. But the inconveniences, expense, and anxiety
involved in such an arrangement could justify it only in
extreme circumstances ; and on the subject of its necessity there was a difference of opinion between the military officers and the settlers. Subsequent experience
has shown, that had a more determined course of action
been maintained, the neighbourhood of the town might
have been kept clear of marauding parties ; and had
only a portion of the money paid for shipping off the

B *

families been spent in erecting houses, many evils, and a heavy expenditure, would have been prevented. Ships were chartered, agents were appointed, printed directions were issued, arguments were used; military men tried to shew that mothers, wives, and daughters were, not not only useless in war time, but an incumbrance, and must be sent away; but the settlers thought otherwise, and many of the women determined not to go. An amusing battle was fought for some time between Lieut.-Colonel Cary, the Deputy Adjutant General, in behalf of the Commander-in-Chief, and the ladies of New Plymouth. The following is a specimen of the weapons used by the former:—

"PROCLAMATION.

"Much irregularity, delay, and inconvenience to the public service, being caused by families ordered to embark on board the steamers provided for their conveyance disobeying the orders they receive, the Major-General directs it to be notified, that he will be compelled to employ the power with which he is invested, to enforce the embarkation of such persons; but he trusts that the good sense of the inhabitants will render unnecessary his having recourse to a measure so repugnant to his feelings."

But the women, except a few, were invulnerable to proclamations, and garrison orders of various kinds. Their husbands were put into the guard-room for supporting them, and militia officers were put under arrest because they deliberately refused to order their men to remove the families from their houses to the ships by force. The conflict now became still more serious, for some of the women took loaded fire-arms, and locked themselves in their houses, threatening to fire upon the first man who should attempt to dislodge them; and others fastened round them their husbands' belts, with ammunition, took their rifles, and went into the bush to their former homesteads, resolved to suffer anything rather than leave their husbands and brothers, fathers and sons, to the liabilities of war, without a home, and without the comforts with which the troops were provided.

Many of the women remained firm, and a few were not requested to leave; but the greater number gave way. Some went to the sister colonies, some to different provinces of this country, while Nelson became the temporary home of the major part. Sad intelligence was occasionally conveyed to them; for their worst fears were in some cases verified. "Sickness, death, and murder" were words with which many a letter might have been labelled. Some of the men, bereft of their companions and all their home-comforts, became drunkards; and we have seen bills of upwards of £30 brought to their widows, for strong drink obtained by the husbands while the families were in Nelson. On looking back upon the conduct of the Taranaki war, we see many mistakes, much expenditure, and many losses, which might have been prevented. Much suffering— especially by placing the night pickets in very exposed places, without a shelter from the wintry blast—was endured unnecessarily. The extreme allowance of one shilling and sixpence a day, without proper clothing, added to the misery which was generally felt. But we do not forget that we are writing several years after those things took place, and that "it is easy to be wise after the event."

During the winter months, not much was attempted, beyond sending out expeditions—some of them being composed of more than a thousand men, with artillery, and a long train of carts filled with stores—to destroy the pahs, and other native property. The propriety of this course soon became doubtful; for the destruction of crops, the burning of raupo houses, the breaking of machinery, and the demolishing of pahs, was not so complete as to reduce them to want, while the irritation which they caused led the Maories to retaliate in a further destruction of the settlers' property.

As the summer approached, preparations were made for more determined measures, and an opportunity was soon afforded to discover the intentions of General Pratt. For some time, a turbulent party from Waikato wished to distinguish themselves, and not content with the banks of the Waitara, they resolved to take up a position at Mahoetahi, some miles nearer New Plymouth. The leader of this daring attempt was Wetene Taiporutu, one of the greatest chiefs of Waikato—a man who cherished the worst feelings against the white race. Before they had time to entrench themselves strongly, General Pratt determined to give them battle. Expecting a determined resistance, a strong force was mustered, comprising troops, Militia, and Volunteers, with field-pieces drawn by bullocks, and carts filled with ammunition. On the approach of the army, the Maories invited them to the conflict, shouting, "*Haere mai, haere mai!*"—"Come along, come along!"—feeling confident, apparently, that they should have no trouble to maintain their position. But they were mistaken; for soon after the firing began, the civilian forces were ordered into the pah on the one side, and the soldiers on the other, and in a few minutes the combatants were within a few yards of each other, dealing out destruction at a fearful rate. The Maories rushed from the pah into the neighbouring swamp, where a heavy fire awaited them. Throwing away their garments and guns, they ran *for their life* towards the Waitara, the soldiers pursuing, and sending the swift messengers of death among them as they ran. The fighting was soon over, and a search for the dead and wounded was commenced. Twenty-eight Maori bodies were brought into the pah, and laid side by side, among which was the body of Wetene Taiporutu. In all, forty-five natives were found killed and wounded, and several of the latter died within the next twenty-four hours. The remains of the principal chiefs were brought into the town for burial; the others were interred near the spot where they fell. Care was taken of the wounded men, among whom was one whose former position as a teacher under the direction of the missionaries, and who declared that he came to Taranaki more in the capacity of a chaplain than to fight, caused much sympathy towards him. He was treated with the utmost kindness, and, when recovered from his wounds, was escorted back to his own people. A fine young man, who had been trained in the excellent Wesleyan institution at the Three Kings, was brought into the hospital with a severe bayonet wound, but died after a few hours. One man was taken prisoner without being wounded. He was discovered feigning himself dead, and was laid across a cannon, which was soon after fired, when the man started up, and was taken prisoner. On our side, four men were killed, and sixteen wounded—two of the former being soldiers, and two civilians.

The return of the forces in the evening caused no

little excitement in New Plymouth. The men covered with sweat and dust—the guns ornamented with green branches and wild flowers—carts filled with wounded men, and others with dead bodies—the shout of victory which rent the air—the prisoners, marched between fixed bayonets—and the general feeling that, for the present, the town was not in danger of an attack from the Waikatos—produced a scene which will not be soon forgotten. An inspection of the bodies of the chiefs—pierced by bullets and bayonets, or smashed by heavier missiles—was very affecting. Military funerals followed, in which the regular troops and the Militia intermingled. But the military pomp, the solemn music, the firing at the graves, could do but little towards soothing the breasts of the bereaved.

Supposing that the Waikatos would attempt to revenge the death of their friends, and particularly of their chiefs, by an attack upon Auckland, a large number of the troops were removed thither, leaving New Plymouth to be defended by its civilian forces and a few soldiers; but this does not appear to have been necessary, as the following extract from one of the Auckland newspapers will shew :—" A most important meeting of the natives has lately taken place at Coromandel, in consequence of several near relatives of Wetene, who was killed at Mahoetahi, having expressed a determination to go to Taranaki to revenge his death; according to the native custom, they, as the representatives on the father's side, were obliged to take up the case, except otherwise decided on by the natives as a body; to prevent them from doing so this meeting was called, and all the natives and Europeans were invited to attend. A feast was prepared by the natives on a grand scale, about five hundred natives were present, a most substantial dinner o roast beef and pork, plum pudding, &c., was prepared, and got up in good style, for five days successively; for the first two days about two hundred Europeans sat down to dinner in a canvass house eighty-four yards in length, the natives at one end and the Europeans at the other, no spirits were allowed on the ground, tea being substituted in its place, and the greatest harmony and good feeling existed. The meeting will no doubt be a lasting blessing to both races."

In the month of December a more direct course of action was commenced at the Waitara. Wiremu Kingi had been reinforced by large numbers both from Waikato and the South, and it became evident that they were prepared to resist the progress of the troops. The names of Huirangi, Matarikoriko, and Kairau will long be remembered as scenes of struggle and death. Not depend-
ing on the strongly fortified pah, from which they might harass our men, they adopted the plan of rifle-pits, and so well were they constructed that our officers were suspicious that some persons who had seen the rifle-pits at the Crimea must have given them instruction. Some of these were dug in the high fern so that the soldiers were within a few yards of them and shot down before their danger was discovered. They were so constructed in many places as to afford complete protection from artillery, and temporary houses were connected with them underground where they could both sleep and store provisions. To charge these pits was deemed madness as it was supposed that the charging parties would be instantly shot down, but this has since been found errone-
ous under the command of General Sir Duncan Cameron, both in Taranaki and Waikato. The course adopted

was extremely laborious, and, notwithstanding the care
taken to preserve our men, a great many lost their
lives. The mode of warfare determined on was sapping.
We will describe the " sap " as it appeared to us on one
of our visits to the " front." It consisted of a trench
several feet wide with a depth, together with the embankments, sufficient to defend our men from balls fired
across it, and of course it was so constructed that the
fire of the enemy could not sweep it, the embankments
were built up with gabions made of the vines of the
supple-jack being filled with earth, and the whole made
impervious to rifle balls. At the head of the trench
where the work was going on there was a " sap-roller,"
which was a circular roll of wicker work made of the
supple-jack so thick that a bullet could not pierce it.
The length and diameter of it was such as to form a considerable defence for the men who were using the pick-
axe and shovel, and was moved forward at pleasure.
Where both sides of the sap were deemed to be in danger
from the enemy, the embankment was made on both
sides and was called a double sap ; but when only one
side of the trench was exposed to the fire of the natives
only one embankment was constructed, and this was
called a single sap. Sharp shooters were placed within
a few yards of each other with their rifles resting on
bags of sand on the top of the embankment, pointed to
the cover from which the Maories were firing. The
soldiers engaged in this duty were exposed to the fire of
the enemy. The trench was strewn with sleeping soldiers having their belts on and arms in their hands,
this being the only way in which tired nature could be
restored by balmy sleep. The poor weary men were
sunk into slumber as sound as could have been obtained

on a bed of down. A line of pickets was placed in advance of the works so as to cover the working party as much as possible and prevent a sudden attack, this was the most dangerous part of the service, many of the pickets being shot dead or wounded. One of these was mortally wounded on the day of our said visit, and died within a few hours. We met a man belonging to the working party coming in the rear holding up his hand which had been slightly wounded, he was laughing and seemed to enjoy his wound as a capital joke. At irregular distances redoubts were constructed in which were the encampments of the men, the sap forming their ingress and egress. In this way the troops made sure but very slow progress towards the Te Arei hills where the natives had fortified their position by a pah and long lines of rifle pits.

For some time the works were left by night, and the Maories supposing that an ambush might be laid for them prudently kept away, but after a while they ventured to visit the sap, and finding no men near threw down some of the embankment, burnt the gabions, and took away the sap-roller to their pah as a trophy, over which much rejoicing was made. The embankments were soon repaired, and another sap-roller got into position, which was protected by placing concussion shells in such a manner that an attempt to remove the roller would cause the shells to explode. This was a terrible mode of defence, but of course it fully answered its purpose.

On the 23rd of January, 1861, a resolute and daring attack was made upon one of the redoubts. The natives knew that it was full of men, but supposed it possible to surprise them before the light of day, and cut them off before much resistance could be offered. Their plans were laid with much care, covering parties being placed in different directions, and the storming party finding their way into the ditch while it was dark, cut holes in the embankment to assist them to scale it. At the first dawn of day the signal for attack was given, but the soldiers were under arms and met them with fixed bayonets; yet such was the daring spirit of the natives that they seized hold of the bayonets of our men to pull themselves to the top of the parapet, where they instantly met their death. A perfect storm of bullets was poured into the redoubt from all sides. Colonel Leslie, of the 40th Regiment, commanding the redoubt, ordered the bugle to sound for assistance, which was promptly given by Colonel Whyatt, of the 65th Regiment. The natives fled, pursued by the soldiery for some time, but after about an hour and a-half from the commencement of the attack the fight was over. Thirty-six Maori bodies lay dead, among which were those of several influential chiefs, and six others were wounded. We had five men killed, including Lieutenant Jackson, of the 40th Regiment, and eleven wounded. Among the men who fell was Corporal Howard, whose career was short but checkered. He was the son of a noble family of England, but, for reasons unknown to us, enlisted as a soldier, and conducted himself honourably. He was foremost in the charge when he fell, mortally wounded; and his body rests, without a coffin, in the lowly grave of a common soldier. His family will probably remain ignorant of his death, as Howard was an assumed name, to prevent his connections from being recognized.

After this daring attempt the fears of the officers that an attack would be made upon the town were revived,

and orders were again issued that no family must sleep
outside the trenches ; but as it was scarcely possible
to prevent this, children were laid in bed with their
clothes on, while their parents sat up ready to move at
the first sound of the alarm bugle. As we now look
back upon those times we see the goodness of God in
preventing the natives from making a rush upon the
town ; for hazardous as it would have been to them, the
danger would scarcely have equalled that at the redoubt
already named, while the destruction of life among our
women and children might have been considerable.

In the second week of March the "sap" was carried
so near the native position that a change of tactics was
inevitable. The most likely course was to storm the
Te Arei hills, but this was deemed very dangerous on
account of lines of rifle pits and other defences ; and as
the Maories could easily retire with plenty of provisions,
and had increased their ammunition by picking up the
rifle-balls with which the hills had been strewn, and
taking powder from shells which had not exploded, the
probability of peace was not apparent. But at this stage
William Thomson and others from Waikato arrived,
and urged the propriety of a truce for the purpose of
arranging terms of peace. On the morning of March
12th a white flag was flying at Te Arei, and at the
request of the natives an interpreter was sent to them,
and three days were spent in discussing terms of peace
without success, after which the white flag was hauled
down. The natives then hoisted the red flag again,
which was the signal for fighting, and fired the first
shot. Three more days of sharp fighting followed, and
several men fell on both sides. The Armstrong guns
were got into position. Lieutenant McNaughton, R.A.,

fell as he was laying a Cohorn mortar on the 17th, the anniversary of the commencement of the war. The first shot was fired by this officer, and he had been in every subsequent engagement; his excellent character and gallant conduct had won such esteem that his death was greatly lamented. On the 19th the flag of truce was again hoisted, and negotiations in reference to peace were commenced. While these were going on, the utmost good-will prevailed among the natives from Te Arei and the soldiers; the former bringing baskets of potatoes, peaches, melons, &c., into the camp as presents. A garrison order was issued on the 22nd, stating that a cessation of hostilities had been granted; that active operations would cease; and that the most amicable spirit must be shown to the Maories; but that no persons must go beyond the lines of defence without a pass from the Commander of the garrison. The Governor and suite arrived on the 27th. Gentlemen engaged in the civil service went freely about the places which had so lately been the scene of carnage; many objects attracted their attention, but the appearance of the men who had sustained the labour of the campaign was the most interesting. "It was a gratifying sight," they wrote, "to contemplate those noble fellows, whose gallant bearing shone forth through all the motley and parti-coloured array of their well-worn, threadbare, curiously clouted raiment; scarce two jackets were alike, and of the whole there were but two of scarlet hue; caps with the regimental number were at a discount; whilst a trusty cutlass in many cases did honourable duty for the officers' holiday swords."

Hapurona and others belonging to the Ngatiawa tribe, having expressed a desire for peace, the Governor offered it upon the following terms:—

" 1. The investigation of the title, and the survey
of the land at Waitara, to be continued and completed without interruption.

" 2. Every man to be permitted to state his claims
without interference, and my decision, or the decision of such persons as I shall appoint, to be
conclusive.

" 3. All the land in possession of her Majesty's forces,
belonging to those who have borne arms against
her Majesty, to be disposed of by me, as I may
think fit.

" 4. All guns belonging to the Government to be
returned.

" 5. All plunder taken from the settlers to be forth-
with restored.

" 6. The Ngatiawa who have borne arms against the
Government must submit to the Queen, and to the
authority of the law, and not resort to force for the
redress of wrongs, real or imaginary.

" 7. As I did not use force for the acquisition of land,
but for the vindication of the law, and for the
protection of her Majesty's native subjects in the
exercise of their just rights, I shall divide the land,
which I have stated my intention to dispose of,
amongst its former owners; but I shall reserve the
sites of the blockhouses and redoubts, and a small
piece of land round each, for the public use, and
shall exercise the right of making roads through
the Waitara district.

" On your submission to these terms, you will come
under the protection of the law, and enjoy your
property, both land and goods, without molestation."

We have quoted these terms in full, to enable our

readers to examine them, as they supply the best
explanation of our object in this war. It has not been
for the acquisition of land, but for the preservation of
law and order. Hapurona and a portion of his tribe—
the Ngatiawa, to which Wiremu Kingi belongs—accepted
the Governor's offer; the Waikato and the southern
people returned home; the labours of the troops were
brought to a close; and the war, for the present, so far
as the Waitara was concerned, was ended.

During these negotiations, on March 30th, Major-
General Cameron arrived, to take the command. The
troops were removed, except from the blockhouses, and
pic-nic parties of ladies and gentlemen from New Plymouth, were soon seen rambling over the ground which
had lately been stained with blood.

CHAPTER XVI.

"Thus, after storms, the rainbow hangs the shifting clouds beyond."

THE circumstances connected with the New Zealand war have invested it with more than ordinary interest both in the United Kingdom and the Colonies. For more than a quarter of a century, these islands have been noted as a successful mission field, many arguments *ad hominem* had been drawn from the effects produced by the Gospel among a people whose name was a synonym for a man-eater, whose coasts had been often strewn with the wrecks of British ships, the crews of which had been murdered, cooked, and eaten. When the erection of a colony became necessary, it was determined to adopt a course of proceeding which would not only prevent the destruction of the Maori race, but lift them up to the full participation of civilization. The object was noble, but the means used to promote it were very defective; they arose not from a wish to ignore the rights of the native people, but partly from a fear of irritating them by an interference with their national customs, and, it must be confessed, partly from neglecting the opportunities of introducing into native districts the blessings of law and order. In the course of a few years the hopes of the best friends of the Maories were likely to be accomplished. The outward forms of religion were carefully observed, the New Testament—almost their only book—was diligently studied. Many of our customs were adopted, they clothed themselves in our manufactures, and acquired property by industrial pursuits. Some alarm was felt in the fact that the race was decreasing, notwithstanding the efforts which were made to prevent it. A change of food, of clothing, of habits, and of employment, endangered the race; new forms of disease, over which we had no control, swept off many, and it must be added that strong drink and vicious diseases made fearful havoc. Large numbers of their women became sterile, children were sickly and died, so that although infanticide, in the general acceptation of the term, had ceased, the number of children reared was small. Yet many persons clung to the hope that this was only a transition period in their history, that it would soon be passed over, and that as the native constitution became accommodated to the new order of things which had grown up around them they would rise in the social scale till an amalgamation of the races might take place. But the war has unsettled these notions, our hopes for their welfare are blighted, our fears of their destruction are excited.

The great subject of dispute is the land. Men who have lived many years on intimate terms with the natives, whose familiarity with their language and customs entitle their opinions to respect, have lately attempted to illustrate the tenure upon which their lands were held. But so difficult and complicated is the subject that various and, in some cases, opposite conclusions have been arrived at. We will give a few statements as specimens of the difficulty which is felt. In a pamphlet recently published by Mr. Bushby, who was appointed to New Zealand as British Resident as early as the years 1833, it is stated that the distinctive rights of land with reference to sale had no existence before the treaty of Waitangi, that the regulations which the natives have since observed in the disposal of their land have been derived from us, that the idea of selling land was as far from the native mind, before their connexion with the European race, as that of selling the water of the ocean, or the rain of the atmosphere, and that in reality no law was observed in the disposal of their land but the law of might. The Rev. T. Buddle says, concerning the Maori word *mana*, which is supposed to express the authority of a chief over the land of his tribe, " It certainly did not originally mean that which is now claimed for it, viz., a chief's manorial right. The use of the word was not heard of until this Maori King movement originated it. . . . . A man took possession of territory by the strength of his arm, and rested his claim on his conquests. . . . . . If land exchanged hands it was not by sale, but by conquest—by might disregarding right." Mr. Clarke, one of the early missionaries of the Church of England, and in later years an active Government officer, insisting on an extensive knowledge of the Maori language, their customs and modes of thinking, as being necessary to understand the native titles to land, admits that " on the subject of tribal right there is room for a difference of opinion as to the extent of its privileges or powers." Mr. J. White, an officer in the Native Department says that there is not a part of New Zealand that was not owned by some tribe, not a stream, wood, or mountain, but had a name attached to it as an index of some point in their national history. Yet their land often changed hands, some of the titles by which it was conveyed as related by Mr. White being sufficiently amusing. If

c*

fishhooks were made of the bones of a chief and the insult was discovered, his tribe took possession of the land belonging to the offenders. If a temporary hut, built by a chief while on a journey, were used by any other party, he claimed a part of the district in which it was situated. The land on which a child was born was claimed as the right of the child. If a chief dropped one of the feathers from his head while travelling in the forest, and made an enclosure round it, without the owners of the land objecting to it, he claimed a part of the land in the neighbourhood. To call a man by the name of any eatable thing was accounted a great curse, and gave the insulted man a claim to land as a mode of redress. Land was sometimes ceded as payment for assistance in war, and was often claimed on the ground that their dead was buried there.

A Bill was brought into the British Parliament in June, 1860, by his Grace the Duke of Newcastle, the Secretary of State for the Colonies, by which it was vainly supposed that the difficulties of the land question might be met. That Bill was dropped. When the attempt to pass it into law was known in the colony some indignation was felt and expressed, the presumption being that the Imperial Parliament were suspicious of the motives which influenced the Colonial Government. This was expressed in the General Assembly, when the Honourable William Fox moved—"That this House desires to repudiate, in the strongest possible manner, the allegations which have been made, that the colonists entertain any but the most friendly feelings towards the native race; that they are in any way indifferent to their welfare and conservation; or that they entertain any such sentiments on the subject of acquisition of the native lands as have been attributed to them."

It soon became evident in the colony that a strong feeling of distrust was growing in the native mind, our most sincere assurances of kindness and honesty had but little weight; while they spoke of the Queen as their mother, who was feeding her children with cannon-balls. The Governor determined to convene a meeting of the chiefs from all parts of the country, for a free and open conference on the subject of their complaints, with a special reference to suggestions for their future government. At a considerable expense a number of chiefs were gathered together from distant places; the meeting was held at Kohimarama, a few miles from Auckland. Those who were determined to oppose the government did not go; a few who were undecided were present, but the greater part consisted of friendly chiefs. Many speeches were made, and native chants were sung, dissatisfaction was expressed, and sentiments of loyalty were declared; there were friendly greetings, the *hongi* and the *tangi* were called into frequent requisition; but it is very difficult to define the benefits which flowed from the conference. It, however, brought the chiefs into contact with his Excellency, and raised a hope that such gatherings might be beneficial when the chiefs became more accustomed to order, and might be led to express their sentiments with less reserve; an arrangement was therefore made to convene a similar conference annually, but before another year transpired Governor Browne was superseded, a different line of policy was adopted, in which the Kohimarama conference had no place.

The General Assembly of the colony was convoked,

to devise measures to quell the rebellion that seemed likely to spread. Various opinions were entertained on the best plans to insure order among the disturbed tribes. The idea of war, continued for any considerable time, was very repugnant to the feelings of the most influential men in the colony. The loss of life which it might involve, not to mention the heavy expenditure which must be met, led many to express their views of the native question with zeal and distinctness. Letters were addressed to the chiefs by the Government, and messengers were despatched to the tribes, to assure them that the war would be confined to the people who had assumed an attitude of defiance ; but many of the letters were treated with contempt, the messengers were slighted, the old men doubted the Governor's sincerity, and the young men were anxious to show their prowess in the field. All classes, except a few persons whose principles had no weight in the colony, were anxious to prevent the destruction of the natives, while the necessity of shewing the evils of insubordination was evident. Various persons published their views of the difficult question ; the newspapers teemed with lines of policy ; some thought that, if the insurgents were cut off from all communication with the colonists, while the defiant attitude was maintained, the want of such articles, both of food and clothing, as they had for many years been accustomed to enjoy, would induce their submission with but little or no destruction of life.

When the Taranaki war was first known, a general expression of sympathy for the settlers was heard, not only in all the provinces of this country, but in the neighbouring colonies also. Public meetings were held, and pleasant words were uttered. Subscriptions were raised, to be expended in finding shelter and articles of clothing for those who had been driven from their homes. The newspapers were full of the usual circumstances of war. The province of Taranaki was brought into view, and the intrepidity of its inhabitants held up to admiration. The colonies of New South Wales, Tasmania, and Victoria sent the troops which were stationed for their protection, and the Government of Victoria sent their colonial war-steamer Victoria to our aid. The ladies of Lyttelton, Canterbury, employed themselves in the pleasant and honourable work of making articles of clothing, for the comfort of the Taranaki settlers who were engaged in the war, and transmitted them, with a cheering letter of sympathy.

While those pleasing occurrences were taking place, which demand our gratitude, a painful reflection was forced upon us in reference to many of our young men. They had been trained to sobriety and industry; the example of their parents, and the success which had attended their plodding habits, led them along in the same course, and held out a promise that, from this class would spring the most substantial men of the province. Many of them were correct in their moral character, and if their language lacked refinement, it was happily free from vice; others were under religious influences, had been trained in Sunday-schools, and enjoyed the advantages of pious parents. But a military life brought them all together; the picket-room endangered their morals, but far worse was the block-house, where many were kept for months together. There, amidst oaths, card-playing, and other vices, their early restraints were weakened, till, in many instances, they were almost entirely thrown off. Many of the young men learned to drink; they became idle; their Militia pay was spent at the public-house, and we fear that their future life will be affected by the vices learned in their military career.

The elderly men were exposed to hardships which they were not able to bear. The night duties often exposed them to the storm of wind and rain, and their being without an opportunity of removing their wet clothes, they contracted disease. Some were hurried into the grave; others still live, but their health and strength are gone. They were less able to sustain the calls of military life, and more liable to consumption and other diseases, when their usual habits were interrupted, on account of the severe labour they had sustained as pioneers in colonial life.

Commissioners were appointed to examine the claims which the settlers were invited to present for losses sustained during the war. These included houses burnt, fences destroyed, and farms laid waste; and horses, cattle, and sheep lifted. A large amount was awarded them. The pomp of war was removed, and men breathed more freely. General Pratt received an ovation on his arrival at Melbourne, and was soon after knighted by his Sovereign. Other honours were bestowed, and many hearts were glad that the conflict between such unequal parties was brought to a close. But in this there was a mistake; hostilities had ceased, but the war was not ended.

CHAPTER XVII.

CESSATION OF HOSTILITIES.

"And many who suffered, are now calmly sleeping
The slumber of freemen, borne down in the fight."

IT was not unlikely that the submission of Hapurona and a few followers would be so construed as to mean the conclusion of the New Zealand war; the colonists would gladly have entertained this sentiment, had the circumstances with which they were familiar permitted them. But the fact is, that only a small section of the wide-spread Ngatiawa tribe accepted the Governor's terms; the other tribes which had taken part in the war retired in sullen silence, or tried to justify their late proceedings. Hapurona was immediately honoured with the charge of one of the blockhouses, erected not far from the Waitara, with a good salary attached to his commission. For a short time he was often seen in New Plymouth, apparently satisfied with the position he occupied. But the waters soon became troubled, for his son was roughly used by an officer into whose tent he had intruded, and the insult stung the irritable nature of Hapurona; in his excitement he threatened great things, exposed himself to a temporary arrest, and a few days after, throwing up his commission, he allied himself again to his old companions in rebellion.

The terms offered to the Taranaki and Ngatiruanui tribes were as follows:—Entire submission to the Queen and to the law; the return of all plunder then in their possession, and compensation for that which had been

destroyed; all mails to be permitted to pass through the
country without molestation; persons, goods, and cattle
to pass through the country without interruption; with
a distinct understanding that all parties concerned in
the murder of boys and unarmed men were to be tried
by the Supreme Court, whenever they could be arrested.
It was easy to issue terms, but difficult to secure them
respect and observance. They were simply treated with
contempt. Trusting to their generalship, their extent
of country, and the dense forest in which they could
obtain shelter from any number of troops, together with
the abundant provisions which could be easily produced
both inland and along the coast, the tribes between New
Plymouth and Wanganui maintained a defiant position.

Better things were expected from the Waikato tribes;
they had credit for superior principles, and were making
rapid improvement in the usages of civilized life before
the idea of a king distracted their attention. The best
construction was put upon their words and acts; efforts
were made to induce them to acknowledge again the
Queen's supremacy; while serious fears were entertained
of the consequences which might issue from the general
agitation. The danger increased, it was not possible
any longer to ignore it; and some steps were deemed
necessary to stop the course of evil. A numerous and
influential native meeting was arranged to take place at
Ngaruawhahia; as the principal chiefs were to be present,
the Governor considered this to be a favourable opportunity to lay before the Waikato people a firm declaration of the line of policy which he intended to carry out
in reference to the king movement and other subjects of
dispute. A long declaration was drawn up with considerable judgment, reminding them that in setting up

a king in opposition to her Majesty's Sovereignty, in levying war against the Queen, in burning and otherwise destroying the property of her Majesty's peaceful subjects ; by interrupting the free course of the law through war parties, by stopping the mail, and by usurping jurisdiction over Europeans ; they had violated the Treaty of Waitangi. The Declaration concluded by demanding from all—"Submission without reserve to the Queen's authority and the authority of the law. From those who are in possession of plunder taken from her Majesty's European or native subjects, restoration of that plunder. From those who destroyed or made away with property belonging to her Majesty's European or native subjects, compensation for the losses sustained."

The Ngaruawhahia meeting was convened on the 6th of June, 1861 ; ceremonial visits were paid to the tomb of Potatau, likewise to the present king ; speeches were delivered as usual, and food was distributed. The next day a tangi (lamentation) was held for Wetini Taiporutu, who fell at Manoetahi. On the 8th the Governor's Declaration was produced, and parts of it read. Contempt was expressed by some, and others determined to " stop their ears " against it. Several clergymen were present, who urged the propriety of considering the Declaration through courtesy to the Governor, as well as on other grounds. But it was in vain, for Wiremu Tamihana and others, on rising to reply, justified the proceedings of the Maories in the course which they had taken.

A reply was, however, sent to the Governor from the meeting, informing him that a report had reached them that the General had insisted on a war with Waikato, and concluding with the following words :—" O friend, restrain your angry feelings against all parts of New Zealand. Let our warfare be that of the lips alone. If such be the course pursued by us it will be a long path, our days will be many while engaged in fighting that battle. Let it not be transferred to the battle (fought) with hands. That is a bad road, a short path ; our days will not be many while engaged with the edge of the sword. But do you, the first-born of God's sons, consider these things. Let not you and us be committed to the short path ; let us take the circuitous one, though circuitous, its windings are upon firm ground." Wiremu Tamihana also replied to the Declaration of the Governor by a long letter, in which he argued that his Excellency's prohibition was founded upon the relation subsisting between master and slave, and was contrary to the directions given in Deuteronomy xvii. 15.

As the time was approaching when the Governor intended to convoke the General Assembly, and with a view of gathering together the chiefs of various tribes for the purposes of a conference, the subjects of dispute between the two races, and the measures best calculated to settle them, naturally occupied much of his Excellency's attention. Accordingly a memorandum was published by the Governor, dated May 25th, 1861, taking a comprehensive view of the dangers and difficulties attending the present state of the native people, and suggesting a line of policy which, if properly carried out, seemed most likely to restore peace and preserve harmony. His Excellency suggested that " native territory should be divided into districts, and if possible one or more chiefs in each should be appointed to act as organs of communication with the Government ; that the Runangas, lawfully constituted, should have power to recommend regulations for the local affairs of the district; and that measures should be taken to ascertain and register tribal rights. To carry out these regulations it was suggested that a particular chief should be selected to act in each district between the Governor and the people. A description of the Hapus (sections) of each tribe, with a list of all the families belonging to each and the chiefs who represent it, with the boundaries of the land belonging to each Hapu, should be carefully made and registered; and certain chiefs, to be chosen by the people, were to be made trustees of such land, with the assurance that it should not be sold without their consent. The General Assembly should confer the power upon the Governor, or upon some other persons, subject to her Majesty's approval, to clothe the native title with a Crown grant. His Excellency further stated that a much larger staff of officers will be required if the Government really undertake the civilization of the Maori people; as Hokianga, Kaipara, Taupo, the Ngatiruanui, and Taranaki tribes, and the country about the east coast, have rarely been visited by an officer of the Government, and some of them not at all; the consequence is that "the residents in those districts have never felt that they are the subjects of the Queen of England, and have little reason to think that the Government of the colony cares at all about their welfare." In the opinion of the Governor the native service should be entirely remodelled and made efficient; for which purpose a central school should be established for the instruction of assessors and young men who might wish to enter the native service; and that schools, adapted to the wants of the people, should be conducted in the Kaingas.

The General Assembly met in June. All felt it to be the great work of the session to arrange conditions which the Maories would accept, and which should secure a lasting peace. Different opinions were expressed concerning the policy of the Governor, and quite enough was said in justification of Wiremu Kingi. The most important incident which occurred, was the arrival of despatches, appointing Sir George Grey, K.C.B., lately the Governor at the Cape of Good Hope, to supersede Colonel T. Gore Browne in the government of New Zealand.

The fame which Sir George Grey had won in the management of aboriginal tribes, both in this country and at the Cape, was the cause of his re-appointment. Very high expectations were formed of him in England ; an honourable member of the House of Commons declared that his presence among the Maories would be equal to ten thousand troops, and Mr. Gladstone, then a member of the Imperial Cabinet, called him a great Proconsul. Many persons saw a smooth path before them, through his influence. Wrongs would be righted, the natives would be cared for, disaffection would cease, and the prosperity of both races would roll on in one mingled stream. Others were more considerate. Being aware of the honourable intentions of Governor Browne, and the obstinacy of the insurgent natives, and supposing that the former would not be exceeded, nor the latter abated, the change of Governors was not accepted as the panacea of all our evils. Yet all classes received Sir George Grey heartily. The act of the home Government to relieve our distresses by this extraordinary appointment, was appreciated, and the Premier determined to object to no plan which his Excellency might wish to adopt, but to assist him to obtain whatever measures he might desire, and whatever money he might deem necessary to enable him to carry them out.

Sir George Grey arrived at Auckland on September 26th, 1861, in H.M. corvette Cossack, 20 guns, Captain R. Moorman. His landing was the occasion of great excitement. Offices were closed, shops were shut, and demonstrations of welcome were general. His Excellency was installed as Governor of New Zealand on the 3rd of October, 1861, his Honour the Chief Justice administering the oaths. Addresses were presented to him from both Europeans and natives. Some of the latter were so interesting, that we will quote some specimens. Soon after it was known that Sir George had been re-appointed, a few chiefs near Auckland prepared a long address, in which they said :—" The dogs of Governor Browne and Potatau are here, biting one another. Their keepers have acted foolishly. The chains of the Pakeha dogs have been loosened, and they have bitten the Maori dogs, which have turned upon seeking satisfaction, after they felt the pain. . . . Do you search out the meaning of this our song :—

" Thou comest back in grief,
O youngest and best-beloved son.
Once were the people sportive,
Like the tide which ebbs from off the strand.
Alas ! The influence like unto that
Which women hold o'er men
Has vanished ; and the people now
Are wanderers in the world—wide world—
Subject to its capriciousness and hate,
Like withered plants, scorched by the noontide sun.
Thou wert drifting [*i.e.*, the Government],
Borne along by tidal streams,
Whose waves ran high,
And overset the prows.
Now thou art broken—cast upon the shore."

Taraia, the principal chief of the Thames, an old warrior, said—" Here have I been during your absence, lonely, weeping for you. . . . The waters of my sea, Houraki, were quiet when you left, and now, upon your return, they are still calm. The waves of other places have been rudely dashing ; but you will quiet them. . . . Welcome to the shore, O father of the Maori and Pakeha!" Similar sentiments were expressed by the chiefs of Coromandel and of the Bay of Plenty.

We have already shewn that a better organisation was deemed necessary by the preceding Governor — an organisation in which the natives might be largely employed as officers. This view obtained favour in the eyes of the Home Government, and in despatches to Sir George Grey, dated June 5th, 1861, the Duke of Newcastle says—" I look forward to the introduction by you of some institutions of civil government, and some rudiments of law and order, into those native districts whose inhabitants have hitherto been subjects of the Queen in little more than in name, notwithstanding the well-meant colonial legislation of the last few years.

In the latter part of the year, the Governor visited the Waikato, where many gave him a hearty reception. As he stepped ashore at Kohanga, he was welcomed by the war-dance, and shouts of " *Haere mai! Haeri mai!*" On the 16th of December, a meeting was convened at Taupari, composed of about seven hundred persons, to whom his Excellency stated that he intended to act impartially for the good of both races, and to put an end to war, and that, for this object, a very large force, which might be increased at his pleasure, had been placed at his disposal. He urged them to restore the plunder taken from Taranaki as stolen property. The

value of having roads was pointed out, showing that
their produce could then be conveyed in carts, instead of
continuing to burden their women, and so to risk the
future health and strength of the race. The importance
of allowing travellers to pass without molestation was
insisted on. His Excellency treated the Maori king and
his flag as being child's play; but stated that they might
lead to bad consequences, and promised that no land
should be purchased without all persons concerned in it
being consulted. A sketch of the future form of Government was given in which districts were to be proclaimed,
Runangas held, native magistrates appointed, and sala-
ried officers employed. Medical gentlemen, also, were
to reside among them; clergymen were to be increased,
and schoolmasters were to be spread through the districts; and, in addition to these improvements, openings
were to be found for superior young chiefs in the Government service, which would ensure their respectability
and influence.

Another meeting was held at Kohanga on the following
day, in a large native building. The representatives of
five tribes were present. Considerable efforts had been
made to decorate the house for the occasion. A wooden
image, elegantly tattooed, representing Tipa, the ancestor
of the tribes present, was placed above the seat of the
Governor. A beautiful mat hung around the image, and
a very old and highly-prized stone weapon was suspended
from its hand. At this meeting the usual amount of
speech-making was heard; but the anxiety of the
Maories to obtain arms and ammunition, with their
opposition to the making of roads, indicated the approach
of evil times.

The tribes residing in the Taranaki province retained

their spirit of opposition to the Government in the most unmistakeable manner. No Europeans were allowed to travel on their land; the over-land mails were stopped, and his Lordship the Bishop of New Zealand was turned back. Then, to allow a little variety in their policy, a "toll gate" was set up, past which natives and Pakehas might go on the payment of a stated sum, varying from a shilling to six hundred pounds sterling.

In Waikato and other places the working of the Runangas was very unsatisfactory. Men, women, and children constituted these gatherings, whose proceedings were not conducted on any recognised principles. They were often held late in the evening, when each endeavoured to out-talk the other. But their inability to adjust their own differences was not the only evil, nor was it the least, resulting from them. Industrial habits were broken up, wide fields lay uncultivated, ploughs and harrows, machines and mills were suffered to rust and rot through disuse and exposure. Great poverty prevailed as the consequence, which was occasionally relieved by exorbitant fines, demanded of Europeans, if any of their cattle, sheep, or horses, happened to stray upon the waste land of the Maories.

Many of the young men were trained as soldiers, after the military style of England; and their behaviour at drill, their uniform—consisting of blue coats and white trousers, with white caps, having a red cross embroidered in front—and the discipline maintained, were striking instances of their ability to copy what they deem valuable in a superior race. Could we have seen those young men as fully determined to imitate the English in the arts, and industry, and virtues which the Government and the religious bodies endeavoured to place within

their reach, they might soon have become men of substance and influence. But where are they, while we
write? Many have fallen upon the battle-field, and
others are wanderers, driven by the war which they have
evoked from the land of their fathers, with an uncertain
future looming before them.

The subject of Native Schools occupied an interesting
place during the cessation of hostilities—not that there
is much to admire in the effects produced by them,
but they serve to shew the desire maintained to raise
the race, and the difficulties which attended the work.
A Board of Education was instituted by the Government,
and large sums of money expended, with various results.
The assertion which we have heard, that the schools
established by the Government really provide a good
education for all the youth of the Maori race, is simply
incorrect. But few parents avail themselves of the offer,
nor are they calculated to meet the wants of all. This
has been acknowledged by gentlemen whose long residence in the country, and intimate acquaintance with
the people, entitle their opinions to respect. George
Clarke, Esq., Civil Commissioner at the Bay of Islands,
after stating that those schools "leave the bulk of the
population untouched and uneducated," suggested the
institution of village day-schools, to be supported by
Government, under proper inspection; intelligent natives
to be appointed teachers, with a small salary; the
instruction to be given chiefly or entirely in the Maori
language, and confined to an elementary course. From
these schools it was proposed to select intelligent boys
and girls for admission into the Central Schools, which
would be expected to teach the higher branches of a
good education, together with the English language.

There is much to recommend in Mr. Clarke's scheme, and there are many difficulties lying in its way. We could point out probable causes of failure without being able to suggest anything which would be more likely to meet the case. Desirable as native education is, and desirous as we are that measures should be taken to educate and raise the Maori race, we despair of seeing much accomplished in it before the complete return of peace.

CHAPTER XVIII.

RE-COMMENCEMENT OF THE WAR.

"The line advances ; shot on shot,
And ever true and steady."
FREILIGRATH.

IT was in the beautiful month of March, 1863, when
Sir George Grey and his Executive Council deemed
it right to "re-instate the Taranaki province." On the
4th of the month his Excellency, with Lieutenant-
General Cameron, the Colonial Secretary, and the
native minister, landed from H.M.S. Harrier, under
an appropriate salute. The news of his Excellency's
arrival soon spread southward, producing some excitement, in which the natives concerted measures for their
future conduct. Before determining his course the
Governor was understood to have received letters from
some of the Waikato chiefs, consenting that Tataraimaka
might be re-occupied. It was not grateful to the feelings of the settlers that the consent of native chiefs
living more than a hundred miles away should be considered necessary to the peaceful occupation of their
former homesteads, which had been bought with their
own money, cultivated with their own hands, and for
many years before the war had been the scene of peace
and plenty. Still, if they could have entered upon their
farms with safety, the native feature in the Governor's
policy would not have greatly injured them. But instead
of sanctioning the re-occupation of Tataraimaka, the
spirit of suspicion was evoked concerning the intentions

of the Government among the Waikato tribes. On the 20th March an outrage was committed at Kohekohe, on the Waikato river. At the request of Te Wheoro, Sir George Grey had consented to erect a court-house and a police-station at Kohekohe, as a part of his plan to introduce law and order among those tribes. Soon after the buildings were commenced the natives imagined that the real object was to erect barracks for the introduction of the troops; and determining to stop this at once, about two hundred men went unarmed, broke up the works, floated the timber to Maungatawhiri, the nearest military station, and sent off the carpenters, without inflicting personal injury.

Significant as this act was, a still more hostile spirit was shown at Otawao only four days after it. Some time before, the Governor had originated an institution of great value, regardless of expense, at Awamutu, Otawao, on the extensive property which had been given by Potatau and others to the Church Missionary Society. It was intended to exhibit, on a scale which had not been seen before in a Maori district, the advantages of civilization. In addition to superior educational advantages there was a model farm, tradesmen were employed to teach carpentry, shoe-making, smith's work, and printing. The convenience of these trades being carried on in the heart of a native population was great, and the consumption on the establishment secured a ready market for the neighbouring produce. The domestic arrangements were most satisfactory. There was a printing-press also, from which a newspaper was issued in the Maori language, and widely circulated. Some articles in this journal, relating to the evils attending the Maori king movement, increased the jealousy and dislike of the natives to the institution; notwithstanding the number of Maori youths whom they knew were well fed and clothed, and learning useful trades. Rewi, the principal chief of the Ngatimaniopoto tribe, determined to break up the establishment, and endeavoured to inspire his men for the work by chanting a *waiata*, of which the following translation is a part :—

> " Cast them down, dash them down.
> Fling them upon the trees.
> Let them be as prey to be cast down ;
> As prey to be dashed down ;
> As prey to become the property of the far-famed.
> Arise ! gird on !
> It is to be cast down ; it is to be dashed down ;
> It is to be brought into collision—
> The collision of army meeting army ;
> It is the prayer to overset them,
> To lash them.
> O Tangaroa, file your teeth,
> Sharpen your teeth ! "

The spirit of this song will not be mistaken, although it has nothing else to recommend it to notice ; nor was it lost upon the followers of Rewi, who formed a taua—war party—and broke up the Awamutu institution: This was done on the 24th of March, in the temporary absence of J. E. Gorst, Esq., the civil commissioner residing at the station. Two bullock-carts were taken to convey the spoil to a distance. The printing-house was forcibly entered, the press and other articles were placed in the carts a nd driven off, the fence was partly destroyed, and an armed sentry was placed over the premises. Firebrands were procured to burn down the buildings, but happily were not applied. Mr. Gorst was urged to leave, and threatened with death if he refused. It was said that all the Waikato people were agreed in this work of destruction; but this was incorrect, for the utmost loyalty and friendship were shown by some in their endeavours to prevent the outrage. By these proceedings twenty-two native lads were hindered from pursuing their respective callings, in which they were deeply interested, and the most complete civilizing institution which had been formed among the Maories came to an end. Aporo, one of the most active chiefs in this affair, was apprehended soon after in the city of Auckland, tried for the offence, and sentenced to a long imprisonment. The principal aggressor, however, was Rewi—a chief who has since distinguished himself in war—as the following letter, addressed to Sir George Grey the next day, will show :—

Friend Governor Grey,—Greeting.—

"This is my word to you :—Mr. Gorst has suffered through me. They are my men who took it—eighty armed with guns; the reason whereof is to turn off Mr. Gorst, in order that he may return to the town; it is on account of the darkness occasioned by his being sent here to stay and deceive us, and also on account of your word, 'by digging at the sides, your king movement will fall.'

"Friend, take Mr. Gorst back to town; do not let him stay with me at Te Awamutu. Enough; if you say that he is to stay, he will die. Enough; send speedily your letter to fetch him in three weeks. It is ended. From your friend,

"From REWI MANIAPOTO."

At Taranaki circumstances became still more threatening; road parties were stopped, a rumour prevailed among the friendly Maories that war would soon re-commence, and the few settlers who had ventured to their farms seeing cause for alarm, removed their families into the town. His Excellency and suite were in New Plymouth ; they ignored the danger, and tried to banter the settlers out of their fears. But this did not avert the peril. On the 20th of April an ambush of forty-five natives, divided into three parties, was placed by the side of the road leading from New Plymouth to Tatara-maka, whose object was to cut off the first European whom they might see ; the plan of attack was for the middle party to fire ; and the others to prevent escape. The *Taranaki Herald* of April 25th published a state-ment of the danger, and drew upon itself the temporary ridicule of the Auckland newspapers. But on the 4th of May another ambuscade was laid, with fatal effect. Dr. Hope, Lieutenant Traggett, Sergeants Ellers, and Hill, privates Flynn, Kelly, Banks, McCarthy, and Ryan, belonging to the 57th Regiment—were the victims. All were shot and tomahawked except Kelly, who made his escape after receiving a ball through his trousers. Flynn, we believe was the only married man who fell; consequently much sympathy was shown to his widow. Sir George Grey gave her a valuable building site, sub-scriptions towards re-erection of a cottage were raised, amounting to £79, of which Lieut-General Cameron gave £25. A gold medal was presented to private Kelly, as a memorial of his escape, and reward for his bra-very. It was barely possible that this might be murder, a private crime, rather than a declaration of war ; the Government wishing to consider it in this light directed a coroner's inquest to be held, but the movements of the natives very soon placed their intentions in the clearest light. On the 29th Lieutenant Waller was fired at from an ambush on the same road, not far from a redoubt ; his horse fell and was despatched with the tomahawk, from which fate the rider had a narrow escape. Assistance being immediately obtained, one of the ambuscade was apprehended : he was a half-caste, named Hori (George) ; upon his person and near the spot where he was taken Dr. Hope's watch, chain, locket, and ring were found, with a rifle and some of the accoutrements belonging to the murdered soldiers. A session of the Supreme Court was held at New Plymonth in the early part of July, when Hori was placed on his trial for the wilful murder of Dr. Hope and the attack on Lieutenant Waller. The peculiar circumstances under which the Court was held occasioned some special remarks from his honour the Chief Justice. He described the event—the Supreme Court convened in a garrison town, under martial law—as being an anomaly ; for until a recent period the civil power had been so jealous of the military, that no soldier was allowed to remain in a city where the Queen's judges were holding assizes ; and that still later it was an act of great indulgence to a soldier to be allowed to leave his barracks and appear before the public during an assize ; while in the present case the Supreme Court was really sitting under the protection of the military power. Hori being found guilty on both charges, was condemned to be hanged, which sentence, however, was commuted to imprisonment for life.

The natives boldly attempted to take up a strong position on the banks of the Katikara river, that forms the south-west boundary of the Tataraimaka block, within a few hundred yards of the troops, which led to the first battle after the re-commencement of hostilities. This took place on the 4th of June; the troops with Armstrong guns were marched to the neighbourhood on the previous night, H.M.S. Eclipse, having Sir George Grey on board, being ready to take a part in the action. Soon after daylight the natives were surprised by the fire of the Armstrong guns; before they could recover themselves, the Rifle pits were taken in a rush with fixed bayonets, followed by a terrible slaughter. In their infatuation some hid themselves in the *raupo wares*, and were burnt to death! Twenty-eight native bodies were interred, including the remains of those which were burnt, and many were wounded. One soldier was killed and nine wounded, some of whom died soon after.

The event so long dreaded had now taken place, hostilities were renewed. To what extent would it spread? How far were the Waikato tribes committed in the course taken by the Southern natives? Could the settlers in the wide-spread provinces be protected if a general rising of the natives took place? What treatment might be shewn to our women and children should they fall into the hands of the Maories? Would it be a repetition of the horrors of the Indian mutiny on a smaller scale? Such questions as these were natural, but no one could answer them, our fears were aroused, and, while praying for the Almighty's protection, defensive measures were promptly taken.

The development of the war has revealed a spirit of hostility which justified those fears, as the following pages will show. From Whanganui to Auckland, with but little exception, the country has been laid under the ban of war. Waikato, Waipa, the neighbourhood of Auckland, Tauranga, and Whanganui, as well as Taranaki, became the scene of battle and slaughter. Yet there are many tribes that have not drawn the sword, particularly northward of Auckland, nor are they likely to do so. This is a subject of thankfulness, as is also the fact that only one European female has been killed, and she was not tomahawked.* Additional barbarities have been perpetrated lately by the insurgents of Taranaki and Whanganui, the heads of victims having been cut off and taken away. It was feared that if the war were prolonged this phase of horror would be followed by others, till they would revert to cannibal abominations. It was supposed with some reason that this loathsome custom had already been revived, at least in one instance, as portions of a human body—that of a soldier—were found under circumstances which justified suspicion, but we soon learnt that our worst fears were unfounded.

This darker feature of Maori warfare was commenced at Aua Aua, a few miles from New Plymouth, in April, 1864. Captain Lloyd and a few men were suddenly attacked, thrown into confusion, and shot down. In addition to other mutilations five bodies were found decapitated. This was a cloudy and dark day. All that military pomp could do to shew respect to the departed, and cover the scene with the array of glory, was done, but the inhabitants of New Plymouth having closed their shops and offices followed in a truly mournful procession as the headless bodies of their countrymen were carried to the grave. The head of Captain Lloyd—who left a widow and two children in New Plymouth—was taken down the cost to Whanganui, by the

* Since the above was written a terrible slaughter of women and children has been perpetrated by the natives of the east coast.

Maories, for a purpose similar to that of the Levite, whose shocking history is recorded in Judges xix.—to stir up the people to deeds of revenge. It was with much satisfaction that the head of· the gallant Captain was recovered by peaceable means and deposited in his grave.

We have said that the country southward of Tataraimaka was shut up from the Pakeha, and from any of the Maories whom the resident tribes did not wish to see on their lands. The boundary line was marked by the erection of a board containing a statement of tolls, which were to be paid before any one was allowed to pass. This constituted the " gate," which proved a serious hindrance to the military officers and others, when they were desirous of reaching the ship-wrecked passengers and crew of the " Lord Worsley," but the safety of their lives was considered most probable if the " gate " were not forced. The supposition was no doubt correct. As a curiosity of its kind we will present the reader with a partial copy of the tolls demanded in the name of King Matutaera Potatau, translated, of course, into English :—

TOLLS PAYABLE AT THE MAORI GATE.

Minister of the Gospel ...	...	...	... £50	0	0
Newspaper mail ...	...	...	...	... 300	0	0
Maori disciple of the governor ...		...	... 200	0	0
Pakeha policeman	...	...	...	... 500	0	0
Maori policeman ...	...	...	...	... 5	0	0
A preaching Maori minister	...	...	... 55	0	0
(Letter) badly tempting (the tribe) seize it and make the bearer pay ...	...	...	... 500	0	0

The above is the law for the Pakeha people.

Tolls of the Maori people are as follows :—

Things carried on a man's back ...	..	...	0	0	1

A pig carried in a cart	...	...	...	...	0	0	6
Pig driven ...	...	...	...	...	...	0	0	6
A cow or horse, each	...	...	...	...	0	2	0
Fine for trying to evade these tolls	...	...	5	0	0

The gate with its tolls may be considered as a clever piece of policy, for it completely shuts out the settlers from going in search of their cattle and horses which strayed beyond the boundary, or which had been taken away by hostile natives, while it permitted the Maories of the south to visit the town to sell their produce and buy what they wanted, on the payment of a small sum, during the two years that hostilities were suspended.

Among those who took most interest in the Maories in England were the noblemen and gentlemen who composed the committee of the Aborigines' Protection Society. The moral worth, the high position, and the indomitable zeal of those gentlemen, could not fail to secure respect to any course of action which they might adopt. But it is quite as likely that they might damage the cause which they sought to promote, as it is that the colonists might prevent by ill-advised acts, the speedy and lasting settlement of the dispute. That their interference proceeded from the most honourable motives no one can doubt, but it is more than doubtful whether it accomplished any good for the native people. That the war has been prolonged, the native people reassured in their determined opposition to the Government, the course of his Excellency the Governor interrupted, and that the loss of many lives among both races have been the result of that well-meant interference, can hardly be denied. In a memorial addressed to His Grace the Duke of Newcastle, the Secretary of State for the Colonies, they denounced the Confiscating

Act as a sweeping and indiscriminate measure without a parallel in the history of modern colonization, an indelible blot upon the British name, unless the Imperial Government prevented its enforcement, and calculated to drive the natives into hopeless rebellion and despair.

An address was also sent by the same committee to Sir George Grey, as the Governor of New Zealand, regretting the confiscation of the land belonging to the insurgents, and expressing a hope that his Excellency would lose no favourable opportunity of making peace. To this the Governor replied in a firm and respectful manner, stating that the proposed confiscation would increase the value of the land belonging to the loyal natives, while it would convince the insurgents that rebellion is a dangerous enterprise, for a European population would supply a market for a native produce and offer a high price for any surplus lands which the Maori owners might wish to dispose of, and while the people who have been in arms against the Government would find a sufficiency of land set apart for their use, they would not fail to understand the superior circumstances of the tribes that had not disputed the Queen's sovereignty.

His Excellency transmitted the address to his Ministers, requesting them to favour him with their observations on it. Accordingly an official memorandum was prepared in which they state that up to that time—May 5th, 1864—the natives in rebellion had not made the smallest overture of peace, that in the opinion of many natives the Maori king would be eventually triumphant ; that according to native customs the party that makes advances of peace acknowledges itself, by such an act, to be beaten ; that the efforts which the Government have already made in this direction had been construed as an expression of weakness; that the opportunity to return to the Queen's allegiance has always been open, without any personal punishment whatever—an opportunity which a considerable number have embraced. That to urge the Maories to come to terms of peace would at once arouse their suspicions and deter them from it, and that no hopes can be entertained of a permanent peace till the hostile tribes acknowledge the supremacy of British law. On the subject of confiscation the official memorial remarks: that in Maori warfare the conquered tribes forfeited their lands, and that the Government of New Zealand has always recognised this title to lands as valid; that the Maories had intended to appropriate the houses and farms of the settlers to their own use, by right of conquest; and that the confiscation of a large portion of the waste lands of the natives in arms against the Queen, in order that they may be peopled by the white race, was necessary, not only to preserve the colony from destruction, but to prevent the native feuds which have proved a very serious barrier to the advancement of the race. The land which was to be set aside for the use of the natives would be very much increased in value, as a certain portion, more than sufficient to supply their wants, was to be conveyed to them in families or as individuals by a Crown grant, and by this means it was hoped that the land disputes would be settled for ever.

On a careful consideration of the circumstances through which we have passed for the last seven years, we cannot see how the renewal of the war could have been prevented. The re-occupation of Tataraimaka before the claims to the Waitara were given up might be the occasion, but it certainly was not the cause of the outbreak. Of this we think the desolation of the Taranaki province, the exclusion of the Europeans from the country southward of New Plymouth, and the conduct of the natives in connection with the wreck of the "Lord Worsley," are conclusive. Nor were the tribes residing in the neighbourhood of Waikato less determined against the continuance of British rule. The Maori king might be a foible, a thing which would please for a while and then fall to the ground by the weight of its absurdity. So Sir George Grey treated it, hoping that by ignoring its power he should destroy it, but in this he was mistaken. Yet allowing the Maori king and the so-called Maori Government, the application of the latter to European traders and settlers could not be permitted. To levy taxes, to execute Maori-made laws, to distrain under enormous fines the cattle which happened to trespass on native waste lands ; to take away by force the native women who had been married to white men, together with the half-caste children, the issue of these marriages ; to stop the Government mails and destroy the contents of the mail bags at pleasure ; to form a taua—a war party—and march them into the settled districts, to redress real or imaginary wrongs ; to slaughter the troops and settlers, both in open warfare and in a more private manner, and then expect to be treated with all confidence and kindness in the next province are things altogether inconsistent with the honour and safety of a British Colony. This is the course which the adlerents of the Maori king have pursued, the settlers have borne with it, the Government have wished to ignore it as much as possible, hoping for a

favourable turn in these affairs, but all in vain. According-
ing to the statement of the Maories themselves, they
waited till they were tired, expecting that the Governor
would commence the war afresh, but being disappointed
in this, they determined to re-open hostilities in the
manner just narrated.

CHAPTER XIX.

" Balls whistle ; stones fly left and right ;
  Stout arms are standards bearing !"
                                    FREILIGRATH.

FOR many years the native tribes inhabiting the
Waikato district have occupied a distinguished
position. The extensive and fertile plains produced
abundance of food, the rivers afforded an easy mode of
travelling from the coast to the interior parts of the
island, the number of fighting men which could be
quickly brought into the field was large, and the energetic chieftains who had swayed their councils won the
respect of many other tribes. This was increased by
the raids made upon distant parts of the island, the
cruelties practised, and the slaves secured. The approach of a Waikato *taua* was the signal of distress, followed by flight or desperate resistance ; the threat of
such a visit, long after the colony had been formed, led
to the complete fortification of the pahs, and storing
provisions for a siege.

The Waikato chiefs were desirous of a simultaneous
attack upon the provinces in the southern part of the
island, while they themselves would deal out destruction
to the town and district of Auckland. Northward of
Auckland the natives were anxious that the honour of
the Waikatos should be laid in the dust ; this arose
partly from ancient animosities, buried but not destroyed,
and partly from their anxiety for the safety of the colony.

E*

The Hokianga Maories wrote to Sir George Grey:—
"O Governor, be strong to strike the fire that is blazing.
Strike, extinguish, trample, and put it out, lest it come
blazing here, and burn your children." In carrying
the war therefore into the Waikato country, the Governor was not only consulting the safety of Auckland,
but by striking at the root of the evil he endeavoured to
prevent hostilities from being opened among distant
tribes, and in districts where the Queen's supremacy
was still acknowledged.

On the 12th July, 1863, Lieutenant-General Cameron,
with three hundred and eighty men, crossed the Man-
gatawhiri stream—the boundary between the Government and the native land—and for the first time invaded
Waikato. Two days after, an elderly settler and his son,
both unarmed, were murdered at their work. The next
day, twenty-five natives, who refused either to remove
or to swear allegiance to the Queen, were apprehended.
A proclamation was published, threatening to confiscate
the land of any Waikatos who might join in the war.
The settlers became alarmed, many families left their
homesteads for places of refuge, and a collision seemed
imminent. On the 17th the Maories attacked the escort
at Shepherd's Bush with considerable spirit, and were
gallantly met by our men, though with great disadvantage, under the command of Captain Ring. A gentleman who visited the scene before the rencontre was ended,
observes,—"We saw men lying dead among the felled
timber. One poor soldier had his face frightfully tomahawked, and his tongue was nearly plucked up by the
roots. We passed by pools of blood; horses lay dead in
their traces; and the household goods of the settlers
were strewn on the road. Five soldiers were killed and

twelve wounded. The losses sustained by the natives could not be accurately ascertained."

On the same day the battle of Koheroa was fought. As this was the first engagement fought by Her Majesty's troops in Waikato, more than usual interest was excited by it. On July 16th the natives assembled in force on the hills in front of the camp, and commenced fortifying their position with rifle pits, thus giving a challenge to the troops for a trial of arms. Lieutenant-Colonel Austen, of the second battalion of the 14th regiment, in charge of the Koheroa camp, marched out with five hundred men, without artillery, in the forenoon of the 17th, and a spirited destructive action followed. The rifle pits were charged—General Cameron, it is said, rushing forward twenty yards in advance of the men, waving his cap in the air with a cheer,—and directly after the pits were cleared at the point of the bayonet. The main body of the enemy fled in confusion, and were pursued by the troops about five miles. The victory was complete, but it was purchased with a considerable loss of life among the Maories. The statements of their losses are various, but it is certain that not less than fifty men fell. Among the things left by the natives in their encampment were spades, tomahawks, spears, double-barrelled guns, flint muskets, green-stone *meres*, ammunition, and a large quantity of good clothing. The troops suffered less than might have been expected ; only one man being killed in action, and twelve wounded, but some of these soon after died in consequence of their wounds.

This was followed by the murder of several settlers, families were attacked in their houses, one woman was shot, the only white woman who had fallen during the war;* and the destruction of property was very great. The most melancholy instance occurred in a family named Trust. A youth, aged seventeen years, with his younger brothers, one aged twelve and the other nine years, endeavoured to make their escape from a house which the Maories attacked. As he ran with his little brothers, one in each hand, the Maories pursued and fired upon them; one of the little children fell wounded, and a few moments after was despatched with the tomahawk; then the other child was shot down, and met with a similar fate; the youth was also shot in the shoulder, but succeeded in getting away.

After a hot fight at Mere-Mere the next stand made by the natives was at Rangiriri, a few miles higher up the river. This place will long be remembered as the scene of a hard-fought battle. After the discoveries made at Mere-Mere the greatest preparations were deemed necessary in the attack to be made at Rangiriri. The action was commenced at three o'clock p.m., on the 20th November, 1863, with the Armstrong guns, and was replied to by the natives with small arms—the only kind they possessed. After working the guns for about an hour and a half, the General gave orders to charge the rifle pits, determined to force his way to the centre of the pah. The order was obeyed with such impetuosity, under a heavy fire from the front and flank, that the natives ran from the first line of defence. The soldiers fought their way to the central works, which they could not carry. These consisted of a square redoubt, with a ditch nine feet wide and a parapet twenty feet high, protected by rifle pits on the front and flank. Here, a

* This was written before the massacre of women and children on the East Coast.

tremendous firing was kept up, with terrible effect. Several attempts were made to storm the redoubt without success. A detachment of the 40th Regiment made the first trial, we believe under Colonel Leslie ; then the Royal Artillery, led by Captain Mercer, made a desperate effort ; General Cameron then requested Commodore Sir William Wiseman to supply a strong party of Marines and Blue-jackets from the force which was acting on the river, which request was immediately complied with, and the men dashed up to the redoubt in the highest spirits, but were driven back with great loss. By this time the day was nearly ended, but the firing was continued by moonlight. The enemy was shut up in a small redoubt, and surrounded by the troops, so that escape seemed impossible. In this manner the night passed away, the General expressing his determination to carry the redoubt on the following morning at all hazards. Many of the officers and men lay in their blood through that long night, while the cold air and the occasional showers added to their sufferings ; and within sight of their companions in arms, who could render them no relief, on account of the incessant fire kept up by the natives. Many a man thought of wife and children, and many a fervent prayer was offered up for divine protection. Soon after daylight, when the order was about to be given to storm the works, the natives hoisted a white flag—there was an unconditional surrender. The effect produced cannot be described.

Nearly a hundred natives were killed and as many wounded, according to the most reliable accounts. Our own loss was severe : two officers were killed and thirteen wounded, some of the wounds being so severe that death soon followed; thirty-five rank and file were killed, and eighty-five wounded; making our loss in all one hundred and thirty-five. It would be a melancholy pleasure to linger over the memory of several who met their death at Rangiriri, but it may be better to ask the reader's attention to one case only—that of Captain Mercer.

Captain Mercer's gallantry in the field of battle, and Christian conduct in private life, will not soon be forgotten. He had command of a battery of Armstrong guns. While in Auckland he devoted as much time and attention to the Young Men's Christian Association, the Bible Society, and the Sunday School belonging to one of the Independent Churches, as his military duties would permit. He was severely wounded in the early part of the action, in an attempt to force his way into the redoubt, and lay all night in unutterable agony. The next morning he was found with his head resting upon the dead body of a gunner. Both jaws were shattered, and his tongue was torn out, but reason retained her seat. Mrs. Mercer, on the eve of her confinement, hastened to the camp, to render him the tender offices which might if possible smooth the last hours of life. Not being able to speak, he took a pencil and wrote the following memorable words:—"My darling, do not grieve for me. I have peace, the most perfect peace in Jesus —deep, deep as a river! He doeth all things well." A few hours after this he died, leaving a disconsolate widow and four small children.

On the 31st of March and 1st of April, 1864, the battle of Orakau was fought. The Maories were said to be only three hundred, and we know that they defended themselves with small arms only, but they were probably the flower of their fighting men. Their position was very strong, with flank defences and deep trenches, and was nearly covered by flax bushes, high fern, and peach trees. The usual appliances of artillery were tried, but without much effect.

When General Cameron arrived, and, on learning that women and children were in the pah, he directed the firing to cease for a short time, and requested the Maories to consider the value of life to their wives and children, and submit; but the answer returned was that they would never submit, but would "fight for ever and ever and ever." The artillery again poured upon them a tremendous storm of shot and shell, and a breach was made through which the soldiers rushed into the redoubt. The Maories then leaped the parapet and trenches in front of the troops, dashed through the lines formed by the 40th Regiment, and ran in the midst of a shower of bullets. The troops pursued them for about six miles, strewing the course with killed and wounded, both men and women. It must not be forgotten that the Maories had been entirely destitute of water for about three days, and that the pah was surrounded by overwhelming numbers, that they were cut off from all hope of success, and that they did not leave their position till the slow but certain process of sapping, together with the incessant use of guns and rifles, made it evident that they must either submit or flee. The General declared that "it was impossible not to admire their heroic courage and devotion in defending themselves so long against such fearful odds."

Nearly twenty bodies had been buried by the natives inside the pah, and numbers lay along the route which they took, so that about one hundred Maories were supposed to be killed. Thirty-four prisoners fell into our hands, but of these twenty-seven were wounded. On our side sixteen were killed and fifty-two were wounded. The losses sustained at Orakau contributed a good deal towards a desire for peace among some of the influential chiefs. There was little hope of eventual success. The natives were not desirous of another battle, the positions already occupied were left in sullen silence—this proved to be the last battle which decided the fate of Waikato.

The war in Waikato will always be remembered as a very unequal contest. The number of men constituting the Maori force was perhaps not more than the seventh of the number employed against them. Nor could their weapons of war bear any comparison with the various and formidable implements of British warfare. Much of their powder was of their own manufacture, and of course was an inferior article; for shot they used marbles, copper coin cut in pieces, and pellets of wood. They made gun-caps of the phosphorus taken from lucifer matches, embedding it in the eyelets which are used in lacing boots. The loss of their three pieces of cannon was greatly in their favour, as in addition to the difficulty of conveying them to distant places, they could ill spare the quantity of powder necessary to make them effective, and we have already seen that during the little time they had them in position the most effective shot consisted of a seven pound scale weight.

But their perfect acquaintance with the country, the assistance in conveying provisions which they received from their women, the ease with which they could cross the well-known swamps, or glide through the tangled forest, gave them a great advantage. They are naturally impetuous, fond of excitement, and very superstitious.

These things were the means of sustaining them, for if they were driven from one position some pretended prophet foretold success on a future occasion, which led them to continue a contest which there was not the slightest reason to suppose could be brought to a successful issue.

CHAPTER XX.

" Thine arm from peril guards the coasts
Of them who in Thy laws delight ;
Thy presence turns the scale of doubtful fight,
Tremendous God of battles, Lord of Hosts."

WORDSWORTH.

EARLY in the year 1864 indications of rebellion were seen in places remote from Waikato. Ominous signs began to appear at Tauranga, in the Bay of Plenty, on the east coast. It was deemed necessary, therefore, to send a detachment of troops thither. It was soon found that men as brave as those who nobly defended their position at Rangiriri were to be met at Tauranga. Challenges were sent to Colonel Green, stating the time when they would be ready to fight, and, that they were determined to defend their hills and plains till the last.

A resolute attempt was made to drive the enemy from the Pukehinahina pah, commonly called the Gate pah. In a description of the pah contained in the dispatches of General Cameron to his Excellency the Governor, dated May 5th, 1864, we learn that " it was constructed on a neck of land five hundred yards wide, the slopes of which fell off into a swamp on either side. On the highest point of this neck they had constructed an oblong redoubt, well palisaded and surrounded by a post and rail fence." The assaulting column was composed of one hundred and fifty seamen and marines under Commander Hay, of H.M. steamer " Harrier," and an equal number of the 43rd Regiment under Colonel Booth. A breach having been made by the artillery, a desperate attempt was made to storm the redoubt, which was as desperately defended. Within a few minutes almost every officer of the column was either killed or wounded. Suddenly the troops fell back to the nearest cover, which gave the enemy a great advantage. We had sixty-four killed and forty-six wounded. The superior conduct of the natives, compared with those of the west coast, should not be forgotten, not a dead body was mutilated, nor a wounded man ill-treated, nor was anything taken away, although watches, gold rings, money, and other valuable articles were entirely within their reach. The insurgents lost about thirty men, many of whom had been long known in the neighbourhood as quiet inoffensive persons, till the war-demon inspired them.

The vigilant commander of the troops endeavoured to prevent the completion of another pah. This led to the spirited and decisive battle of Te Ranga, a few miles from the Gate pah. On the morning of June 21st, a strong body of troops with an Armstrong gun went to meet the enemy, whom they found at work in their rifle pits. After a consultation among the principal officers, it was decided to make an immediate attack, the bugles sounded the "charge," the men cheered with a will, and with fixed bayonets rushed upon the rifle pits. The natives remained firm, defending themselves with great coolness and determination, till a large number was lying in the trenches either killed or wounded, when the remainder endeavoured to escape followed by the soldiers who shot them down as they ran.

The number of Maories supposed to be at Te Ranga was about six hundred, embracing men from distant parts of the country. The victory was decisive. Not less than seventeen principal chiefs were killed, several of whom had been highly respected for their superior intelligence and good conduct before the excitement of the war. One hundred and seven Maori bodies were laid along the trenches which their own hands had prepared as places of defence—so that they had literally dug their own graves—the friendly natives wrapping the body of an old friend or a relative in a shawl or blanket as a last expression of affection.

In the latter part of July decisive measures for peace were adopted, Colonel Green, who had been in command through the painful proceedings already narrated, now came forward with buoyant steps to welcome the first overtures to loyalty. In this pleasing work Mr. Rice, of the Native Department, took an honourable place. At the appointed time one hundred and fifty men came in canoes to lay their arms at the feet of the Colonel and take the oath of allegiance to Her Majesty the Queen.

On the fifth of August his Excellency the Governor, with the Premier, the Colonial Secretary, Lieutenant-General Cameron, and suite, and other gentlemen, arrived at Tauranga, to receive the submission of the natives *pro forma*. The utmost preparations were made by the Maories in honour of the occasion. Some of the men were dressed in good broad cloth ; the women displayed a fine assortment of crinolines of large size, silk dresses and elegant head attire. But all were not so fortunate, for the blanket was the principal article of clothing worn by many persons, whose shrunken and careworn countenances shewed that they had known what hunger was. When all were seated, and a few minutes had passed in respectful silence, Pencanimi

Taku gracefully addressed his Excellency :—" Welcome, welcome, O my Father. Welcome that which is good, welcome that which is right, welcome truth, welcome to Tauranga ; welcome love, welcome to you and our great Mother, whose laws we have trodden underfoot !" The Governor, after Puoka te Whanake and Hokohoka had spoken, then delivered a short address, and the meeting was adjourned till noon the next day.

At the appointed time Sir George Grey, General Cameron, and a number of other gentlemen met the Maories for further proceedings. Two hundred and fifty natives were present, divided into two companies— friendly natives and surrendered insurgents. After a few words of welcome from a friendly chief, the Governor delivered the following address :—" Although I am not acquainted with the boundaries or extent of your lands, or with the claims of individuals or tribes, what I shall do is this : I shall order that settlements shall at once be assigned to you, as far as possible in such localities as you may select, which shall be secured by Crown grants to yourselves and your children. I will inform you in what manner the residue of your lands will be dealt with. But as it is right in some manner to mark our sense of the honourable manner in which you conducted hostilities, neither robbing nor murdering, but respecting the wounded, I promise you that in the ultimate settlement of your lands the amount taken shall not exceed one fourth of the whole land. In order that you may, without delay, again be placed in a position which will enable you to maintain yourselves as soon as your future localities have been decided, seed potatoes, and other means of settling on your land, will be given to you." At the close of the address the natives rose and bowed, the two principal chiefs expressed their entire satisfaction, and the meeting terminated.

The expedition to Tauranga was short, sharp, and decisive. It will lie in the memories of the people for generations yet to come. Tales will be told of the prowess, and of the compassion too, both of the Pakeha and the Maori. The cemetery at Te Papa, situate on the southern peninsula of the mission station of the Ven. Archdeacon Brown, will long be clothed with melancholy interest. It had been the burial place of the Maories for many years past. Here a spear and there a skull; in one place the figure-head of a canoe, and in another a block of stone, mark the resting places of natives of fame. There also, by some large weeping willows, lie the bodies of our troops who fell at the Gate pah, with a neat fence to preserve their graves from unnecessary intrusion. Walks have been tastefully laid out, covered with sand, and bordered with shells. The graves of several of the officers are distinguished by tombstones, while the remains of humbler men who fell with them sleep securely by their side. Many whose remains are interred there had distinguished themselves at the Crimea, in some of the most exciting scenes of the Indian Mutiny, and at the Cape; for those services they had received the plaudits of their country, and wore medals and clasps, the gifts of various sovereigns; and then, while assisting to quell the rebellion in this island, met their death in a Maori pah. Scores of natives also sleep at Tauranga the sleep of death, which suddenly overtook them in the heat of action. How different will be their circumstances when all there shall hear the clang of the Archangel's trumpet, summoning all to the bar of the Great Judge, to be tried according to the deeds done in the body, whether they be good or evil.

But before then what a change will pass over our world! The weapons of war will be mere relics of the past. Nations, and tribes, and races, will love one another. The war-spirit which now destroys so widely will be looked at as an infatuation. In the midst of the millennial light and glory our history will appear a history of madness and blood. We wonder at it while we write; we dread the few first years of the future; we scarcely know what to hope for, in the turbulence which many of the tribes delight in; but we earnestly pray that the scenes which have been witnessed at Tauranga may not be enacted again in other parts of our disturbed colony.

CHAPTER XXI.

"For they have learnt to open and to close,
The ridges of grim war."

THE coast lying between New Plymouth and the mouth of the Wanganui river, extending about a hundred and eighty miles, and inhabited by the Taranaki and Ngatisuanui tribes principally, is the tract of country to which we now invite attention. The extent of beautiful land, well watered, capable of supporting a vast population, was held by a comparatively small number of natives, and having a market for their produce in the European settlements above named, they had a fair opportunity of becoming rich.

The extent of country, the dangerous rivers which intersected it, the proximity of the dense forest, the uncertainty connected with landing stores by surf boats, the thick scrub and the numerous gullies which were found in what was called the open country, to which must be added the want of roads by which guns and military stores might be conveyed; securing great advantages to the natives, but presenting formidable difficulties to the troops, made the west coast hostilities an object of general dislike to the soldiery.

In January, 1865, General Sir D. A. Cameron proceeded to Wanganui, where a considerable body of troops were awaiting his orders. Preparations were also made by the insurgents, so that the first movement of the soldiers was the signal for hostilities. The first men

men who fell were five friendly natives, shot down rather unexpectedly. The following account of one of them named Rio will show the determined character of the insurgents. His companions having been killed with bullets and tomahawks he swam his horse across a river, but while climbing the opposite bank the poor beast was shot. Rio immediately afterwards received a ball in the thigh, and then another ball passed through his body. He then submitted to the enemy, but instead of taking him prisoner, a man approached and shot him through the forehead.

A military road-making party was attacked, chiefly for the purpose of plunder, and very successfully too, for the natives secured prisoners and ammunition, clothing, working implements and food.

A signal victory was obtained by the loyal natives over a strong body of the insurgents at Ohoutahi on the 23rd of February. Besides the pah seven redoubts were thrown up and a flag staff was erected, showing that some importance was attached to the place. After some very spirited firing the order was given to charge, which was soon followed by the retreat of some and the submission of others. Pehi, an old and very influential chief, was among the rebels ; his wife shouted " O Hori Kerei, when will light come out of this darkness ?" and immediately appeared with a white flag, at the sight of which the firing ceased. Pehi, with eighty men besides their families, then become prisoners of war, but retained their arms ; the chief, however, contended that his submission had reference to the Wanganui only, and that he had a right to assume a hostile position in any other place. He soon after gave up this singular claim, and with several of his followers signed a declaration of allegiance to the Queen; but a few men of his tribe refused to do so, among whom was Topia, his own son.

The daring spirit of Topia when confronted by the Governor illustrates the difficulty of subduing the most determined natives, by either kindness or war. In reply to the question from his Excellency, whether he was willing to renounce the Maori king and the Pai Marire delusion, Topia said—" Te Kawana, kahore ahau e pai ki te houhou i te rongo ki akoe, kore rawa rawa, a ake, ake, ake," &c. In English it is, " O Governor, I will not make peace with you, never, never, never, neither now nor at any other time hereafter for ever. My enmity against you will constantly endure. It was I who brought my Hauhau worship to the inland districts of Wanganui. I cut off the head of the pakeha who was murdered at Wanganui, and sent it to Tauranga. My karakia [the Pai Marire worship] shall not be given up till I die." At this unexpected statement of his sentiments and intentions Sir George Grey ordered him out of the house, telling him that at the expiration of twenty-four hours he would offer a reward for his capture and hang him. Topia coolly replied,—" Very well, take me now, shoot me, hang me at once." The reader will probably wonder why the Governor allowed such a dangerous man to escape; he could not in honour have done otherwise, as the Maori chief came at the special invitation of his Excellency.

On the third of April a hazardous step was taken by the occupation of Pipiriki, as a military post. This place lies about seventy miles from Wanganui. The roads from the East Cape, Taupo and Waikato converge here. It has been the boast of the Maories that Pipiriki was never captured in the native wars. The only means of traffic is by the river, which the encampment completely commands. The unpleasant old chief Pehi had occupied the spot, and his redoubtable son Topia, was not likely to give it up without some fighting; but a little management accomplished the purpose, and enabled Major Atkinson, at that time minister of Defence, to locate there two hundred military settlers, and eighty friendly natives. The men with their tents and stores were conveyed in canoes, and contrary to general expectation not a shot was fired at them.

Intelligence was received on the 23rd through a native who came from the enemy, that the Ngatimaniapoto warriors, under Rewi, were expected at the Waitara, to prevent the survey of that district. Prompt measures were therefore taken to occupy Pukearuhe at the white cliffs, situate about twenty-five miles north-east of New Plymouth ; that being the only line of traffic at present available, on account of the swampy and hilly nature of the country in that neighbourhood.

In the middle of June an expedition was led southward by Colonel Warre, to meet the forces coming from Wanganui. A native prisoner was released and sent with a message to the Maories residing in villages inland of Warea, inviting them to meet the Colonel on friendly terms and intimating the unhappy consequences of their refusal. A watch was lent to the messenger that he might not mistake the time allowed for a meeting, but neither watch nor messenger was seen again. Consequently the forces marched up to the villages, and a skirmish ensued.

On the 19th of July intelligence was brought to the Governor, who was then at Wanganui, that the force under Captain Brassey at Pipiriki was in a very critical position, and as it was scarcely possible to send a sufficient reinforcement before the redoubtable Wereroa pah was subdued, Sir George Grey determined to take the field himself. With a force of four hundred and seventy-three men, most of whom were natives, with four hundred of the regular troops, encamped about nine hundred yards from the fortress as a moral support only—his Excellency managed to obtain possession of the pah at daylight on the 22nd, without losing a man. Fifty prisoners were captured, the greater part of the garrison escaped, and the position which the Governor had been so many months anxious to occupy fell into his hands under circumstances which considerably redounded to his honour.

Major-General Trevor Chute, of the Australian Station, assumed the chief command in New Zealand soon after the departure of General Cameron, and, on account of the contempt offered to the Governor's efforts to establish peace, he was soon seen at the head of his forces in a hostile attitude. His march from Wanganui to New Plymouth in the month of January, 1866, excited general hopes that the rebellion would 'be soon crushed.

On the 3rd of January, 1866, Major-General Chute left the camp at Wereroa with a force of about seven hundred men. The day following the Ototuku pah was attacked. Three sides of this fort were protected by its situation, while a line of palisading and rifle pits defended the front. Lieutenant Keogh and three men fell wounded in the advance, but as the natives beat a hasty retreat the pah was taken without any further loss. One of the insurgents was left dead, and five others are said to have been killed in the bush. The pah was destroyed, and the growing crops either pulled up or cut down. On the 6th the force halted before another rebel pah called Putahi. When the troops were seen a red flag was hoisted by the insurgents as the signal for fighting, about two hundred of the garrison came out and fell into ranks with military precision. As the General did not attack them that day a detachment of the enemy left the pah, and under cover of the bush fired upon the troops, but were driven off by the native contingent. Seeing the pah to be strongly defended General Chute secured a reinforcement from the camp at Patea, and on the 7th the attack was made. After the engagement had continued about an hour the rifle pits were charged, the natives fled and the pah was gained. Several small native settlements were destroyed on the 12th, including Whareroa, where the great meeting-house called Taiporohenui, measuring about one hundred and thirty feet in length by about forty feet in breadth, was situate, shewing this place to have been a central spot for the purposes of rebellion.

Search was then made for Otapawa, the stronghold of the Ngatiruanui tribe. It was built in the forest on a spot which secured to the garrison great advantages; much labour had been spent in palisading, entrenchments, and an underground means of escape, and it was strongly defended not only by the men belonging to it, but by those who had been driven from their pahs a few days before. Lieutenant Carre got his Armstrong six-pounders into position, but his practice, effective as it was, elicited no reply, so that many thought the pah was abandoned. On a nearer approach the rifle pits behind the palisading and a bush at right angles with

the pah swarmed with Maories, determined to reserve
their fire for the deadliest range.   The order rang out
" The 57th advance; rangers clear the bush."   The
bush was cleared, the pah was gained, and in less than
half an hour the flames were fiercely completing the
work of destruction.

The General then determined to proceed to New Plymouth by the native path behind Mount Egmont.   This
was extraordinary and unprecedented.   The force consisted of five hundred and fourteen men, all told, with
tents and other military stores.   A large number of
pack horses were provided, but to get them through the
dense and entangled forest a roadway had to be cut.
In some places the steep gullies with soft bottoms were
found more difficult than the bush.   As no more than
three days' provisions were taken, several horses were
killed and served out as rations.   A few natives were
seen and some of them shot, a little girl was captured and
adopted by the native contingent, and the wet weather
made bush marching very disagreeable; but after a few
days they all emerged in good health, rather hungry,
but elated at the feat which they had achieved.

When the extraordinary march and the signal success
of General Chute became known in New Plymouth a
public meeting was called, a triumphal arch was erected,
and a dinner was given to the non-commissioned officers
and men.   The force then moved on, supposing that
more work awaited them on their southward march.

The achievements won in such an intrepid manner
were not followed up by equally decisive measures, the
consequence was that the rebels soon rallied and determined to maintain their hostile position.   But their
numbers are becoming less, for sections of the tribes have

sworn allegiance to the Queen, and others are likely to do so soon There may be some skirmishes for a little time to come, as ambuscades are occasionally laid, especially to cut off the surveyors, but we cherish the hope that not much time will pass before peace and prosperity will be found along this blood-stained coast.

CHAPTER XXII.

" Vice and misery ramp and crawl.
  Root them out, their day has pass'd :
  Goodness is alone immortal ;
  Evil was not made to last."
                          CHARLES MACKAY.

THE subject upon which we now enter is in some
respects the most melancholy part of Maori
history. Amidst all the horrors of war, with its Sabbath
desecration, its destruction of property, the sufferings
of wounded men, and the sudden departure of the slain,
the value of true religion may be found, so that the gory
field of battle may be the scene of spiritual conflict and
victory to the dying saint. The correctness of this
statement has been repeatedly proved in this country,
by both the Pakeha and the Maori. This is in some
small measure a redeeming feature of the otherwise
execrable character of war. But the subject of the
present chapter admits of no mitigation of its evils ; it
affords nothing to hide its hideous deformity, as an
object of faith, nor has it anything to soften the harsh
and cruel measures by which its advancement has been
accomplished.

This is not the first time that the Maori mind has
been made the dupe of religious imposture. Some years
ago a man announced that he was Jesus Christ, and
endeavoured to conduct himself agreeably to this remarkable distinction, but either the mind of the people

was not suited to the occasion or he did not act his part cleverly, for the only benefit resulting from the venture was a sobriquet, under which the pretender winced all the days of his life. It is easy and natural to condemn such delusions in unmeasured terms, and to attribute them to the ill-taught mind of a people just emerging from the miseries of savage life; but we must not forget that in the present age the Mormon invention has drawn tens of thousands away from their homes, their Christian sanctuaries, and the honour of domestic life, both in Great Britain and America, by vagaries as heartless and foolish as those which now disturb the peace of Maoridom.

The reader will be interested with a sketch of the founder of the Pai Marire faith. His native name was Te Ua Tuwhakararo; his Christian name is Horopapera —*i.e.*, Zerubbabel. He is often called Te Ua, but Horopapera is the name by which he is usually known. He belongs to the Taranaki tribe, and was taken into slavery during one of the raids made upon their southern neighbours by the Kawhia and Waikato tribes, a few years before the planting of the New Plymouth settlement or the arrival of the missionaries in this district. At Kawhia, which was for some years a flourishing Wesleyan mission, Te Ua heard the Gospel, learned to read and write, and received Christian baptism by the hands of an excellent missionary, the Rev. John Whiteley. At the commencement of the war in 1860 Horopapera espoused the cause of Wiremu Kingi, and fought against us at the battle of Waireka. There is nothing disagreeable in his personal appearance, nor is there any indication at present of insanity, or of natural shrewdness; his features are heavy, his face is not tatooed, and no one without knowing him would suppose him capable of exciting the greater portion of his race.

In the history of Te Ua we may learn a useful lesson. No one, looking upon him as he was borne away from his mother's care into slavery, when only three years old, could have imagined that after a few years the disconnected thoughts of *his* mind, and the meaningless words from *his* lips, would be the cause of grief in both hemispheres,—yet so it is. It is important that our prayers should be daily offered for the young, for a few years hence they will become the chief actors upon the stage of life.

It is impossible to describe the advantages which the Pai Marire were supposed to convey. Some pretended that they could draw ships ashore through its influence, and have been seen repeatedly gesticulating for this purpose. Others imagine that it will act upon them as a charm to protect them from danger. The Bush Rangers have occasionally met with a solitary old woman, fetching water or firewood, as they have approached a pah, and with her hair standing more than usually upright through fright, she has continued repeating ' *Pai Marire, Pai Marire* ' while the men passed by, attributing her safety, no doubt, to the magic power of the words. Warriors, supposing that the Pai Marire spirit constituted them invulnerable, sometimes walked fearlessly up to a redoubt strongly garrisoned. An instance of this occurred at Sentry Hill, a few miles from New Plymouth, on the last day of April, 1864. About three hundred men, after interesting themselves with the war dance, marched boldly in front of the redoubt commanded by Captain Shortt, of the 57th Regiment. But they had to pay dearly for their presumption, their

Pai Marire power failing them when it was most needed, thirty-one were killed and buried by the troops.

In April, 1864, a new and most revolting practice was resorted to by the adherents of the Pai Marire faith — that of cutting off the heads of the white men who fell into their hands. In some cases the heads were left near the spot where the horrible deed was done, in others they were carried to distant tribes as trophies of war and proofs of the great influence of their peculiar spirit, and were useful in exciting a wider extent of sympathy; and in a few instances the heads of our countrymen were supposed to be a medium through which the Angel Gabriel favoured them with further revelations. For this purpose the head of Captain Lloyd, of the 57th Regiment, who, with several of his small reconnoitering force, fell at Aua-Aua, was taken down the coast and into the pahs on the banks of the upper Wanganui. Since then it was no very unusual thing if a man were missing to find his body without its head. It was not likely that atrocious mutilations would stop here, nor did they. In some instances men were disembowelled, in others the bodies were so chopped that a description cannot be attempted, and missing parts led to serious fears that the Maori oven again steamed with human flesh. A darker day seemed to hang over the race; such unprecedented things had transpired that no one could tell what might follow. The missionary societies in England were condemned as political organizations, whose principal object was to secure the land of the Maories for colonial purposes, and the missionaries were looked upon as spies in the interests of the Government. Human heads, and flags prepared for the purpose, were carried hundreds of miles;

agents with untiring zeal urged the advantages of the new faith, as the means of uniting the tribes against the colonial foe; the miracles of its founder were considered conclusive regarding its claims for homage, and the predictions of Maori triumphs in distant lands, when the honour of England should be laid in the dust, appealed to the love of pre-eminence natural to the human heart.

The writer was standing under shelter one morning during a shower, in the month of March, 1865, when a Maori came up and told him that on the East Coast the natives had murdered a missionary, cooked a part of his body, and eaten it. This shocking intelligence we immediately made known in the town of New Plymouth, but no one really believed it, as during fifty years no missionary had fallen by the hand of a New Zealander. But the truth soon startled the community. The blow had indeed fallen; the first New Zealand martyr had sealed his high and holy calling with his blood. The particulars of this shocking tragedy—this exhibition of Pai Marire hatred to the Gospel of Christ—we will endeavour to describe.

The Rev. Carl Sylvius Volkner, the proto-martyr of New Zealand, was a native of Cassel, in Germany. After studying in the Hamburg Missionary College he came to New Zealand, about the year 1847, as an agent of the North German Missionary Society. Some years after he united himself with the Church Missionary Society, and received ordination both as a deacon and as a priest. His labours were commenced in Taranaki, and afterwards transferred to Waikato, and thence to the East Coast. The last four years of his useful life were spent at Opotiki, where he erected a handsome church and commodious schoolrooms chiefly at his own expense.

Mr. Volkner had been on a visit to Auckland, where his wife resided after being removed from her home for safety from the war, and shortly after his return to the scene of his missionary enterprise and toil he was cruelly murdered, as here narrated. During his absence the natives, in connection with some emissaries from Taranaki, determined upon his death. His house was entered by violence, and his furniture and other property were put up to auction, and sold to the highest bidder. Having committed themselves so far, they waited in daily expectation for his arrival to complete their horrible design. At length, on the 1st of March, a schooner, under the command of Captain Levy, a Jew, having on board the Rev. Mr. Volkner and also the Rev. Mr. Grace, of Taupo, belonging to the Church Mission, arrived at Opotiki. Among the novelties of the Pai Marire faith there was one which proved useful at this time—a claim to identify themselves and their religion with the people and religion of the Hebrew race. On this ground the captain of the schooner and his brother, who kept a store at Opotiki, were at liberty through the days of evil tidings, which slowly passed. On their going ashore the missionaries and crew were made prisoners, their baggage and the cargo of the schooner were landed and locked up. The next day Mr. Volkner was summoned to the place of execution, which was under a large willow tree, on a branch of which a block and cord were fastened. His coat, vest, and shirt were taken off, and worn by Kereopa, a chief of the Maketu tribe. The devoted missionary maintained a calm spirit and shook hands with the natives as they were bandaging his eyes. Without pinioning his arms and legs they hauled him up with the block by a cord placed round his neck. There hung the messenger of mercy, slowly dying by the hands of the people he had come to save, a spectacle on which they gazed with feelings which outraged the worst features of savage life. While the body hung, and before life was extinct, his boots and trousers were drawn off and appropriated. When the body was taken down the head was chopped off with an old axe. Kereopa scooped out the eyes and swallowed them. A line of infuriated savages was then formed, and the bleeding head passed slowly over their open mouths, that both men and women might taste the missionary's blood! The body was still more foully mutilated, and portions thrown to the dogs. In the evening a meeting was convened in the Catholic Chapel, and their abominable orgies were practised, with the bleeding head of the martyr placed on the pulpit before them, after which the head was taken away to be dried for future use. Thus fell, honourably fell, in the front of the battle, the faithful servant of Christ, while in robust health, and in the forty-sixth year of his age. His name will be embalmed among all the churches; he has experienced the fulfilment of the words of Jesus, " He that loseth his life for my sake, shall find it." The blow fell heavily upon his affectionate widow, who had been prevented by the advice of friends from returning with her husband to their station, where she would probably have shared his fate.

The star of the Pai Marire fanatics was now in the ascendant; they had commenced a new campaign, the object being the destruction of mission stations and the murder of missionaries.

Several soldiers who had fallen into their hands were compelled to carry heavy burdens, and what was far more distressing, even the heads of their countrymen who had been killed, were borne from place to place as proofs of victories gained over white men. Our poor fellows were fed on the coarsest food, the barest rags covered them, their sleeping places were of the most revolting kind, and they were coolly told that when their services were no longer needed they were doomed to be struck on the head with a death-blow, and left where they might fall.

It is probable that Horepapera became alarmed at the progress of Pai Marire events, for they had certainly exceeded in deeds of violence any of his anticipations; but he had let loose a stream which he could not stem. He has lately complained of additions made to his revelations. Any excited persons, having a white man's head in their possession, could obtain fresh communications from the Angel Gabriel, the result of which might be at any time seen in the most atrocious deeds of darkness.

The Government was now determined to put down the fanaticism with a strong hand. A proclamation had been issued some time before prohibiting its practices, but such a step was perfectly useless where there was no power to enforce its observance. A military campaign was determined on, to be continued till the principal murderers of Mr. Volkner should be brought to justice. Several of them were soon after captured, tried by a court-martial and condemned to death. It was deemed better policy, however, to try them also before the Supreme Court; this was done, and several of them were declared guilty, and condemned to be hanged; while we write they are confined in the Mount Eden prison, at Auckland, their hair cut short, with irons on their legs, and in their prison dress; they feel that disgrace has fallen upon them to the uttermost, so that death would probably be preferred to a commutation of their sentence.* The principal means used to exterminate the Pai Marire faith and practices will be described in the next chapter.

* Several of those unhappy men have since been executed.

KEREOPA.

MURDERER OF THE REV.ᴰ Mʳ VOLKNER

CHAPTER XXIII.

WAR WITH THE HAU HAUS.

"To meet proud Europe's flashing guns,
And fight like warriors nobly born :--
Then come, ye chieftans bold,
With war plumes waving high ;
Come, every warrior, young and old,
With club and assagai.
The vultures from afar
Are gathering at your Prophet's call."

T. PRINGLE.

HAU HAU is the name by which the professors of the new faith are known. The words Pai Marire express the religion itself, and Hau Hau is the designation of the devotee. The murderous proceedings of the Hau Haus made it necessary to put them down with a strong arm. Had they contented themselves with their foolish vociferations, without endangering the public peace, it is not likely that the Government would have interfered, however much every right-thinking person must have deplored their delusion; but when the settlers were driven from their homes, their property seized and scattered among the tribes, their very lives threatened, and a highly-esteemed missionary savagely murdered, the resolution was formed to pursue them by an armed force, until the murderers should be apprehended and the peace of the country restored.

August 2nd, 1865, was distinguished by a determined attack upon the stronghold of the Hau Haus. When the colonial forces and their native allies marched up to within a short distance of the pah and opened fire, the

G*

enemy bravely manned their trenches, and kept up a steady fire. After attempting in vain to dislodge them with the rifle, Captain Fraser ordered a charge; the bayonets were immediately fixed, and with a cheer, such as is heard only on a battle-field, our men rushed upon the rifle pits, in front of a volley of bullets; the enemy were scarcely prepared for such a dash, only a feeble resistance was made before the trenches were cleared and the pah was taken. The ground was strewed with twenty-five bodies of the Hau Haus—twenty-five souls hurried from the wicked and foolish Pai Marire faith to meet the just and holy God—and seven women were taken prisoners. No time was lost in reducing the place: the flag-staff was cut down, the whares were burnt, and the fences were levelled. Provisions were found in abundance—wheat, potatoes, and kumeras,—and horses, cattle, and sheep fell into our hands. The fight lasted scarcely half an hour; it was indeed 'short, sharp, and decisive.'

In his official dispatches, dated August 14th, 1865, the officer commanding states that the number of Hau Haus killed from the commencement of the campaign was eighty-seven, and the number of prisoners taken up to that date was forty-seven, of whom forty-two were wounded. Fifteen of the native allies had been killed, and fourteen wounded; of the colonial forces none had been killed, but ten were wounded.

A very shocking event transpired at Whakatane, on the 22nd of July, illustrative of the growing determination of the native mind. The cutter "Kate," commanded by Captain Pringle, arrived at the Whakatane Heads from Auckland, viâ Tauranga, on the evening of the 21st. Mr. J. Fulloon, a highly respectable half-caste, employed as a Government interpreter, was a passenger. The arrival of the vessel suggested the idea of securing *utu*—*i.e.*, compensation—for their friends who had fallen in battle, by capturing the vessel and murdering the crew. The next morning a number of men went on board, with arms in their hands as usual, and had breakfast with the crew. Mr. Fulloon was asleep in his berth, with a revolver lying by his side, for fear of a surprise, but this was removed by the soft tread and careful hand of a native, without awaking him. The object of the Maories was so completely hidden that no one appears to have suspected it. At a given signal each Maori singled out his man, and within a few minutes every person belonging to the vessel, except one, was murdered. Mr. Fulloon was shot several times, as he lay in his berth, with his own revolver. The captain and mate were felled to the deck with the tomahawk. The escape of Mr. B. White was very remarkable. His little son, a half-caste, eight years of age, had just been taken on board to meet his father, and was the means of saving his life. As an infuriated Maori was in the act of firing upon Mr. White the little fellow knocked aside the barrel of the musket, and the bullet passed ; and when a second attempt was made to shoot his father the noble boy rushed between him and the musket, and received the shot in his own person, but, as we understand, without severely injuring him. The savages then let Mr. White live, but made him a prisoner ; after a few days he made his escape, and having suffered some hardships for about a week he arrived at a place of safety. The ill-fated vessel was plundered and then burnt.

A considerable portion of the Arawa tribe distinguished themselves against the rebels on several occasions. By their energetic movements the Hau Haus were harassed and many taken prisoners, among whom was an alleged murderer. An attack upon the Pukemaire pah was deemed desirable, but as its position was remarkable for strength and favourable for defence, more than usual caution was needed. During the first week of October a force, consisting of Pakehas and Maories, started on a reconnoitring expedition, with the intention of attacking it if success were probable. They found its natural and other fortifications quite equal to the report. About four hundred yards from it stood a church, showing that other scenes had been witnessed in this neighbourhood. The officer in command ordered an attack, and so disposed his force that a fire was opened on several sides. To this the Hau Haus resolutely replied, and a military settler, who had recently joined the force, was struck with a bullet, which entered his waist and came out at his back. During the few hours which he lived he spent his time in earnest prayer, conscious that eternity was just before him. The sergeant of the little covering party had two fingers shot off, as they were conveying the wounded man to the rear. But the sergeant was not to escape so easily, for a bullet penetrated his chest, so that he also had to be carried to the rear, where the ball was immediately extracted. Lieutenant Biggs greatly distinguished himself by getting into the pah with a small body of men, but as he had not sufficient support, and his ammunition was expended, he was obliged to retire. A few days after the natives deserted the pah, and fled to another strongly fortified, more than twenty miles away. Lieutenant Biggs resolved to follow the fugitives, and again

won the admiration of the public by a dashing achieve-
ment, with a hundred and thirty men. Without a com-
missariat, and with no more ammunition than they could
carry, away went the little force across the country,
where there was no road, forcing themselves a pass
through dense bush, climbing steep hills, and walking
along the beds of creeks, till they reached Kawa Kawa,
where they rested a few hours. At two o'clock the next
morning they renewed their journey, skirmishing with
the enemy when they came to the river, which was
crossed several times, and at an early hour found themselves in front of the Hungahungatoroa pah, where the
garrison which fled from Pukemaire had ensconced
themselves.

This pah was situated on the top of a hill, two sides
of which were so precipitous that it was almost impossible to scale them, the other sides being defended in the
usual way. An attack was commenced in front without
much impression till a few volunteers and native allies
managed with much risk to climb up on one side and
secure a position so high that a fire was pointed down
into the pah, which appeared to dispirit and surprise the
garrison. About noon the firing ceased, and an offer
was given to the natives to preserve the lives of themselves and their families by immediate submission, and
an engagement to sign an oath of allegiance to the
Queen of England. Some were desirous to do this,
others, among whom were a few Taranaki emissaries,
strongly opposed it; but after a considerable contest of
words and feelings their submission was declared.
Patara (Butler) and Kereopa, the chief disturbers, were
still at liberty, their word was sufficient to kindle the
flame of contention in many breasts, and to determine

their followers not only to fight for their new religion, but to seek revenge for their friends already fallen in battle. The utmost vigilance was necessary to prevent a surprise against the troops. It was necessary to drive the enemy from a pah at Wairengaahika.

This pah was built near the residence of the Bishop of Waiapu. The barns and other outhouses had been burnt, the dwelling-house was much damaged, paper was torn from the walls, books were scattered with their leaves strewn about, and the complete destruction of the entire premises by fire was barely prevented by the arrival of the troops. The first attack on the pah was unsuccessful, for after keeping up a heavy fire several hours the troops were glad to entrench themselves in the vicinity of the pah for the night. Our losses this day included two native allies killed, an ensign shot through the head, and a private shot severely through the shoulders. The battle was strongly contested on the next day. The following day, which was Sunday, the natives tried the effect of a ruse. About eight o'clock in the morning some two hundred of the enemy advanced armed, in three bodies, close to our main position under a flag of truce, but instead of being thrown off his guard, the Major commanding suspected the stratagem, and a fire was instantly opened from both sides, and a fair hand-to-hand fight with about equal numbers in an open place and without the aid of trenches took place. In this struggle the enemy had thirty-four killed and as many wounded, while our only casualty was one man wounded. The pah was not yet taken, but the natives were so dispirited at their losses and their prospects that a few days after they surrendered unconditionally; a hundred and twenty guns and a quantity of ammunition were given up, and a hundred and eighty men became prisoners of war. The other pahs in the neighbourhood were evacuated, so that if the contest must be continued the seat of war would probably be removed. The men were amused with the adroitness of a Hau Hau named Renata Tupara, who, feigning himself dead as he lay beside two bodies while the troops passed over the ground, immediately after rose, snatched the two guns from the bodies of his comrades, and reached the pah in safety.

The war in Poverty Bay was now supposed to be ended. The natives residing in the upper Wairoa and on the borders of Lake Waiharemoana remained in a hostile position. They probably trusted to the difficulties which their rugged country would present to the approach of troops, to the abundant provisions which their crops supplied, and to the facilities for escape which the lake offered if they should be closely pressed. To follow them into their strongholds was necessary for the safety of the country. The native allies were selected for this work, accompanied by several European officers. The enemy was prepared for their approach and opened fire from rifle-pits covered with fern. Though at great disadvantage our natives set fire to the fern, and when the rifle-pits were exposed—forming a semi-circle—a skilful and energetic attack was made, by which the enemy was routed and a running fight towards Onepoto followed. The great body of the Hau Haus escaped in canoes across the lake during the night. Fourteen prisoners were taken, over whom the chiefs held a Runanga—a council of war—the next morning, and deciding that four of them should die on account of some circumstances which were deemed aggravating, they were taken out and immediately shot.

Soon after hostilities ceased on the East Coast, the natives with few exceptions acknowledged themselves beaten and placed themselves at the disposal of the Government. Sir George Grey determined to transport them in considerable numbers to the Chatham Islands. Several ship-loads were sent, and one of H.M. ships was stationed to prevent their escape.*

But notwithstanding the cessation of hostilities in the East Coast and the transportation of a number of the people, some fears are still entertained that the sword will be drawn there again. The principal cause of this fear lies in the fact that the chiefs Patara and Kereopa are still at liberty ; the former possesses great influence, and was the moving spirit which stimulated the people at Opotihi to execute their horrid purposes, and the latter was the chief actor in the shocking tragedy of the murdered missionary. Large sums of money have been offered to the loyal natives for the capture of those men, and spirited attempts were made, but as often as the friendly Maories were at the point of succeeding, something favoured the escape of the outlawed party.†

That the Pai Marire delusion is dying out we have written elsewhere, and every month confirms the statement ; they will not like to confess it, but many a native regrets the course he has taken, and would be glad to occupy the place he filled a few years ago, when the missionary was welcomed to his pah, when the Bible

* The Maori prisoners have since the above was written escaped from the Chatham Islands, massacred a number of men, women, and children, and have been the cause of a fresh military campaign.

† Kereopa was apprehended towards the close of 1871, and executed by hanging last January, 1872.—Eds.

was carried by his side, and when he joined in the morning and evening worship of the Lord Jesus Christ. We pray that those times when the Maori worshipper worshipped in spirit and in truth may soon return, then will the land yield her increase, and God, even our own God, will bless us.

CHAPTER XXIV.

MILITARY SETTLEMENTS.

" Yon pictur'd chart
Of lawn, and stream, and mountain's shadowy height,
And rocks in quiet verdure meekly bowered,
Rebukes the pomp of cities and the strife
Of competition, and the lust of gold. The rude native
tribes
Fast by the borders of the gentle stream,
Carv'd out their heritage, with rival heart,
And hand uncourteous."

L. H. SIGOURNEY.

A VIEW of New Zealand must necessarily be defective without a distinct notice of the military settlements, seeing that they include several thousand persons, are spread over large portions of the country, and form the nuclei of towns and forming districts which will grow into importance. The order originated with Sir George Grey, or rather the idea of applying it to this colony belongs to his Excellency. It is well known that Rome adopted a similar course in settling countries over which her victorious arms had been carried, where the inhabitants were likely to be troublesome to the empire. Nearly twenty years ago Sir George Grey determined upon this plan of defence for the safety of Auckland, when that neighbourhood was menaced by the redoubtable Hoani Heki. The force raised for that purpose was composed of discharged soldiers. Onehunga, Otahuhu, Panmure, and Howick were settled by them. Happily the force was never called into the field. But the fact that they were there was so far satisfactory to the Governor that in more troublous times the idea was revived, with such modification as the circumstances of the day required.

The confiscation of land owned by the rebels was deemed necessary, both to make the natives feel the evils of their doings and as sites for such settlements as might preserve the future peace of the country. This is confessedly the most sensitive point in the conduct and consequences of the war. Much fair reasoning has been published on the step, and highly exaggerated statements have been made concerning it. At one time it was proposed to confiscate sufficient land to pay the expenses of the war and to form settlements of defence, and yet to allow ample provision for every person of the native race. But this pleasing dream soon vanished before the startling expenditure which the war was causing. And the fact was forced upon the Government that to confiscate by proclamation was one thing, but to place a body of industrious men upon a disputed block of land, so that their families and property would be safe, was quite another affair. The word confiscation too was an ominous term. It might mean much or little, it might afflict the innocent with the guilty. In its application it might involve our national dishonour, it could be safe only under the most prudent control. Persons were not wanting either in the colony or in Great Britain who demurred to the scheme as a nefarious attempt to wrong the natives, and memorials against it were presented by philanthropic societies of the highest worth for benevolence and general intelligence to the Secretary of State and to the Governor of the colony.

It may safely be admitted that the Maori mind is more sensitive on the subject of losing his land than on any other. Warriors may be shot down on the battle field and buried by strangers, but this is an incident of war which the excitement of the day will palliate, and *utu* may possibly be obtained which will satisfy the survivors, and cause them to look upon the death of their chief from a point of honour. But when the land is gone the loss is complete, there is no redeeming thought or feeling growing out of it. Does it remain in its general features the same as when they called it theirs? Then every hill and headland, every stream and gully, every remarkable tree and patch of bush, reminded them of happier times. Or is the ground dotted over with cottages, or parted into fields in which cattle are grazing or corn is growing? Then the changes, however pleasing to the European eye, suggest the fact that the Maori people have submitted to a strange race, whose habits and objects differ widely from their own. It can hardly be expected that the noblest principles of colonization—of peopling the waste places of the earth, of improving an unformed race till it be amalgamated with the most refined portions of mankind, or if remaining distinct yet standing on equal terms with the Anglo-Saxon race—should be freely acknowledged or clearly perceived by them. To contend, then, for their landed rights as seen from the Maori standpoint, or forced to retire to pine in sullen silence, is so natural to the native mind that it should not excite our wonder.

The persons by whom a large portion of these lands are to be settled occupy a prominent place in the present state of the colony. They have been collected from various and distant places. Agents were sent by the Government to the chief towns and gold fields of the Middle Island to enlist for a limited period able-bodied men to risk the chances of war, and at the restoration of peace to settle upon a grant of land.

The military settlers have secured a name for their patience under fatigue and privations, and for their prowess in the field. Disappointed of settling upon their lands so soon as they had expected, by the protraction of the war, and having to leave their wives and children for several months together, while hundreds of miles lay between them, they yet looked cheerfully forward to their homes of peace and plenty. But many already sleep in a soldier's grave ; we look over a long list of names representing men who came to this colony with bright hopes, that they should form a pleasant homestead, and build up a family, but they have fallen a prey to the bullet, or the tomahawk, or disease, the wilderness affording them a grave, but leaving hardly a trace by which a mourner may discover the spot.

By the Government returns, made up to the close of 1864, we learn that the number of military settlers was then 6,382, including 1,243 females ; and in the number of males there were 1,118 persons under twenty-one years of age. More than 5,000, including women and children, were in the province of Auckland ; nearly 1,100 were in Taranaki ; 49 were in Wellington province ; and 122 were in the province of Hawke's Bay. Since those returns were completed other persons have been added ; whether more settlements will be formed than are now contemplated it is difficult to say, if it be not so the present numbers will maintain a respectable position in the colony.

CHAPTER XXV.

A FRESH OUTBREAK.

"Then more fearful grew the fray;
The swords that late flash'd to the evening sun
Now quenched in blood their radiance.
The frequent groan
Of death commingling with the storm was heard,
And the shrill shriek of Fear."
                                        SOUTHEY.

ON the West Coast a redoubtable enemy appeared in the person of Titokowaru, before whom the settlers on the banks of the Patea trembled, and some even fled. A colonial force was enlisted, and without having time to learn the duties which would be required of them were hurried into the field. They were led by officers who had distinguished themselves both in the Maori war and in more sanguinary fields of strife; but they fell before the enemy, increasing his prestige, and spreading alarm through the country. The names of gallant officers who stood firm till the rifle brought them down, and exposed them to the gash of the tomahawk, will not soon be forgotten.

On the East Coast the war was conducted on the side of the insurgents by Te Kooti. This man was of no extraordinary note till the struggle of which we write made him famous. The most shocking massacre which has disgraced the native rebellion was perpetrated by his orders. In the early hours of the morning, before the families were awake, the bands of Te Kooti approached the houses of the settlers on the East Coast, and shot

down the men as they arose at the first alarm. Cower-
ing women in their night dresses begged for their lives,
but were shot or tomahawked with savage delight. Little
children met the same fate. Mothers trying to screen
their infants from the horrible tomahawk were laid dead.
A lady who was left wounded lingered in dreadful
suspense and in want of all things for many days, and
afterwards died of the ghastly wounds inflicted. We
care not to open the scene, and, if we could, would draw
a curtain over atrocities which are a disgrace to our
common nature.

The news of this dark tragedy aroused alike both
colonists and friendly natives. The offer of the latter
to take the field was accepted, and for the activity displayed several of the Maori chiefs were raised to the
rank of major. Even the determined Topia, who had
told Sir George Grey some years before that he would
not make peace with him, "never, never, never, neither
now nor at any other time hereafter for ever," took the
field against Te Kooti, and now enjoys the title of major.
With the friendly natives the colonial forces were engaged, much hardship was undergone, the enemy was
not a little harassed, and many prisoners were taken,
but Te Kooti eluded their grasp.

In connection with these disturbances we must record
the murder of the Rev. John Whiteley, an old and
highly esteemed Wesleyan missionary. The excellence
of his character, the length of time that he laboured in
New Zealand, the esteem in which he was held by the
native tribes on the West Coast—where he fell,—and
the intimacy that subsisted between him and the writer,
inclines our pen to linger over this melancholy subject.
Coming to New Zealand in the service of the Wesleyan

Missionary Society about the year 1832, he shared in the joy which the first years of success excited in the self-denying men whose lives were devoted to the Maori race. Many of the best years of his life were spent at Kawhia, and very satisfactory were the results of his labours. He rendered good service as a peace-maker when the natives were incensed both against each other and against the Government. The latter part of his ministry was exercised in the province of Taranaki, and though the honours of age had crowned his head, and the labours of thirty-eight years of missionary work had reduced his strength, he still performed an amount of Sabbath exercises which would make many a younger minister blush. It was usual for him to ride into the country on a Saturday afternoon from twenty-five to thirty miles, and early on the Sunday morning, commencing his work, he would hold six or seven short services during the day among colonists and Maories, civilians and military men, drawing their minds away from earth to heaven, and then, worn and weary with bad roads and crossing dangerous rivers, he returned to town in time to conduct the evening service or to listen to the sermon of his fellow-labourers. It was on such an errand of love that he left his home for the White Cliffs, twenty-five miles north of New Plymouth, on February 13th, 1869, and there, at the White Cliffs, on the evening of that day he was met by the cruel and cowardly foe and shot dead, and his horse was shot also. When found, five bullets had pierced his body, his coat was taken away, and the saddle was removed from his horse.

Both the Church and Wesleyan Missionary Societies can point to martyrs for Christ—men who counted not their lives dear when called to lay them down in e service of their Master. Our wonder is not that two missionaries have fallen by the hands of wicked and cruel men, but that only two have fallen in fifty-six years. Had the early missionaries been sacrificed, as they seemed again and again likely to be, few would have been surprised, but in our own day the height of wickedness was reached by the murder of men whose life had been devoted to the welfare of their murderers. The blow fell heavily upon the few Maories who remained faithful to Mr. Whiteley's ministry. They could only exclaim, "Alas! our father!" It was touching to see the tangi which was held over his grave, for sincere were the tears shed and the lamentation which was uttered. We have pleasure in adding that the Colonial Government marked their appreciation of Mr. Whiteley's character by granting a yearly pension of £100 to his widow, and after her decease to his unmarried daughter.

The curiosity which the presence of our troops excited among the native people led to amusing descriptions for the benefit of those who had not seen them. "The soldiers," said a Ngapuhi chief, "wear red garments; they do not work, or buy, or sell. They practise every day with their weapons, and some of them watch constantly as if they expected to be attacked every moment. They are a very suspicious people, and have stiff hard things round their necks to keep their heads up, lest they should forget and look too much downwards and not keep their eyes continually rolling about in search of an enemy. They will attack any one their chief orders, and they will not on any account run away, but will fight till the last man of them is killed. They are fine handsome people, all looking like chiefs. The

H*

sailors are a different tribe, but are brave. Their clothes
and arms are different from the soldiers, and they talk
and laugh more." For the brave men whose graves are
in our own colony, and for others equally brave who
have left us for other lands, we cherish a sincere respect,
and anticipate a meeting with many of them in the
realms of everlasting peace.

Instead of being disheartened by the hostilities of the
past, the session of our Colonial Parliament in 1870
will be remembered on account of the gigantic measures
proposed for the improvement of the country. These
included railways which should connect distant provinces
and afford facilities for conveying the produce of corn
growing districts to market. Telegraph communications
were to be extended, and water races to be conducted
through the gold-fields. Immigration was to be invited
on a large scale, the working-classes were to be largely
assisted in the transit from the Fatherland, and how
many other good things were to be added we know not.
When the Bill was brought before the House of Representatives honourable members were taken by surprise,
and some denounced the whole as visionary. But as
the details were unfolded and the principles on which
the policy was founded were explained, objections were
withdrawn, and the Bill passed with some modifications
by a large majority. To carry out these measures the
Government intends to borrow several millions sterling,
the range of operations extending to ten years. Supposing that this policy can be carried out, without en-
tailing upon the colony an ungainly debt, we cannot
imagine a scheme more likely to make these islands the
home of a numerous enterprising and prosperous people.
The House was in session when the first intelligence

reached the colony of the war between France and Germany, and it was at once seen that our colonial policy must remain in abeyance for the present. When, however, the billows of war subside we anticipate a large increase to our population, abundance of work, and a fair measure of prosperity.

Within about thirty years the population of the colony has risen to nearly a quarter of a million, not including the Maories, and notwithstanding the injurious influences of the last ten years, its prospects are more cheering than they have been before. In the years gone by a few rich men have lost all that they had, and many poor men belonging to the working-classes at home have become rich. As the country is opened opportunities will be afforded to others to lay the foundation of family respectability, if that respectability be properly defined, and not mistaken for the false notions which have caused the failure of many. We are proud of the colonists of New Zealand, vicious persons and some that are indolent are found amongst us, but the general conduct of the people command our esteem and raise our expectations of future propriety.*

* From New Zealand we learn that the Government has succeeded to a great extent in its endeavours to conciliate the natives, and it is stated that many of the Maories "who had embraced the tenets of the Hau Hau religion, are returning to the belief in Christianity." The experiment of employing native labour in road making, telegraph extension, and other public works, has been very successful, and has had a most conciliatory effect. Te Kooti is still uncaptured, but it is said that Kereopa, the murderer of Mr. Volkner, the missionary, divulged his retreat shortly before his execution, and a party has started in pursuit. The initiation of public works in almost every province in the colony has given great satisfaction. Abundance of employment is now

CHAPTER XXVI.

CONCLUDING REMARKS.

"How leapt my heart with wildering fears,
Gazing on savage Islanders—
Ranged fierce in long canoe,
Their poisoned spears, their war-attire,
And plumes twined bright, like wreaths of fire,
Round brows of dusky hue!
What tears would fill my wakeful eyes,
When some delicious paradise—
Freshening the ocean where it shone,
Flung wide its groves of gold!
Serene in silent loveliness,
Amid the dash of waves."—"Isle of Palms."—
PROFESSOR WILSON.

WHAT New Zealand will really become we of course do not know, any further than inferences may be permitted to guide us. But only let the course of events flow on for a century, equal in value to those which have marked the last thirty years, and it will be readily granted that a numerous, energetic and powerful people will be found here.

The Maori race does not at present include more than 40,000 persons men, women, and children. They are not

afforded every one. The success of the gold fields has added to the general prosperity. The gold export for 1871 was 730,029 oz. as against 544,880 oz. in 1870, being an increase of 185,140 oz. With the view of encouraging the establishment of colonial industries, the Government have offered a reward of £2,500 for the first 100 tons of printing paper manufactured by machinery in the colony.—EDS.

destined to occupy the place long which they now fill; they must improve, the means used professedly to raise them to a higher standard will not be continued in vain; and the natural love of imitation will determine them to seek a higher level. One of the great hindrances to their social improvement, is found in the custom which appoints their women to perform the hard labour of the field. This prevents them from bestowing the attention upon their houses which is necessary to insure comfort. On this account principally perhaps the substantial houses of the opulent chiefs, houses well-built by colonial tradesmen, are found with scarcely any furniture other than that of a Raupo whare. The dream of amalgamation of the two races will not be a reality for many years to come; but while they retain their own language, and some of their national customs, we believe that the Maori people will occupy an intelligent and influential position in the country.

There is no probability that the war when once fairly over will ever be renewed. The number of settlements in almost all parts of the country and the application of law to the native people, will be among the means to preserve the peace of the colony. Restrictions such as must gall a people have in fact been taken away, others will follow, till the Maori will be able to dispose of his land in the best market, or retain it at his pleasure. Some years of sullen silence may follow the sharp crack of the last rifle fired with the hope of hitting a fellow man, but another generation will soon look upon a scene which will have sufficient attraction to engage them among the chief actors, in spreading abroad the blessings of peace. The Pai Marire delusion will be remembered only with shame; already it is drooping, we seldom hear it mentioned ; in New Zealand there will be but " one Lord, one faith, one baptism."

We have said but little about the political constitution and working of the colony, as our thoughts have not been turned strongly to this subject, and the changes through which our helms-men are endeavouring to conduct the political barque, may cause a description of our present political status to be inapplicable to the condition of the colony a few years hence.

Many of our leading men in political life are well educated and thorough statesmen, and would compare favourably we believe with those of any other colony ; others, men of good common sense, have lifted themselves up from the working classes to fill a place in the parliament of their country. For some years the complaint was loudly uttered that the Maories had no voice or vote in enacting the laws which they were expected to obey ; this complaint has now been silenced, and honourable members of our House of Representatives, of the Maori race, take their part in legislating for the colony. The part they take, however, does not extend far beyond their vote, for ignorance of the English language, as well as their crude ideas of law and order, prevent them from being of much real service in the senate house.

The political relations of England with Europe and America afford an interesting study to all classes of our community. For in addition to the fact that 16,000 miles cannot separate our hearts from the Fatherland, the great emporium for our produce, and from whence, we derive the clothing which we wear, the principal tools of our labour, and the most valuable of our home luxuries, make it very desirable that the ocean highway be not disturbed by a hostile flag. The steady flow of English literature into our colony, and the monthly interchange of letters, are doing much to mould the character of our youth, and to preserve intact the sterling virtues of the British nation in her most distant colony. Through the present postal route, across America by rail, we are brought into regular communication with the United States, and within a month's intelligence from England by the telegraph, privileges which we did not dream of in the first years of our colonial life.

It be readily seen that this book has been written from a colonial point of view, and by one who has seen much which is here described. But the author ventures to hope that the fact will not lessen the interest which may be felt in his pages. He lays no claim to infallibility ; errors may possibly be found, but he is not aware of having distorted any truth through a desire to please or from a fear of giving offence. Not being a partisan to any political or other project he may not be likely to present an unfair picture of facts, which interested writers of the highest honour may over colour or over shade. Nor has he ignored the value of spiritual religion in forming the character of colonial life in its best phases, but knowing that " rightousness exalteth a a nation" he has given this subject a prominent position. The war was a subject contrary to his taste, but he was compelled to write of " garments rolled in blood," of the flashing sword, the cannon's roar, of slaughter and of death, without which he could not have presented his readers-with a proper view of New Zealand affairs during the last ten years.

Facts will continue to accumulate, changes will occur, the colony will advance, and in this advancement fresh features will be developed, which future writers will use for the benefit of the public in both hemispheres. Larger numbers in pursuit of noble objects will be reported, an increase of wealth will be displayed, the value of imports and exports will be greater, population will increase, manufactures will occupy a higher place; but the facts which we have described will not lose their interest, and the consequences of these facts upon the Maori and the colonial races will be found in their future history. Lights and shadows have marked the past, it may be so in time to come, to some extent at least, but we cherish the hope of a happy future for our colony; and we will end our pages with the prayer that God may direct all our future movements, and build up of both races a people that shall honour Him.